First Edition

Personal Financial Stewardship

A Practical, In-depth, Christian Perspective

E. C. Anthony

Heavenslink Ministries
Old Hickory, Tennessee

Personal Financial Stewardship, 1e

3rd Printing

Edward C. Anthony

Printed in the
United States of America

ISBN: 1-59744-016-7

For permissions or supplements please contact:

Heavenslink Ministries
109 Woodside Ct.
Old Hickory, TN 37138
heavenslink@att.net.

All Bible verses are taken from either the New Translation by J. N. Darby (JND) or the King James Version (KJV). Cover Design by Joshua Lomelino.

Note to the Reader

The author has attempted to verify all information contained in this text as of the time of publication. The area of finance can change quickly. Financial instruments and laws are created and change on a daily basis. The book looks at financial issues from a Biblical basis rather than the perspective of which will make the most money. The author suggests that readers seek Godly, professional counsel where appropriate that will take into account their specific situation. The author does not assume any liability whatsoever for the reader's financial decisions as they are between the individual and the Lord. The biblical insights provided in the text are based on the Bible alone and do not necessarily reflect a particular tradition or denominational viewpoint. The author takes the Biblical perspective and uses the generic "he" to represent an individual when the context is not gender specific.

Dedication

To the Lord Jesus who has saved me from death and has given me a new life – may He receive any glory for any blessing resulting from this work. To my wife Barbara who has always been there as a support in all I undertake. To my son Paul and his wife Jen, as newlyweds may they find the truths from His Word a guide to their new life together. To all the gifted Bible teachers that have shared the Word and provided an understanding of the Scriptures from which I can teach others.

Preface

Purpose of the Book

The question may rightly be asked why the author undertakes a book on personal finance when there are others already on the market. The key of this undertaking lies in the perspective it takes. It unashamedly takes a Christian, Biblical perspective. The author was unable to find a single textbook on the market that thoroughly looks at personal finance from a Biblical perspective. There are many good Christian finance books written for the mass market but none is developed in such a way that it would make an excellent classroom, study, or financial seminar text. There is a small book entitled Biblical Financial Study from Crown Financial Ministries that provides a good starting point for a college level class but is better suited, due to its brevity, to a Bible study group looking to take a brief look at personal finance. In this text we seek to take an in-depth look at the issue. My interest was peaked to write this book after having a discussion with colleagues on the text that Trevecca University uses for its Financial Stewardship class that is required of all undergraduate students. It was interesting to note that a significant portion of the text was not being used and the part that was being used had to be augmented to be sure students understood, that as Christians using the Bible, how we view our use of resources is much different than that of the world. That more universities, and especially Christian universities, are adding personal finance as a core course is important and I expect the trend to continue in order to better prepare students entering a world whose motivation is, for the most part, about money. To help these universities and students in their quest for a better understanding of Biblical finance the author has created this work. It is the first major textbook on Christian financial stewardship available and it is the author's hope that Christian universities will be able to take advantage of this resource to support their curricula. The author welcomes constructive comments, ideas, and corrections. He can be reached at destinyslink@att.net. May the Lord receive the glory for any blessing that accrues from this work.

Audience for the Book

This text can be helpful for anyone desiring a thorough, methodical review of personal stewardship and all that it encompasses. The book serves two significant audiences. First it serves the Christian teaching institution and its students. The primary objective was to develop a text that would prove helpful in engaging students in dialogue concerning real-world financial decisions that they will face as they enter the career they have been called to. Thus, the text would make an excellent tool for Christian high schools, colleges, and universities. The second audience is the Christian who is already in a career but desires to better understand the way of freedom from financial worries that seem to envelope most in the world. Thus, the text could also serve as an excellent tool for churches, finance seminars, conferences, bible studies, and personal use.

Organization of the Book

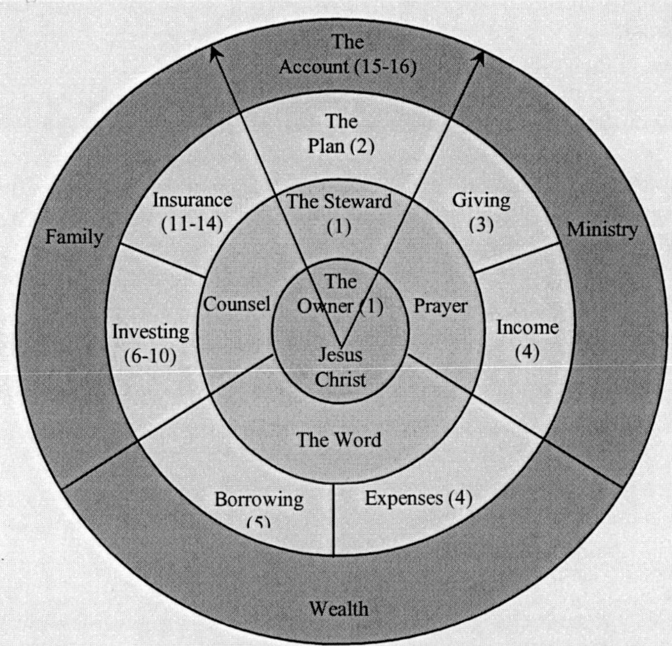

Exhibit I-1. The Christian Financial Stewardship Model.

The organization of the book is based on the Christian Financial Stewardship Model developed by the author. It is a model composed of four concentric circles as shown in Exhibit I-1.

The text works from the inner circle toward the outside. The first two chapters help to establish the foundation on which to successfully build a financial plan. Chapter one emphasizes the preeminence of Jesus Christ as creator and provider of all and how God works through us as stewards of His great resources. The three key components that God has provided to help us live a life of freedom to serve Him by His Spirit are His Word, prayer, and the Godly counsel of others that are older in the Lord. Chapter two then builds on this foundation by discussing how the truths discussed in chapter one are used to help us build our plan for financial stewardship. It is in this chapter that the basic financial planning process is covered.

Starting in the third chapter we are operating from the third circle of the model. This circle deals with the implementation of our financial stewardship plan. We start by looking at Biblical giving since that is one of the most important topics discussed in the Bible. In chapter four we will undertake a substantial amount of work in the area of cash flow management. This deals with determining the sources of our income as well as the destination of those same funds or resources. We will learn a great deal about how we spend and how we can substantially reduce what we spend in this section.

Chapter five helps us to take an in-depth look at the use of credit for borrowing and debt from a Biblical perspective. We will also investigate issues dealing with bankruptcy in this section. This chapter also provides a substantial section on how to go about making major purchases. These include homes, automobiles, education, appliances, and weddings. This section will prove invaluable as you consider major purchases in the future.

Chapters six through ten provide a significant look at investing. The Bible has a great deal to say about investing as a steward and there is much to learn about what constitutes an investment. Of course, in order to create a good return for the Master, we will need to understand what investment opportunities are available and which ones are good. The section will include information on tax-advantaged instruments, stocks, bonds, mutual funds, as well as other investment vehicles.

Following the learning about investments we will look at the issue of insurance. This is covered in chapters eleven through fourteen. We will discuss the Biblical perspective for insurance and how insurance, as we know it, came to be. We will also investigate the many types of insurance and discuss which ones you should consider purchasing and what they might cover. Key insurance instruments discussed include life, health, property, auto, disability, and liability. There are many insurance products today that are unnecessary and we discuss which ones you should avoid.

As you can see, most of the text covers issues that deal with our financial plan and its effect on our cash flow. When we get toward the end of our lives we might reflect back on our stewardship plan and think about how all of the resources we received, especially financially, have been used. The last circle in our model emphasizes how the interaction with the financial plan deals with an account. That is, God has made us stewards and has provided over the years many resources (the account) for which we have, hopefully, carefully planned their usage. As we look back and give account we will have likely received over a million dollars in our lifetime. In chapters fifteen and sixteen we take a look at the key areas that will determine your return on that investment; including the effect on the family, the ministry, and our estate or wealth. It is in this section that we also investigate issues of retirement and estate planning.

A number of special features have been added to the text to make it a useful reference for the professional, counselor, or elder. These include:

🕮 The Bible Speaks

There are many Bible texts noted throughout the book. These are identified in the margin by an open Bible. A chronological list of verses used and where they are referenced in the text is also given in Appendix C.

ⓘTips

As with any text on finance there will be key financial tips that need to be emphasized that you should not overlook or perhaps might be normally overlooked. The author brings your attention to these "Tips" by identifying them with an information icon.

Think About It…

The world of finance involves numbers and so there will be many interesting numbers and statistics provided throughout the book. The author will highlight especially interesting or telling statistics or formulas for your consideration by identifying them in the margin by the money bag.

? What is the Meaning of…

There may be many new terms that you encounter as you read the text. To help identify key word definitions in the text, the location of definitions will be identified by a question mark in the margin.

Getting Connected

We live in a highly connected society via the Internet. The author has tried to identify for you some of the best web sites to check for financial information and assistance. This will be a great help in light of the shear magnitude of the information available on the Web. These key web sites will be identified by a small networked computer icon.

Supplements to the Book

There is an instructor's CD available with the text that includes an exam bank. It is expected that the supplements will be expanded in future additions based on feedback from students and faculty.

Acknowledgements

This work would not be possible without God leading other able individuals by His Spirit to teach the truths of God's Word to me and educate me in the area of personal financial stewardship either via an itinerant ministry or through writing. Except for a few noted exceptions all that is written here comes as the Lord has led me to write. Though the writing is original, no doubt some of the phrases, thinking, topics, graphs, and sequencing will also be reflected in other works as would be expected in any field where there is some common body of knowledge and I acknowledge my indebtedness to others who have run the race before me in writing, teaching, and providing me much of my learning. Anything that has been adapted based on other data or works is noted at the point of use. Anything that the author has directly taken from another work is noted at the point of use based on permission of the copyright holder. My thanks to those who provided permission for usage of such material.

Special thanks to those who have played a role in the preparation and publication of this work. In addition to those mentioned in the dedication I acknowledge the encouragement and support of my colleagues James Agee, Jon Burch, and Moosa Valinezhad who have been extremely helpful in reviewing and editing the work and thank them for sharing their insights on how to make the work even better. I also thank the research committee at Trevecca which provided some of the funding for the work. Special thanks to Joshua Lomelino and his new bride, Bethany, for their work in designing and creating the cover of the book. I'm sure you will have a great life together in the Lord. May God bless each of those who had a hand in this work and may all the glory abound to Him.

About the Author

Dr. Ed Anthony is a Bible teacher, professor, and speaker devoted to making a difference in the lives of those he comes in contact with. As a former elder, church treasurer, and financial counselor he has many years of experience in the area of personal financial planning. He also teaches at Trevecca Nazarene University in Nashville, Tennessee in the areas of financial stewardship, management, and information technology. He ministers as an itinerant Bible teacher at local churches around the country as the Lord leads. He is an award-winning speaker and member of the National Speakers Association and is regularly invited to speak at seminars and conferences. Originally from Connecticut, he now resides in the Nashville area with his wife Barbara. He hopes that this book will make a difference in your life and if it does please feel free to email him to let him know at destinyslink@att.net.

Contents Overview

Contents

Part Two Managing and Following the Stewardship Plan

Chapter 5 Managing Credit, Borrowing, and Debt, 142

Part Three Investing for the Future

Chapter 6 Introduction to Investing, 196

Part Four Determining and Managing Insurance Needs

PART ONE

Laying the Foundation for Financial Stewardship

Chapter 1
The Biblical Perspective

Chapter 2
The Financial Stewardship Planning Process

CHAPTER 1

The Biblical Perspective

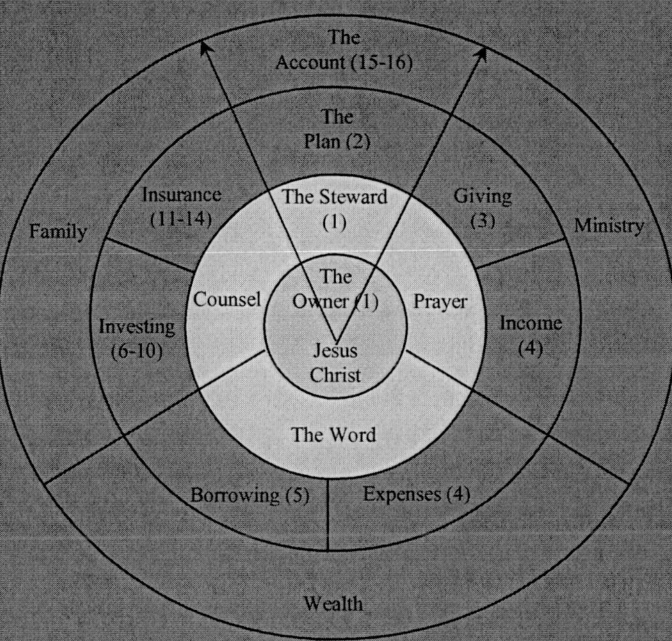

Learning Objectives

1. Identify the Biblical basis for financial planning and the three key factors in preparing a financial plan.
2. Explain the key differences between how the world views personal financial planning and how the Christian views it.
3. Understand from a Biblical perspective what it means to be a steward of what God, as owner, has given you.
4. Describe the "counting the cost" perspective described in the Bible from both a Christian financial and discipleship view.
5. Examine and understand the three components that should influence the direction of your Christian financial planning.

Lord, I commit myself to you.

Lord, help me to be the steward you would want me to be. I desire to know thy Son, and to know Him better, that I might walk as He walked in this world recognizing that I am just a pilgrim passing through this wilderness. May I seek, by your Spirit, to recognize how your ways are different from the world's ways. Help me to understand how to properly count the cost in all that I undertake that I, according to thy will, might be blessed with all spiritual blessing in thy Son. I thank you even now for what you will do in my life and with the resources you provide. As I undertake this study of Biblical stewardship I commit to being a faithful steward of all that you give me according to thy Word.

Getting Oriented to God

Our first section heading above clearly sets this personal financial planning book apart from others. You may be a student taking the course because it's required and so you see it as something that you must do. Perhaps you are one who has experienced the ravages of the world's insatiable desire for riches and realize there must be more to life. Whatever your situation, to gain the freedom from the world that the Bible speaks about, you must understand what the Bible has to say about it. The Bible is very clear on what is needed to be able to understand it. It says: "*But we have received not the spirit of the world, but the Spirit which is of God: which also we speak, not in words taught by human wisdom but in those taught by the Spirit, communicating spiritual things by spiritual means. But the natural man does not receive the things of God, for they are folly to him; and he cannot know them because they are spiritually discerned*" (1 Corinthians 2:11-14, JND). The caveat is that one must have the Spirit of God to understand what God has to say. Without the Spirit of God within, the things of God appear as foolishness. Some of the things we will touch on together in this book are looked on as foolishness to the world because they can only be discerned or understood by the Spirit of God.

Notice that understanding comes via the Spirit of God and not by the wisdom of men. When it comes to the things of God it is the Spirit of God that enlightens us. It does not matter how many degrees whether theological, financial, or otherwise we have earned. It's not that God cannot use education or degrees, in fact, in many cases He does, but when it comes to teaching the things of God, He uses men gifted by His Spirit to teach and preach what the world calls foolishness. It is interesting to note that most business or Bible schools today would not hire most of the New Testament writers or apostles because they would not have the man-made requirements to teach the things of God. Thankfully despite these things, the Spirit of God still works and can show even the most unlearned what God has to say.

This is what is great for us. No matter what our background or education God, by His Spirit, can enlighten us to how we should live our lives, and that includes being stewards of the resources we receive. Now the question that may come to mind is: How do we receive this Spirit of God so we can understand what is conveyed in the Bible about financial stewardship? Well, we can be assured that it is not difficult. In fact the work has been done. Remember the historical facts about Jesus? That Jesus came as the Son of God, as a man lived a perfect life, died, and rose again. These are historical facts that few will try to argue with. But assenting to those facts does not mean believing them. The key to receiving His Spirit within you is believing that He came and died **for you**. See, there are two paths in life, the path that leads to destruction (which by default we are all on because of sin) and the path that leads to life, which can be had by recognizing and believing, by faith, that Jesus Christ died for your sin and rose again by the power of God that you might have a hope, which is life everlasting with Him. Consider John 3:16-18. It states: "*For God so loved the world, that he* *gave his only-begotten Son, that whosoever believes on him may not perish, but have life eternal. For God has not sent his Son into the world that he may judge the world, but that the world may be saved through him. He that believes on him is not judged, but he that believes not has already been judged, because he has not believed on the name of the only-begotten Son of God*" (JND). Are you judged (condemned) or do you have life? The key is faith. "*But without faith it is impossible to please Him. For he that draws near to God must believe that He is and that He is a rewarder of them who seek Him out*"(Hebrews 11:6, JND). Now, if we receive Christ by faith, which is required to enter heaven, as well as understand His will for our lives, where is the Spirit that will give me understanding and wisdom that concerns God? It comes by faith in Christ. Romans 8:9-16 makes this very clear. 1 Corinthians 3:16 notes: "*Do ye not know that ye are the temple of God and that the Spirit of God dwells in you*?" Paul is pointing out that the local church at Corinth had the Spirit of God dwelling in them and that this was an indication that each believer, in the church, was indwelt by the Spirit. Romans 8:9 is emphatic concerning the connection between the believer and the indwelling Spirit: " *if any one has not the Spirit of Christ he is not of Him"* (JND).

So in simple faith, believing that Christ died for you and took on Himself your sin, you too can receive His Spirit so you can begin to understand all that He has in store for you from His Word. With that Spirit you can begin to have true understanding and wisdom that comes from above. God has changed many a life. Will you let Him change yours today?

The Preeminence of Jesus Christ

The Owner

Jesus Christ

At this point we assume you know Jesus Christ as your personal Savior and as a result have been indwelt by His Spirit. With that in mind you will now be able to understand that the first key in financial planning is that Christ is preeminent in all things. The world would have us think that "we are #1" and that we need to "look out for #1" but the Bible shows quite the contrary. All that we have we owe to what Christ has done.

Christ – the Creator and Sustainer of All

As Christians who are interested in pursuing God's will for our lives and handling our financial matters according to His insights we must first recognize fully who it is that has created all that is available to us and who keeps this world afloat (or in space for that matter). We want to first note that Christ as one with God and uncreated was involved in the creation of the world. Concerning Christ's involvement in all creation Paul writes "*Who is the image* (not likeness) *of the invisible God* (God in a form we can see), *firstborn* (first in rank or position) *of all creation* (as uncreated He heads all that is created); *because by Him were created all things... all things have been created by Him* (implying that He has always existed) *and for Him. And He is before all and all things subsist together by Him...that He might have the first place in all things"* (Colossians 1:15-18, JND).

The whole book of Colossians emphasizes the preeminence and sufficiency of Jesus Christ in all things. After coming to Christ the first key lesson for us to learn concerning the world of Biblical finance is that Christ must be recognized as preeminent in all things in our lives. If other things such as school, career, family, and the like are more important in your life than Christ then you will not be able to fully take advantage of the peace and freedom (John 8:36) that the Bible offers when it comes to your finances as well as other areas of your life. This is the very issue that the Lord deals with in Luke 14 where He says "*If any man come to me, and shall not hate his own father and mother, and wife, and children, and brothers and sisters, yea, and his own life too, he cannot be my disciple; and whoever does not carry his own cross and come after me cannot be my disciple."* (v. 26-27, JND). This may appear to be a very harsh verse and without the Spirit of God, that is what it appears as to the world. Yet, by the Spirit we can understand what this verse means. The issue is one of preeminence and place. That is, in order to put Christ first in our thinking requires us to deny that first place that others may normally secure in this world. This is nearly impossible to do in the flesh but by the Spirit of God we can take up our cross and give Him His rightful place as first in our lives. Bearing the cross is often misunderstood as bearing some kind of burden but that is not the issue at all here. The issue is the preeminence of Christ by denial of the world's desired place in our lives. The cross is the instrument of death. When you take up your cross you are symbolically putting to death the world as having first place in your life.

If you truly want to have freedom and peace in this life concerning your personal finances it is imperative to put Jesus Christ first in your life. If you're unwilling to do this then your financial plans are bound to go awry because the world and its techniques will find a way to influence the flesh. The world spends millions trying to understand how the human body, mind, and emotions work so that they might create the best techniques to get you to do financially that which you really should not do. In this book we will touch on some of the things that the world does, to try to influence you to make decisions that sometimes you don't even realize your making. God has given us a marvelous mind with the ability to reason properly and weigh alternatives. Be sure to commit to putting Christ first so that you will use that mind as God intended, not only for your peace and freedom, but for Christ's glory.

Christ – the Owner and Provider of All

Now that we understand that by Jesus Christ all things were created and subsist, we can now take the next step and understand that as the creator He in reality owns everything and if He owns everything then what we have is by His providing it. Now before you run off and stop going to school or working, we need to keep in mind how God works in providing what He owns to us, for our use. For instance, we know that one of the ways God provides for us and our families is through our working in the world at various trades. This is Biblical and the Bible makes it quite clear that if a man does not work then he should not eat (2 Thessalonians 3:10). So it would seem that as long as you don't eat you don't need to work ☺. Of course, the intent of the verse is the opposite. Otherwise, not eating would lead to death. The point is clear that God desires that men acquire some of His resources through work in order to provide for their own needs in the world. This, of course, is only one way God provides but it does illustrate that He provides by various means and some of those require action on our part.

That the Lord owns all is an important concept that is much different than the world's perspective. If we understand that He is the owner of all, we take a far different view of how we manage resources than if they were our own. The same would likely be true if I were to ask you to manage a million dollars while I'm away for a year, especially in light of the reward I will give you for handling it well. You are likely to be much more careful about how you use those funds than you would normally be of your own. I'm not saying you should not manage your own funds as well as mine but our view naturally changes when the owner changes. Interestingly, after being a steward of another's resources and seeing the possible return, you might want to handle yours much differently. 1 Corinthians 10:26 notes that "*for the earth is the Lord's, and the fullness thereof.*" Paul is quoting the phrase from Psalm 24:1. It specifically states that "*the earth is the Lord's and the fullness thereof; the world and they that dwell therein*" (KJV). There are many other verses that support the fact that God is the owner of all. For further study consider verses such as Deuteronomy 10:14; 1 Chronicles 29:11-12; Psalm 50:10-12; and Haggai 2:8.

If God is the owner then how does He provide us with these things that He owns? We have already noted that He often can do this by our work. Paul was a tentmaker and God at least partially provided for him through that work (Acts 18:3). Ever since the fall in the Garden of Eden it appears that man receives God's provision, for the most part, through work. It appears that before the fall the work was not as toilsome as after (Genesis 2:10, 3:19).

There are other ways that God provides as well but we must keep in mind that He is in control and the way He works with one person may be substantially different than another. It should be noted that one who lives in physical poverty can have as much peace and freedom as one who lives in great wealth because it is not the material things that make the difference to either. They both have spiritual riches that go far beyond the physical. This is something very important for the Christian to understand. Some Christians have pained themselves through with many sorrows thinking that God wants them to be physically rich in this present age. 1 Timothy 6:9 notes: "*But those that desire to be rich fall into temptation and a snare, and many unwise and hurtful lusts, which plunge men into destruction and ruin*" (JND). Many Christians have taken what was meant for literal Israel as true for the Christian. As a result many have made a shipwreck of their faith. Faith by its nature deals with that which cannot be seen. For Abraham and Israel faithfulness was rewarded with physical wealth and blessing. That is quite clear from the Old Testament. But when we get to the epistles the teaching concerns the Christians and the church and the emphasis is on the spiritual blessings. The obedient faith of a Christian leads to an abundance of spiritual rather than physical blessing. Now God may see fit to abundantly bless physically as well, as He has done with many Christians but a lack of physical wealth is not an indication of a lack of obedience nor is wealth an indication of obedience. That is a view of man, not of God. Man looks on the outward appearance but God looks at the heart (1 Samuel 16:7). The Christian's blessing is being, as it were, with Him right now. This is why Paul notes in Colossians 3:1-4 where our affections are. They are where Christ is. If that's the case then physical wealth certainly cannot be a guide for the Christian as to whether he is blessed of God. Elsewhere Paul says: "*Blessed be the God and Father of our Lord Jesus Christ, who has blessed us with every spiritual blessing in the heavenlies in Christ*" (Ephesians 1:3, JND). There is no question that the Christian is blessed but it's always seen as spiritual and in the heavenlies.

Peace and freedom in your personal finances will come in realizing that wealth in this world does not determine whether God has blessed you. The question may then arise why be a good steward? The issue is future reward. We will discuss this more when we look at being a consumer versus being a steward but the results of our stewardship here will be reflected by what we gain as a future reward in heaven and in His kingdom. Our desire is to use the resources and talents the Lord has given us on account to build "the account." That way we can look forward to giving an account as was apparently the case with two of the stewards in Matthew 25:14-29. Those who have life desire to give a good account of what is in the Master's account at the end of their lives. This account focuses on three areas that we explore in more detail in part five of the book. These areas are family, where we expend resources in return for maintaining and growing lives of service to Him; ministry, where we use resources to further His work; and wealth that is saved for future uses and an inheritance. Paul speaks of the "account" in Philippians 4:17 and Romans 14:12 notes that each man will give an account. The key reminder of this accounting for the Christian, though, comes in 1 Corinthians 3:11-15 where the issue is not salvation but the work; that is, the results of the use of resources given to him will be tested by fire to determine if a reward is to be given. Faithfulness in stewardship will lead to greater reward as seen in the parable of the steward in Matthew 25.

God does provide by means other than work. That God miraculously intervenes at times in the affairs of men based on His own volition and in answer to prayer is clear from scripture. That is, God does not use us as robots but allows men a sphere within which they can exercise free will. God knows the ultimate ends and He has ultimate control. Although men's ways for the most part lead to evil God's intervention is always good and just. This intervention at times includes divine judgment. Some verses to study that emphasize God's control and intervention include Psalm 135:6, Proverbs 21:1, and Acts 17:26. Sometimes God can take that which is intended for evil and use it for good as in Joseph's case (Genesis 45:4-8, 50:19-21). Of course, Christians often quote Romans 8:28 recognizing that all things work together for good to those that love God. That God will provide for all our basic **needs** is clear as can be seen in Matthew 6:31-33 and Philippians 4:19. In fact 1Timothy 6:8 notes that it is with these things that we should be content. God directly intervened to provide for the needs of the nation of Israel in the wilderness (and for Elijah who was fed by the Ravens (1 Kings 17:4-6, KJV)). The key is to seek Him first.

Besides work and direct intervention, God often provides through others for your needs. The church at Macedonia provided for others liberally (2 Corinthians 8:1-2). 1 Timothy 5:18 speaks of the church providing for widows. These same widows are to be those who have helped others (1 Timothy 5:10). Of course, there are many cases in the gospels where individuals ministered to the Lord Jesus.

In summary, then, God provides the resources He owns to you in one of three ways. They are by your efforts such as work, by the assistance of others, and by direct intervention. The frequency that God uses these three, based on the external evidence, is in the order given.

The Christian as a Steward versus a Consumer

Have you ever noticed how often we are identified as "consumers" in the world? In fact, it appears to have become engrained in our thinking. Even the measurement of inflation, or the increase in prices of goods, is reported by the Consumer Price Index (CPI). If we see ourselves as merely consumers then the world has us where it wants us. Have you ever considered what the term consumer means? The word comes from the root – consume, which according to Webster's dictionary means to destroy or expend by use; use up; to eat or

? Consumer

drink up; devour, to spend (money, time, etc.) wastefully. So a consumer is one who undertakes these things. Now, using that definition, would you want to have the constant title of being a consumer? We understand that we do consume food and water to keep our bodies alive but would you use the term in general to identify your life?

The Bible takes quite a different look and emphasizes that we are stewards rather than consumers. Stewardship involves not only using up some resources but developing and making others grow as well so that over a period of time the result of their use leaves something of greater worth than when you

? Steward

started. Webster's defines a steward as "one who manages another's property or financial affairs; one who administers anything as the agent of another or other." Now this is the Biblical view of who you are as a Christian. There are many examples dealing with stewards and stewardship in the Bible. For study look at Joseph as a steward in Potiphar's house (Genesis 39:1-4) and later in the land of Egypt (Genesis 41:39-44); the parable of the stewards in Matthew 25:14-29; the parable of the wise steward in Luke 12:42-44; and how the elders must demonstrate good stewardship of what God has given them (Titus 1:7).

The property is not always money as can be seen in Titus but whatever the Lord provides. There are some other key things to notice as well. God recognizes that there are differing levels of skill and talent in each individual. For instance in Matthew 25 one was given five talents, one was given two, and another one. Have you ever noticed what he says to the first two concerning what they received in the first place? The issue was not who was more talented or had more abilities or gifts but their faithfulness to use what the Lord gave. Although the sums were different that were given to the first two stewards the Lord calls them both "a few things." Both were commended in the same way because the result (a 100% growth of the resource) was the same. The Lord knows the steward and He only desires that we be faithful in the little He has given us here on earth. Notice also that the property belonged to their lord just as what we own belongs to our Lord.

We are taught in the Scriptures to be good stewards and not good consumers. The world makes a significant effort to get you to use your resources as quickly as possible even if it means more waste so that you will spend more or need to purchase again. Just look at the efforts of merchants, advertisers, and creditors and you can see that it appears that they are acting in unison to help you destroy the resources rather than grow them. The Bible says it best in 1 Corinthians 4:2 – "*Here, further, it is sought in stewards that a man be found faithful*" (JND). In this book we will see how we can be faithful stewards of what the Lord has given and thus be able to give a good account. A consumer has nothing to show for his consumption but the faithful steward has much to show for his stewardship.

The Love of Christ versus the Love of Money

Perhaps you have heard the adage "money is the root of all evil." Many Christians have learned that this is not what the Bible says. 1 Timothy 6:10 notes that "*the love of money is the root of every evil…*" As, perhaps you know, money is not the issue, but the love of it. It all comes down to coveting or desiring that which you don't have. The world says not only to look out for yourself but that it is a great desire to be rich and have the best. Again the world is at odds with the Bible. As we have already noted the verse preceding verse ten notes that "*those desiring to be rich fall into temptation and a snare, and many unwise and hurtful lusts which plunge man into destruction and ruin.*" Verse 10 finishes with, "*which some having aspired after, have wandered from the faith, and pierced themselves with many sorrows.*" Yet, this is exactly the way the world wants us to think so that our desires and dreams can be fulfilled.

The Bible would rather you seek after the things of Christ. In verse 11 of this same section Paul writes "*But thou, O man of God, flee these things, and pursue righteousness, piety, faith, love, endurance, meekness of spirit*" (JND). Now, I realize that may not sound all that exciting to some of the young people reading this text. But if you truly know Christ and desire to serve Him this should at least tug at your heart so that you have an interest in pursuing the things of Christ which have eternal value. We really need to keep in mind that we do not own anything, it is the Lord's. If it is the Lord's, then we need to keep in mind that He will ask: What have you done with it? What is the return?

See, if we follow the Biblical perspective we could lose all our physical possessions tomorrow and still have peace and freedom in Christ because the return is more than the growth of financial resources as we have already noted. But, from the world's perspective of becoming rich, if we lost it all tomorrow we would be living in fear because we have lost what we had owned. When we recognize He is the owner we recognize His right to take it back, as well, and still find peace. Job recognized this when he said "*the Lord gave and the Lord hath taken away, blessed be the name of the Lord*" (Job 1:21, KJV). Job recognized all that he had belonged to the Lord and even in such a loss his heart was right. Would we be able to do the same? We can, if we recognize our love must be focused on Christ and not on the mammon of this world. As the Bible notes, you can only serve one master, and it should be God (Matthew 6:24; Luke 16:13).

As young people you will be pressed to seek after the riches of the world. Allow the Spirit of God to help you restrain the flesh that would succumb to its enticements. Paul says concerning all others but Timothy "*for all seek their own things, not the things of Christ*" (Philippians 2:21, JND). Will we be counted, like Timothy, as those who truly seek the things of Christ?

The Wisdom of God versus the Wisdom of Men

The final key in dealing with the preeminence of Christ deals with our ability to reason about financial things. It is another area in which the Bible has something significant to say. When looking at financial issues we may be inundated by help from the world. We can be assured that the world's true desire is to relieve you of some of your funds or resources. In the next section, on the plan of the Christian, we will detail the three resources that will be of importance to you in making the right decisions (assuming that you have decided to make Christ preeminent).

The world's mechanisms are not always, and perhaps I should say rarely, the mechanisms of God. The world, composed of unbelievers, views things from a perspective of self and "what is in it for me." As a result, their thinking emphasizes schemes that enrich themselves. Do we need to go into the obvious greed that has overtaken many in the corporate world to make the point? Whether WorldCom, Enron, or some other smaller firm the façade may be to help the "consumer" but the heart is really with the money. We have already noted that our affections should not be on the mammon of the world, for who can serve two masters? The same is true of the world's wisdom. That is, the wisdom of God seems as foolishness to men since their master is different (1 Corinthians 1:25, 2:14) and the wisdom of the world is seen as foolishness to God (1 Corinthians 3:19). If our master is Christ then our view of the way we should do things will be different. Keep in mind wisdom from a Biblical perspective is more than just knowledge and understanding. Knowledge involves knowing the facts. Understanding involves using that knowledge or being able to synthesize various known facts and previous experience and weigh possible alternatives. Wisdom not only involves weighing the alternatives but making the right decisions or taking the right path

The question may be raised as to whether we should use our minds then. The answer is a resounding YES! The key is that the mind must be used as guided by the Sprit of God. *For let this mind be in you which was also in Christ Jesus that who subsisting in the form of God did not esteem it as an object of rapine* (to be coveted) *to be on an equality with God but emptied himself, taking a bondman's form, taking his place in the likeness* (not image) *of men* (Philippians 2:5-7, JND). Read Ephesians 4:17-24 and see if you can identify how the important the mind is. In verse 17 it notes that we should not walk as the rest of the nations walk in the vanity of their mind that is corrupt but to, as verse 23 notes, be renewed in the spirit of our mind. The mind is a powerful thing that can do great things for God's glory when used by the Spirit of God, but can also be extremely corrupt as can be evidenced by what we see in the world today.

You don't have to go far to see the world's desires. As I am writing this chapter my wife stopped by to let me know what she had just heard about on an investment show. The story is of a 71 year old woman who thought an insurance agent who had been a friend of her late husband was helping her by setting up a 17 year annuity for her. What she did not realize was that to receive any money out of the annuity required a 25% payment of the funds withdrawn. Although I don't know all the details of this transaction it became quite clear where this agent's mind was and it was not about helping the woman but helping himself to her money or to a good portion of her needed funds. Basically she would lose 25% of the annuity meaning that she would be losing money on the investment. This is an example of the wisdom of men crafting something that is corrupt and of the flesh. I'm pleased to note that there is a happy ending for this story since she had called this investment show and the man eventually went to the president of the insurance company to get it straight. Even though it was legal the president recognized right away that it was not right and worked with the woman to get it straightened out. How many others, though, never have that happy ending, because of the covetousness of the mind and not being guided by the Spirit of God.

As we begin to delve into the details of financial planning in this book please pray for guidance from God by His Spirit to do that which is right rather than that which is expedient in satisfying some desire. It may not be easy, especially if you are a young person in high school or college with many dreams. Be sure they are dreams that God has for you as well.

The Plan of the Christian

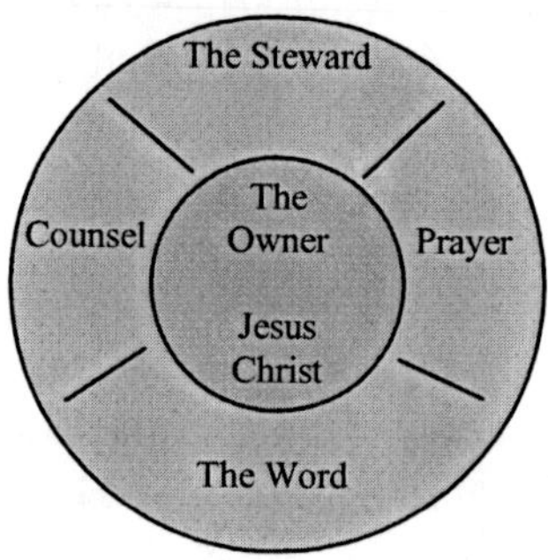

Understanding God's involvement with man is important because it helps us to see that He expects us to use our minds and wills to glorify Him. The key is to be sure that the Holy Spirit is having an influence on these. With the influence of the Spirit in the life the correct decisions can be made. If only it were that easy. As you know even if you are a Christian you don't always do as you should. Basically we are doing one of two things when we do not allow God through His spirit to have the rightful place in our lives: we either grieve or quench the Spirit. When we grieve the Spirit we basically do that which the Spirit is telling us not to do. To quench the Spirit is not to do that which the Spirit suggests to do. The first issue of grieving the Spirit occurs in Ephesians 4:30. The context describes the things that occur when you let Satan or the flesh have influence in the life. This of course is not what the Spirit desires for your life and so He is grieved when you partake of these very things. The issue of quenching the Spirit occurs in 1 Thessalonians 5:19. The context of this verse is dealing with positive things such as rejoicing, praying, and holding fast. These are the things that the Spirit certainly would have us do and if we don't He is then quenched. The leading of the Spirit is reduced or put out like a fire.

Your Plan – God's Direction

The next logical question that you then might ask is how do I really know if the Spirit would or would not have me do something from a financial perspective? We will get to that later in this section but we want to first recognize and discuss the fact that based on how God works among men our wills have a substantial role. As a result, God expects us to think, plan, judge, and do. This is certainly true of us as we begin our journey into understanding what God has to say about personal finances. If God is working in our lives we may well do the planning but it is God by the Holy Spirit that does the directing. This is brought out in Proverbs 16:9 which notes "*A man's heart deviseth his way, but the Lord directeth his steps*" (KJV). God allows us to do the planning but He wants our planning to have direction from Him so that the steps we take are within His will. This does not mean that God does not give us options to choose from. If you are looking to buy a home and you find four that meet your needs and any of them would fit within your budget, is God going to be upset because you chose the one with the brown wood exterior because you happen to like that style? Not likely. God has given us a mind and a will to make appropriate choices. We make choices every day dealing with what we will eat, what we will wear, and what we will do for the day. Does this mean that God can not use your choices to your and others' benefit? Does this mean that God can not work miraculously using appropriate choices you have made? Of course not.

Once we have established that we are Christians willing to be led by His Spirit we can begin the journey to financial freedom and peace. The first step in the plan is to recognize that your part is vital. Financial plans do not grow on trees nor are they one size fits all. We must make the effort to come up with a plan. The old business adage is quite applicable here: "plan or be planned for." If you don't plan with God's leading then the world has a plan for you which usually involves relieving you of all that you receive. Make a commitment to plan today.

You as Steward and God as Owner - Accountability

We have already noted that we are called to be stewards and not consumers. We learned an important truth from 1 Corinthians 4:2 – "*Here, further, it is sought in stewards that a man be found faithful.* " That is, stewardship is about faithfulness. We also learned that there is a unique relationship of the steward to the resources he has – they belong to another. We earlier emphasized that their owner is Christ. The goal of the steward is to earn a return on the Master's resources and we identified that there were three major areas that encompass the accounting of the stewardship. They were the family, the ministry, and the estate that is left.

In this section we want to explore the importance of the accountability of you as a steward. If we do not understand there is accountability then, unfortunately, the resources will likely be squandered. Accountable means having to give a report of your work. What if your professor at the beginning of the semester gave all the assignments and readings that were to be done throughout the semester and trusts that you will do them? The professor mentions that he will not be collecting the work or reviewing the things that you read. You get an A by just coming to class once in a while!! Now, after the hallelujahs die down I have this question. How many of you will have completed all the assignments and readings that the professor assigned at the beginning of the semester? Based on my experiences there would be few that have. What if the professor said there would be one exam based on the assignments and readings given sometime the last 3 weeks of the semester and that would count for your entire grade? Experience again shows that most will attempt to complete most of the assignments and readings. When there is no accountability for what needs to be done our natural mind may quickly dismiss

? Accountable

the relevance of doing all the work without considering the possible benefits that are lost by not doing it.

This all gets back to using our minds as guided by the Spirit. If you believe that God has allowed you access to a college education then you would want to be a good steward of that which is provided by that education. Yet, it never ceases to amaze me how many students, many very well intentioned, lose focus on the stewardship of their education and don't nearly receive the return that they should on it. Invariably it is accountability that determines the return on your education. Those who are dedicated to receiving the most out of their education usually are being held accountable in some way. Perhaps it is mom and dad who are paying for college, or a scholarship committee, or an employer. The key is, as stewards, they are accountable.

So, another important thing to understand is that as stewards we are accountable to the Master for what He provides us. Faithfulness involves accountability. How we use our resources is important and we want to be able to look forward to giving an account. In Luke 16 is the well known story of the unjust steward. (v. 1-13). There is much to be learned from this parable about finances and especially financial stewardship. In the first verse the steward of a rich man is accused of wasting the master's goods. This turned out to be true. The steward was really being a "consumer" of the master's goods and not a steward. In verse two the master appropriately requests of the steward an accounting: "give an account of thy stewardship." Literally he is to give a reckoning. Now, the steward is in a real pickle, as we might say, because he can no longer have the stewardship and yet he is quite used to living the high life. As a result he is unwilling to work and too ashamed to humble himself and beg. Before we continue we see some very important truths for ourselves. We are handling the Master's goods so always keep in mind that you will be called to give an account of your stewardship of those goods. Never waste the Master's goods as a consumer as this steward did. Never put yourself in this type of situation.

Notice that the master does not bail him out by giving him more goods. As a steward you must be faithful in a little to be faithful in much (Luke 16:10). So what is the steward to do? Interestingly, you would think that the steward lacked intelligence to get himself into this mess but the steward actually was quite intelligent as can be seen by his plan for after he loses the stewardship. He basically strikes deals with all those who are debtors to his lord for less than what they owe so that when he gives the actual account to the lord and is put out of the stewardship he will have many friends in these debtors to help him out. It's sad to see that the steward didn't use his intelligence in the first place.

Perhaps you know the rest of the story, the lord commends the steward for his wise plan in taking care of **himself**. The Lord in using this parable was not condoning the dishonesty of the steward for He actually is the one that calls him "unjust." It is the master in the story that commends the steward. The purpose of the parable was to show the importance of using present opportunities for future blessing. The children of the world, whose god is mammon, seem at times to be wiser than those who are not of the world. Here the unjust steward was wise in using his present opportunity to ensure his own future blessing. We need to take hold of the present opportunities that God has given us to be a steward of what He has given that we might look forward to giving account. As we have noted before, our blessings are for the most part spiritual, and many are future. But are we using present opportunities, financial and otherwise, to prepare for that future? 1 Peter 4:10 makes clear that these resources are more than physical but include our spiritual gifts that God has given. Luke 16:12 emphasizes that on earth we are stewards of another's things but in the future of our own. But if you have not been faithful in another's then you certainly will not be faithful with your own that would be given you at the Bema (2 Corinthians 5:10). Of course, it all comes back to whom we give the preeminence. That is the point of Luke 12:31-34. Seek first the kingdom of God – that will show where your treasure is and your heart as well. You will then look forward to giving an account of all that God has given. Luke 12:42-43 states "*And the Lord said, who is that faithful and prudent steward whom his lord will set over his household, to give the measure of corn in due season? Blessed is the bondman whom his lord on coming shall find doing thus*" (JND).

Planning and Counting the Cost

In the next chapter we discuss in detail the steps involved in financial planning and creating a plan. In this chapter we are continuing to lay the foundation so that you will be successful in the undertaking. Another important Biblical truth related to planning is that it involves intelligently counting the cost. When the Lord explained that discipleship required taking up our own cross He was emphasizing that it meant putting to death or denying the world as having the first priority. He explained this concept using several parables that deal with counting the cost. These same truths dealing with discipleship apply to us as financial stewards.

The parables come from Luke 14. The first concerns the building of a tower (vv. 28-30) and the second with determining whether to go to war (vv. 31-32). In each case the Lord is trying to point out that to be His disciple requires a cost – He becomes preeminent. Likewise when making a decision we must plan and count the cost. A lack of planning means you may start out strong but run out of funds and have a building half completed. The sad part is not just the ridicule of others for your state but the likelihood that another will receive all that went into the project. This is what happened in the late eighties when the real estate market had a "major correction" as some might call it. Many buildings went unfinished and were auctioned off in bankruptcy proceedings, the original owners receiving nothing after all they had put into it. Most, if not all, had not counted the cost or if they did, used a wrong perspective in counting the cost.

Planning means doing more than writing down a few things you would like to do, it means understanding how to properly calculate the cost. You don't need to be a mathematician or an engineer but you must be willing to take the time to count the cost. The world would rather you not count the cost of your decisions. That is why the world's emphasis is on getting you to buy now before it's too late. Research shows that those who take time to consider the cost of a deal don't normally take it. The merchants and advertisers know this and you need to be aware of it as well. Do any of these sound familiar? Time is limited! Call today, space is limited! This deal is only good today! Be one of the first 15 callers! And that's not all; if you order in the next 15 minutes you will receive...! They contradict the Biblical perspective of counting the cost. Taking advantage of those offers lacks planning. The Bible tells us to plan and count the cost. We need to disregard that which would violate that rule. Any deal of the world that sounds too good to be true likely is too good to be true. That is, there is more than meets the eye. You will learn a great deal in this book on how to count the cost and you should find it a great benefit to you as you seek to be a good steward of the Lord.

Setting and Implementing Financial Plans

We can now summarize this section so far by saying that God expects the Christian to plan and implement financial plans as a good steward. This involves making Christ preeminent and pondering carefully using the mind that God has given us. I sometimes call this the combination of seeking and thinking. There is one last component to setting in place and implementing successful personal financial plans. I call it the doing or performance phase. See, we need all three parts: preeminence, pondering, and performance or in the vernacular; seeking, thinking and doing. Leave any part out and our plans will fail.

That brings us to performance or doing. In order to have a plan or to make a plan of any use requires doing something. But that brings us back to the question I posed earlier that I promised to get back to. How do I really know if the Spirit would or would not have me do something from a financial perspective? I suggest that there are three mechanisms by which we may know the mind of God concerning a matter. These can only have instrumentality if it is the Spirit of God providing the insight. That is, these three mechanisms are based on the power of the Holy Spirit. They are the Bible, prayer, and Godly counsel.

We should be able to see by this point that the Bible has a great deal to say about financial matters and, in fact, it is my understanding from another that it is the second most touched on topic in the Bible, next to love. Although I have not confirmed this point I would certainly not be surprised. A great deal of our time is spent in stewardship type activities (working, shopping, selling, investing, etc.). It's no accident that many of the parables of the Lord used money or riches to teach a lesson. If the use of resources was so important to God to include so much in the Bible it would seem to behoove us to use it as a source for counsel and wisdom in this very area. Paul, in writing to Timothy, noted that "*every scripture is divinely inspired, and profitable for teaching, for conviction, for correction, for instruction in righteousness; that the man of God may be complete, fully fitted to every good work*" (2 Timothy 3:16-17, JND). These two verses say it all concerning the applicability of the Bible in determining and implementing our financial plans. Do we wish to be a fully fitted and complete steward of God? Then use His Word. There is no better source of wise counsel in this world today. Throughout this book we will draw on the truths of the Word to help us understand the direction we should take when it comes to our financial planning.

In addition to the Word as a guide, there is prayer. God communicates to us through His Word and we communicate to God through prayer. Prayer serves several purposes. Perhaps first and foremost it keeps us in fellowship with and thinking about Him. It's like the accountability of stewardship, if we are not vigilant we soon lose track of things and begin to wander off the path. The same is true with prayer. There are many examples of prayer in the Bible but in summary they fall into four key areas. They are worship (adoration) because of who He is, confession, thanksgiving for what He has done, and supplication and requests of Him. This is not a treatise on prayer so we will not go into too much detail, except to say, that all of these are an important part pf prayer. We want to emphasize that God certainly wants us to pray and it is one way by which we gain knowledge of what He would like us to do. The Word says, "*the fervent supplication of the righteous man has much power* (James 5:16, JND). Again we will not go into all the details of prayer but reading His Word helps us understand how and what to pray for. Praying that the Lord make us multi-millionaires will not be answered in the affirmative since it is clear that this is a wrong desire. It will seem as if the Lord is not answering since you have requested an answer to prayer that He has already given you in His Word. No better verse makes this clear than James 4:3, "*Ye ask, and receive not, because ye ask evilly (amiss), that ye may consume it in your pleasures*" (JND).

The opposite of asking amiss of course is asking rightly, in faith knowing that whatever God answers is best for you. The Scripture states "*if ye shall ask anything in my name, I will do it*" (John 14:14, JND). Now this is where we go astray. We see the "ask anything" and right away think God will give every desire of our heart. But as we have already noted, the Bible also notes that we can ask amiss and such prayers will not be answered. The whole counsel of God shows the importance of prayer but also praying rightly. We do not always know how God will answer prayer but as Christians filled with the Spirit we know when it has been answered and sometimes we realize that the answer may be "no" or "wait." Sometimes the answer comes through other brothers and sisters in Christ, or perhaps God uses someone we don't know. At other times He may answer in a miraculous way and other times His silence on a question is an answer. However He answers we need to keep in mind that prayer is another way by which we can know God's will.

The last way God speaks to us is through the Godly counsel of others. Now, please note I said "Godly" counsel. The world's counsel is often tainted by its perspective on life. As is mentioned on the copyright page of this book it is wise in light of the rapidity of change in our world and each individual's unique circumstances to seek appropriate financial and legal counsel before making major decisions. I would suggest that counsel, if possible, should come from a Christian professional. Be careful though, there are many who use the term "Christian" in their business because they go to a church and want the members' business. There are many who profess to know Christ in this world but few who have confessed Him as the one who has died for them. The testimony of others concerning an individual may be able to help you find the right Godly individual.

Godly counsel, of course, is scriptural. The Bible says "*where no counsel is, the people fall; but in the multitude of counselors there is safety*" (Proverbs 11:14, KJV). The key here is again in the type of counsel. The worldly wise may be helpful and very knowledgeable in the financial maze of rules or in the legalese of the day but they have little understanding of the Biblical perspective. So, use the world's experts if necessary to understand its requirements but when it comes to knowing what God wants consider Godly counsel.

In summary, then, our Christian financial planning and implementation is influenced by the Holy Spirit in three ways. They are by His Word, by prayer, and by Godly counsel from others. It is by using these we truly understand God's will for our lives in the area of finance.

Men and Women are Different!

Perhaps you have seen or heard about the book *Women are from Venus and Men are from Mars*. I have not read the book but the title alone indicates to me that the author understands there are differences between men and women. This is another area where the Bible and the world often differ. The world tries to make women and men appear the same or perhaps interchangeable. Despite the world's attempts to make the two genders appear the same or equal in every aspect God has made them different. The physical differences are quite evident and some of the ways men's and women's bodies work are different. The fact that the woman bares the children is a significant difference. We could also go into how the women's role from a Biblical perspective is different and how quite often the emotional makeup of the two genders is different. That is, we could write a whole book on how we have learned from God and experience that men and women are different. We will not try to undertake that dialogue here but want to recognize that these differences also generally have an effect on how women and men view financial matters.

For instance how often do men purchase something for the kitchen? How often do women purchase tools for the garage? Now some may, but generally this is not the case. Send men and women into a grocery store and see what they come out with. I'm sure it will be different even if given the same list of things to buy. We point this out here because many of you are or will get married and it's best to realize now that you and your spouse will have differing views on just about all aspects of finance. You will need to discuss this issue candidly with one another.

Even the emotional makeup and how individuals deal with problems are different and can affect the financial plan. Let's say you get into a major argument with the one you love. How does that affect the finances? Interestingly, it does. It has been found that often people will try to get a release from the stress by shopping. What is interesting women will do it more frequently at the malls buying clothes and the like but men will go out and buy major things such as cars and boats to assuage the hurt. Neither is good but men really bust the spending plan when not in the right frame of mind.

The key point here to keep in mind as you enter into the marriage relationship is that how men and women view financial matters can be significantly different just because of their makeup. In addition, the environments that each person grew up in can have a significant impact on how they view financial matters. Be sure to keep these differences in mind and discuss the issue up front and learn to work together on the differences.

One final note, the advertisers realize there is still a difference and so often they will market to the sexes differently even for the same product (such as a car). It's good to keep this in mind as well. A great deal of money goes into researching consumer behavior and they know what buttons to push to get you to buy something even though you may not really need it.

Outcomes and Chapter Summary

In this first chapter there were five learning objectives that we identified to help us understand the Biblical basis of personal financial planning. To understand God's ways we first learned that we need to be oriented toward God and have the Spirit of God within to effectively understand what He has for our lives. We learned that both God and we play an important role.

Learning Objective 1. **Identify the Biblical basis for financial planning and the three key factors in preparing a financial plan.**

We found that the three key factors in this planning are preeminence, pondering, and performance. That is, seeking, thinking, and doing. The first involves making Christ preeminent in our lives, the second involves using our minds or intellect, and the third involves making an effort to do something. If we miss any of these our plan fails. We learned that two important factors emphasize making Christ preeminent in our lives: that He is the creator and sustainer of all and that He is the owner and provider of all.

Learning Objective 2. **Explain the key differences between how the world views personal financial planning and how the Christian views it.**

In relation to the preeminence of Christ we also looked at differences between how the world views financial things and how God views them. Here again, three things were identified that characterize the different views. The world views us as consumers while God views us as stewards. Secondly, the world has a love for money and mammon is its god whereas the Christian has a love for Christ and He is their God. Last, the world seeks the wisdom of men while the Christian seeks the wisdom of God.

Learning Objective 3. **Understand from a Biblical perspective what it means to be a steward of what God, as owner, has given you.**

We also took an in depth look at what it means to be a steward and found that the key is accountability and reward. That is, using current opportunities for future blessing. We learned that being a steward involves being the administrator of another's goods. In this world we are the administrators of God's goods that He has given us. We also noted that it is more than financial resources but also time, talent, spiritual gifts, and other resources as well.

Learning Objective 4. **Describe the "counting the cost" perspective described in the Bible from both a Christian financial and discipleship view.**

We also learned that as a steward we must count the cost much like when we count the cost of becoming a disciple of Christ. Our priorities are changed and the cost means putting aside or putting to death the things of the world that used to have first place in our lives so that Christ is preeminent in our thinking. Similarly, when taking on financial planning we must count the cost of taking certain actions.

Learning Objective 5. **Examine and understand the three components that should influence the direction of your Christian financial planning.**

Finally we looked at the three mechanisms that God uses to communicate with us concerning our planning and implementation of financial plans. They are His Word, prayer, and the Godly counsel of others. These three things together help in our thinking to make decisions concerning the wise use of the resources that God has provided. These are all efficacious by the Holy Spirit dwelling within.

We have now set the foundation for the coming chapters of the book where we can in earnest look at the financial planning process and discuss the details of how to manage your plan including financing, investing, and insurance. Together we will see there is much to learn and with an open mind and the Spirit within we can see what God has in store for us.

Bible Texts Referenced

Genesis 2:10	Genesis 3:19	Genesis 39:1-4	Genesis 41:39-44
Genesis 45:4-8	Genesis 50:19-21	Deuteronomy 10:14	Job 1:21
1 Samuel 16:7	1 Kings 17:4-6	1 Chronicles 29:11-12	Psalm 24:1
Psalm 50:10-12	Psalm 135:6	Proverbs 11:14	Proverbs 16:9
Proverbs 21:1	Haggai 2:8		

Matthew 6:24	Matthew 6:31-33	Matthew 25:14-29	Luke 12:31-34
Luke 12:42-44	Luke 14:26-27	Luke 14:28-32	Luke 16:1-13
Luke 16:13	John 3:16-18	John 8:36	John 14:14
Acts 17:26	Acts 18:3	Romans 8:9-16	Romans 8:28
Romans 14:12	1 Corinthians 1:25	1 Corinthians 1:26	1 Corinthians 2:11-14
1 Corinthians 3:11-15	1 Corinthians 3:19	1 Corinthians 3:16	1 Corinthians 4:2
2 Corinthians 5:10	2 Corinthians 8:1-2	Ephesians 1:3	Ephesians 4:17-24
Ephesians 4:30	Colossians 1:15-18	Colossians 3:1-4	Philippians 2:5-7
Philippians 2:21	Philippians 4:17	Philippians 4:19	2 Thessalonians 3:10
1 Thessalonians 5:19	1 Timothy 5:10	1 Timothy 5:18	1Timothy 6:8
1 Timothy 6:9	1 Timothy 6:10-11	2 Timothy 3:16-17	Titus 1:7
Hebrews 11:6	James 4:3	James 5:16	1 Peter 4:10

Exercises and Research Activities

1. Take a careful look at the Bible and what we discussed in this chapter and see if you can answer the question; why isn't every Christian rich?

2. We looked at Christ as the Creator and sustainer. Why is this important in the context of financial stewardship?

3. Why do you think that God has us work in order to secure possessions from Him?

4. Find an article or advertisement that emphasizes the individual as a consumer and write a short summary of what it attempts to accomplish and what the Christian reaction or perspective should be.

5. Write a two-page summary about where "love" fits into Christian financial stewardship.

6. Explain how God directs us if we are the ones who are supposed to be doing the planning. Isn't our plan guiding us?

7. Research and present an example of accountability, or the lack of it, in relation to finance.

8. Research and present an example of a financial situation where counting the cost was an issue that was either not considered or was ignored. Discuss the ramifications of the decision.

9. Research and present at least one way women and men are different when it comes to financial issues.

10. Prayerfully consider and select someone to help you be accountable for your personal finances.

11. Take some time to research the Scriptures and try to write a short paper on how God interacts with the world and how that is evidenced in financial stewardship.

References and Resources

Books:

Burkett, Larry. *The Word on Finances*. Moody Press, 1994.

Web Sites:

Crown Ministries. www.crown.org.

CHAPTER 2

The Financial Stewardship Planning Process

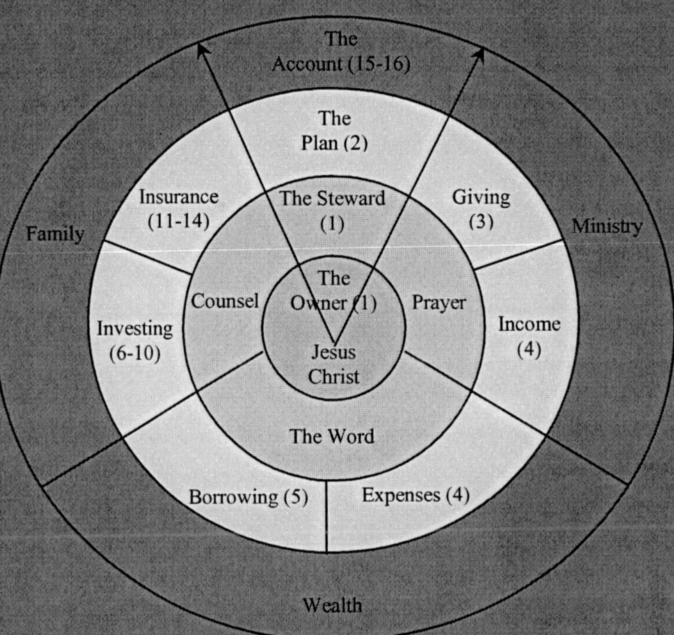

Learning Objectives

1. Define opportunity costs and identify and describe the five key influences that help determine the cost or value of something.

2. Explain how time affects the value of money and be able to calculate the future value of a sum invested now or periodically and determine what would need to be invested now in present value, or periodically to reach a projected sum in the future.

3. Identify and explain the four tradeoffs when considering the cost of something.

4. Be able to review and determine whether a financial account, transaction, or resource relates to being an asset, a liability, an expense, and/or income.

5. Describe the financial planning process.

6. Develop a personal wealth and net worth statement.

7. Develop a personal debt assessment.

8. Develop a personal cash flow and spending plan statement.

9. Develop a set of financial goals.

Lord, I commit to planning.

Lord, I realize that according to thy Word you have given me a mind to use for your glory, including planning for the future. Please let your Spirit guide me as I commit to setting appropriate goals and plans. I want your will to be done so please direct my steps. Keep me from seeking the world's riches as I plan and help me seek to plan wisely that which you would have me plan for. Thank you for your love and for the resource of life you have given me.

Opportunity Costs and the Value of Time

You may not have heard of "opportunity cost" but the phrase itself may give you an idea. Every opportunity has a cost associated with it. It is not the specific cost of an item we purchase but the cost of the missed opportunity of the alternatives. So opportunity cost is what we give up as a result of a financial decision. If I buy tickets to a Red Sox game then I give up not just the price of the tickets but the opportunity to use those funds for other purposes such as saving for the future or buying some books. Opportunity cost deals with this second part – that is, what we give up that we could have done.

? **Opportunity Cost**

Cost is important when discussing the value of time as it relates to money. It is sometimes called the "time value of money." It is as if time itself has an influence on increasing the value of money. Now we need to be careful here because this is only true if the money is gaining a return. If I take the money I would have used for purchasing tickets ($100) and put it under my mattress for 20 years", time will likely have a negative effect on the money and it will be worth less because prices will likely have increased reducing the amount I can buy with that hundred dollars. If, instead of buying the tickets, I invested the money at a 5% annual rate of return, paid monthly, for 20 years then I would have $265.33. In a sense by buying the tickets I missed the opportunity to have $265 twenty years from now. Again, price increases or inflation as we call it, may still have an effect on that sum. So we can see that the decisions we make today can have a profound effect on our future. That is what the Lord is showing us in the parable of the unjust steward (Luke 16:1-8). We need to take advantage of present opportunities that will lead to future blessing. Before we learn how to make calculations dealing with the time value of money we need to understand some other factors that influence pricing, value, and return.

? **Time Value of Money**

The Issue of Scarcity

One factor often ignored when considering financial decisions is the issue of scarcity. In fact, if you have children or in the future have them, be sure they learn this concept. As children, we often grow up thinking there is an endless supply of whatever it is we want, or we have little understanding of the cost related to something. If you needed a pair of shoes your parents bought them. If there was no more milk in the fridge then mom or dad went and bought some. The difficulty for many children is that for the first eighteen years of their lives most of their needs or wants are taken care of. We define scarcity from an economic perspective as the inability to satisfy all needs and wants at the same time. Basically we only have limited funds and so must choose which needs to satisfy among many relevant needs.

? **Scarcity**

As you reflect on your finances there will be times that there are many relevant needs to be taken care of but you must choose one over another due to limited financial resources. This is the part you may not have seen as a child (although some have) and this is what scarcity is about. Conceptually we understand that money is limited but we don't really understand it until we need to make choices from among many good and deserving needs. Scarcity is a factor that not only significantly influences our financial situation but also the value of the goods we see. If through tradeoffs among needs or wants many in the community can not afford the automobiles at the local dealership then it is likely the dealership will need to make some decisions on the pricing of its product. A lower price on the product might help in winning some of the tradeoff decisions. Without getting too bogged down with the whole realm of economics and supply and demand, it is important to understand that when resources are scarce they influence the value of various financial transactions and instruments.

The Issue of Inflation

? **Inflation**

? **Deflation**

Another factor that influences pricing, value, and return is inflation. Most of you will be much more familiar with this term than scarcity. Inflation is basically a rise in the general level of prices. The reverse of this is called deflation where prices in general are falling. Generally, over the years, prices have gone up. The general reason for this is that there are more people, thus there is more demand for goods. If the supply of goods does not keep up with the demand then prices go up which will take some of the demand away as people make other choices, which relates to our previous discussion on scarcity. You can now see that these are related. Another possibility, of course, is that the demand may persist but workers will seek higher wages in order to meet the higher price. The difficulty with this, of course, is that it will increase the cost of producing goods which will in turn make the prices of goods higher. I think you see how at times inflation can be self-perpetuating.

? **Purchasing Power**

The inflation factor is important to us because it reduces what we call our purchasing power. Purchasing power is a measure of the goods and services we can buy with whatever income we have. For a simplistic example, if my favorite cookies, Keebler fudge sticks, are currently $2.00 a package and I have $10 to spend on them I could buy five packages of cookies. If next month I go to purchase the cookies with another $10 and the price has increased to $2.50 a package I can now only buy four packages. My purchasing power has been reduced as a result of the price increase of the cookies. Instead of buying five packages I can only buy four. I either need to live on the four packages or take $2.50 from somewhere else to purchase the extra package or secure an additional $2.50 in income to buy it.

Now, many of us hope to get an annual increase in our income to not only offset the increase in prices but give us some extra income to use. In times of higher inflation this is rarely the case. If you live on a fixed income inflation may prove to be difficult to deal with. If your income this past year was $30,000 and you just received a 10% increase you might be quite excited since this coming year you will be making $33,000. But what if the inflation rate is

15%? Then in real income terms you have taken a 5% reduction of $1,500. You will be making the equivalent of $28,500.

We touch on this factor because it is one of those things you must be thinking about as you do financial planning. A logical question here then would be, how do we know what the inflation rate is or will be? Inflation is measured by the government using the consumer price index (CPI). Most of us have heard of this term before and it is a measure of the cost of living for the average "consumer." The CPI is composed of a "basket" of over 400 goods and services that the government tracks prices for from all over the country. The base of the index was established during the time period of 1982-1984. The value of the basket during that period was assigned an index of 100. From that point forward you can easily calculate the total inflation rate from the base by subtracting 100. At the end of 2004 the CPI was 190.3 and by subtracting 100 we see that prices have risen 90.3% since 1984. So the cost of living, as we call it, has gone up 90.3%. As we noted before, as prices rise our purchasing power decreases. The decrease in our purchasing power, percentage wise, is different since we are looking at some amount of income we have that can purchase less, rather than looking at what is being purchased and costs more. They are two different ideas. For you mathematicians out there you can take the base CPI (100) and divide it by the current CPI and subtract that result from 1 to find out the percentage decrease in purchasing power you have had. Of course if your purchasing habits are different than the "basket" of the CPI then your inflation rate may vary. For further `information on the CPI, its current value, and its history see http://www.bls.gov/cpi/home.htm.

? **Consumer Price Index**

As far as knowing the future inflation rate we must be honest and recognize that no one really knows for sure. That being said, we can be intelligent and estimate it based on historical norms and current trends. Inflation estimates are offered by many entities, including the government Office of Management and Budget (OMB), various economists, and private organizations. Of course, inflation affects interest rates and predicting future interest rates is also difficult. We still need to at least make an estimate of interest rates as well as inflation if we are to make sound financial decisions. We will cover more on interest rates later when we get to borrowing and investing. Check the end of the chapter for resources that provide estimates of inflation and interest rates.

The Issue of Risk

A third factor that influences pricing and value is risk. We are familiar with risk in several ways. We sometimes look at risk as taking a chance like in a lottery or doing something that is dangerous such as canoeing over the Niagara Falls. We call these risky because there is a significant possibility of loss. Our financial decisions are also influenced by risk. Should I buy the lawn mower used or new? Should I take that promotion? Should I buy that painting as an investment?

? Risk

From a financial perspective we define risk as a measure of the degree of uncertainty. Thus, different risks will result in correspondingly different prices or values. For example, you would not expect to pay the same amount of money for a used lawn mower as you would for the same version of a new one. The price of the used one, no matter how little it was used, will be less because there is more uncertainty as to its capability, how long it will last, or how the previous owner used it. If you want greater certainty and less risk you might buy the new mower which may also have a warranty. But you will pay more for having less risk. Now, we may ask the question which we should purchase? I will leave that to the chapter on borrowing when we talk about making major purchases. The promotion we noted also involves risk. If I take the position what happens if it doesn't work out? If I take it, will that same position be there a year from now? Risk is involved. The riskier the decision to take the promotion the more likely there will be greater financial rewards. The painting as an investment has a different type of risk but still deals with uncertainty. The issue with it is whether you will be able to sell it for more in the future. This is what we call return risk which we will cover in more detail when we get to the chapters on investing. Suffice to say here, the risk factor plays an important role in our financial decision-making.

The Issue of Perception

? Perception

A fourth factor that influences pricing and value is perception. This is the most volatile factor and is closely related in some ways to risk. In the financial world we would define perception as decisions based on intuition. Perception can involve the senses but the intangible aspect of intuition is also included. Some may call it guessing but we will not go that far. Perception plays a significant role in the pricing and value of markets and goods. For instance, gasoline prices recently have been over $2.00 a gallon in some parts of the country. What caused them to go up by 70 cents a gallon or more? Increased demand? No. The war in Iraq? Perhaps a little but since we were not getting much oil from there in the first place it probably isn't the issue. OPEC cut production? No. Did all the refineries burn down? No. As we look at it nothing has really changed that should make oil prices so much more expensive except the perception factor. With the unrest in the world, market traders perceive that there may be a shortage so almost immediately prices go up to account for the perception. So really, fear often influences perception. The fear is that current world events will interrupt supplies so that results in the bidding up of the price of oil.

Another recent example is mortgage rates. They have risen over 1% since they reached historic lows in 2004. Why are they going up if the Federal Reserve has not increased rates yet? There is a perception that they may raise them in the near future (which they did). Unlike the oil issue here it is a mixture of the senses and intuition. That is, the stronger economic numbers and comments from the Fed are scrutinized to see what indications there might be for future interest rate trends. Rates have already gone up far more than the Fed is likely to change the prime rate at one time but perception fuels the increase and makes the markets volatile. How else do you explain a company reporting record earnings and then have its price go down? Traders perceive something negative so the stock goes down. Some of the perceptions turn out to be correct while others do not. Unfortunately, the markets don't wait around to find out which ones are correct.

Let's say the CEO of a major company sells most of his stock. What will the markets do? They will perceive that there may be some problems with the company and begin to sell. The price of the stock will then go down since there will be more sellers than buyers. What the market assumed could be incorrect. They later find that the CEO sold to cover a major debt that he was determined to get rid of. The price of the stock may inch back up but the market cannot really undo (put things back exactly as they were) what has been done by perception.

The Issue of Time

The fifth and last key factor that affects value and pricing is time. Again risk also plays a role in relation to this factor. Very few of the readers of this book will question the fact that their time is of some value. It may be different for each of you but there is likely some value that you would place on your time. If you are a consultant you might place a value of $125 hour on your time or perhaps $1000 a day.

What many younger people miss is that time does indeed influence the value of your account in the future. Let's say you are 20 today and find some way to save $100 a month until you are 65. Without interest you would save $54,000. Now that $54,000 we calculated does not include the value of time which is paid via interest or return on your money that as a good steward you have invested. Even if we are conservative and invest it at 5% a year compounded monthly the value of your account when you are 65 grows to $202,643.73. Did time make a difference here? What if the return was even greater? Let's say 8% per year. The value then grows to $527,453.99. Now there are factors that influence return including risk and inflation. But the important thing here is that time with the effects of compounding (reinvested interest or interest on your interest) substantially increases the value of your account. Also, the length of the term can increase the rate of return but we will get more into that later when we get to investing. Here the goal is to encourage you to consider the factor of time when you make financial decisions. We will see when we get to borrowing this truth has the same effect where you end up paying much more than you borrowed back to the lender. The exception here is it's the bank getting the benefit, not you.

? Compounding

Now you may be a little nervous about what is behind all of these numbers I just rattled off in that last paragraph. In reality the math is not difficult and the formulas have already been developed. There are also books that have been published that have compound interest tables to make it even easier. Check your local book store for a copy. A smaller version of these types of tables is provided for you in Appendix A of this text. There are four basic formulas that can be helpful if you want to do your own calculations or want to go beyond the entries listed in most tables. For instance, most tables will have up to 30 years, but in our example above we needed 45 years so I did the calculation.

Future value of a one time payment. The first formula is the future value of a one time payment. For example, I put $100 in the bank today and the annual interest rate is 6% on average for 10 years. We will assume the bank applies interest to your account on a monthly basis. The formula is like this:

$$\text{Future Account Balance} = \text{the base amount} * ((1+i)^n)$$

i = the interest rate for each of the periods that the bank applies interest to your account. So, the annual rate is 6% or .06 and the compounding is monthly (12). Then we take .06 and divide it by 12 to get .005. Basically the bank will give you interest of a half percent each month which, of course, equals the annual rate of 6%.

n = the number of interest periods that the bank will credit to your account which in this case will be 10 years times the 12 months each year which gives 120.

1 = the number one

Now you can plug the numbers in the formula:

$$\text{Result} = 100 * (1+ .005)^{120}$$

$$\text{Result} = 100 * 1.81940$$

$$\text{Result} = 181.94$$

So assuming I place $100 in an account today and add nothing to it, it will grow to 181.94 in 10 years. This type of calculation can be quite useful in determining different financial alternatives that may result in a one time savings that could be set aside versus being spent. For instance, we would like to get a new bedroom set. We can afford $2000. Now we could spend the whole sum or we could decide to be a bit more frugal and find something that meets our needs that only costs $1000. We could then invest the $1000 difference. This formula will help me determine the value of this alternative in the future. Table A-1 in Appendix A provides a table of values to make it easy to calculate the future value without having to use the formula.

Future value of a payment per period. Another important financial formula is the future value of an amount that is saved every period. For instance, you have decided to cut back on living expenses to the tune of $75.00 a month (you stopped buying CDs, drinking Dasani water, and cancelled your fitness club membership) so you can save for your next car. Let's assume monthly compounding with a 7% rate of return and you want to buy your next car in 5 years and want to know how much you will have. The formula is slightly different and is as follows:

$$\text{Future Account Balance} = \text{the base amount} * (((1+i)^n - 1)/i)$$

The values to plug in the formula are calculated as before except in this formula we subtract one and then divide by the i (applied interest rate; .07/12=.00583). n = 5*12=60.

$$\text{Result} = 75 * ((1+ .00583)^{60})\text{-}1)/.00583$$

$$\text{Result} = 75 * ((.41734)/.00583$$

$$\text{Result} = 75 * 71.5855$$

$$\text{Result} = 5368.91$$

In 5 years you will have over five thousand dollars available to help in the purchase of your next car. This formula can again be quite helpful in evaluating purchase tradeoffs. For instance if you were considering buying season tickets to attend your favorite sports team's games you could compare the purchase to saving the funds. Let's assume that it costs $250 a month for the next 5 years to keep season tickets for your team. If the average interest rate is 6% then the cost of purchasing the tickets is actually 1409.27 instead of the $1250 (5 * 250). That is the amount you would have if you invested the money instead.

Present value of a future sum. There are two similar formulas for determining what you need to invest now to have a certain amount in the future. The first is often called the present value formula which calculates the present value of a future sum. It lets you know what you need today to invest to get what you need in the future. Let's say you just received a small inheritance and would like to set some aside for a future car purchase. To figure out how much you should set aside you can use a present value formula that uses one payment up front. You expect to need $8000 in 6 years for your purchase and expect that you can get at least 5% compounded monthly on your money.

The formula looks like this:

$$\text{Amount needed to invest} = \text{base amount} * (1/((1+i)^n))$$

We already know how to calculate i and n so we can plug in the numbers and do the calculation.

$$\text{Amount needed} = 8000*(1/((1.00417)^{72}))$$

$$\text{Amount needed} = 8000*(1/1.34934)$$

$$\text{Amount needed} = 8000*(.7411)$$

$$\text{Amount needed} = 5928.80$$

You would need to set aside $5928.80 of the inheritance today to have $8000 available in 6 years. Table A-3 in Appendix A supplies present value factors to make it easy to perform these calculations.

Present value of a sum of future per period payments. The second formula is sometimes called the sinking fund formula. It allows you to calculate how much a month you must set aside at a particular rate to achieve some sum in the future. Let's say that the previous result of setting aside $5928.80 is more than you can do and you decide you want to know how much a month you would have to save to have the $8000.00 in 6 years assuming the 5% interest rate.

The formula looks like this:

$$\text{Amount needed to invest} = \text{base amount} * (i/((1+i)^n - 1))$$

We already know how to calculate i and n so we can plug in the numbers and do the calculation.

$$\text{Amount needed} = 8000*(.00417/((1.00417)^{72}-1))$$

$$\text{Amount needed} = 8000*(.00417/.34934)$$

$$\text{Amount needed} = 8000*(.01195)$$

$$\text{Amount needed} = \$95.60$$

You must invest $95.60 each month for 6 years at 5% to get the desired amount of $8000 within the six year time frame. Table A-4 in Appendix A can be used to help make this calculation. Again, these are not hard formulas and can be easily determined on a calculator. They can be extremely useful as you do your planning and that is why we cover them here rather than under investing. We will remind you of them there but knowing them before we get into the planning process will be a great asset. There are other formulas that we will look at when we get to the investing chapters. These four should be all you need to get you started in making relevant comparisons of alternatives.

Purchase Tradeoffs

We have now seen that there are at least five factors that influence the price, return, or value of something. They are scarcity, inflation, risk, perception, and time. In this section we also want to look at tradeoffs we make every day when considering whether to purchase something. There are at least four of what we might call purchase tradeoffs. They are cost, quality, quantity, and time. Here we are taking a slightly different view. We are not specifically looking at how any of these factors influence price which, as we know, they can. We have already looked at time and indirectly looked at quality when discussing risk and perception influences to pricing. Here we want to focus on what tradeoffs we make so that we can understand how these may be of help in keeping our financial plan in order.

Cost is an issue when doing financial planning. We do not need to be scientists to know that if our plan shows more outflow than inflow that we won't stay afloat very long. Often we will seek ways to reduce costs by making a tradeoff. For instance, if you drink Perrier water you may decide to drink Poland Spring to save on the cost of water. Now, in your mind you may look at the switch as getting a water of lower quality (whether a reality or not). That is the tradeoff you are making for a reduced cost.

Let's say you decide you can't give up the quality offered by the Perrier product. You may then decide to buy less water or buy it in larger quantities at a reduced price. Now the tradeoff is not quality but quantity. You are willing to give up buying the product in the quantity you normally do in order to keep on drinking it.

If you can't bring yourself to change the size of the bottle you purchase and you must still have Perrier then the other possible tradeoff is time. That is, you can choose to drink it less often. This, of course, reduces the quantity purchased thus reducing the cost. There are other ways of looking at time as well. If you pay to have your lawn mowed you may find the time saved is worth the cost because you now have time to do something that is perhaps more productive.

The goal here is, again, just to get you thinking. Proper planning can be done on any income but we need to understand the tradeoffs and then be willing to make the necessary decisions.

The Basics: Assets, Liabilities, Income, Expenses

Another area we want to touch on before we learn to create a personal financial plan is what the major elements of the plan include and what they are focused on. That is, what role do these elements play in the plan? If we understand their role appropriately then we can again make the right choices and create a financial plan that works. In this section we define each key element and what it is used for and then note how we personally view it as a steward of what God has given.

Defining the Categories

Most financial reports deal with one or more of four key areas that we will define here. These definitions are based on the standard definition used by most financial people and how a dictionary would usually define the term. In the next section we will deal with how our definitions as stewards might be different.

? Assets

Assets. The Webster's dictionary basically defines an asset as an item of ownership having exchange value. Most texts are very brief and define assets as what you own. Items of ownership include those things that you may still owe money on. These assets can include houses, land, cars, furniture, savings accounts, and the like. I think the dictionary definition is a bit more accurate. The key is that there is an exchange value. Could you sell it and, if so, what is the fair market value? The fair market value is the price that you could expect to get for the item from a buyer, on the open market in a reasonable period of time, assuming that you and the buyer are free and willing to enter into the transaction or not. As soon as you or the buyer are under some compulsion to buy or sell the price will likely change to the advantage of one or the other and thus the "fair" value is not what would be realized by a sale. It may be more or less. What is important here is that an asset must be fairly valued based on the current circumstances. If you must sell that asset in two weeks its value may be substantially different than if you were going to hold it for an indeterminable amount of time. Also, you can't value an asset based on its expected future value since the future is unknown. An asset is valued at a point in time so you can determine your financial status at a point in time.

Assets, at times, are further divided into categories. The term "liquid assets" is often used to identify those assets that can easily be obtained in the form of cash. Sometimes called monetary assets, these include savings accounts, checking accounts, certificates of deposit, and cash on hand. A second category of assets often noted is "tangible assets." It is not as if cash is not tangible but these items are considered non-cash items that would need to be sold to get the cash equivalent or make them liquid. These include houses, cars, furniture, antiques, and the like. The value of these items may go up or down over time depending on the asset and the market conditions. This is why they are valued at a point in time. Another category that is sometimes listed separately is "investment assets." These include stocks, bonds, real estate, and other investment vehicles that may incorporate these, such as individual retirement accounts. These would also need to be sold in order to make them liquid at their current market value, thus, they are also valued at a point in time. Their value can go up or down over time although historically these have experienced an increase in value over time.

In summary, then, assets are things that you own that have some value in exchange for them. They are often divided into one of three categories including, liquid or cash assets, tangible assets, and investment assets. Assets are valued at a point in time so that we can create valid current financial plans and reports. We will learn about how these can be used in a plan later in the chapter.

Liabilities. The basic definition offered by a dictionary would be monies owed, debts, or obligations. Another definition the dictionary gives is "something disadvantageous." This definition, although not actually used in this context by most, in a sense is quite appropriate. These are the items that would be opposite your assets in a financial report. The value of these items is usually predetermined based on an instrument, such as a loan, that you signed to acquire an asset. Whereas assets can change based on various market conditions, liabilities often do not. There are a few cases such as variable rate instruments that can change a liability based on market conditions. Liabilities usually change in value as you repay the obligation. So, liabilities tend to go down in value over time usually based on a predetermined schedule of payments. There are certain situations where even with payments the value of a liability goes up. For instance, when you pay less interest than you owe for a particular period, the value of the liability will increase because the interest not paid is added to the outstanding balance. This is sometimes called negative amortization.

? **Liabilities**

As with assets, liabilities can be, although not always, grouped into categories. The two most popular categorizations are short term liabilities and long term liabilities. Although these categories are not hard and fast, short term liabilities usually include obligations that are a year or less. These may include utility bills, college fees, insurance, rent, and credit card balances. Long term liabilities often include mortgages, car loans, education loans, and other long term purchase loans. By this list you can see why liabilities might be considered a disadvantage. We discuss this in more detail in the next section concerning the steward's view of these things.

Income. From a dictionary perspective income is the returns that come in as a result of your labor, business, investments, and the like. Basically they are cash inflows into the home and could include other items such as gifts, rebates, and refunds. Most individuals who run into financial difficulties try to resolve the problem by increasing inflows rather than decreasing outflows, this is often an error.

? **Income**

Expenses. Expenses are simply costs or charges. These can be incurred as a result of purchasing, or considered reimbursements for previous funds borrowed. These are basically cash outflows from the home.

? **Expense**

We only introduce income and expenses for the sake of the upcoming discussion in the next section on the steward's view of these things but we will certainly get into more detail on these later in the chapter. An important point that is often missed by young people is the relationship between these four categories of assets, liabilities, income, and expenses. Intuitively we know it is good to have assets and not so great to have liabilities, but do we fully understand how to integrate the four categories to maximize our assets and limit our liabilities? Let's continue on and see.

The World's versus the Steward's Perspective

As we have noted in chapter one, the Bible calls us to be stewards rather than consumers. This can be difficult since the world is constantly bombarding us with the message of consumption. The difficulty is that the more we consume the less we will have to show for the return for our efforts in the "the account:"

Exhibit 2-1 shows the four categories in a Financial Picture Model (FPM). You notice first of all there is nothing in any of the four categories. That is, we will start from scratch. Let's say our parents have just given us the "left foot of fellowship" from the home. Where do we start in the figure? The question, then, is where are you at financially? Let's update the figure to show a $1500 savings account and $38 in cash as the only assets we have but we have no liabilities.

Income	Expense
Asset	Liability

Exhibit 2-1. The Financial Picture Model - The Categories Empty – Starting from Scratch

So, in Exhibit 2-2 we have added the savings account. How do the other categories get filled? Now, after hearing our parents' ultimatum, we decide we need a nice cold Coca-Cola while we ponder our future. How will this expense be funded?

We could pay for it in one of two ways: through the cash fund or the savings account. But before considering how cash flows within the picture how do things get into the financial picture in the first place? Where did the cash and savings come from? Where do the liabilities come from? They obviously come from the outside. That is, there are external factors that influence the internal state of our plan. We don't necessarily have to use every possible external factor but there are a number we can look at. Let's look at income. How do we get income? For most of us it is or will be from working at our

Income	Expense
Asset Savings - $1500 Cash - $38	**Liability**

Exhibit 2-2. The Financial Picture Model – The Internal State of Things

profession. So we need to add that to the income side – working for Carabba's (nice restaurant). Carraba's in turn pays us and we consider that to be income. But on the outside we must note that there is some type of skill, talent, or profession that we are stewards of that makes us capable of satisfying the employer's needs so that we get paid. So updating the previous exhibit we now include our skill set that the Lord has blessed us with and our work income.

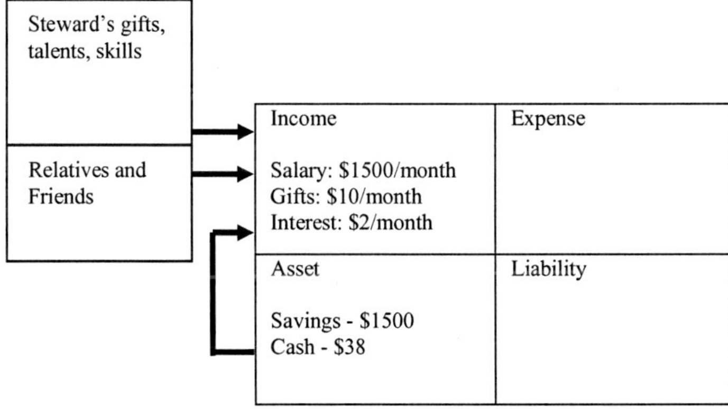

Exhibit 2-3. The Financial Picture Model - Income Included

Are there other ways of getting income into the picture? How about gifts or interest from our savings account? We have added these to Exhibit 2-3. It is interesting to note, now, that an asset can produce income. In fact, as we have seen in the Biblical parables we have already discussed, it seems that an asset should return something. Are we using present opportunities to provide for future blessing? This appears to be one of a number of lessons from the parable of the rich fool in Luke 12:16-21. The rich man's return from the harvest was great but he also misunderstood that asset and its purpose. He saw it as just his asset for making himself merry. He did not recognize God's ownership. As a result, his plan of stewardship, to build bigger barns for

himself would have no future blessing in God's eyes. Of course, often missed is the cost related to the tearing down of the old barns and building the new. Was there truly going to be a valuable return on this type of asset after factoring in the costs? Perhaps if, like Joseph, he decided to build barns for the purpose of providing against a famine, then the possible future blessing would be great. So an asset should have a purpose for future blessing and/or be providing a current return. This is the steward's perspective of an asset.

Assets as the world would see them, as we have noted, are anything of value that can be exchanged for money. As a result, the world by definition includes even items that cost a great deal to maintain and whose function is not truly that of an asset. For instance, the current value of cars is included as an asset on financial statements even though the cost of maintaining and running them annually may outweigh their worth. The same can be said of a house. The world includes the house as an asset but the steward, as with the car, recognizes the home as a substantial liability due to the expenses related to its upkeep.

The problem is not so much where they are listed on the statement but what we think as a result of where they are listed. If we see the home as an investment we think spending more and more for larger and larger homes is a "good investment." The truth is homes are shelters that have substantial expenses related to them, so, although listed with assets, should be viewed as liabilities. Bigger homes just like the bigger barns of the rich fool are not always the way to go. Many people learned the hard way that homes should not be seen as investments when in the late 1980s the real estate market took a substantial correction and many lost their homes. They didn't loose an investment they lost their shelter; their place to live. Exhibits 2-4 and 2-5 now show updated financial pictures from the world's and steward's perspectives respectively.

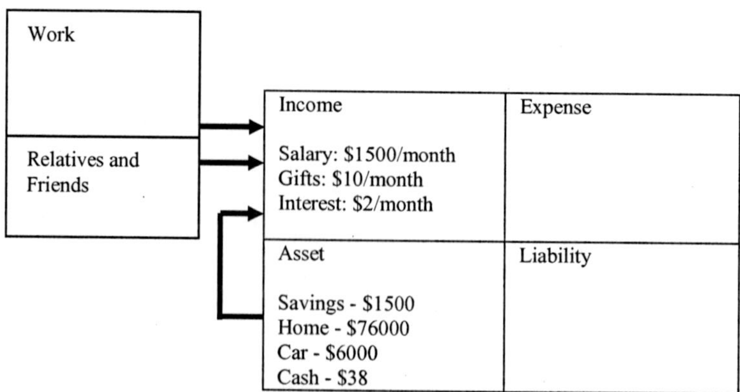

Exhibit 2-4. The Financial Picture Model – The World's View

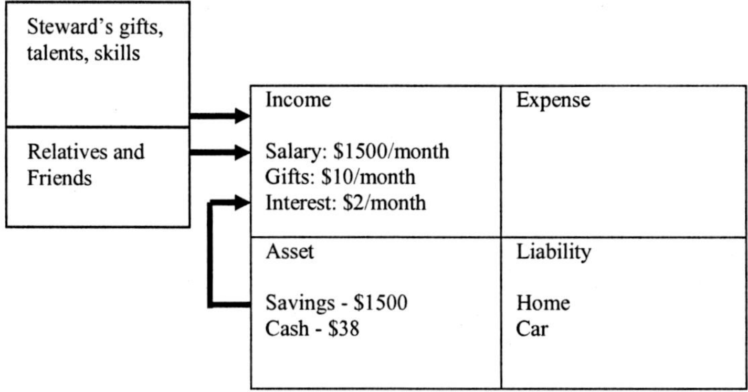

Exhibit 2-5. The Financial Picture Model – The Steward's View

The steward's view sees anything that generates expenses as a liability since it does not create a return to the income box that can then be used to increase assets. Cars and homes don't return anything unless sold. Selling them is not usually a viable option unless you buy another, live on the street, or find a place where someone else foots the bill.

Money also flows into our picture from the outside through credit or borrowing. These become liabilities since they generate expenses that must be paid as well as the repayment of the amounts that are owed. The strange thing about borrowing is that it comes in through the liability quadrant and is really never seen as income. Where do the funds go generated by the borrowing? They either exit through the expense quadrant to be seen no more or generate another asset. Of course, depending on the asset (like a home or car), the steward might view the purchased asset as another liability. What we find as a result of all this is that money only flows out through the expense quadrant. So now we can update our two financial pictures appropriately to reflect this in Exhibits 2-6 and 2-7.

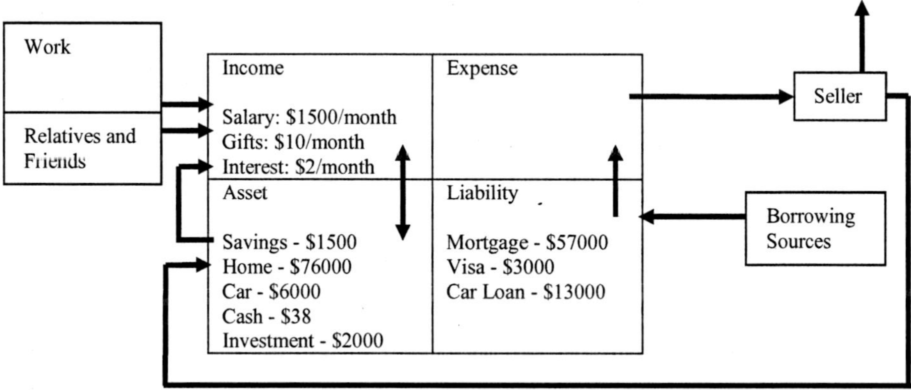

Exhibit 2-6. The Financial Picture Model – The World's View Complete

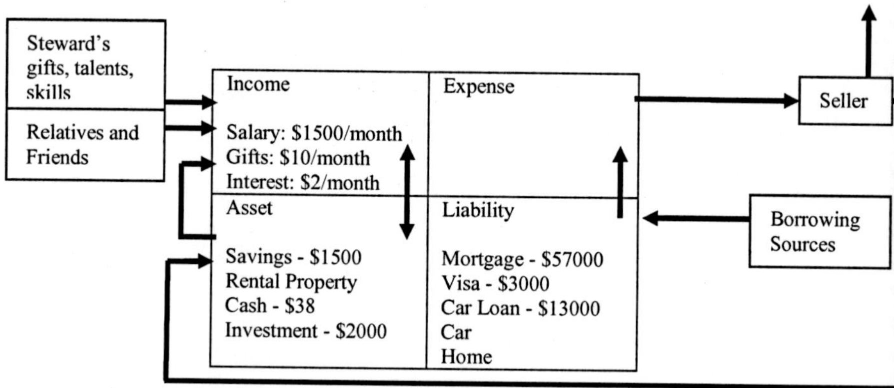

Exhibit 2-7. The Financial Picture Model – The Steward's View Complete

Developing a model like this is very important so that we can understand where the money we generate goes. The world encourages us to increase the size of the expense box. When that happens, and times get tight, the world then says to increase the income box and if that is not possible then increase the liability box. Rarely does the world look at increasing the asset box or reducing the expense and liability boxes. The steward recognizes the need to increase the asset quadrant by reducing the expense and liability quadrants. As good stewards, we really want our model to look like Exhibit 2-8.

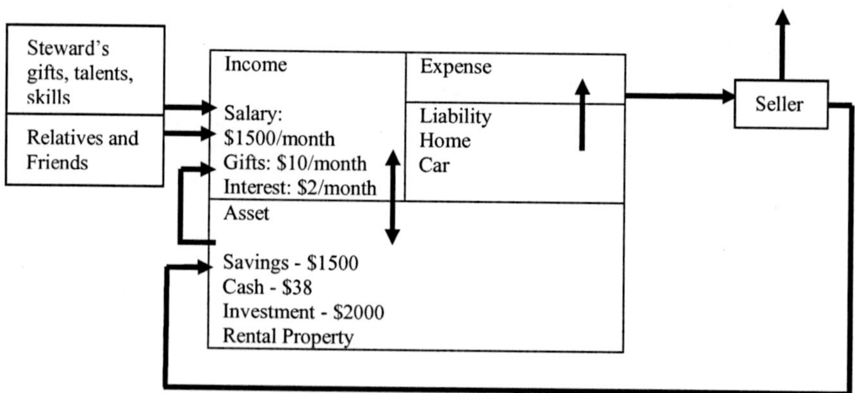

Exhibit 2-8. The Financial Picture Model – As the Steward Really Views It

Note: Although the exhibits in this section are unique many others have used some form of quadrants to portray the issues related to personal spending. For another unique use of this approach see the book entitled *Rich Dad Poor Dad* by Robert T. Kiyosaki. Though the book presents a worldly perspective of becoming a millionaire Kiyosaki does take an appropriate view of assets.

This exhibit shows several important points that we need to keep in mind as we move forward into planning. First, the steward's liabilities are few and relate not to having debt but maintaining the resources. There are no loans on the home or car but there are still taxes, utilities, maintenance, and insurance among other things to be paid. By having few liabilities the steward is able to focus income on the asset area where much return can be developed. The world says to use other people's money to leverage purchases including assets but the Bible says that the lender rules over the borrower. (Proverbs 22:7). Second, the steward keeps the expense quadrant smaller than income in order to use income to develop assets. The world says to increase expenses to look better but the steward wants a good return and is not misled by vanity and short term gains. By having a smaller expense quadrant the steward has the ability to purchase assets without using excessive liability. Third, the assets quadrant proportion-wise continues to grow for the steward. Lastly, if the assets continue to grow then the income from those assets continues to grow and the need for outside income is reduced allowing more time to devote to the Lord's work and the steward's ministry. By the way, I didn't forget about that nice cold Coca-Cola but now I think you understand enough about the model that you can decide where the money will come from.

As a side note, what most people don't realize is that most millionaires in America do not inherit their wealth but rather take the view of the steward above and are careful with their resources. They focus on assets and, though their goal or purpose of being rich may be unbiblical, their wise use of resources makes them successful with the world's mammon. Let us seek to be wise stewards using the resources that we know are a provision from the Lord in a manner that is well-pleasing to Him and we will be blessed and He will be glorified.

Developing a Financial Plan

Up to this point we have sought to lay a good foundation on which we build our financial plans. We continue that in this section but also begin to look at the practical implementation of what we have learned about planning. We start by looking at a basic financial planning process and then look at how to develop the basic plans we will need to be successful in the world.

The Financial Planning Process

Most project planning processes have at least five steps and this is no different for the financial planning process. Most plans involve at a minimum 1) an analysis of the current situation, 2) the design of financial plan possibilities, 3) selecting and putting the plan in place, 4) running with the plan, and 5) evaluating progress on the plan and updating as necessary. You might also break the first step into two, the establishing of financial goals and the analysis of your current position. Sometimes the last step will also be broken into two steps consisting of separate review and revision steps. Others may combine some of the steps. So, generally there are 3 to 7 steps in the financial planning process. Occasionally you may see a plan with fewer or more steps. In this text we explore a six-stage financial planning model. Exhibit 2-9 shows the process diagrammatically to make it easy to grasp.

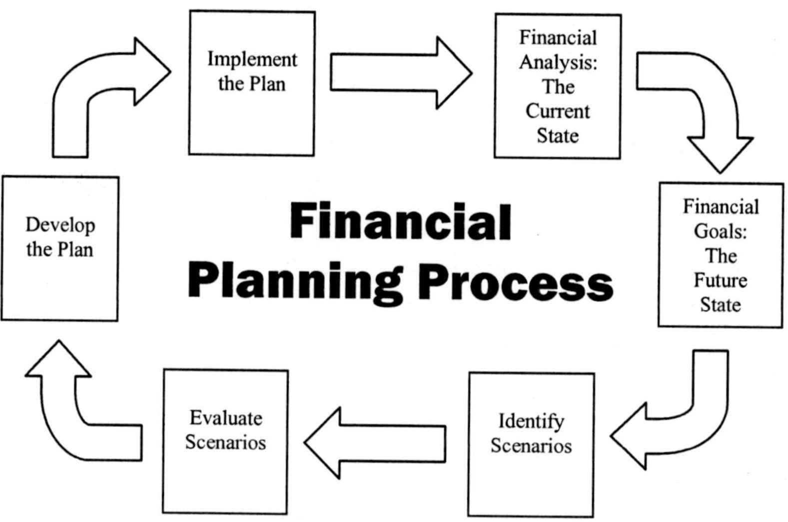

Exhibit 2-9. The Financial Planning Process

Note: Just about every financial text book has some diagrammatic or tabular view of the financial planning process. Although each is presented in a unique way they usually provide for a series of 3 to 7 steps. See Personal Financial Planning, Tenth Edition, by L. J. Gitman and M. D. Joehnk, © 2005 South-Western, or Personal Finance, Seventh Edition by J. R. Kapoor, L. Dlabay, and R. J. Hughes, © 2004 McGraw-Hill for different models using a similar six-step process.

There are six steps to the process. It does not pay to skip the steps. Remember our discussion under the biblical perspective that we need to seek, think, and do. Each of these also should be considered as a part of this process. Here we will briefly discuss each step of the process and what is involved in making them a reality.

Financial Analysis: The Current State. It's amazing how many people attend to their financial affairs without really knowing what their current state is or how they are using their current income. Most don't bother to look at the current state of financial matters until they are in very deep trouble. The importance of analyzing our current financial situation cannot be understated. How can you plan your financial goals or other goals, for that matter, unless you know how things currently stack up? Have you ever noticed how Paul was often sending brethren to the local churches in the New Testament? Did you ever notice why? Let's take a look. In Philippians 2:9 Paul says "*But I hope in the*  *Lord Jesus to send Timotheus to you shortly, that I also may be refreshed, knowing how you get on*" (JND). The KJV actually uses the term "know your state." Paul obviously is concerned as to whether things are going well with the Christians at Philippi. It's not a financial issue although I'm sure Paul would be just as interested about that as he was for the financial state of those at Jerusalem.

What is important here is that Paul, by knowing their state can then determine what the next step might be. Based on the findings he could exhort, encourage, teach, send others to minister, or take a collection. It is clear in Colossians 1:7-8 that Epaphras has given a report on the state of things at Colosse. As a result Paul is writing the letter to the Colossians to deal with some of the needs he is hearing about. Again the important thing here is that we need to know the state of something before we can make plans and act. Proverbs says, "*also, that the soul be without knowledge, it is not good; and he that hasteth with his feet sinneth*" (19:2, KJV). See the connection between knowledge and planning? The one who does not plan and goes full speed ahead is headed for failure. Before taking steps with the feet analyze your financial situation. Create a net worth and life wealth statements as we show you later in this section.

Financial Goals: The Future State. The second phase of the financial process is to establish where you would like to be in the future in relation to financial goals. Here again, it is better to brainstorm a little first then try to narrow down your actual goals. (We discuss the clarifying of goals later in the chapter.) This way you avoid missing something that may well be important to you or your spouse, if you are married. Keep in mind that this process is a cycle and changes will occur as you go through different stages of life. The stages of life also will influence which goals you emphasize in your planning. This does not mean you cannot think ahead, of course. The earlier you look at future goals the more likely you will be able to achieve them. Exhibit 2-10 shows an example of a financial planning life cycle that compares what the typical world-view is versus what might be the best view for us to take.

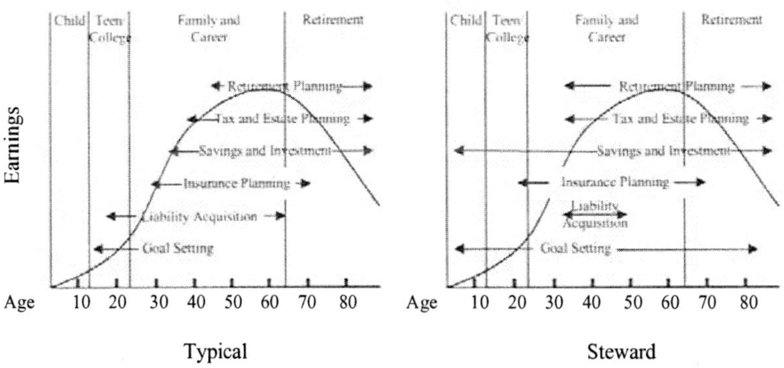

Exhibit 2-10. The Typical versus the Steward's Personal Financial Life Cycle

Note: Adapted from Personal Financial Planning, Tenth Edition, by L. J. Gitman and M. D. Joehnk, © 2005 South-Western, and Personal Finance, Third Edition by A. J. Keown, © 2003 Pearson Education.

In this exhibit the curved line on the graph represents the average income stream. It starts out small in the early years and then grows until just before retirement at which point the income stream begins to decline as fewer hours are worked and more reliance is placed on income from assets. During the various stages of your life you will likely have a number of different planning goals. This together with the income stream is what is presented. The steward's perspective starts planning earlier in the life-cycle and has other and sometimes different planning priorities.

Financial goals often fall into several groups and categories. The categories are usually short-term and long-term, and the groups usually include purchase management, credit management, risk management, investment management, and estate management. These are the key areas the book tries to cover as noted earlier. Later in this chapter we go into more detail on establishing financial goals.

Identify Scenarios. In step three you want to identify possible actions you could take to reach your goal. There may be many or there may be few but be sure to note all the possibilities that come to mind. This, again, is more like brainstorming. Don't evaluate the possibilities now - that will be done in the next step. Just write down the ones that come to mind. For example, you have set a goal of saving $6000 within two years so you can purchase a used car. What scenarios are possible to help you achieve that goal? Several possibilities include working an extra 25 hours a month and saving the extra $250 in a car account; reducing expenses by $250 a month and putting the savings into the car account; have a tag or yard sale once a month to create $75 income to save toward the car account; sell the old boat that is sitting in the back yard for $1000; and the list goes on. One or perhaps several of these in combination may accomplish the goal. The key is keeping an open mind and being creative on determining what you can do.

Evaluate Scenarios. Once you have identified various scenarios for meeting each financial goal you now must evaluate them and their effect on each other to come up with a set of goals and scenarios that you want to use to reach those goals. There are worksheets for doing this provided in Appendix B. Carefully weigh and pray about each goal and the alternatives that are available. Make sure the alternatives are biblically sound and follow the guidelines we have discussed so far in this text. Once you have chosen the alternatives you will have a complete list of goals and how you expect to accomplish them. This is the preparation you will need for the next step.

Develop the Plan. Step five involves taking your list of financial goals and the various alternatives that you have chosen to use to reach those goals and formulate them into a plan. This plan will be your spending plan or budget. Notice we didn't start with the budget but much of the detail that would have gone into the budget would have been identified in step one of the planning process where we did the analysis of your financial situation. The spending plan and the related worksheets in Appendix B will be discussed in detail later in the chapter. Here we are just noting that this is an important step in the planning process.

Implement the Plan. Now we come to the exciting point where your plan is implemented. You can do all the planning in the world but if you don't do something then you will not reach your desired goals. Keep in mind just doing anything is not the key but doing what your financial plan calls for. This can be a difficult time in the process but also can be the most rewarding. You need to be committed to making the plan work. If you see the need for changes due to unforeseen events then go back to phase one and re-evaluate the situation, with the new insights in mind, and go back through the process. Once you have gone through it once, the process should go a bit more quickly and smoothly.

Review the State. The last step (or the repeat of step one) is to keep an eye on your goals and see if you are making progress toward them based on the measurements you decided to use when making them specific. Are you making appropriate progress toward them? Is there any need for changes? Are there any unforeseen difficulties? If everything is going well so far then continue to monitor them, otherwise take your new found knowledge back to phase one and start again by including the new information and revising your plans. You will become quite accustomed to doing this and it should not be seen as a burden but as a help in keeping you on the right track.

Determining Expected Wealth and Net Worth

As we promised we have now come to the section that will explain how to do the financial analysis that we need to do if we are going to successfully set and implement financial goals. In order to begin your financial planning journey we need to look at your current state of affairs (financial, that is) and put together what we call a Net Worth Statement or Balance Sheet. There is a worksheet in Appendix B to help you accomplish this.

Do a complete review of your circumstances to understand what it is you own and owe. Be careful and do not forget anything, no matter how small. In counseling people I have found that there are additional debts that they had forgotten about. Tuition owed a school, money owed parents, and appliance debts are examples that are often missed. Remember we need to know all the assets and all the liabilities. We will count your home and car, if any, as assets keeping in mind how we should really view them. Even if you are in college you may have a few assets without realizing it. Consider the following areas to see if you have missed any assets and remember to use the fair market value:

Cars. Use the Kelly Blue Book (www.kbb.com) for value. To be safe subtract 10%. Don't forget to adjust for added or missing accessories or excessive mileage. Most people over-value their cars so be sure to be careful. Other valuation guides commonly used can be accessed at www.edmunds.cim and www.nada.com.

Homes. Base the value on the prices of homes that have sold in your area in the last year that are comparable in size or features. Several web sites have sales information by neighborhood and street (http://realestate.yahoo.com/re/homevalues/, which uses www.homegain.com, and www.domania.com are two examples). Usually a realtor will perform a market analysis for free so that is another option. Again, most people over-value their possessions and the home is no different.

Furniture. Unless the furniture is antique it loses value quickly. Some furnishings such as Ethan Allen may sustain more value but they are also very expensive to purchase. Most furniture once delivered depreciates significantly, perhaps as much as 30%. Once used the value declines fairly rapidly. If well taken care of, though, furniture is worth something but it is usually 25% or less of the original price you paid. To find out the going prices look at auctions, estate, tag, or yard sales to see what some comparable furnishings might bring.

Collectibles. Antiques, paintings, and other collectibles would need to be appraised professionally to know their approximate worth. You may be able to price some items based on past sales you have seen or through antique catalogs or auctions. But the best way is through a professional. This is worth doing occasionally for insurance purposes as well. If you can find a store that might give you a ball park figure on the conservative side for free for purposes of your financial report that probably would suffice for our needs here.

Accounts. All bank and investment accounts are considered assets and should be itemized for your net worth report. The company with which you have the account will periodically give you a summary and the value of your account. These are often available online as well.

Cash. If you keep cash in the house, purse, or wallet then that should be totaled and added to your report. Don't forget those jars or banks of coins that are often missed. They should be counted and added as itemized items under cash. Quite often people have a substantial amount in coins in their vehicles. Count that as well.

Money Owed to You. Have you lent money to others? Then that would be considered an asset. Whether it is a small loan to friends or a larger one to a relative these should be included as assets. If they have become uncollectible or you have forgiven them then do not include them.

Savings Bonds. This is an item often missed by young folks. You may still have savings bonds that have not matured or your parents may be holding some for you that you may not be aware of. Check it out. The current value can be determined by using the savings bond wizard available from the treasury department web site. The wizard can be reached at http://www.publicdebt.treas.gov/sav/savwizar.htm.

Life Insurance. If you have any cash-value insurance include the current value of that in your list. This amount should be available from your insurance company. Keep in mind if you are young your parents may have a policy that is yours so be sure to check it out and include it.

Other. If you have other items of value such as jewelry and electronics then itemize those in your list as well. Be careful though, especially with electronics such as computers, which lose their value quickly. Use the fair market value.

The assets have covered the positive side of the ledger, now we need to gather information together on liabilities or what monies you owe. Some of the areas to consider are:

Credit Card Debt. Be sure to get the current balance of all credit cards for this report and while you are at it get the minimum payment and the current interest rate on the account for later use. Don't forget store cards such as J.C. Penny and Sears. Itemize each of the credit cards, even if they have a zero balance, and their respective balances for this part of the report.

Loans. Itemize all loans that you have. Also note the interest rate and minimum monthly payments for later use. Include home and car loans, student loans, home equity loans, home equity credit lines (even if zero), loans from friends, relatives, and parents, and other non-secured loans.

Bills. List all accounts for which you have outstanding balances. This would include utilities, doctor's, child care, school expenses such as tuition, and other purchases made on account. Also note the interest rate being paid for future use.

Once you have gathered the information needed you are ready to calculate your net worth using the worksheets. These calculations are quite straight forward and Exhibit 2-11 is provided here as an example. Total your assets and enter the amount in the row marked "assets total." Do the same for your liabilities; total them and enter the amount in the row marked "liabilities total." The third and final calculation is to take the liabilities total and subtract it from the assets total. Enter the result in the row labeled "net worth." If it is negative you can add a minus sign in front of the total or put the total in parentheses.

Net Worth

Assets	Estimated Value	Liabilities	Estimated Value
Personal Property Assets		**Loan Balances**	
Home	$ 135,000	Mortgage loan	$ 67,000
Vehicles	$ 9,800	Home equity loan	
Jewelry		Car loan 1	$ 2,000
Artwork		Car loan 2	
Furniture	$ 8,200	Student loans	$ 3,000
Electronics	$ 2,100	Real estate loan	
Antiques		Other loan 1 - (Dad)	$ 800
Other		Other loan 2 - ( )	
Liquid Assets		Other loan 3 - ( )	
Cash	$ 162	Other loan 4 - ( )	
Checking account	$ 532	Other loan 5 - ( )	
Savings account	$ 945	**Other Outstanding Debt**	
Certificates of deposit		Credit card 1 - (AMEX)	$ 506
Money market account		Credit card 2 - (Discover)	$ 992
Life insurance (cash value)		Credit card 3 - ( )	
Other		Credit card 4 - ( )	
Investment Assets		Credit card 5 - ( )	
Retirement account	$ 16,939	Credit card 6 - ( )	
Bonds		Credit card 7 - ( )	
Mutual funds	$ 1,265	Other debt 1 - ( )	
Individual stock shares	$ 745	Other debt 2 - ( )	
Real estate other than home		Other debt 3 - ( )	
Other		Other debt 4 - ( )	
Assets Total	**$ 175,688**	**Liabilities Total**	**$ 74,298**

Net Worth	**$ 101,390**

Note: Adapted from the Net Worth Calculator Microsoft Excel template available on the Microsoft web site at http://www.microsoft.com.

Exhibit 2-11. Net Worth Statement

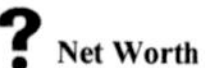

The total net worth indicates what you have accumulated in wealth so far in your life. That is, no matter how much you have earned or received over the years if we were to sell everything and pay off all outstanding liabilities we would end up with a total that represents "all that is left to our name", so to speak. If it is negative it means that even if you sold everything and tried to pay off your creditors you would still not have enough to pay them off. Obviously, that is not a situation you want to be in since it puts you into a place of surety, which according to Biblical principles is to be avoided. But at least by taking this step you now have a better picture of where you are and no matter how bad it looks you can take steps to make it better.

Now, you may raise the legitimate question as to whether the net worth is good or bad or somewhere in between. There are several ways we can get an idea of the condition of a financial situation. First, there is what we call the solvency ratio. It shows you the strength of being able to withstand a decline in assets. The smaller the result the less likely you are to remain solvent (or keep a positive net worth). This ratio is calculated by dividing the total net worth by the total assets.

Solvency ratio = Total net worth/Total assets
Sample ratio = $101,390/$175,688 = 58%

In this example we see that the solvency ratio is 58 percent. This indicates that this financial situation would be able to take a 58 percent decline in asset value before reaching the point of insolvency. Again, the lower the number, the more likely the threat of insolvency.

Another small calculation to view the strength of a balance sheet is the debt to total assets ratio. This indicates what portion of the assets would be used up by the debts if they all were to be paid off. The higher the percentage here the more likely one may become insolvent since more of the assets would need to be used to take care of liabilities. Here is an example of the use of this ratio:

Debt to asset ratio = Total debt/Total assets
Sample ratio = $74,298/$175,688 = 42%

Since the percentage is less than 100 percent the financial situation is solvent but, more importantly, you get a quick indication of how much of the assets would be eaten by the debt if they had to be paid. Here, a little less than half of the assets would be devoured by paying off debt.

A third way of looking at the net worth result is to compare the result with some benchmark based on how much you should have based on your age. To set expectations first we can estimate that if we receive an average salary of $25,000 a year for 45 years then we would earn $1,125,000. Many of us will make more than that so the amount is likely to rise considerably. Even if you work at a fast food restaurant for $7.00 an hour for 45 years at 40 hours a week you will still have earned $655,200. The point here is that you will likely earn a great sum of money over your life of work. How much of what you have earned should already have been accumulated for future blessing?

Determining this amount is what is called the expected wealth amount at the time you calculate it. Stanley and Danko (1996), writers of *The Millionaire Next Door* have done extensive research on the issue of wealth and came up with a basic formula that should give us a good idea on how well we are doing based on their experiences with millionaires. They suggest multiplying your age by your total, annual pre-tax income from all sources (excluding inheritances). Take the result of that calculation and divide by ten.

Subtract any inherited wealth from the result and you have an amount that should closely reflect what you have in net worth. If it is higher you are doing better than average and if lower not as well as average. Here is an example:

> Wealth = (Age * (current annual pre-tax income -inheritances) / 10) -inherited wealth
>
> Wealth = (37 * ($24,000 - $1,000)/10) - $2500
>
> Wealth = (37 * $23,000/ 10) - $2,500
>
> Wealth = $82,600

If the net worth is $101,390, as we have noted before, then this individual is ahead of the game wealth wise. This family would be expected to have a non-inherited wealth of $82,600 but in reality has much more than that ($101,390-$2,500, or $98,890).

The various calculations we have covered are given to help you determine where your net worth places you. They help to identify whether your financial situation needs to be strengthened or not. Based on what you learn here you will begin making some preliminary financial goals.

Debt Analysis Assessment

The next part of your planning analysis includes developing a debt list that you can use when considering goal alternatives and developing your spending plan. We had suggested while you were gathering information for your balance sheet that you also gather information about monthly minimum payments and interest rates for your liabilities. We can now use that information to develop a detailed list of each debt so that when we begin brainstorming and setting goals you will have this to work with.

Exhibit 2-12 shows a sample debt analysis report. Appendix B contains a sample sheet you can use to do this on your own. The list contains the creditor's name, the purpose of the debt, the minimum monthly payment, the balance currently due, the anticipated payoff date, and the interest rate. Everything should be straight forward to fill in except the payoff date. This can be calculated using an amortization table or using a calculator and a simple formula. For a complete analysis on how to calculate debt payoffs, and the various finance charge calculation methods companies use see Appendix D.

Debt Analysis

Extra Amount: 10.00 [Date]

Type of Consumer Debt	Balance	Minimum Payment	Payoff Months	Priority	Interest Rate	Monthly Payment	Months to Payoff
Auto Loans							
Car Loan - Suntrust Bank	2,000.00	98.00	21		8.9%	108.00	19
Education Loans							
Trevecca Student Loan	3,000.00	25.00	120		4.2%	35.00	86
Personal Installment Loans							
Loan from Dad	800.00	20.00	40		2.0%	30.00	27
Home Improvement Loans							
Other Installment Loans							
Credit Cards							
American Express	506.00	10.00	51		18.0%	20.00	26
Discover	992.00	15.00	67		13.0%	25.00	40
Home Loans/Credit Lines							
Washington Mutual Mortgage	67,000.00	332.78	202		6.5%	342.78	196
Loans on Life Insurance							
Margin Loans from Broker							
Other Loans							
Totals	74,298.00	500.78	202			510.78	196

Note: Adapted from the Consumer Debt Payoff Microsoft Excel template available on the Microsoft web site at http://www.microsoft.com.

Exhibit 2-12. Debt Analysis Report.

Developing a Spending Plan

So far we have looked at two critical components to the analysis of your financial state. They are the balance sheet or net worth statement, and the debt analysis statement. We now come to the third, and last critical analysis instrument and that is the current spending plan assessment. Once you have completed this assessment you will have all the information you will need to begin considering your financial goals, identifying alternatives, and evaluating and selecting plans of action. There is a spending plan worksheet available in Appendix B for this assessment as well. Our goal here is not to create a new spending plan but to identify what the current state is. You will modify it later based on your financial goals.

? Spending Plans

A spending plan is basically a statement of cash flows. It is somewhat similar to the balance sheet but the cash flow statement or spending plan looks at an average month and notes all of the income (or inflows), and expenses (or outflows). The total outflows are then subtracted from the total inflows to determine the current cash flow. As with the balance sheet it may be negative, which again is not a good thing. That would indicate that more is being spent than is coming in. Whether that is the case or not at least you will know your state when you are done with this step.

Exhibit 2-13 gives a sample spending plan and the associated cash flows. Previously we had discussed what income and expenses were, now we want to actually identify them and the monthly amounts associated with them. The top part of this assessment is the income section. Here you want to list the average monthly amount you receive as income from any source. These amounts should be before taxes. If you receive pay on a weekly basis then multiply the amount by 52 then divide by 12. If you receive other income quarterly then multiply it by 4 and divide by 12. The key is to get all amounts in monthly ratios. Don't forget interest income, gifts, part time or casual work, and help from outside sources such as government assistance, grants, and scholarships.

Now comes the more difficult part: identifying all of the expenses. To make this section accurate and make your endeavors successful it is best if you keep track of everything you spend for a period of time, such as a month, so that you really know what the expenses are. Most people are quite often amazed at what they are spending their money on when they begin to keep track of it. Again, the goal here is to analyze the current situation and not try to change things. That will come later once we have all the analysis done.

Personal Spending Plan

Income	Projected Income	Actual Income	Difference
Income 1		2250	
Income 2		500	
Interest Income		5	
Investment Income			
Other Income			
Total monthly income		2755	

Housing	Projected Expense	Actual Expense	Difference
Mortgage/Rent		$475	
Real Estate Taxes		$100	
Telephone/Cell		$38	
Electricity		$67	
Gas			
Water			
Sewer			
Cable			
Rubbish Removal			
Repairs		$50	
Supplies		$25	
Other: Condo Fee		$175	
Total Housing Expenses			

Transportation			
Vehicle Payment			
Public Transportation			
Parking/Tolls		$3	
License/Registration		$4	
Fuel		$42	
Maintenance		$45	
Other			
Total Transportation Expenses			

Insurance			
Home/Renter's		$60	
Automobile		$105	
Health/Dental/Vision		$109	
Life		$30	
Disability			
Long-Term Care			
Liability		$25	
Other			
Total Insurance Expenses			

Food			
Groceries		$100	
Eating Out		$60	
Vending		$3	
Other			
Total Food Expenses			

Education			
Tuition			
Books			
Room & Board			
Subscriptions		$12	
Organization Dues		$10	
Other			
Total Education Expenses			

Personal Care			
Medical/Dental/Vision		$75	
Hair Care		$9	
Clothing		$25	
Dry Cleaning/Laundry			
Health Club			
Other			
Total Personal Expenses			

Entertainment			
Movies		$8	
DVD/CD/Videos		$10	
Concerts		$3	
Sports			
Web Subscriptions		$3	
Other			
Total Entertainment Expenses			

Column 1 Totals		**$1,671**	

Giving	Projected Expense	Actual Expense	Difference
The Lord's Work		120	
Charities			
Other			
Total Giving		120	

Gifts	Projected Expense	Actual Expense	Difference
Christmas Gifts		50	
Cards		5	
Other Gifts		10	
Total Gift Expenses		65	

Investing	Projected Expense	Actual Expense	Difference
Retirement Account		150	
Emergency Fund		25	
Investment Account		25	
Total Investment		200	

Miscellaneous	Projected Expense	Actual Expense	Difference
Bank Fees			
Professional Fees		10	
Other			
Total Miscellaneous Expneses		10	

Taxes	Projected Expense	Actual Expense	Difference
Federal Income Rax		250	
State Income Tax			
Local Income Tax			
FICA		155	
Medicare		34	
Personal Property Taxes			
Other			
Total Tax Payments		439	

Loans	Projected Expense	Actual Expense	Difference
Personal Loans		80	
Student Loans		100	
Credit Card 1		50	
Credit Card 2			
Credit Card 3			
Credit Card 4			
Credit Card 5			
Credit Card 6			
Credit Card 7			
Other			
Total Debt Payments		230	

	Total Projected Expense	Total Actual Expense	Total Difference
Column 2 Totals		**$1,064**	
Column 1 Totals		**$1,671**	
Spending Plan Totals		**$2,735**	

Cash Flow Total	**$20**

Note: Adapted from the Monthly Family Budget Microsoft Excel template available on the Microsoft web site at http://www.microsoft.com.

Exhibit 2-13. Spending Plan Assessment – Actual Spending.

Remember we want the average monthly amount so if the expense varies from month to month, such as electricity, then take the last year and add up the charges for each month and then divide the total by 12. Also, don't include anything that is reimbursed by another such as work expenses or some health expenses. Expenses can be categorized into some key areas and this may help you identify what they are.

Taxes. Federal withholding, state tax, Medicare, FICA.

Giving. Gifts to the local church, non-profit organizations, and individuals.

Housing. This includes your shelter which usually is a mortgage payment, rent, or the room portion of room & board at school. It also includes any utilities such as electricity, gas, telephone, cable or satellite TV, water, and sewer. Other items under housing may include maintenance and rubbish disposal. Under this section you list anything dealing with keeping a functioning shelter.

Food. This section would include the groceries and snacks you purchase, the board portion of room and board if you are in school, vending machine purchases, money spent on coffee pools, and eating out that is not part of a vacation or other entertainment. If the eating out is incidental to a vacation or going to the ballpark or some other entertainment then include that under entertainment.

Transportation. Here you would include car payments, gas, oil, licenses, wheel fees, maintenance, emission fees, and any roadside assistance programs such AAA. Also included here would be tolls, parking, and bus, train, and taxi fares not related to entertainment or reimbursed by work.

Insurance: Here you include all insurance payments including medical, optical, dental, disability, long-term care, life, mortgage, credit, home, car, liability, and any other insurance you may have. Be sure to calculate the monthly amount for each of these.

Personal Care/Health. Include all non-reimbursed expenses for medical, optical, and dental. Amounts paid to flexible spending reimbursement accounts can go here but don't include the reimbursements or their related expenses in the plan. All self-paid prescriptions and over-the-counter remedies can go here as well. Vitamins and other supplements should be included here as well. Also identify any personal expenses for grooming, dress, and fitness.

Loans/Debt. All payments for debt should be included here. These numbers can be retrieved from the debt analysis you did in the previous section. Do not include the mortgage or car payments, which were included under housing and transportation respectively.

Entertainment. All recreational and vacation activities go here. These would include food related to the entertainment, school activities and activity fees, outings, camping, concerts, movies, movie rentals, and sports to name a few.

Audio/Visual. This section includes materials purchased such as subscriptions, CDs, DVDs, videos, books (not textbooks for school), newspapers, and audio books, to name a few.

Education. In this section you enter your tuition and other fees not noted elsewhere in the plan: textbooks, supplies, lab fees, tuition for your children, child care and nursery school fees, and seminar fees. Also include dues and organization fees here.

Miscellaneous. Sometimes called other. This is where everything else that doesn't fit well into another category goes. This might include various fees that you may be subject to such as bank fees and professional services fees. An example here might be attorney fees or tax preparation fees.

Savings. Includes funds set aside for emergency, investments, and future purchases.

This list should cover just about every area you might spend money in. Anything not noted can be added to the miscellaneous category or under one of the others where space has been left for your additions. Please be careful and try to cover every penny you spend on average each month. Often, well-meaning people will say that $30 or $50 for frivolous spending, that is not tracked, is necessary so you won't go crazy. This seems like worldly advice rather than that of a Christian. As ones who want to give account we want to know where the funds are going.

Now that you have the income and expenses that you currently have filled in, you can total them into the appropriate entries on the worksheet. After this, just subtract the total living expenses from the total living income and enter the total in the provided space on the form. If it is negative you can put a minus sign in front or enclose the amount in parentheses.

Developing Financial Goals

Now you have completed all three planning worksheets and are ready to take a serious look at where you are and then identify financial goals, alternatives to reaching those goals, and choosing from among those alternatives. Once you have chosen the road you wish to take you can then update these worksheets to reflect your new plan. These new worksheets along with your financial goals will be the documents that form the basis of your financial plan. In the ensuing chapters we want to work with you to understand all the different facets of the spending plan you just created so that you can identify appropriate alternatives and make intelligent choices to meet the financial goals that you will now create.

Before moving on to the next chapter, review the notes on establishing financial goals covered in this chapter. Then, based on your analysis of your current situation and your desired blessing for the future, write down a set of financial goals using the worksheet in Appendix B. Exhibit 2-14 gives examples of short and long-term goals related to the financial life cycle covered earlier. These goals relate to purchase management, credit management, risk management, investment management, and estate management. When setting financial goals:

Be Biblical. Goals such as: I want to get rich or have a luxurious house like the Jones', or do nothing when I retire are goals that should be foreign to the Christian, as far as physical riches go.

Be Specific. Goals should be measurable. How else will you be able to count the cost and evaluate whether you can reach or have reached the goal? Saying I have a goal of saving a lot on my expenses may never be met if I don't define what "a lot" is. Perhaps it would be better to say I will save $200.00 a month on my expenses within 3 months.

Be Timely: Notice how I put a time frame on that last goal. Putting a time frame on the goal will help you determine when to begin implementing steps to get there, and whether you will be able to, in light of other goal priorities. This will also help if one goal is reliant on another being achieved first. Don't underestimate the importance of putting a time limit or an end date on a goal.

Be Realistic. Setting goals that cannot be realistically met are likely to lead to financial plan failure. I want to be the owner of the Boston Red Sox is just not a realistic business goal for me, as much as I may enjoy rooting for the team. There would be business availability, time, and money issues that would make such a goal unrealistic. It does not mean I can't establish a goal that might seem difficult, but prayerfully consider each goal and then as God leads add it or leave it off the list.

Be Written. All financial goals (as well as other life goals) should be written down as a way of reminding you of what they are. Research shows that those who write goals down are much more likely to accomplish them. Goals can be posted and easily carried with you so that you'll have something to use as a reference as you pray for God's will in these areas.

Be Prioritized. You will likely have many financial goals and it is not surprising that at times they conflict. The issue could be insufficient funds or other resources such as time. Sometimes you will have two very important goals that cannot be satisfied at the same time. This is where prayer and Godly counsel can help. In the end, though, you will likely need to make some difficult choices. Be sure to set a priority on your goals in order to keep track of what your current objectives are. If you try to work on too many goals at once you may get frustrated and ignore the plan that you very much need.

Those who would undertake developing financial goals themselves need to have two key attributes:

Be Content. Don't make financial goals out of being discontent with what you have. Making them because you are discontent with the debt you have is a different story. But it is important to keep a biblical balance. We should plan but also be content. Paul says in Philippians 4:11 "*not that I speak as regards privation, for as to me I have learnt in those circumstances in which I am, to be satisfied in myself*" (JND). Paul found contentment in whatever state the Lord put him in. Does this mean we should not plan? Of course not. James

Financial Goals Worksheet

Date Set	Goal	Priority	Target Date	Cost	Biblical	Specific	Realistic	Measured
Near-Term Goals								
3/1/2005	Pay off credit cards	High	3/1/2006	12500	Yes	Yes	Yes	Yes
1/1/2005	Save $500 for Christmas gifts in order to pay cash at Christmas	Low	11/1/2005	500	Yes	Yes	Yes	Yes
4/1/2005	Build an emergency fund of $2000	Med	4/1/2006	2000	Yes	Yes	Yes	Yes
5/1/2005	Buy new sofa for under $300	Low	9/1/2005	300	Yes	Yes	Yes	Yes
Mid-Term Goals								
12/25/2003	Become debt-free	High	2/1/2008	43000	Yes	Yes	Stretch	Yes
1/1/2005	Start a retirement funds with at least $5000	Med	11/1/2009	5000	Yes	Yes	Yes	Yes
Long-Term Goals								
1/1/2005	Purchase a home in the Nashville area	High	1/31/2012	163000	Yes	Yes	Yes	Yes
5/15/2000	Earn a doctorate degree in Digital Multimedia	Med	6/1/2010	37000	Yes	Yes	Stretch	Yes

Exhibit 2-14. Financial Goals Worksheet

takes the right perspective when he states "*Go to now, ye who say, to-day or to-morrow we will go into such a city and spend a year there, and traffic and make gain, ye who do not know what will be on the morrow, (for what is your life? It is even a vapour, appearing for a little while, and then disappearing,) instead of your saying, if the Lord should so will and we should live, we will also do this or that*" (4:13-15, JND). To plan without God in the picture will lead to failure for the Christian. So there is a balance of seeking the Lord, being content, and planning.

Be Willing. Although you may not yet know what steps you want to take to achieve a goal, after you have brainstormed scenarios and chosen alternatives you will want to return and fill in that remaining portion of the goal. That is, what steps are you going to take to make the goal a reality? Remember "doing" is a key aspect of how God uses us. We are not very useful servants of the Lord if we are unwilling to take action. Another aspect of this is that sometimes as you look at your alternatives there are none that are very palatable. The question is, will you, in the will of the Lord, do what it takes? It may mean selling the car or the home, or canceling the cable or satellite TV. If that is what God is showing you must be done to achieve the goals you believe are in His will, will you do it?

Use the examples in Exhibit 2-14 as a guide to stimulate you to think about some of the key financial planning areas. As we proceed through the other chapters and discuss each of these areas you may be motivated to change your goals. That is not a problem and you should feel free to return to this point at anytime.

Once you have completed a preliminary list of financial goals, continue on into the next chapter and we will discuss many insights into the various alternatives for securing the financial peace that God would like us to have. Based on your learning from the other chapters you will be able to decide what steps you would like to take to implement your financial goals. Keep this financial goal worksheet handy to fill in what steps you will take as you learn and make these decisions.

Outcomes and Chapter Summary

In this chapter we focused on financial stewardship planning basics. We started by looking at the issue of opportunity costs and factors that influence value, return, and pricing. We took an in depth look at the future value of money and learned the mathematical equations that allow us to intelligently look at financial alternatives. We studied the basics of financial reporting looking at the asset, liability, income, and expense components. We then focused on the financial planning process and the key tools in developing a financial plan. This learning now sets the stage to examine the components of the spending plan in detail and learn how to develop alternatives that will meet planned financial goals.

Learning Objective 1. **Define opportunity costs and identify and describe the five key influences that help determine the cost or value of something.**

We learned that opportunity costs are what we give up as alternatives to purchase something. We learned that there were at least five factors that influence pricing, return, and value. These were scarcity, inflation, risk, perception, and time. Although there is some interaction among these, they play an important role in determining what it is we pay for an item, what we get in return for an item or investment, and the general value of pricing in the market place.

Learning Objective 2. **Explain how time affects the value of money and be able to calculate the future value of a sum invested now, or periodically and determine what would need to be invested now in present value, or periodically to reach a projected sum in the future.**

We learned that our time is valuable and if someone uses it we would expect to receive appropriate compensation for it. This idea, though, gives us insight into the fact that time in some sense itself has value. In reality it is the ability to have money you save earn interest in a periodic basis that in turn also receives interest for the remaining term of the investment. This is called compounding. It shows the power of time in growing savings.

Learning Objective 3. **Identify and explain the four tradeoffs when considering the cost of something.**

Generally, there are four factors that we tradeoff when considering the purchasing of something. They are cost, quality, quantity, and time. It is the interaction of these in differing amounts that determines the final purchase cost. We learned that what we give up is basically a type of opportunity cost.

Learning Objective 4. **Be able to review and determine whether a financial account, transaction, or resource relates to being an asset, a liability, an expense, and/or income.**

We defined and examined assets, liabilities, income, and expenses. Assets are what we own and that can be exchanged for some cash value. Liabilities are amounts owed to others. Income is what is received of cash value from another or what we call cash inflows into the home. Expenses were defined as the cash outflows from the home. We also learned that the steward views cars and homes as liabilities because they do not actually return any income to the home and have many expenses related to them.

Learning Objective 5. **Describe the Financial Planning Process.**

We learned that the financial planning process usually has anywhere from 3 to 7 steps based on various financial planning processes that have been advocated over the years. We learned a six step model that works in a cyclical fashion and includes: identifying the current state, identifying the future state, identifying alternatives, examining and selecting alternatives, developing the plan, implementing the plan, and we then return to step one to once again review the current state.

Learning Objective 6. **Develop a personal wealth and net worth statement.**

We learned how to develop a net worth or balance sheet statement that identifies the basic current state of our financial situation. It included taking the sum of all liabilities and subtracting it from the sum of all assets. The result was our total net worth. It was the first of three tools used in giving us a total view of our financial situation.

Learning Objective 7. **Develop a Personal Debt Assessment.**

The personal debt assessment was the second tool we used in understanding our current financial state. It identified all of our creditors, the amount owed, the interest rate, the minimum monthly payment, and the expected payoff date. It gives us a more complete picture of our liabilities than the balance sheet.

Learning Objective 8. **Develop a personal cash flow and spending plan statement.**

The personal spending plan or cash flow statement was the third and final tool used in evaluating our current financial state. It itemized all income and expenses. In addition, the sum of the expenses was subtracted from the some of the incomes to provide a net cash flow.

Learning Objective 9. **Develop a set of Financial Goals.**

Finally in this chapter we learned about developing financial goals using a financial goals worksheet. Financial goals need to be biblical, specific, realistic, timely, written, and prioritized. In addition, those making the goals need to be content in the Lord and willing to do His will.

Bible Texts Referenced

Proverbs 19:2	Proverbs 22:7
Luke 12:16-21	Luke 16:1-8
Philippians 2:9	Colossians 1:7-8

Exercises and Research Activities

1. Identify something that is scarce and explain how that impacts its current cost.

2. Do some research and find an example of someone who took a financial risk and why. What was the result? Should a Christian take the same risk?

3. If I place $3500 in an account that earns 6% and do not touch the account for 40 years how much would I have at the end of the time period?

4. Your grandmother has given you $9,000 so you can purchase a car. Are you better off spending all of it on a car or should you save some of it?

5. You have decided to save money so you can pay cash for your next car. You have figured out that by cutting back on expenses you can save $97 a month. How much will you have in 6 years when you are ready to buy another car assuming you can save at a 7% rate of interest?

6. You and your wife have decided to save so you can pay cash for your home rather than take a mortgage. Together with careful spending you both have committed to saving $440 a month. You plan on buying in 8 years. How much will you have assuming an 8% rate of return?

7. Your uncle has given you a choice of taking $7,000 now or $10,000 in ten years when you will need the funds to help fund your child's education. You expect that you could earn 8% compounded monthly if you were to take the cash now. Should you take it now or wait? Explain your answer.

8. Find some one who owns a home (yourself, your parents, or another) and research how much it currently costs to make it available for living. Include repairs, utilities, taxes, and interest on the mortgage. Consider how much that cost would be for a 10 year period. Compare that cost plus the original price of the home to the current value of the home. What did you find? What would you suggest the rate of return on this investment was? Would you consider it a good investment? Would the rate of return increase or decrease over time?

9. Create a set of financial planning documents for yourself. Include a net worth statement, a spending plan, a debt assessment worksheet, and a financial goals worksheet.

10. If you have a $200,300 mortgage on a home worth $245,215, $4,000 on credits cards, $4,395 loan on a car worth $3,650, $3,000 in savings, $315 in cash, and $900 in an IRA, what is your net worth?

11. Develop in detail a set of financial goals for the next 20 years. Include some thoughts on how you expect to accomplish those goals.

References and Resources

Books:

Gitman, L. J. and M. D. Joehnk, *Personal Financial Planning*, Tenth Edition. South-Western. 2005.

Kapoor, J. R., L. Dlabay, and R. J. Hughes. *Personal Finance*, Seventh Edition. McGraw-Hill. 2004

Keown, A. J. *Personal Finance*, Third Edition. Pearson Education. 2003.

Kiyosaki, Robert T. *Rich Dad Poor Dad.* Warner Business Books. 1998.

Stanley, T. S and W. D.Danko. *The Millionaire Next Door.* Barnes & Noble. 996.

Web Sites:

Bureau of Labor Statistics. www.bls.gov/cpi/home.htm
U. S. Treasury. www.publicdebt.treas.gov.
Home Gain. www.homegain.com
Domaina.com. www.domania.com
Kelly Blue Book. www.kbb.com
National Automobile Dealers Association www.nada.com.
Edmunds. www.edmunds.com

Excel Templates:

Microsoft Corporation. http://www.microsoft.com

Calculators:

The Finance Center. www.financecenter.com/products/calculators
Saving Bond Wizard. www.publicdebt.treas.gov/sav/savwizar.htm.

PART TWO

Managing and Following the Stewardship Plan

Chapter 3
Stewardship Basics

Chapter 4
Managing Inflows and Outflows

Chapter 5
Managing Credit, Borrowing, and Debt

CHAPTER 3

Stewardship Basics

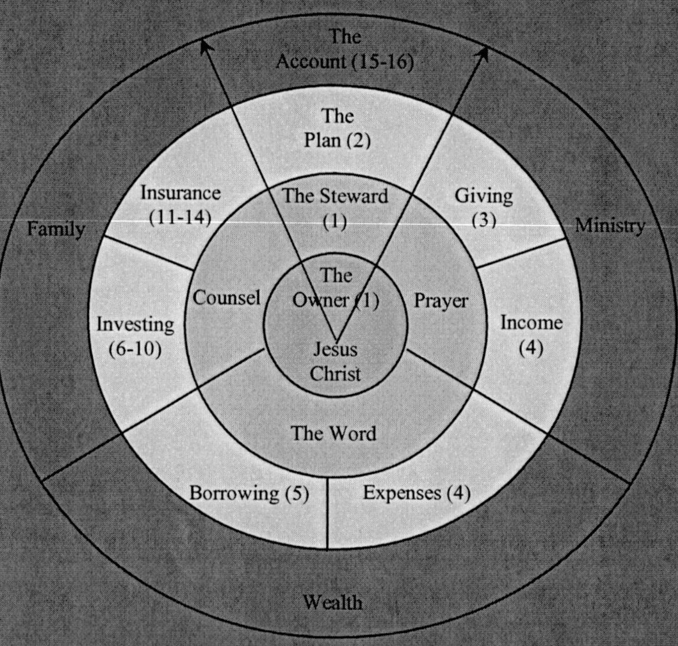

Learning Objectives

1. Describe the biblical perspective on giving and explain why it plays such an important role in the Christian life.

2. Analyze and choose the best bank for managing personal cash flows.

3. Identify and describe the role children play in financial planning and how they also can influence another's financial planning.

4. Understand and explain the trade-offs that are made in relation to saving as a steward and explain why saving is an important aspect of stewardship.

Lord, I commit to giving and saving.

Lord, I need your help in making the right priorities in my life. There is so much in the world that would attract me to use the resources that you have provided to me in the wrong way. Lord, I commit to giving to you out of the love of my heart for what you have done for me in sending your Son to die for me. I also commit to saving some of the resources you provide that I might have a storehouse from which to bless you, my family, and others as you guide by your Spirit. Thank you for your generosity to me in all that you have provided. You are a great and awesome God and there is none that compares to you.

In this chapter we want to learn about some of the basics related to being a steward and analyzing your financial plan to make sure you can reach your financial goals. The following chapters will get into more details on each section of the spending plan. This chapter will deal with the two important broad issues of giving and saving. In addition we will look at the role of children and get acquainted with banking in preparation for the following chapters. By covering these issues up front in a separate chapter we hope to be able to make better decisions when looking at various other areas of finance in coming chapters.

The Value and Blessing of Giving

As Christians one of the first things that come to mind as we analyze our situation is how much we give to the Lord's work. Because of its biblical basis few Christians will not at least think about it when contemplating either financial goals or its priority in relation to the rest of the spending plan. I am often asked if God requires Christians to tithe; or whether gross pay or net pay should be used in determining giving; or is giving only to the church; and a host of other questions. Of course, it is not really all that important what I think but it is very important what God has to say, so in this section we will look extensively at the Bible for our answers on the purpose and methodology of giving.

Biblical Giving – the Christian Perspective

In this section we try to understand what the Bible has to say about giving. The key here will be to open our minds and hearts to what God has to say and not necessarily what we have been taught as a practice. They may end up being the same or they may not but we should follow God's Word.

So, what does the Bible say about giving? Well, a great deal and so we should start with the first time we see an offering made to God. In the scripture the first occurrence of a word, phrase, or symbol is usually quite informative. Now, many of you may rush to Genesis 14 where the first occurrence of the word "tithe" occurs, but that is not where giving to God starts in the Bible. It is Genesis 4:3-5. This is the first use of the word offering in the Bible and should give us some insights to what giving is all about. Here we have the story of Abel and Cain's offerings. It is clear from the context that God had revealed to them that when they bring an offering it is to be one that requires the shedding of blood, which is clearly a type of the offering of Jesus Christ. This is why Abel's sacrifice was acceptable and Cain's was not. But what do we learn about giving here? First that giving was brought to God. The giving, if appropriate, resulted in acceptance of the offering by God. Second, and related to this, is that the giver did not give expecting something in return. Third, the gift was a form of worship – a sacrifice sweet-smelling to God and so we learn worship is giving

to God. Fourth, the gift is of Christ. The sacrifice of the flock was symbolic of Christ and so when we give we give that which is of Christ. Fifth, it appears to have been voluntary. Although they knew what type of sacrifice was to be given the issue of when they brought it was not developed here. There could have been a particular time but we are not told here. It certainly was not based on the law of Moses since that hadn't arrived yet. Interestingly, two things we don't learn about here are the frequency and the quantity. Yet those are the first things we might think of if someone were to preach to us on the subject.

The first occurrence of the word "offered" in the Bible is in Genesis 8:20-21. This describes the offering Noah made to the Lord after he left the ark. Again there is no mention of frequency or quantity. In fact, we see the same elements as we saw in Genesis 4. This appeared to have been a voluntary offering of thanksgiving to God as an act of worship – a sweet-smelling savor unto God.

Next in Genesis 12:1-8 we see that Abram, after his call by God, built an altar to the Lord. We are not told what he did on the altar but I think we have a good idea based on the previous two examples.

We now come to Genesis 14:20 where we see the use of the word "tenth." Here again there appears to be no prescription. Abram out of thankfulness gives to the priest of God an offering of the spoils of battle (this is noted specifically in Hebrews 7:4). Here again it appears voluntary, out of love for God and an amount chosen by Abram from the spoils of war. We know the spoils consisted of goods and food (v. 11) and Abram gave a tenth of these spoils to the priest. If we were to use this section alone (which many do) to understand giving, men would only give a tenth of what they earned in warfare. But I think we see a trend of what giving is about. By the way, this is the only time Abram is reported giving a tenth of anything to God.

There are many mentions of offering in Genesis as in the offering of Isaac in Genesis 22:1-14. There we also see the first occurrence of the word "worship", but the only other mention of tithe is in relation to Jacob in Genesis 28:20-22. It is a vow and so we don't see an actual offering. Although voluntary we would be hard-pressed to use this section for the basis of giving since Jacob was not really giving but making a deal with God. The happenings of Jacob in the proceeding chapters indicate he was not in a place of blessing.

When the Mosaic law came along giving was instituted as a requirement of the law. What did the law require? First there was the Lord's tithe in Leviticus 27:30. This appears to be what is described in Numbers 18:10-11, 17-18, which belonged to the Levites and is sometimes called the Levites tithe. The Levites ministered for God and did not earn a living on the outside so the other tribes gave a tenth of their flocks, grain, and fruit to help support the Levites. In a sense it was like supporting the government of Israel (theocracy).

Deuteronomy 12:10-18 speaks of a second tithe that was instituted on the taking of the promised land to be taken to Jerusalem to be eaten together as a family. This is often called the festival tithe. In Deuteronomy 14:28 we have a third tithe offered every three years for the welfare of those in the city such as the fatherless and widows. It is not clear if this was a modification of the second tithe or in addition to it. Other offerings and taxes included: not gleaning the fields (Leviticus 19:9); Nehemiah 10:32-33 speaks of a temple tax; every seventh year all debt was to be forgiven and the land lie fallow (Exodus 23:10-11).

What we basically find when we look at tithing is not a gift to the Lord as a form of worship but a requirement by God as the king to fund the government of Israel. This was the equivalent to our tax system today. But if that is the case where is the giving under the law like we saw in Genesis? Well, it is still there. That is, Israel still gave free-will and firstfruits offerings as gifts to the Lord beyond the required amount to fund the government. I estimate that the Israelites gave 20-25 percent of their production to the Lord to support the nation's government and welfare programs. But there was firstfruits and free-will giving beyond this (Exodus 35:4-10; Numbers 18:12; Leviticus 22:18-23; Deuteronomy 16:10).

Deuteronomy 16:10 says "*and thou shalt keep the feast of weeks unto the Lord thy God with a tribute of a free-will offering of thine hand which thou shalt give unto the Lord thy God according as the Lord thy God hath blessed thee*." Exodus 35:5 says "*take ye from among you an offering unto the Lord; whosoever is of a willing heart, let him bring it, an offering of the Lord: gold, and silver, and brass*." Now this is giving. In fact it seems to speak in the same fashion as we saw in Genesis. A voluntary gift in proportion to what God has given. These are noted at a particular time but there are numerous free-will offering passages that show God's desire for man to give voluntarily as he has been prospered. All seem to have the attribute of worship; giving that is a sweet-smelling savor to God.

So, thus far we have learned that tithing and giving are two different things in the Old Testament. Giving relates to free-will offering and tithing to funding the government of the nation of Israel. Israel was supposed to do both, giving up to 25% for funding the theocracy, and free offerings on top of that out of love for God as an act of worship. The difference between the two thoughts under the law and the plain examples of free-will offering in Genesis make it clear that these are different things.

That brings us to the New Testament. What is the Christian supposed to do as far as giving goes? Not surprisingly giving has not really changed. Before getting into giving in the New Testament let's look at the role of tithing. There is no surprise here either and it is just like the Old Testament. The tithes funded the nation of Israel and the Lord Jesus himself said that this was proper for the Jew to do. In fact, there are only four passages where the term tithe is used in the New Testament and not surprisingly they all deal with the nation of Israel and not the Christian. We have already noted Hebrews 7 where it speaks of Abram and Melchisedec (1-9), showing Melchisedec as a type of Christ and really is not intended to show anything about tithing and even if it were we have looked at what the intent was there.

Two other occurrences deal with the same situation with our Lord. The Lord tells the scribes and Pharisees they should have done the tithing but not left the weightier matters of the law undone (Matthew 23:23; Luke 11:42). This, again, deals with tithing to support the Jewish nation's government that had not ended yet since Christ came to offer them the kingdom (which they subsequently rejected). As Jews they should have been tithing but were lax in other areas. The only other mention in the New Testament is Luke 18:12 where the self-righteous Pharisee is praying to the Lord how marvelous it is that he tithes all that he has. Obviously this is not teaching that the Christian should tithe but that it was customary for the Jews to do so based on the law.

That is all the New Testament says about tithing (we use the word not to mean a tenth so much any more but the action of giving what you have set aside). Nothing is written to the Christian or the church concerning tithing. That is because tithing is different from giving. Tithing of 25% or so was for the funding of the theocracy. This makes sense since the Christian is not funding the nation of Israel. That is, the church has no government as we know it because Christ is its head and we are all members of that body. Christians live in the world under various forms of human government but not a theocracy. Thus, they pay these forms of government taxes to provide for the nation in which they live. So, what Israel paid then we now end up paying as taxes to fund government programs. Israel is a little different because at times it was a government that was governed by another such as in the Lord's time. The Romans were in power so Israel not only paid for their own government but also helped Rome by paying taxes.

The issue is often raised that tithing came before the law so it applies to all. This is not true. The idea of a 'tenth' came before the law but tithing as defined in the law was unique starting with the law. Nonetheless, even if tithing as defined in the law came before the law, it does not necessitate it applying to the Christian. Animal sacrifices came before the law and yet we do not continue to perform them. The Sabbath came before the law and yet we do not observe it although the Lord did. The key is understanding that which applied to Israel quite often does not apply to the Christian or the church. This is why Paul often in the epistles had to keep reminding the saints not to get hung up in the ordinances of old. They had been put aside and Christ had presented a new and living way.

Well then, what is the Christian to do? The same as free-will giving in the Old Testament. Let's look at the New Testament perspective on giving and we will find it is no different than the old. When tithing is properly understood, then giving as the Bible describes it is consistent. From the gospels, which don't deal with the church or the Christian specifically, and the epistles, which are written to the Christian believers in various churches, we learn the following key things about giving:

Do It Willingly. Mark 12:41-44 is the passage concerning the widow casting her gift into the treasury. This widow didn't just give a certain percentage nor was she compelled to give what she gave. In fact, most would have been quite understanding if she didn't give because of her financial situation. The issue isn't how much she gave (two mites) nor how much of her living (100 percent). The issue was the heart. She gave willingly out of love to the Lord, and as a result, she is blessed to be recorded in the scripture as having done so. The same thing applies to Zaccheus when he gave half of his goods to the poor (Luke 19:1-10). That still likely left him a wealthy man yet the Lord did not condemn him for not giving more nor for giving too much. The issue once again was the willing heart. The epistles also show the same idea in 2 Corinthians 8 where Paul speaks on giving. He says "I speak not by commandment" (v. 8). He is not commanding giving. In fact, several times he notes the importance of willingness "*...that there was a readiness to will...*" (11) and "*for if there is a willing mind...*" (12). In 2 Corinthians 9 he continues "*each according as he purposed in his heart...*" (v. 7). I believe we see that giving is to be done willingly just as it was done in the Old Testament. It is not an issue of law or government, but of love.

It Involves Everyone. Paul says "*let each of you…*" (1 Corinthians 16:2). That does not seem to leave anybody out. No matter how rich or how poor everybody should be a giver to God. Even if you're a student at school God is including you. He wants everyone to experience the opportunity to give out of a loving heart.

Do It Cheerfully. Going back to Zaccheus, did you notice how excited he was? Now, part of that was just having an opportunity to be with Jesus, but look at what it says about Zaccheus when Jesus tells him to come down "*...and received him with joy*" (Luke 19:6, JND). That joy of coming to know the Lord overflowed in liberality. Paul again in 2 Corinthians 9 says about giving "*not grievingly, or of necessity, for God loves a cheerful giver*" (v. 7, JND).

Do It From What You Have. God does not expect us to go borrow money for His work. He already owns everything. God has allowed us to be instruments in His work rather than doing it Himself directly. This allows us to show our love to Him. Even the widow who gave the two mites gave from what she had – in her case it was all she had. Paul in 2 Corinthians 8 notes in relation to a man giving "*a man is accepted according to what he may have, not according to what he has not*" (v.12). In the previous verse as well it says "*…out of what ye have*" (v. 11). 1 Corinthians 16:2 says "*…as God hath prospered.*" There is no specified sum but we are told it comes from what we have been given and should be done in liberality (2 Corinthians 8:2).

Do It as a Sacrifice-As Worship. Some people do give in what we might term a sacrificial manner as the woman with the two mites, but this is never a requirement of the giver. When we see sacrificial giving in this way, we see it as it must be difficult to do, to be accepted, or cause a hardship to be true giving. I believe this is not what sacrificial giving is about since to do so is putting a constraint on the giving which negates all of the other Scriptures we have just noted. It is not the amount of the gift or how much of a sacrifice it is, but it is a sacrifice as in worship. All Christian giving should be seen as giving to God in the form of worship. In this sense all giving is sacrificial, if done in the spirit of worship. This was the problem with the Pharisees. It's not that their giving was wrong, but they did it for others to see, it wasn't a sacrifice of worship to God. This is why Paul exhorts that the laying in store be done on the first day of the week (1 Corinthians 16:2). This is the Lord's day and the day on which we worship Him. As we saw in the Old Testament when we come to bring a gift to God it is worship. It is no different for us as Christians today. Don't focus so much on yourself (making a gift sacrificial) but on Christ (offering a gift as a sacrifice).

Do It Regularly. We just noted 1 Corinthians 16:2 where Paul notes that we should lay in store on the first day of the week as God hath prospered. It appears that since worship is done on the first day of the week on a regular basis and giving is part of that worship we are to do it then.

I realize what has been presented here may be a surprise for many who have been taught that we are to tithe or give through various quota systems and fund-raisers. Until I studied the issue for myself and saw what the Bible said I followed the same traditions that most others have followed. In reality giving in the Bible is free-will and examples range from very small up to everything a person has. If you find giving ten percent is what the Lord would have you give, that is fine but keep in mind that He may also have you give more based on how He has prospered you.

The Value and Blessings

We should take a moment to understand why giving to God is important. That is, why does the Bible encourage us to give? As with all things in God's plan there is a purpose and this is no different. We learned a great deal about what the Bible has to say about giving in the last section and so we saw glimpses of His purpose in it there. The key reasons for giving are:

As Devotion or Worship. That is, giving is done to demonstrate our love to God as He has done to us. 2 Corinthians 8 says "*for ye know the grace of our Lord Jesus Christ, that for your sakes he being rich became poor, in order that ye by his poverty might be enriched*" (v. 9, JND). Paul was showing that giving was an expression of the saints' love to God as Christ giving His life was an expression of His love to the saints. We see an example of this type of love given by the woman that anoints Jesus' feet with the ointment and wipes them with her hair (Luke 7:37-38). Hebrews 13:15 notes that we should not neglect doing good and sharing, for with such sacrifices God is pleased. It can't be any plainer than Philippians 4:18 that states concerning the Philippians' gift to Paul "*But I have all things in full supply and abound; I am full, having received of Epaphroditus the things sent from you, an odour of sweet savour, an acceptable sacrifice, agreeable to God* (JND).

To Help Others. 2 Corinthians 8:4 speaks of the gift from the churches in Macedonia to help minister to the saints. 2 Corinthians 9:12-13 notes that the gift from the Corinthians would be for that which is lacking among the saints but also an avenue of thanksgiving to God, which relates back to our first point. In Acts the saints did not view their goods as their own but God's and as there was need they sold something and brought the proceeds to the apostles to minister to those who had need (Acts 4:32-35). Paul makes a general pronouncement that emphasizes that Christians are to help the saints saying "*so then, as we have occasion, let us do good towards all and specially towards those of the household of faith*" Galatians 6:10, JND). John also makes clear that helping other believers is important saying "*but whoso may have the world's substance, and see his brother having need, and shut up his bowels from him, how abides the love of God in him?*" (1 John 3:17, JND).

To Help Those in the Ministry. Another purpose in giving is to support those who minister in the Lord's name. In the New Testament church the teachers and evangelists were supported this way. Elders (sometimes called bishops, pastors, or presbyters) and deacons, of which there is always a plurality in the local church, helped to keep order in the church and watch over the saints and feed them from the word as well. The elders focused on the spiritual aspects of the ministry and the deacons on the temporal ministry. Although there is nothing noted about financial support for deacons in the Bible some of the same concepts we note here may well apply to them. Paul emphasizes, though, the support of those in the spiritual aspect of the work. The teacher clearly is to be ministered to as we see in Galatians 6:6 that states "*let him that is taught in the word communicate to him that teaches all good things*" (JND). Support for the evangelist is appropriate as is noted in 1 Corinthians 9:14. In 1 Corinthians 9:9-11 Paul, in using a quotation from Deuteronomy 25:14, is noting the importance of his legitimate claim to support from the source of those who received his ministry. Verse 11 says "*if we have sown to you spiritual things is it a great thing if we shall reap your carnal things?*" (JND). The same truth seems to apply to elders in 1 Timothy 5:18 which quotes from the same verse in Deuteronomy 25:14. Paul says "*let the elders who take the lead among the saints well be esteemed worthy of double honour, specially those labouring in word and teaching...*" (JND).

For Spiritual Blessing. God emphasized to Israel that if they were obedient and gave as directed they would be blessed. Jesus confirms this same thing to the Jew. But the key was their attitude of heart. This is why the Pharisees, though they may have given generously, were not blessed. Their purpose in giving was to be blessed, not by God but by men. 1 Corinthians 13:3 states "*and if I shall dole out all my goods in food...but have not love, I profit nothing*" (JND).

The Bible does note that as Christians we need to sow bountifully that we might reap bountifully (2 Corinthians 9:6). Luke 6:38 also seems to envision this same thing where it states "give and it will be given to you." Now we see that Luke 6 really relates to the kingdom Christ was offering to the Jew but there are lessons for us as well. But we are hard-pressed to see the physical nature of the things applied to Israel as relating to the believer. Paul is always emphasizing the spiritual blessing and reward for the believer in Christ in this age after the kingdom was rejected by Israel. Where were Christ's blessing in giving his life? They are in the heavenlies. He is our example, He gave all that there might be a great spiritual harvest of blessing. We have already seen that giving with the desire to get rich via a return is not God's plan unless the believer desires to be rich in spiritual blessings in Christ. Paul makes this clear in Philippians 4:17 where the saints' giving was not because Paul desired a gift but he desired to see their giving so it may abound to their account. Verse 18 then emphasizes the spiritual aspect of the gift. Then verse 19 emphasizes that God shall supply all their needs. Not only does the Christian have rich blessing in heaven, but God will take care of his needs (not necessarily desires, or giving riches) on earth. Perhaps it is best said that we are to set our affections on things above which means when we give, we give that He might be glorified and then we are blessed in knowing that God is satisfied with the gift.

The Role of the Church

We have already noted a number of verses that relate to giving and the church and so we will summarize here how your giving relates to the local church so you can be sure that you are being a good steward of what God has entrusted to you. We learn the following key points concerning giving and the church:

Church is a Storehouse. The church is the conduit for Christian giving to saints in need and to the ministry in general. Paul notes in 1 Corinthians 16:2 that we are to lay up in store each week. Some will suggest this could be at home, others within the local church, but in either case the context shows that the church together is giving the gift.

Funded by Believers. There is no indication that the local church and the ministry are ever funded by the unbeliever, as we often see today with fund-raisers and the like. Paul says in the same verse "let every one of you." He is speaking to the believers. Thus, as a believer it is important that you give.

Helps the Saints and the Ministers. We have already looked at the details of the purpose of giving so we will not cover them again here. It is clear that the local believers support the needy such as widows indeed (1 Timothy 5:16) and the ministers of the word (1 Timothy 5:17).

The Focus is People. Most, if not all, of the funds spoken of as gifts in the New Testament were focused on helping people in need or working in the ministry. A large portion of the funds you give to a local church should be for that purpose. Often today we see huge sums being spent on construction and upkeep of buildings that are perhaps used several times a week. I know of churches today that still meet inexpensively in a home or hotel so that more funds can be given to those ministering or in need as Paul shows in the Scriptures.

Determining to Whom We Give

The last section of our discussion on giving is an important one. How do we determine where to give? There are so many "ministries" looking for funding that it seems impossible to determine where the real needs are. If this is how you feel then you are right. The truth is there are many ministries whose purpose is well intentioned but not of the Lord. In addition, there are many non-Christian organizations in the world that do honorable things that seek our support as well. What are we to do?

Well, it would be best to look to the Bible and, interestingly, everything that we learn about giving in the Bible we have pretty much covered earlier. That in itself should tell us something. In reality our giving can be very focused and if the local church through its deacons are good stewards and are spiritually mature, the proper needs of the ministry would be met. Based on what we see in the Bible we need to look at the following:

First determine that the local church is following sound stewardship principles as we have discussed in this book. A church's stewardship of its funds is an excellent indication of its spiritual health. If a majority of the funds go for buildings, grounds, and staffing (other than support for teachers and elders laboring in the Word) then you may want to investigate a church that is more biblically sound.

Second, once you are serving in a church that is sound, do your giving through that local church. Let the mature deacons and elders of the church who should have mature spiritual minds determine whether a particular ministry should be supported. Since there are a multitude of elders and deacons there is a thorough review of the use of funds and to what needs they are going. They can look beyond the methods of men to see what is spiritually strong and sound.

If you desire to determine these things on your own you will need to review each ministry very carefully looking at 1) its spiritual state, that is, does it follow Biblical teaching?; 2) the financial reports to see if it is a good steward of what God has already provided them; 3) its leaders to see if they are setting biblical examples in how they conduct themselves and how they seek funding; and 4) praying and seeking Godly counsel from others as you try to ascertain which ministries to support.

Third, anonymously support the needs of teachers, evangelists, and individuals in need by suggesting or designating a gift to them through your local church. If a church does not allow this then find a local church that does. The only reason a church should not be willing to do this is if their analysis has found some spiritual issues that prevent them from doing so.

I do not have time to go into a full-scale discussion of how to look at a ministry. The only ones noted in the Bible are the local church, the individual in need, the teacher, the evangelist, and the elder, especially if he is a teacher. That is the extent of the supported ministry in the New Testament. Any individual or ministry should be along these lines. Organizations whose emphasis is political or social reform, although well intentioned, should not be the recipient of your gifts. There is no biblical basis that I can find for these.

Be careful of fund-raising letters. Most "ministries" today spend more time raising funds than they minister to those they support. Quite often these are professionally written letters by marketing agents who know how to word it just right to get you to send in a donation. Most have pre-written letters ready to send out for the next donation as soon as they receive the first. They are using the methods of men to try to fund God's work. There seems to be a constant bombardment from Christian ministries saying that without our support they will fail. A ministry occasionally letting the saints know of their needs is fine, but for most it is a daily or weekly call. Is the ministry really of the Lord if it is constantly soliciting funds? It would at least cause me to raise the question. In the New Testament, the servants of the Lord were serving and letting God do the providing.

You may occasionally desire to help an organization in the world. Again I recommend that support to the world be done through the local church. This way God can receive the glory for any help given. Also keep in mind that worldly organizations, though perhaps well intentioned, may not be the kind of stewards you would like of the funds, nor necessarily use them the way you had hoped.

In summary, then, give carefully and for the most part do it through a biblically sound local church that supports the ministry of individual teachers and evangelists, as well as Christian organizations.

Managing Bank Accounts

The second key area we want to deal with under the area of basics is banking. Understanding how to find and use a bank is quite important even if it seems simplistic. Banks are finding new ways to get your money through various fees and we need to be vigilant in avoiding these extra costs.

Shopping for a Bank

To be an effective steward in our society usually requires the use of a bank or a similar institution such as a savings and loan or a credit union. Some are able to use just cash if their spending plans do not call for large sums of cash. But for most, check-writing to make payments is required due to where the money must be sent or the amount involved. Also, we may want to look at some banking instruments for purposes of investing, but that we will look at in later chapters.

Although we often use the generic term "bank" for financial institutions that offer checking and savings accounts, how are they different? Let's briefly note how each of these is different.

Banks. These are what we refer to as full-service financial institutions. They offer just about anything you would want in a basic financial instrument. These would include credit cards, loans, and safe deposit boxes in addition to the standard accounts we cover below. Most banks also offer special services such as investment services, trust services, and insurance services.

Savings and Loan Associations. As their name implies these institutions have for the most part focused on savings and loan services for customers. Because of the changes in banking laws many of the differences between these and banks have disappeared. They were once known as "thrifts" emphasizing their lower overhead. One area of difference is that these institutions can only offer interest-bearing checking accounts. Also, 70% of their loans must be for home mortgages if they are federally chartered. You may also find that they offer slightly higher rates on savings accounts due to their lower overhead. There are different types of saving and loans and in the Northeast something similar called savings banks. The differences are technical and we really don't need to go into them here. From our customer perspective they all operate the same way.

? **Credit Union**

Credit Unions. Are non-profit organizations that are owned by, and formed for the benefit of its members. As a result you must meet the qualifications of the particular credit union to join. The key difference is that credit unions are for consumers and so do not venture into the commercial arena like the other financial institutions. Most accounts at credit unions have the word share in them and may use slightly different names such as "draft" for "checking." One nice thing about credit unions is they often have higher savings rates and lower loan rates than other institutions.

Brokerages. As we mentioned, banking laws are constantly changing and so investment firms, also called brokerages, can now offer banking services and banks can now offer investment services. The goal, of course, is to increase competition and thus improve the cost to the consumer for various services. The main benefits of a brokerage are that funds can be easily moved between your investment and cash accounts and you receive a single statement showing the balance of all accounts.

Online Banks. More recently there have been entries into the marketplace that use the web for offering services to its customers. These banks use the Internet, mail, and the phone to handle all bank services. There are no physical locations although some are associated with another institution such as an insurance company that can handle some items at a physical location. State Farm Bank is an example of this. It is an online bank but does allow some basic transactions through their insurance agency locations. Online banks generally pay the highest savings rates among the banks because of the low overhead associated with running the bank and perhaps as well to entice people to try something that may not seem practical. I am an experienced user of an online bank and have found it to be a great benefit.

Bank Accounts

So, now that we have an idea of the types of institutions that are out there, other than investing services, what basically does a bank have to offer? Let's briefly note the choices available to you at the average bank. Keep in mind when we use the term bank we mean any of the institutions we have noted above. Exhibit 3-1 following this discussion shows a comparison of the features of the various accounts we will discuss here.

Checking Accounts. These accounts let you make deposits and funds are withdrawn when you write checks to others. They do not normally provide interest on the balance thus any funds left in the account the bank is free to use for its own investment until you need them. That is, the bank gets free use of your money until you request it. Automated Teller Machines (ATM) also give you access to your account.

N.O.W. Accounts. These accounts are basically checking accounts that earn interest. NOW means Negotiable Order of Withdrawal. Of course, the negotiable order is the check that you write to have funds withdrawn from the account.

? NOW Account

MMA or MMDA Accounts. These are not money market mutual funds although they are often confused with them. We get into those when we get to the chapters on investing. Money market accounts (MMA) or money market deposit accounts (MMDA) are also checking accounts that earn interest but do so at a higher rate but not as high as money market mutual funds. In exchange for a higher rate you are required to keep a minimum balance in the account or in a related account or combination of accounts with the same institution. There are sometimes limitations on how often you can access or transfer funds in these accounts and there may be stiff fees for going below the minimum.

Savings Accounts. Savings accounts are instruments that allow us to earn interest but there are no checks available to withdraw funds. Funds can be withdrawn either in person or at an ATM. There are usually two types of savings accounts. The passbook savings account is, as its name implies, an account that tracks the balance using a passbook that records entries as deposits and withdrawals are made at the institution. These sometimes pay a slightly higher rate than other savings accounts because you must bring the passbook to the bank in order to access your funds. As a result, the bank is more likely to keep your funds longer and not have to worry about the overhead related to processing many withdrawals. The other type of savings account is called a statement savings account and, as its name implies, involves sending you a statement each month that shows the transactions and current balance on the account.

? CD

CD Accounts. The other type of account that is popular at a bank is a CD or Certificate of Deposit. These are sometimes called timed deposits because the funds are left with the bank for a predetermined amount of time. To withdraw the funds before the time required has elapsed incurs a penalty of usually at least one month's interest. Because of the limitation on the withdrawal of funds and the penalty, the rates are usually higher than savings accounts. The rates also are higher as the term of your deposit grows. So a 2-year certificate will pay a higher rate than a six-month certificate.

Type of Account	Return	Risk	Liquidity	Convenience	Balance Requirement
Checking	0%	Low	High	High	Low
NOW	0-1%	Low	High	High	High
Savings	.5-1.5%	Low	High	Medium	Low
MMA	.5-2.5%	Low	High	Medium	High
CD	1.5-4%	Low	Medium	Medium	Medium

Exhibit 3-1. Comparison of Bank Account Features.

Account Features

There are a few other things related to bank accounts we should note that might be helpful if you have not done much of your own banking up to this point.

Checks. The checks you get when you open your checking account can be used to pay bills and withdraw funds from your account. It may be surprising to some to know that many students going to college have never written a check. For those who haven't got a clue how to write one we have provided a sample in Exhibit 3-2. Keep in mind you may be charged for your checks when you open the account and anytime in the future that you need to order more.

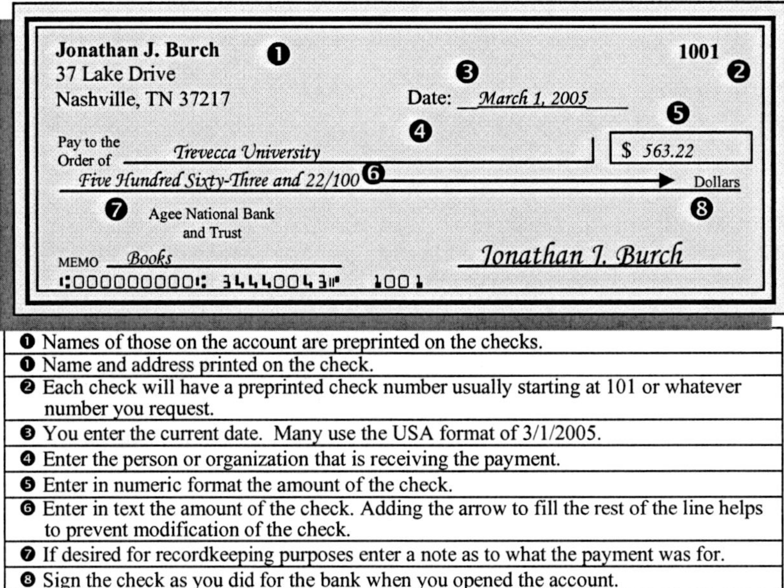

❶ Names of those on the account are preprinted on the checks.
❶ Name and address printed on the check.
❷ Each check will have a preprinted check number usually starting at 101 or whatever number you request.
❸ You enter the current date. Many use the USA format of 3/1/2005.
❹ Enter the person or organization that is receiving the payment.
❺ Enter in numeric format the amount of the check.
❻ Enter in text the amount of the check. Adding the arrow to fill the rest of the line helps to prevent modification of the check.
❼ If desired for recordkeeping purposes enter a note as to what the payment was for.
❽ Sign the check as you did for the bank when you opened the account.

Exhibit 3-2. Sample Check.

? Cashier's Check

Cashier's Checks. A guaranteed check that the bank makes out to a particular payee and is signed by an officer of the bank. You must provide the funds for the check. Banks usually charge a fee for this service but if you do substantial business with your bank or keep a minimum balance in a savings or CD account they may waive the fee.

? Certified Check

Certified Checks. These are checks that you write that the bank has certified as having the funds available to cover it and has indicated this by marking the check as "certified." As with the cashier's check, there are usually fees but they may be waived depending on the account or the business that you do with the bank.

? Money Order

Money Orders. These are like checks that you purchase with your funds and can be helpful for those who do not have checking accounts or only write a few checks a month. They are usually written for small amounts and can be cashed like a check. You must, of course, pay the amount of the funds to the issuer of the check. There are fees for each money order which can run as much as $3 at a bank. The U. S. Post Office does money orders fairly inexpensively at 85 cents each. Again, if you are a good bank customer the fees may be waived.

? Traveler's Check

Traveler's checks. These are prepaid checks that can be used as cash at most business establishments. Each must be signed when you purchase it and then signed again when you cash it. It's a good way of verifying that the check is yours since they can be easily used as cash. Unlike other check instruments they have certain denominations ($20, $50, and $100) and are issued by major financial organizations such as American Express or Visa. They can be purchased at most financial institutions we have noted. As with other special check instruments these carry a fee, which may be waived for some bank customers. Other organizations such as motor clubs (e.g.. AAA) also provide this service, which may be free for certain members.

? Debit Card

Debit Cards. These look just like a credit card and now are offered by most financial institutions. As the name implies, its use creates a debit or subtracts the transaction amount from your account that is connected to the card. Unlike a credit card the transaction is immediate and your funds that were used for a purchase are no longer available for use. Unlike a credit card that may have a specific limit at which you can no longer use the card the debit card is limited by the funds available in your account. Basically, these replace check writing and most merchants accept them for purchases. Keep in mind many banks are beginning to assess charges for using debit cards since they do not make as much money as with credit card transactions. That is, there is no balance to assess finance charges on, nor is there a fee paid by the retailer if you use the debit card with your personal identification number (PIN). Also, if you have a newer ATM card, it likely could be used as a debit card.

? Credit Card

Credit Cards. We cover these in detail in a separate chapter but these are card instruments that allow you to borrow funds quickly based on a pre-approved limit of funds that are available. Most merchants accept at least one of the major credit card company cards such as American Express, Discover, Visa, or MasterCard. You are then billed monthly for all transactions you have made to the card. If you are required to pay the balance in full each month then the card will sometimes be called a "charge card" rather than a "credit card." With that exception they operate the same.

? Smart Card

Smart Cards. These are much like debit cards or credit cards and look much like them. They allow you to make purchases at most merchants. The difference is that the funds available for use are not borrowed or deducted from an account, but are stored on the card. That is, you give a bank funds and they in turn update your card to show what is available to be used. This allows the bank to use the money until you use the card and the merchant gets it from the bank. Of course, it helps you since you don't need to carry cash on you. If you run out of money on the card you can then reload it with more funds from the institution that issued the card. These are becoming very popular and are used at universities, copy shops, and even by merchants in the form of gift cards.

What should you look for in a bank? Look at what your individual needs are in relation to account usage, service, and convenience and then begin looking. For most of you the key will be "free checking." Now in our society "free" has many meanings at least based on the advertisements I see. It's like getting an advertisement for a free CD if you send in $9.99 shipping and handling. Is the CD really free? No. To mail a CD might cost a $1 or so. I guess the other $8-$9 must be the handling. I would suggest that you look for the following when looking for a checking account:

1. No monthly fee for having a checking account.
2. No per-check fees for writing checks.
3. No fees for using the bank's ATMs.
4. Free online access to view, transfer, and pay bills.
5. Free transfers of funds among accounts.
6. Convenience in accessing ATMs and branches.
7. Free or low cost checks.
8. Insured.

Keep in mind there may be other legal fees that a bank can charge even if it is considered free checking. Exhibit 3-3 provides a list of factors to consider when choosing a bank, in general.

Factors	Bank 1	Bank 2	Bank 3
Fees/Cost			
Convenience			
Safety			
Location			
Products			
Interest Rates			
Service			
Compare banks by comparing these features. You may wish to use a point system to more objectively evaluate them. Take 100 points and divide them among the factors based on how important they are to you and then rate each bank on a scale based on the points you gave for each factor. For instance if you gave 20 points to the fee factor then you would score each bank on a scale of 0-20 on that factor. The more fees and costs the fewer the points. Total the points for each bank and compare the totals.			

Exhibit 3-3. Factors to Rate when Choosing a Bank.

You will notice I didn't put anything about interest rates in the list above. That is because for the most part the interest rates being offered on interest bearing checking accounts are so tiny it is almost ludicrous. There are a few exceptions but the key is to focus on eliminating the fees, which can easily eat up any interest you earn plus much more.

Many interest bearing checking accounts require a minimum balance to avoid fees. For instance, as of this writing one Tennessee bank requires $25,000 to avoid fees and the interest on the checking account is .10%. Yes, you are reading that right, that is a tenth of one percent. If you go under the minimum you are hit with a fifteen dollar service fee. This account is not a bargain. $25,000 invested at 5% somewhere will gain you over $100 a month, whereas at their rate you will make a little over $2 a month. So the moral is buyer beware. If there is a minimum balance requirement, be sure it is relatively small, perhaps $500 or less, and be sure the fees are not exorbitant if you go under. If you go under the limit they may also penalize you the interest for that month. State Farm currently offers checking where you earn significantly higher interest than most banks if you keep a balance of $2500 and there are no fees if your balance falls below that amount.

Watch out for ATM fees. Most banks will charge you for out of network use of other banks' ATMs and that other bank is likely to charge you as well. These fees can be as much as $5.00 when put together, just for obtaining a small amount of cash at the bank.

Watch for other fees such NSF (not sufficient funds) fees and overdraft fees. Some of these fees are now an exorbitant $30 or more. Many banks automatically add overdraft protection to your account and you may not be aware of it or the costs involved.

Some banks may require direct deposit. Direct deposit involves your employer, or other institution that would normally issue you a check, to send the check deposit directly to the bank to be credited to your account. Employers usually still provide a direct deposit receipt showing the details of the transaction. Find out what happens if you no longer do direct deposit.

Some banks are now charging a debit card per transaction fee. Bank somewhere else if this is the case.

Don't automatically take the checks the bank gives you. Look at the cost and see if you can get them made cheaper elsewhere. You may find some banks provide an initial box of checks free and then you will have some time to shop for a better price on them for the future.

You may want to visit www.bankrate.com to get a basic comparison of accounts for your area. They also note ATM fees, NSF fees, and minimum balance requirements for both interest and non-interest bearing accounts. Always verify the information with the bank and check local banks for specials. In Florida for instance, Bank Atlantic as of this publication was offering "Totally Free Checking." Bank of America is currently offering free checking for life. Keep your eyes open for opportunities such as these. Forget deals that give a free gift. The gift will be long gone while you will likely still be paying bank fees.

Check your local banks carefully, as well, since they may offer accounts with fewer fees than the big name banks and may have more time to service your needs as an individual.

The checking account is the key area of comparison shopping for various banks. See Exhibit 3-4 for a sample comparison worksheet. Use it to help find the best deal for a checking account. You may also want to look at savings rates, especially if you wish to connect your savings with your checking for overdraft protection. Be careful though, there is usually a fairly stiff fee for using the feature even though it is your own money. The fee is less than an NSF fee but still, some charge $10 or more to use the overdraft feature.

Factors	Bank 1	Bank 2	Bank 3
Monthly fee			
Per check fees			
Minimum Balance			
Interest			
Online banking			
Overdraft protection			
Cost of checks			
Direct deposit			
ATM access			
Compare checking accounts by comparing these features. You may wish to use a point system to more objectively evaluate them as in the bank comparison in the previous exhibit or you may decide to create a spreadsheet with the actual results of your analysis. You will need to take into account your extent of usage of the account as you make comparisons.			

Exhibit 3-4. Factors to Rate when Choosing a Checking Account.

Setting Up and Using a Checking Account

Once you have chosen a bank you will want to visit it to complete the paperwork required to open the accounts. You will likely need to bring one or two forms of identification to the bank that include your current mailing address. The key piece of paperwork signed is usually the bank's signature card. This will identify who is allowed to access the account and the signatures of each individual will be on the card. You can open the account as an individual account, where you are the only signer and user of the account, or you may open a joint account with another person where either may sign, or, if desired, both must sign to access the account.

Be careful to read the bank signature card since it will also identify what happens to the account if one of the individuals on the account dies. There are usually two ways of holding an account jointly. The most common way is Joint Ownership (or Tenancy) with rights of Survivorship (JTWROS). This allows the surviving individual to continue to access the account and gain full ownership of anything in the account. The other form is called Joint Tenants in Common (JTIC). This means that the surviving account holder only gets a share of the account, usually half unless otherwise specified. Laws do change frequently so be sure to check with your state. Another possibility that some states, such as Florida, allow is to have a beneficiary assigned to the account so that when the account holder dies the beneficiary receives what remains in the account. The beneficiary cannot touch the account while the owner is still living. This is sometimes called a Payable on Death (POD) account. We'll note this in more detail when we get to estate planning toward the end of the book.

When you open the account the bank will usually let you pick out the checks you would like to use. Keep in mind there are all types and styles of checks and some can be quite expensive. Sometimes the bank includes the first

100 checks at no cost, but check. If not, you can elect to purchase them from the bank or wait, and purchase them elsewhere. The bank will usually give you a few blank checks and deposit slips to get you started. Don't be coaxed into spending too much on checks. Remember the less you spend here the more you have to save for other important things. Current check prices range from $3.95 to over $50.00 for 200 checks depending on how elaborate they are and whether they create duplicates or are made for computer printers. Go with the cheapest on these since they are eventually destroyed. The per check price drops as you purchase more, but if you order more make sure you are likely to use them. If you plan on moving or changing banks for some reason then ordering fewer will be better. Figure on your usage and your plans and buy accordingly. As a guide, on average people write 10 checks a month, or 120 a year. So, 600 checks will last five years at that rate.

If you will be paying most of your bills online you can stick with a very small number of checks and save on the cost of the checks, envelopes, and stamps (assuming you have free online bill pay). Even if you don't use checks, unless you opened your checking account with a few million dollars or you connect to a savings account that has online transfer you will need deposit slips. The bank will usually print booklets of these at no cost.

Savings accounts will either have deposit and withdrawal slips (which you get for free at the bank) or a passbook, which is free as well. CD accounts usually don't have any regular deposits or withdrawals (although there may be exceptions for special types of CDs) so you won't have any paperwork to deal with after you have opened the account.

Once you have opened your account the bank will also send a checkbook cover (take the cheap, free one) and a register or ledger to record when you make transactions against your account by writing checks or making deposits. You can use this register or use a computer financial product such as Quicken or MS Money to keep track of it on the computer. These products also provide the ability to print checks. Keep in mind, though, that these checks will be more expensive than the standard checks you can get. It's better to go with free online bill pay than spending money on computer checks and envelopes. Of course the big plus of financial software is that it can be helpful in balancing your accounts, which we cover in the next section.

Perhaps by now most of you have seen or written checks but for those that have not you can review exhibits discussed previously in the chapter. Exhibit 3-5 provides a sample of a transaction register for an account along with notes on the key entries in the register. No matter what you use for recording your transactions, be sure to use something. Do not get in the habit of writing checks and then filling in the register later. Too often people forget to enter it later and then find out too late that they have a $30 overdraft fee because they thought they had more money in their account than they actually had. These types of charges are too much of a waste of your funds as a steward and they can be avoided.

Trans. Type Check #	Date	Description	Payment		Fee	Deposit		Balance	
	2005							894	34
1001	1/2	Trevecca Books	563	22				331	12
Deposit	1/4	Gift from Mom				100	00	431	12
Transfer	1/7	From Savings				600	00	1031	12
1002	1/11	Rent	475	00				556	12
ATM With.	1/11	Cash	35	00	2.50			518	62

Exhibit 3-5. Account Transaction Register.

Some other key points to keep in mind when dealing with your bank accounts include:

- Avoid automatic recurring withdrawals from your bank accounts. By avoiding automatic withdrawals you retain control of your resources rather than someone else.
- Don't forget to record ATM, debit, and other electronic transactions in your register.
- Write your checks in ink so someone cannot change the amount easily.
- Be sure that dollar amounts that you have written in text and in digits match. Mismatches do happen. If it does, the bank usually takes the amount written in text.
- Banks will usually return unsigned checks that you have written. This takes time and can result in late payment fees from those for whom the check was meant. I did send an unsigned check once that the payee (it was a utility) was able to cash; I was surprised it got through.
- Don't forget to endorse (sign on the back) checks that you will be depositing. There are actually federal regulations now in place on how your check is supposed to be endorsed.

Balancing Your Accounts

One very important aspect of finance is knowing the status of your finances. It is difficult to make sound financial decisions if you are unsure of your current resources or obligations. An important part of keeping abreast of your situation is balancing your accounts regularly and as soon after receiving a statement as possible. The process of balancing your accounts is sometimes called "reconciling" your account. That is, you want to see if what you have in your records matches that of the institution from which you received the statement. Account reconciliations should be done for all bank accounts, credit cards, loans, and investment accounts. This should not be taken lightly since over time you will uncover errors that either you or the institution have made. Also, for credit cards, it is a good way to keep an eye on whether someone has compromised your account information and is illegally using your card. Here are some examples of problems I have found in the last 10 years of reconciling:

A bank double charged my account for a check that I wrote. That is, the check had been accidentally processed by the bank twice. I could have lost $50.00.

A bank accidentally withdrew the wrong amount from my account for a check. The check coding the bank placed on the bottom of the check (called Magnetic Ink Character Recognition or MICR) when processing it showed that the amount was different from what the check was written for.

I found an incorrect charge on a credit card that I had never made. About a month later I found another and realized that someone likely had my card information but was being careful not to raise suspicion by creating lots of charges in hopes that an occasional charge would be ignored or something that might be overlooked because I was unable to remember what I bought.

I made a deposit to a bank that had checks totaling more than what was on the deposit ticket. The bank caught the error before I did.

Several times restaurant personnel have changed tip amounts on credit card receipts to give themselves more money. In each case I have caught it and had it corrected.

I closed a bank account and then the bank tried to send a statement with maintenance fees showing that I owed a balance. I called the bank to correct the error.

As you can see many things can go wrong with accounts, including errors on our part, errors by the financial institutions, deceptive practices by institutions trying to get extra fees, or by others just trying to take advantage of your account information. Invariably, as you see from the above, mistakes will be made on your accounts. The key is keeping track of the accounts so that you can catch the errors. A good steward will do this and as a result be able to give an accurate account of that which is entrusted to him.

Reconciliation should occur monthly for most accounts with the exception of retirement or investment accounts where the frequency is more likely to be quarterly or perhaps, annually. Balancing or reconciling an account is not all that difficult. You need your statement of the account from the financial institution as well as your own record of the account usually in the form of a ledger. You might also find it helpful to use a software product such as Quicken or MS Money to make it easier to complete this task. If you do use the computer for your register be sure to regularly enter all of the data that is not automatically created as a result of printing computer checks or the like. Don't forget to enter in your ledger ATM transactions including fees, automatic transactions against your account, and debit card usage against your account.

Exhibit 3-6 shows a sample bank statement. Exhibit 3-7 shows a sample register for a checking account. Be aware that new regulations allow

Bank Statement

Acccount: 00117711 Statement Date: ____________________

Begiing Balance on 01-20-2005: $2,825.54

Deposits and Other Additions:

Date	Description	Amount
01-25	Trasnfer (3322113)	$300.00
02-14	Trasnfer (3322113)	$2,200.00
02-18	Interest Payment	$3.17

Total Deposits and Other Additions: $2,503.17

Withdrawals and Other Charges:

Date	Description	Amount
1-26	Check 334	$26.06
1-26	Check 335	$105.10
1-26	Check 337	$109.90
2-10	Check 338	$16.74
2-15	Check 339	$114.00
2-15	Check 341	$761.62
2-15	Check 342	$1,181.64

Total Withdrawals and Other Charges $2,315.06

Ending Balance on 02-18-2005 $3,013.65

Exhibit 3-6. Sample Bank Statement.

Trans. Type Check #	Date	Description	Payment		Fee	Deposit		Balance		R
	2005							894	34	
Deposit	1/18	Speaking Income				2000	00	2894	34	R
331	1/19	Wal-Mart	100	00				2794	34	
332	1/21	Water Bill	28	80				2765	54	R
333	1/21	ATT	40	00				2725	54	R
Transfer	1/25	From Savings				300	00	3025	54	
334	1/26	Bellsouth	26	06				2999	48	
335	1/26	Nashville Electric	105	10				2894	38	
336	1/26	Discover	328	91				2565	47	
337	1/26	J. C. Penny	109	90				2455	57	
338	2/8	Metro Services	16	74				2438	83	
Transfer	2/13	From Savings				2200	00	4638	83	
339	2/13	Eye Doctor	114	00				4524	83	
340	2/13	Trevecca Books	563	22				3961	61	
341	2/13	Discover	761	62				3199	99	
342	2/13	American Express	1181	64				2018	35	
Deposit	2/18	Interest				3	17	2021	52	
Deposit	2/18	Refund Check				25	00	2046	52	

Exhibit 3-7. Sample Check Register.

banks to keep checks so that you may not receive the originals back. Most banks are likely to take advantage of this to reduce the costs related to processing and sending checks back to the consumer. Exhibit 3-8 shows a sample reconciliation for the account in the previous exhibits. This type of form is quite often provided on the back of your statement or as an additional page in your statement to help you accomplish the task. Of course, computer software, will have automated reconciliation components that make it quite easy to accomplish this. Appendix B also provides a worksheet for performing an account reconciliation.

In summary you need to take the following steps to reconcile the accounts:

Be sure to enter in your ledger any fees, interest, or other receipts or charges that the bank has added to the statement that have not yet been added to the ledger.

Account Reconciliation

Date: 3/1/2005 Bank Statement Date: 2/18/2005

Line 1 **Ending Balance from Bank Statement:** $3,013.65

Subtract Outstanding Checks and Other Payments:

Check Number	Amount	Check Number	Amount
331	$100.00		
336	$328.91		
340	$563.22		

Line 2 **Total Outstanding Checks and Other Payments:** $992.13

Line 3 **Subtotal (subtract Line 2 from Line 1)** $2,021.52

Add Outstanding Deposits and Other Credits:

Deposit Date	Amount	Deposit Date	Amount
2/18/2005	$25.00		

Line 4 **Total Outstanding Deposits and Other Credits:** $25.00

Line 5 **Reconciled Balance (add Line 4 to Line 3)** $2,046.52

Line 6 **Balance from Your Account Reguster:** $2,046.52

Line 7 **Difference (should be zero)** $0.00

Exhibit 3-8. Sample Reconciliation.

Enter the balance on the bank statement on line 1.

List payments that you have on your account that the bank does not have listed on the statement. Total these "outstanding" payments and put the total on line 2.

Subtract line 2 from line 1 and put the total on line 3. What you have done thus far is take the bank's balance and adjusted it for the payments that you have made but have not been received by the financial institution for processing. If they had been received the account balance reported would be lower. Since they have not received them yet, we make the balance lower to match what it would have been if they had. This way both the bank balance and your balance will reflect all payments.

Next we need to do the same thing for deposits or receipts that you have in your ledger but the bank has not processed yet. List and total all outstanding receipts that you have on your ledger but the bank does not. Put the total on line 4.

Add line 4 to line 3 and put the total on line 5.

The total on line 5 should be the total that you have in your ledger.

If these do not match there are several things to check:

- Be sure you have entered any interest or fee debits and credits and that they match what the bank statement shows.
- Be sure you have included all electronic transactions including ATM, automatic, and online bill pay.
- Be sure the amounts listed on the statement for each transaction match what is on your ledger.
- Check to see if there are entries on the statement that may be on your statement in error or are perhaps duplicated.

Most times the balance you have will match what the bank has. If not, figure out why not. Do not assume the financial institution is right and just change your balance. Too many people do this and may well be losing money as a result. If you perform these reconciliations as a habit immediately after your statements come in you will be far better off for doing so and may catch fraud related to your account much more quickly.

The Role of Children

Children play a key role in our financial planning in several ways. Most authors in financial books will note little about children and when they do it is usually concerning how expensive they are to raise. That is certainly one area to look at but there are also the issues of how children influence our financial practices and teaching our children about financial planning. Even if you are young and currently do not have children or do not plan on having children you may find this section interesting, especially if you are one who enjoys helping others who have children.

The Blessing of Children

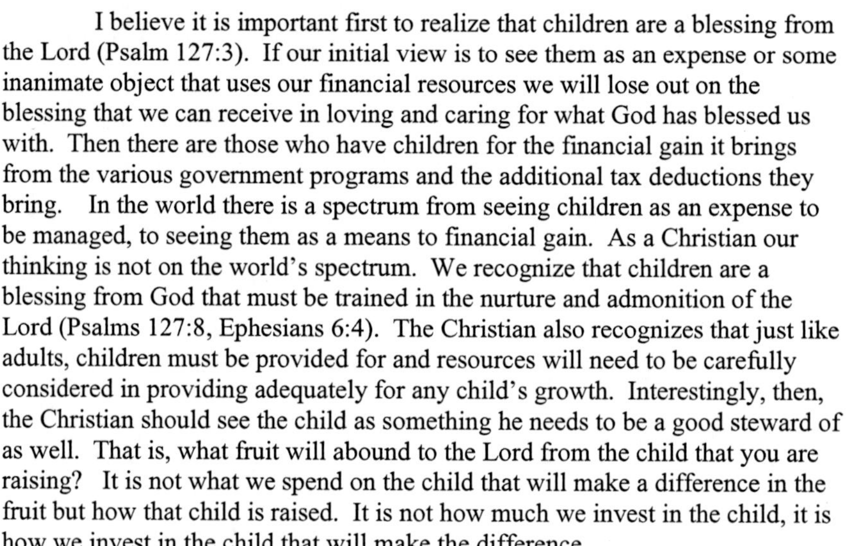

I believe it is important first to realize that children are a blessing from the Lord (Psalm 127:3). If our initial view is to see them as an expense or some inanimate object that uses our financial resources we will lose out on the blessing that we can receive in loving and caring for what God has blessed us with. Then there are those who have children for the financial gain it brings from the various government programs and the additional tax deductions they bring. In the world there is a spectrum from seeing children as an expense to be managed, to seeing them as a means to financial gain. As a Christian our thinking is not on the world's spectrum. We recognize that children are a blessing from God that must be trained in the nurture and admonition of the Lord (Psalms 127:8, Ephesians 6:4). The Christian also recognizes that just like adults, children must be provided for and resources will need to be carefully considered in providing adequately for any child's growth. Interestingly, then, the Christian should see the child as something he needs to be a good steward of as well. That is, what fruit will abound to the Lord from the child that you are raising? It is not what we spend on the child that will make a difference in the fruit but how that child is raised. It is not how much we invest in the child, it is how we invest in the child that will make the difference.

The Cost of Raising Children

Although as Christians we do not view a child as an expense we recognize that they do require care and feeding. Of course, to provide this requires expending some resources. It is hoped of course that by expending those resources there will be a return on that investment in the child. Certainly we need to keep in mind that if we desire to have children that we are agreeing to make a commitment of resources to invest in that child to help him to grow. Investments in food, clothing, and health care are examples of this. You might be surprised to learn that there are many calculators on the web for determining the cost of raising a child. You can go to www.bankrate.com or www.babycenter.com to check out a couple of the many that are available. Many articles have been written on the topic and usually there is an update done by some organization each year. Usually the costs produced exceed $200,000 before college education.

Like all things financial we need to carefully consider what the basis of these calculations are to see if they are realistic. Usually they will take some average for a particular expense area and divide it by the number of children or individuals in the family. If we take housing, as an example, many will divide up the cost of rent (or taxes and interest on a home) to come up with a child's housing cost. To the author this makes little sense unless having a child requires you to spend money to modify your current home to accommodate the child or to move to a larger home. In many cases having a child does not incur any additional housing costs. When we had our son there was no change in our housing costs by adding the child since we had another bedroom in the home. If you have a second child and they can share a bedroom then the same thing is true. Keep in mind that the idea that every child must have his or her own room is relatively new and can lead to much greater expenses by forcing you to buy a larger home. There are benefits in children learning to share a room. Today, too many couples overspend to provide a separate room for each child.

Another category of cost will be food. There will be some incremental cost for each child added to the family. That cost will likely grow as the child ages and eats more. Also, keep in mind as you add children, the cost of eating out increases much more dramatically than does your grocery bill.

A third category of expenses that is usually part of the formula is transportation. As with housing, many of these formulas automatically assume it will cost you more because you will need to buy a larger vehicle. Again this may not be the case. The idea of families with children needing an SUV or a mini-van is also relatively new. A sedan or small wagon is usually sufficient for small families of four individuals or less. If you do buy another vehicle (used or new) because of the addition of a child then your costs may well increase substantially. The additional car payments, if any, the increased consumption of gas for a larger vehicle, and the increased taxes for a newer vehicle in some states will all apply. The biggest cost may end up being the additional driving that results from having a child especially as the child grows. This may include doctor visits, school activities, and other outings or sports.

Clothing is another category often included in child cost calculations. If you decide to clothe your children with only new clothing or the name brands, be ready to spend a great deal (although unnecessarily). In reality families really do not need to break the bank on clothing. There are loads of great used clothing available regularly at yard sales, auctions, or at great discounts at clearance sales. You should never pay retail for clothing and never buy an expensive brand name because the other children's parents are doing it. Often you can get great clothing for free from members of your church. It is amazing how much is spent on clothing and this is why these cost formulas appear so large and overstated.

A fifth area that will certainly play a role and that is the area of healthcare costs. Especially in the first few years, well baby care, immunizations, and various illnesses will likely increase your costs in this area. Healthcare expenses have climbed, and it appears will continue to climb, rapidly. It is likely that the premiums that you pay for your health insurance will climb if it is your first child. After the first child there usually is no increase since you will already be on the family plan of your insurer.

Of course, no child cost would be complete without a miscellaneous category. This usually includes items purchased specifically for the child such as toys, books, and bigger things, as they get older. This area of expenses is not mandatory and there is usually room for much savings here.

Well, that gives you a view of the costs that you may encounter as you invest in your children and that the calculators usually include. There may be additional costs included where both parents work such as childcare. Some calculators will account for this as well. We discuss the issue of whether both parents should work in chapter four under "Managing Income." It is imperative that parents assist children in establishing a fund for their college education while the children are very young. By having a fund available students can avoid getting into an unbiblical position of being unable to repay student loans. We look at this issue in more detail in the section on making major purchases in the chapter on managing credit. We also look at saving for a child's education in Chapter 7 under "Using Tax Advantaged Investments." The key is to realize that children can indeed increase expenses but they are better seen as an investment in something that grows (your child) and should produce value and blessing down the road. Also, it is important to realize that the investment expenses don't need to be outrageous and usually can be significantly under what is produced by the various cost calculators.

The Influence of Children

Another key area for young people to understand is the profound influence children have on our spending habits and priorities. Quite often when we have our first child we are so excited that our emotions take over and we will spend much more than we should so our child "can have the best." We will often buy the best of everything whether or not that might help to care for the child. We also have a tendency to go overboard on toys even as the child grows. I'm sure you can tell your own stories of children who have had so many toys there could never be enough time to use them all, and in reality many are only used a few times and then put in a toy box never to be used again. What is sad many of these toys are then sold at yard sales for pennies on the dollar. The key point to bring out here is that we need to "think" before we spend in whatever we do. It is no different when it comes to our children.

There are several ways in which we unconsciously spend more because of the influence of our children in addition to wanting the best for them. First keep in mind that if you bring children to shop with you, you will likely spend more than you intended. Children will see many new things and be asking for some thing every few minutes. What usually happens is the parent gets tired of the constant requests for things and buys something for the child, even if the child already has two of the item that he never uses. Don't bother to bring children shopping unless they are old enough to understand that you have a spending plan and that they need to help you stay within it on the shopping trip.

The second area of a child's influence is his or her peers. You will undoubtedly be told by a child that they need Tommy Hilfiger shirts or Air Jordan sneakers (oops, got to be careful, they are athletic shoes) and the like. The key reason they need the overpriced wardrobe or other items is that their friends are wearing them or using them. Horrors!!! You don't want your child looking like a freak so you go out and buy them. Don't be tempted to do this. The child needs to learn not to be conformed to the world's view of what is best. It may even hurt the child not to have the same things their friends may have but the key is helping them to see why. That is, don't just say "no" but explain why and show how the savings in not doing so is a benefit to the family. Show how the tradeoffs that we have discussed work. Too many worry about the child's self esteem when with peers but it is those who learn to stand against the world view as youngsters that will be strong Christians as adults. Don't be one of the many parents who overspends as a result of peer pressure your child is receiving. Most of the items you buy will last for a very short time and then are worth little afterwards.

Another area of indirect influence on you is the advertising today that is directed toward children. The goal of the marketers is to reach the children because they know that if they successfully reach a child they will often reach an adult to buy their product for the child. These marketers are not stupid and have done much research in this area. They know exactly how the individual will react to various stimuli and thus how to present their message. It is important, again, here to help the child learn at a young age the financial tradeoffs that must be made in this life so they can make intelligent choices based on thinking through the options.

The Financial Training of Children

Our discussion on children to this point has emphasized showing children how to think from a financial perspective. Our final topic, then, under this section is to provide insights on how we should train our children in financial stewardship and help them acquire this ability to carefully analyze a financial issue and make appropriate choices. By so doing they will be well prepared to make the right choices when they are living on their own. We will try to touch on the key highlights in this area. You may wish to do further reading in a book that deals specifically with this whole issue. Crown Ministries has many good Christian finance books for young children as well as teens available at www.crown.org.

There are 7 key steps in training up a child to be able to deal with personal financial stewardship. They are:

First, the child needs to commit his or her life to Christ as the foundation. As we have already noted, to understand Biblical truths one must have the Spirit of God and this is only available through faith in Jesus Christ. It is important for children to recognize what Christ has done for them at Calvary and what He has saved them from. They need to able to rest in His finished work and allow the Spirit of God to make them a new creation. This will enable them to follow the things of God.

Second, the child must understand that God is the creator and owner of all and that we are stewards of what He has given. If children learn that they are only stewards of what another owns and to whom they will need to give an account, then they will handle finances much differently. We have discussed this aspect in detail earlier in the book.

Third, the child should be able to understand the difference between being a steward and being a consumer. It is important to help children to understand that the world seeks consumption and as a result they will be influenced and encouraged to do so. As parents you must emphasize what the steward does.

Fourth, you need to be a Godly example to your children. Perhaps you have heard the axiom "the nut doesn't fall far from the tree." The idea is that those you produce will be like you. This is no different in the realm of finances. How you train or bring up your children in finances is likely how they will view it when they are on their own. If you provide a Biblical example and involve them as we note here they are likely to follow that example.

Fifth, make financial planning and decisions a family affair. Children will learn a great deal if they participate in the family finances and understand how decisions are made. As long as they can understand that the information is for the family and not for those outside they can learn a great deal by seeing the family spending plan and what is truly involved in running a home and the tradeoffs that must be made. They also get an opportunity to see decision-making in action. Children may also have interesting questions and ideas to contribute.

Sixth, provide income opportunities and be careful with allowances. Allowances are quite often an area of significant discussion because there are differing views on whether and/or how they should be implemented. These differences of opinion usually arise due to both the positive and negative impact allowances can have. First, if you do use an allowance it must be for the purpose of teaching financial stewardship. Giving allowances to children to consume any way they wish is unbiblical stewardship. When a child is young an allowance for purposes of financial training may be appropriate but it should gradually be replaced by the child becoming more self-sufficient in earning income either from work around the home or outside the home. Keep in mind that children should not be paid for chores that they do as part of the family unit where all share in the work (cleaning the home, washing dishes, taking out the trash, etc.). Pay should be given for those items that are not normally considered part of the chores or perhaps that the parents might normally do or have someone else do. For instance, if dad usually mows the lawn or has someone else mow the lawn then once the child is old enough dad could pay the child for mowing the lawn. Also, don't pay children for partially completed work. If they are struggling with a particular task you can use it as a training opportunity and help them learn how to finish it right. The key is to pay only when it is complete. To do otherwise leads children to believe they can get paid for half a job which is not always the case in the business world.

Seventh, keep the individual child in mind – God has made us all differently. As we already know God has given each individual different capabilities, talents, and spiritual gifts. When training our children we need to keep this in mind. It is not a competition among the children or with others in the world, but whether each has been a faithful steward of what God has entrusted to the individual.

In summary, help children to learn and live the financial guidelines noted in this book and followed by you. As the children grow older you can help them to learn the lessons noted throughout this text. In addition, their involvement in the seeing how the family finances work in the form of spending plans, decision making, giving, emergencies, and the like will be great lessons for them. You need to work with your children actively to make financial stewardship a reality. Most parents do little to prepare their children to deal with issues in the financial world.

The Tradeoffs of Saving Money

Up to this point in the text we have looked at a number of tradeoffs and factors that influence our financial choices including quality, time, risk, inflation, and the like. We have also noted the importance of opportunity cost and the time value of money, and how compounding can have a profound effect on your financial resources either positively if you are saving, or negatively if you are borrowing (covered later). Here we want to make a final point about the tradeoffs that occur when you decide to save money to take advantage of the time value of money. That is to say, we want to emphasize that there is no free lunch. When you make a determination to save rather than spend you have made a tradeoff. Perhaps the tradeoff is running the old clunker for another two years or doing without the Friday night pizza dinner you used to have. Whatever the tradeoff, we need to recognize that the tradeoffs are made intelligently and for a reason.

There are several key reasons for trading off for the savings approach. First, for the most part individuals recognize that saving money means sacrificing other things but the key is to remember that the goal of saving is to provide for the future. By doing so, you find a much better situation in the future than would have been possible.

Second, saving not only allows you to take advantage of the time value of money, but helps you to avoid the reverse when you borrow money. That is, if you can save to buy something then you will not need to borrow funds and end up paying compounded interest to the lender, which works against you.

Third, when things go wrong (not if, but when) and you need to replace something you didn't plan for you will have the capability to deal with those problems and have a lot less stress concerning them. You also won't need to compromise for an inferior solution because you will have the savings put aside to deal with the problem correctly. Also, when you hear of special needs concerning others you will be able to help.

In summary, the benefits of saving are more than initially meet the eye. We need to recognize that there are these other follow-on factors that must be considered when trading off saving to purchase something else. As we can see the issue is often one of taking a short-term view versus taking a long-term view. The short-term view often deals with self-gratification, which is what the business world emphasizes today. The Christian recognizes the long-term view that we learn about in the parable of the unjust steward (Luke 16:1-8).

Outcomes and Chapter Summary

In this chapter the emphasis was on some financial stewardship basics. This included looking at a breadth of foundational areas that included Christian giving, establishing and reconciling bank accounts, analyzing the role that children play in the financial planning process, and taking a final look at the tradeoffs associated with saving and its related benefits. With the first three chapters having laid the foundation we will now proceed to coming chapters that help us to build on that solid foundation.

Learning Objective 1. **Describe the biblical perspective on giving and explain why it plays such an important role in the Christian life.**

We learned that the Bible describes tithing and giving as two separate things. Tithing was a means by which God funded the theocratic government of Israel and was required of its citizens. Giving (offerings) were in addition to the tithing and were freewill and from the heart. Christians are called to give generously out of a loving and cheerful heart and not by compulsion. Since we are to bring something to God, giving is seen as a form of worship where the gift is the sacrifice.

Learning Objective 2. **Analyze and choose the best bank for managing personal cash flows.**

There are many factors that go into choosing a bank including location, services offered, and perhaps most importantly the cost of doing banking. An analysis was given of the different types of banking institutions and the various services usually offered by them. We learned about the many fees associated with banking accounts, how to comparison shop for a bank, how to open an account, and how to keep accounts reconciled with the records of the financial institution.

Learning Objective 3. **Identify and describe the role children play in financial planning and how they also can influence another's financial planning.**

Generally, the world looks at children as an expense while the Christian sees them as an investment and part of their stewardship. We learned some of the key ways that children, either directly, or indirectly, influence the parents' financial decisions. Advertisers and peers influence parents indirectly through children. We also emphasized the importance of training children up in financial stewardship and being an example for them. We identified a set of guidelines for developing children as good financial stewards.

Learning Objective 4. **Understand and explain the tradeoffs that are made in relation to saving as a steward and explain why saving is an important aspect of stewardship.**

We briefly summarized the important tradeoffs that are made in order to save and then identified the key benefits of making the saving tradeoff. These included preparing for the future, less stress, less negative compound interest from borrowing, greater capacity to help others in need, and better decisions in emergencies.

Bible Texts Referenced

Genesis 4:3-5	Genesis 8:20-21	Genesis 12:1-8	Genesis 14:20
Genesis 22:1-14	Genesis 28:20-22	Exodus 23:10-11	Exodus 35:4-10
Leviticus 19:9	Leviticus 22:18-23	Leviticus 27:30	Numbers 18:10-11
Numbers 18:12	Numbers 18:17-18	Deuteronomy 12:10-18	Deuteronomy 14:28
Deuteronomy 16:10	Deuteronomy 25:14	Nehemiah 10:32-33	Psalm 127:3
Psalms 127:8	Matthew 23:23	Mark 12:41-44	Luke 6:38
Luke 7:37-38	Luke 11:42	Luke 18:12	Luke 19:1-10
Acts 4:32-35	1 Corinthians 9:9-11	1 Corinthians 9:14	1 Corinthians 13:3
1 Corinthians 16:2	2 Corinthians 8:2	2 Corinthians 8:4	2 Corinthians 8:8-15
2 Corinthians 9:6	2 Corinthians 9:7	2 Corinthians 9:12-13	Galatians 6:6
Galatians 6:10	Ephesians 6:4	Philippians 4:17-19	Philippians 4:18
1 Timothy 5:16-17	1 Timothy 5:18	Hebrews 7:1-9	Hebrews 7:4
Hebrews 13:15	1 John 3:17		

Exercises and Research Activities

1. Consider the Biblical account of the widow that gave all that she had. Why did she give more than a tenth of what she had? In what ways would you follow her as an example?

2. What are the key characteristics that God looks for in one who is giving to Him and His work?

3. An organization that claims to be ministering in the name of the Lord has asked for a contribution. What steps would you take in determining if this were what God would have you to do?

4. In what ways does worship model the act of giving to the Lord?

5. You are a college student living in the Nashville area and need to establish business with a bank. Carefully research and compare the banks that are available. Consider that you currently have $6,000 to put in the bank and you normally write 10 checks a month. Which bank would you choose and why? What accounts would you open with the bank and how would you allocate the funds you have?

6. Do some research and find the best CD rate available from a bank. Assume you have $10,000 to invest and want to have your money back in 5 years.

7. Assume that you and your spouse, in the will of the Lord, will be having a child. Create a spreadsheet showing what you believe it will cost to raise the child including providing for a 4-year college education.

8. Research a grocery store and complete a short paper on the steps that stores take to encourage shopping with children and explain in what ways the store is configured to influence children.

9. Come up with a novel idea on how you would teach your children about money and share it with others in your group or class. What characteristic of money do you find you are trying to convey?

References and Resources

Books:

Burkett, Larry. Pocket Change Series I and II. Crown Financial Ministries.

Burkett, Larry. Money Matters for Teens. Crown Financial Ministries.

Burkett, Larry. Biblical Financial Study Collegiate Edition. Crown Financial Ministries.

Web Sites:

BabyCenter.com. www.babycenter.com

Bankrate.com. www.bankrate.com

Crown Financial Ministries. www.crown.org

Financial Software:

MS Money. www.microsoft.com.
Quicken. www.intuit.com

CHAPTER 4

Managing Inflows and Outflows

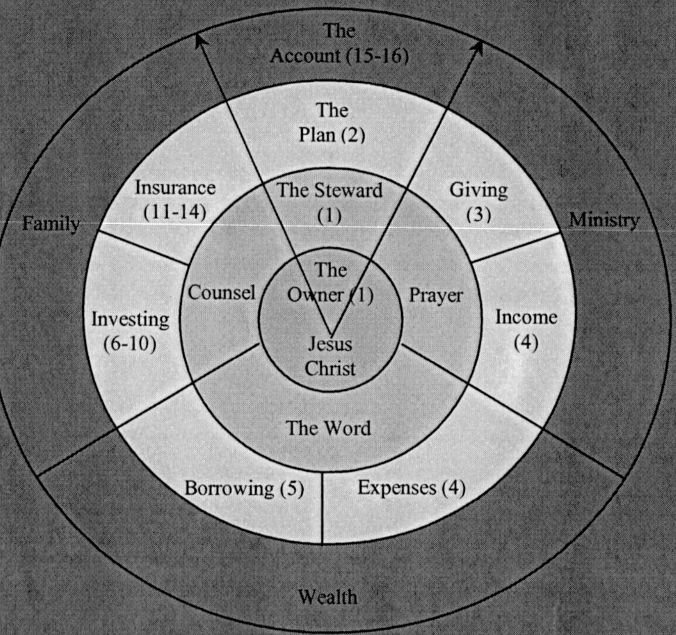

Learning Objectives

1. Identify and describe various sources of income, and identify the tradeoffs and determine the efficacy of both parents working.

2. Be able to develop and analyze spending plans to find ways of reducing spending and meeting financial goals.

3. Understand the effect of outflows to liabilities on the spending plan and net worth.

4. Understand and explain the basics of the American tax system and be able to differentiate good and poor tax planning strategies.

Lord, I commit to spending wisely.

Lord, thank you for the resources you have bestowed on me. I appreciate all that you have done for me and now commit to using those resources wisely. Help me to be a wise steward of my financial resources and to view expenditures from your perspective. Let me by your Spirit make each purchase as if Jesus were physically with me when making the decision. Guide me and encourage me in the right path that the result of my stewardship might receive a "well done" from you. I look forward to that day when I will be forever with you and the Lord Jesus Christ. Until then, I commit to being a diligent steward who need not be ashamed.

In this chapter we want to build on the foundation that has been laid in the previous chapters and develop more fully the reader's capability to identify inflows and outflows in the spending plan and how to increase the inflows while reducing the outflows. We also will look at the role taxes play in our spending plan and discuss some common strategies that are used to reduce income taxes.

Managing Income

In an earlier chapter we dealt with the importance of creating a spending plan and at that time noted that we would discuss in more detail how to look at the income and expense aspects of the plan and identify ways to improve the cash flow from the plan. You will recall that we noted that if you subtract your total outflows from your total inflows you have what is called your net cash flow. If that number is negative that is not a good sign and we will need to improve it. If it is positive that means you have funds that you can invest for the future or to pay off debt, but it is likely that you could also improve this number even more. In this section we focus on the inflows to the spending plan. Generally, the more inflow to the plan, the more that is available for outflow or saving.

Career Related Income

For most individuals or families the majority of their inflows will come from employment in their chosen career or field. This will likely hold true until they retire. For retirees income may come from a variety of sources but for many today it will come from their own contributions to savings and Social Security. This is not a book about job searches and the like so we will not attempt here to show you how to write resumes and cover letters or how to get into a new career to earn more money. There are many good books on the market that can be referenced if you have questions in these areas. You can also search the web for many resources related to this area. Here, we want to identify and discuss factors that can influence your future income flow in general as it relates to your career.

Developing Career Goals

As with financial goals, career goals require some careful thought and effort in order to be reached. Also, in similar fashion, there are certain characteristics associated with career goals that are successfully accomplished.

Be Biblical. For the Christian any career aspirations must be in congruence with the Word of God. There are certain areas of employment or certain employers that are not appropriate for the Christian to be involved with. The Christian must recognize that he is a testimony to the world and one's choices in the area of employment can have a profound effect on that testimony. Any career goals that involve illegal activity should clearly be avoided. Some employment opportunities that may be legal would in many cases not be suitable for a Christian such as bartending and gambling. Another issue for the Christian to carefully weigh would be whether the employer supports that which opposes Christ or supports unbiblical activities. Another area to be considered by the Christian is whether the business operates ethically or requires employees to do things that may be legal but not ethical. For instance, sometimes in the areas of sales or collections companies will require tactics that the Christian would consider inappropriate or unethical. The Christian must look at these various aspects of the employment area and the employer to carefully consider whether the vocation and the employer being supported truly bring glory to God. With these points in mind then, career goals should:

Be Specific. As with financial goals, career goals need to be measurable. That is, you want to be able to determine if and when you have reached a particular career goal. The goal might include the type of work, the employer, the position, and when you hope to attain it.

Be Timely: Career goals need to have a time frame. Just saying that you want to be president of a company someday is not specific enough nor gives you the impetus to accomplish it. When we set a time and we are serious about making it we then are more motivated as the time draws near.

Be Realistic. As we mentioned with financial goals take into account what God has given you for talents and gifts and set realistic career goals. This does not mean you can't stretch to reach something you desire but be sure it is what God would have you to desire in the light of the resources He has provided.

Be Written. All career goals should be written down as a way of reminding you of what they are. As we have noted, research shows that those who write goals down are much more likely to accomplish them.

As we have noted previously, keep in mind that you should seek God's favor in relation to career goals through reading of the Word, prayer, and Godly counsel. Although God allows us to make choices sometimes from among a number of good opportunities, there are others that clearly would be outside His will for the Christian.

Working Diligently

To be successful in your career and bring glory to God you must be willing to work diligently in the field that you have been called to. We are to work heartily as unto the Lord and not unto men (Colossians 3:23). Although there is often physical reward and financial blessing (pay increases, promotions, bonuses, etc.) from working diligently the Christian finds his reward in the heveanlies knowing that he has done a good work for the Lord. Christians are

different than laborers of the world. The Christian, although not a workaholic, works hard and works the required number of hours that have been agreed to beforehand. It is amazing how many, even as Christians, attempt to do as little as possible or even worse short-change their employers by arriving late, taking long lunches, doing non-work related activities on work time, and leaving early. Seek to do that which is right in the sight of God and seek not to follow the ways of men in this world.

Gaining an Education

Research shows that those who earn a college degree earn more income. Exhibit 4-1 shows the correlation between education attainment and income. In addition, the higher the degree attained the more income that is earned. The lesson here is that employers recognize that those who pursue degrees have a greater knowledge of the business or trade and are willing to pay more for it because they will be able to accomplish more and likely at a better quality than one without a degree. If you are able, get a degree that will support you in developing your earning potential in your area of career interest. Today, many companies require a 4-year degree as a minimum. It should be noted that education is Biblical but should not only be considered as a college

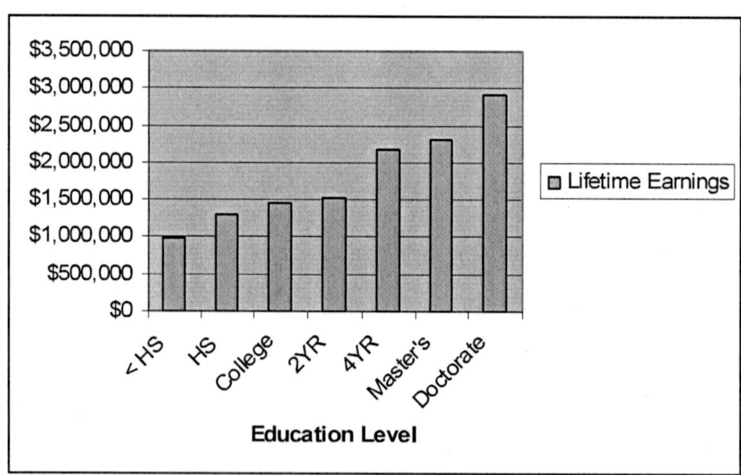

Exhibit 4-1. Lifetime Earnings by Education Level.

Source: Based on data presented by the Employment Policy Foundation at www.educationpays.org.

degree. Education comes in many forms and in many cases you should seek to learn and grow beyond that which you receive in a college education. Paul says to Timothy "*study to show thyself approved unto God, a workman that needeth not to be ashamed*" (2 Timothy 2:15). Paul is speaking of Timothy studying the Word but the implication is clear for all those who would work as servants of the Lord no matter what the work. Interesting, service related to the church in the form of teachers and elders, is one area that does not require a degree (although men often require it) since such ministry that is honoring to God can only be accomplished through the Holy Spirit. This does not mean that education cannot be helpful in the service of Biblical ministry but the Bible never requires it.

Learning to Network

The last key point to make, concerning the success of earning income, deals with networking. By this we mean that you are keeping abreast of happenings in your field of interest and are regularly speaking with others with similar interests. Over 30% of all positions are filled by referrals from others. Unless you make an effort to be involved in your field of interest, you are likely to miss out on greater earning potential. There are many ways of networking. Some include reading the journals and magazines in the field, writing articles for journals, attending and speaking at conferences in your area of expertise, and keeping in contact with those you have met through these efforts. It was through reading the journals in the area of training and education that I was able to move from industry into teaching. I communicated with someone quoted in one of the articles in a training journal and as a result secured a teaching position. I encourage you to take advantage of opportunities that will help you develop this area, including student groups if you are at college.

In summary, individuals who properly set career goals, work diligently as unto the Lord, seek to improve themselves through education, and make an effort to network with their peers earn greater incomes that allow an individual to accomplish more and be of greater help to others. Of course the increased earning is not necessarily to spend more but provides you with greater opportunities to be of service to God and His people either by having more time in His ministry or by helping those in the local church who are in need.

How Many Incomes?

Invariably when giving personal financial seminars or courses the question is raised as to what the Bible says about both a husband and wife working outside the home. The idea of a two income home today is quite common in America. This phenomenon, though, is a rather recent one and certainly is not the primary perspective that the Bible teaches. The Bible as a whole emphasizes the man's role as the head of the home (1 Corinthians 11:2, 1 Timothy 3:4-5, Ephesians 5:21-24) and the woman's role in being a helpmate in the home (Genesis 2:18, Proverbs 31:10-31). Keep in mind I am not saying that woman cannot work outside the home but am just providing a general perspective on what the Bible teaches concerning those who are married. There may be other opportunities for work or service for those who are young or single outside the home. For the most part today, many will dismiss what the Bible has to say about the unique roles of men and women as cultural and thus not applicable to today. This is quite dangerous because then anything that one does

not agree with in the Bible can be dismissed as not relevant on some cultural ground.

Based on the teaching of the Bible it seems appropriate for those who are married (and especially with children) to seriously contemplate whether God would have the wife to take on the helpmate role to nurture the children, if any, and support the husband. This support, of course, might include selling wares made in the home or harvested from a garden or field (Proverbs 31:24). So the answer is not one that says a woman cannot earn an income if married, but when the income is derived to support the family in a way that does not take priority over her role as one who takes care of the home. The virtuous woman of Proverbs 31 provides an excellent example of one who supports her husband, provides meals for the household, works with her hands to create clothing for the household and still finds time to support the home with additional income from creating and selling items that are a natural outgrowth of work she already does in supporting the home. Thus, to say a two-earner family is unbiblical would be incorrect. It is clear, though, that the source of the second income should be a by-product of the work already being accomplished to nurture and support the home itself. Today women are encouraged to take on positions that take substantial priority over the support of the home. As a result young children are put in daycare and other members of the home must take on the role that rightfully belongs to the wife. The decay of the American family is a sad testimony to a number of poor choices that many couples have made including seeing marriage as something that is temporary and not understanding the importance of the wife's role in the home.

Income From Assets and Others

Thus far, then, we have seen how our career planning can influence our income and how having a helpmate can influence income from a biblical perspective. Another source of income that is for the most part put at the bottom of the list is income from assets. Whenever individuals seek to increase income it is invariably by getting a raise, having the spouse go to work, or getting a second job. Another excellent source of income is your assets (not your home and car). These assets might include stocks, mutual funds, bonds, bank instruments such as certificates of deposit, and real estate. One of the key things to learn is building these assets can create income. Many individuals plow hundreds of thousands of dollars into a huge home that will never truly provide income once the costs to maintain it are taken into account.

By building assets that generate income you become less reliant on the world's mechanisms for support and are able to take more time to help in the Lord's work. It takes much patience and determination to regularly set aside something to develop your asset pool. Over and over the principles of building assets are noted in the scripture. The parable of the talents (Matthew 25:14-30), Joseph's work in Egypt (Genesis 41), the parable of the unjust steward (Luke 16:1-8), and many others emphasize the importance of sound investment and the creation of assets that will help support the household and others. We also see the same idea in a spiritual vein in the Bible where the Lord speaks about building up treasures in heaven (Matthew 6:19-21).

Another source of income is through gifts and inheritances from others. Many are quite astounded to realize that they will likely receive over $3000 in cash gifts in their lifetime, assuming cash gifts of $50 a year. Many receive much more than this. Sadly of course, little of this is ever saved and for most it is immediately spent on something. The amount lost actually becomes much larger when we factor in interest if the gifts were saved. If you were to save $50 a year at 6% interest for 50 years you would have $14,516.80. Surprised? Since gifts are not normal and expected income why not save them for when future needs arise?

Inheritances can be a way of passing blessing onto others, especially your children. We will touch on inheritance later in the book but it is also possible you will receive an inheritance at some point in your life. Again, this is an opportunity to carefully consider how this might provide for the future to help your family or others. You perhaps have heard of stories of squandered inheritances and you may find it hard to believe some of them, but the flesh is quick to be greedy and desire "stuff" and before you know it the inheritance is gone. I know one fellow who squandered a $30,000 inheritance on drugs and partying. We even have a parable in the Bible that speaks of the squandering of an inheritance (Luke 15: 11-24). It is almost always best to agree to save the inheritance for a certain period of time. Make sure it is of a good length. It is likely that many of the "needs" you were going to use the inheritance on are no longer needs when the time is up.

Income, then, can be derived by earning it, generating it from assets, or by others giving it to you. Since most of our income is likely to come from our career, carefully setting career goals and improving career prospects play an important role in our total future income. Extremely important is building our assets for future income capabilities. Asset building is often ignored by the average family or they do it in only the smallest measure. Gifts and inheritances should be used to help build assets since they are usually not expected income.

Planning Living Expenses

Now we come to what is likely the most ignored part of the average individual's personal financial planning and that is the area of expenses. Expenses are payments that are made to acquire items or services that are used and do not return income. It's rather interesting to watch how a financial discussion will go when there is not enough money to make ends meet. Invariably, the discussion focuses on how a family can generate more income with little or no consideration of how to create additional available income by decreasing expenses. Scenarios to make ends meet usually involve borrowing money, having a spouse work, or securing another part-time job. We hope in this section to encourage you to take a very careful look at the expense side of the ledger, especially while you are young, so that you can see the difference that careful expense planning can have on your life and that of others.

What is Really Needed?

We have already reviewed the importance of planning for your income and what sources it may come from. Now we want to look at planning our expenses, an area that most individuals and families take little time to look at.

As you look at planning for expenses the first question that you should ask when looking at each expense item is "is it really needed?" Now be careful here. We need to distinguish among needs, wants, and desires. Needs deal with our sustenance and are the minimum costs required to live which includes expenses related to generating income to cover those minimum costs. Wants go beyond the needs and speak of a minimum satisfaction level or a point where we feel we will be happy. So a need may be to have a place to live whereas a want is to have a "nice" place to live. Desires go beyond wants and speak of the long term and are that which we feel will bring the optimum satisfaction. So if the want is to have a "nice" place to live a desire is to have a "luxurious" place to live. Another example is transportation. The need is a basic way that will get us to work. This might be a basic car, bus, or train or perhaps even walking or bicycling. The want moves this to being a nice car with CD player and air conditioning. The desire moves it to a sports car with sunroof, surround sound system, and 500 horsepower under the hood.

Do you see the difference? Needs are immediate issues generally not of the flesh (spiritually speaking) and deal with conditions that actually exist. Wants from a Biblical perspective can have the idea of need, that is, to be in want or lacking. From an English perspective it leans more toward desire. Wants are short term basic desires that usually will more than fulfill a need and occasionally do not fulfill any existing condition or need. They are of the flesh and thus sometimes are called felt needs rather than actual needs. Desires deal with the flesh as well but speak of a longing for that which one does not have and generally, a need fulfilled is incidental to the object itself. Of course, there are good desires such as the longing our Lord had to share the Passover supper with his disciples (Luke 22:15).

With these thoughts in mind the question becomes where should we focus? This is not easy to answer but perhaps the best perspective is to look at your heart in relation to what the Bible has to say about the world's goods. Certainly providing for the basic needs of your family is Biblical and providing for support for the household of faith is important. The difficulty comes in our desire to want the best for our family and friends that can be substantially different than what is needed. Is it Biblical to get the best? The issue is one of intent and reality. That is, what is the intention in what our decision is and what is the real result of what is determined? There are several questions that can be asked in determining whether an expense makes Biblical sense:

1. Is there, at the minimum, a need fulfilled by the purchase?
2. Does the purchase make sense for a good steward? That is, have the tradeoffs been carefully considered (quality, versus quantity, versus cost)?
3. Does the purchase directly or indirectly honor God and His Word or is the focus on self?
4. Would you make the purchase if Jesus were with you when you were making the purchase?

If you can say, "yes" to these four questions you are highly likely to make a sound, biblical, financial decision. For instance one might ask is it biblical to purchase a Porsche? A Porsche certainly at a minimum may fulfill a transportation need if there is one. It is unlikely that it would make good sense for a financial steward and even if it did would it in reality honor God or would it more likely cause ridicule to God's name or cause a stumbling block to others because it is seen as overly extravagant for the Christian? Would the focus not be on you and your nice car – and the fact that "you have made it?"

Keep in mind by asking these types of questions you will likely make decisions that will not be viewed as very popular in the world. They will see you as depriving yourself of the world's luxuries. Their thinking is to "go for the gusto" since you only live once. The Christian perspective is far different. Also, by asking these questions the focus is taken away form the subjective differences among, needs, wants, and desires. The issue is not whether it fits one of the three categories but whether it is a sound, biblical, God-honoring choice. In that case it could belong to any of the three categories. Don't be afraid to ask the questions of each of your expenses and you will find it much easier to follow what is right for the steward.

Spending Plan Busters

There are expense items that occur that can quickly doom any financial plan. It is important to be aware of these and be prepared to deal with them. I call these types of expenses "budget busters." They fall into two categories the "big bang" budget busters and the "silent" budget busters.

The big bang budget busters, as their name implies, have a sudden and substantial impact on the spending plan. These fall into at least four key areas:

1. Insurance
2. Taxes
3. Home repairs
4. Auto repairs

The first two items on the list, insurance and taxes, are not unexpected. The difficulty comes in that they are not paid on a regular basis. Sometimes it is as infrequently as once a year. As a result, if they are not planned for, the bill comes in and all of a sudden there is a scramble to try to pay a significant sum sometimes running into the thousands of dollars. For most families today in America this poses a significant problem. To make the required payment families often make quick ill-advised budgetary decisions that destroy what little planning there may have been when it comes to spending.

The second pair of items on the list, home and auto repairs, are usually unexpected and can occur at anytime. The result is no different, of course, than with the insurance and taxes. There is still a large bill to be paid from a spending plan unprepared to handle it, thus having a profound effect on the family spending plan.

To deal with the above scenarios you must prepare in advance for these possibilities. Be sure to set aside funds each month that can act as an emergency fund for when the auto or home need fixing. It is not a question of "if", but "when" something will fail. Things tend toward decay and after many years of use will fail and need repair. In addition, your spending plan should include an amount for normal maintenance of these items so that major repairs will be less frequent. Usually insurance and tax amounts for the year are known in advance. It is best to divide those amounts by 12 and save that amount each month so that you will have the funds needed to pay the bill when it arrives. For instance, if your auto insurance is $900 every six months then you would need to put aside $150 a month in order to pay that bill twice a year (900/6). By taking these steps families and individuals can avoid poor decision-making based on expediency.

The list of silent budget busters is much longer and we need to carefully consider how each causes havoc to our spending plan. I have identified at least ten expense areas that, without you realizing it, will drain your spending plan resources. Let's review each of them here.

Eating Out. We live in a society that is speed oriented and as a result we are taught to eat out frequently at an early age. The difficulty lies in that while you are learning to eat out it is usually others such as your parents paying the bills. When young people get off on their own they are so used to eating out that it becomes difficult to control not doing it. Eating out can consume large portions of your income and you may not even realize it. Based on figures in the year 2002 the average American eats often outside the home at the rate of over $2200 a year. It can happen without you even realizing it because you are not spending it all at once. That's why it is important to project costs over time so you get a real feel for the cost involved. For instance if you spend $4.00 a day for lunch five days a week you will have spent $1040 annually just to have lunch. That may be fine if you understand the tradeoffs we have discussed in the past but many do not see the scope of the cost of eating out. What if you decided to have dinner out once a week at $20 each? Again you would be looking at another $1040 annually just to have dinner once a week. How about a coffee and donut each morning for $2.50? That's another $650 a year. These numbers don't take into account the lost interest in not saving the money. Carefully consider when you will eat outside the home and how much you are willing to spend. If you do eat out use coupons, look for early-bird specials, or use discounts available with memberships you might have either at work or with organizations such as the American Automobile Association (AAA).

Entertainment. Akin to eating out is the category of entertainment. This is another big area of spending for the average American. This includes movies, CDs, DVDs, sports, and the like. The 2002 statistics for American families shows that the average family spends over $2000 a year on entertainment. The Christian must recognize that the world seeks to have the pleasures of life. Society is becoming more entertainment-based. It has sadly even infiltrated the local churches around the country, so much so in fact, that people now select churches based on how they meet individual needs or entertain them. Most of what we spend on entertainment today would not occur if we just asked the four questions concerning expenditures. This does not mean some relaxation aside to refresh is bad but this type of expense is covered later in the section. In fact the spending given for this category does not include reading materials, cable TV, or vacations. Significantly, then, these numbers just show expenses for pure entertainment.

Cable/Satellite TV. This is an expense that almost all assume is required for a home and some will likely think you have lost your mind if you don't have it. Of course, this is not the case. One of the easiest savings that can be gained in a spending plan is to terminate the cable or satellite TV subscription. You'll be surprised how much more time you will also have for doing other more productive things. The average American home spends almost $50 a month on cable or satellite TV. Do you realize the cost to you over a lifetime just for the sake of being entertained? At $50 a month, and assuming no inflation and not considering the interest that you lose by not saving the funds, during the average adult life of 50 years you will have spent $30,000. That seems like an awful lot of money to account for as a steward and then not to really have a solid purpose for spending it. What is the return? It's something to think about. By the way if you had saved that $50 a month over 50 years even at a small 5% interest you would have a total of $133,433. Is cable TV a good "investment" in light of that number? Again, just something to think about.

Internet Service. Another area that often is missed when considering a spending plan review is the cost of Internet access. Now, Internet access may be appropriate for educational purposes or for work–related efforts. Still, it is important to review the expense. Many individuals overpay for high-speed services that they really don't need at home. The difficulty is that once you get used to the high-speed service it is difficult to switch. Unless you do a great deal of downloading for work at home or have a home business or offer web services from home you may want to reconsider the expense. Currently various DSL and cable access mechanisms cost from $45 to $50 a month on average while dial-up access is around $20 a month on average. This is still a significant difference. If you only need access to email or a limited amount of time on the internet each month then your expenses can be even less. Juno offers free email access and some vendors offer low-cost Internet access for $9.95 or less. Some companies offer communication packages of some combination of local calling, long distance, cell, and Internet. Be aware these plans often include many features you don't need and you my end up paying more than you would if you purchased just the services you need.

Phone Service. As with the Internet services many overpay for what they need. Carefully consider what your communication needs are. Cell phone plans are quite expensive and most will never use all the features or minutes that are provided. In addition many have termination and other fees. The kids likely don't need a cell phone. If you need one for an occasional call then you might want to consider something like AT&T's (recently purchased by Cingular) FreeToGo plan where you prepay for the minutes and then they are good for anywhere from 90 days to a year. I spend about $100 a year for a cell phone that I use mostly when I am traveling. Check your land phone bills and see if there are charges you can eliminate. Some still are paying for phone rentals even though they would have been paid for long ago. Also check your phone bill for unnecessary charges that have been added by the phone company that you may not be aware of.

You can see that many are spending significant amounts on communication. If you figure the cost of cable or satellite TV, Internet access, land phones, cell phones, and all the features and fees that go with them many individuals and families are spending a minimum of $150 a month and a substantial number are paying over $200 a month. Again we are looking at several thousand dollars a year in expense. Is it worth it? Again, just something to think about. As a case in point my wife and I have one land phone line, a basic antenna for TV reception, a single Internet dial-up plan with unlimited use, and one cell phone with nation-wide access. Total cost including all fees and long distance charges is about $60.00 a month.

Christmas Gifts. Another budget buster is in the area of gift giving and especially Christmas gifts. Because of the good feeling connected with giving to others we will likely overspend if we have not carefully considered what the spending plan will be. In addition, you must save each month so that when the time comes you will have the funds available to purchase the gifts. Easy access to credit cards is a huge hindrance to discipline of gift giving since it is easy to charge it if you do not have the funds. Few people actually total how much they spend on gifts each year and if you did you would be significantly surprised by the total. The current average is approaching $500 per household and almost 10% now spend a $1000 or more and this is just for Christmas alone. If we were to add in gift giving throughout the year we are likely looking at double what those amounts are. Some suggestions include cutting back and buying smaller gifts, never pay retail, shopping throughout the year rather than waiting to the last minute when decisions are rushed, and making rather than buying gifts. Remember it is the thought and love that count not the amount or size of the gift.

Vacations. Have you looked at the costs of vacations lately? Depending on the size of your family, costs can run into the thousands. Be careful to plan ahead and avoid the expensive money making locations. The cost of a family or even individuals to get into some of the popular theme parks is getting beyond the reach of many but some do it anyway and hope to find a way to pay later. This is not a good idea. Never charge a vacation unless you can pay it off as soon as you return. When considering vacations consider the purpose and consider the four expense questions we set forth. Will this be an opportunity to relax as a family or is this just a high-priced form of entertainment? Again never pay full price, check with your club memberships for discounts, and consider camping or going to a more out of the way place that doesn't have the crowds or the high prices.

Adult Allowances. A common practice among individuals is to give themselves allowances or play money. Some authors suggest that it can be therapeutic and relieve the stress of keeping track of a spending plan. Of course such a concept is not a Biblical one. A steward is concerned about how funds are used and to arbitrarily use some set amount without any regard to how it is used means there is no accounting for it. Also, any expenses with so called "play money" would escape the four question test we gave earlier, thus creating expenses that otherwise we would not undertake. The whole idea of spending or play money seems ripe for abuse.

Pets. Another area where income can be quietly consumed is with pets. I have counseled, in the area of finances, folks who have had a half-dozen or more pets whose total cost when taking into account food, immunizations, grooming, teeth cleaning, and a host of other services runs into hundreds of dollars a month. Pets are wonderful especially for companionship but they should not allow one to become a poor steward of what the Lord has provided. The Bible speaks about providing for those of your household but I don't think He had pets in mind. Now I do enjoy pets and we have had the same cat for almost 18 years but we are careful to distinguish what is necessary for his well-being. We provide food, drink, and an annual rabies shot (required by law). Otherwise, we avoid other expenses.

Bank Fees. Another silent consumer of the spending plan is the bank fees. Banks are great at finding ways of getting your income. As we have already noted use a bank or banks that will allow you to avoid as many fees as possible. Some folks will spend $20-$30 a month on fees and the bank acquires the use of their money as well. Be sure to check for ATM fees, overdraft fees, per-check fees, account service fees, account inactivity fees, and the like. Most bank fees can be eliminated with careful planning on your part.

Subscriptions. Many people are surprised to find that subscriptions to newspapers, magazines, newsletters, and other club related annual expenditures consume a substantial amount of money. The reason that it is a surprise is because they are paid for throughout the year making the individual expenses seem small, but when they are added up their effect is quite large. Review all organization and subscription expenses you really do not need. Many receive subscriptions that they never read. Consider using the library instead of paying for the subscriptions or share the expense with another believer and share the subscription.

This concludes the review of the largest spending plan busters that will be encountered. Through careful planning and the review of each expense through the lens of the four expense questions provided earlier you can "create" more income than you thought possible and perhaps even more than seeking another part-time job. Taking this section seriously can make a world of difference when you give an account.

The Church as a Community

As we continue our look at planning living expenses we come to another asset that is often overlooked in helping to keep expenses to a minimum and that is the community you have in the local church. In society today we often only meet as a church community for fellowship briefly and then most everyone goes their own way. Yet, there is much that local believers can do together that can help to reduce expenses.

ⓘ **Pool Coupons**. Cutting out and collecting coupons may be tedious but when used properly can result in significant savings in the expense category. Doing it as a group can be even more beneficial. First, it will encourage fellowship with others in the church. Second, you will likely have more of a variety to choose from. Third, you will have the support of others in helping you to reduce your expenses and perhaps provide some sense of accountability in your shopping. It also makes the whole process less tedious when doing it as a group. We discuss the use of coupons later in the chapter.

ⓘ **Shop Together**. Another way of reducing expenses is by church members shopping together. This again not only provides fellowship for the believers but provides additional support and accountability as they shop. You may also be able to buy some larger items together and split the cost that would not only reduce the individual cost but also cut down on food that is discarded because there was too much to be used in the package in a timely manner. Shopping together can be very helpful for single individuals as well for the same reasons and the savings are likely to be greater since larger containers could be purchased and split. Small packages usually are very expensive per unit of product purchased.

ⓘ **Buy in Bulk**. Related to shopping together is buying in bulk. The church as a community might be able to work with some stores or manufacturers to purchase some items in bulk at a lower cost and pass the savings on to the local church members. Products such as paper towels, tissues, toilet tissue, canned goods, pet food, and the like could be purchased in bulk at a discount and then the cost split among the families participating. They would just pay for what they needed at the reduced cost per item. Again this can be helpful for singles and families.

Share the Skills. God has provided many individuals in your local church with a variety of talents and skills. These skills should not only be used for earning an income but for helping the other believers in the local area. Why have believers pay retail costs for services that you could provide at no or reduced cost and thus allow more funding to be available for the Lord's work and savings to support families? Help your local church to start a directory of services that are available for church members at no or reduced cost for its members. Also try to find believers in other local churches who would be willing to participate in areas for which your local church lacks the skills. You might even have days set aside once a month to work together on these areas. For instance someone skilled in automobile repair could hold an auto service day at his home or the church for church members. Perhaps others might get together to cook. Others perhaps can come together to clean or garden. The list can go on but as good stewards we need to work together to reduce the expenses incurred by our brothers and sisters so more is available for His work and for family support through savings.

The local church can play a significant role in helping families reduce the flow of funds out for expenses by working together and supporting each other out of love. The result is not only great financial benefits for the families and the church but great unifying benefits such as the extended fellowship that these opportunities provide.

Determining Expense Necessity

Earlier in the chapter we had discussed the issue of whether a purchase fulfils a need. At that time we asked the following four questions to help determine whether an expense is warranted:

1. Is there, at the minimum, a need fulfilled by the purchase?
2. Does the purchase make sense for a good steward? That is, have the tradeoffs been carefully considered (quality, versus quantity, versus cost)?
3. Does the purchase directly or indirectly honor God and His Word or is the focus on self?
4. Would you make the purchase if Jesus were with you?

Those four questions still remain, but we want to note several other questions that are either related or provide additional insight in making a purchase decision. Also note that the fourth question above is phrased slightly differently than you usually hear. That is, we often hear the phrase "what would Jesus do?" but I submit it is far more telling to ask the question "what would you do if Jesus were with you?" It is interesting to note that as Christians He is always with us by the Spirit so our answer should be the same as if He were physically present with us.

What is the Purpose? This relates to the first of the four questions above. What is to be accomplished by the purchase? Does it deal with a real need? Is it just a feeling that you need to fulfill? As we honestly consider this question we must often realize that most "needs" are not needs at all and the purpose is dubious at best.

Is there a Value? This relates to the second of the four questions above. As a steward we are always looking at the value and return of using financial and other resources. So we need to contemplate the value of an outlay. What would be the result of not making the purchase? Would there be any difference? Would there be a reduction in value of current resources? For instance, to purchase a medication to cure a medical problem would meet a need because without it the value of the human resource is reduced and could cause further harm later.

Is it Necessary? This relates to the third of the four questions noted above and as stated before deals with separating the emotional from the reality of the need. This summer may seem very hot and so you may have the immediate need of cooling off. As a result you may say we have the need for a pool!! But is that what is really needed? It is likely that there is not a real need here for a pool. It is just not necessary. There are many other ways one can deal with heat. Interestingly pools quite often are status symbols that receive little use. There are a number of pools, both in-ground and above ground, in our neighborhood and we have rarely seen them being used, if at all.

Is There a Way of Eliminating or Reducing the Expense? Related to this previous point is trying to consider ways of eliminating the expense or at least reducing it by finding alternatives. Perhaps the need expressed is for a "new car." On further reflection it is not a "new" car that is needed but transportation. So a "used" car would do in this case thus reducing the expense. But you give it further consideration and realize that the transportation is only needed for work, otherwise the car would sit in the driveway. So now it is no longer a "used" car that is needed but some way of getting to work. Perhaps after further reflection you realize that the five mile ride to work could be accomplished with the bike you already own or perhaps there is a colleague who can give you a ride to work. All of a sudden what was a need for a "new car" has been eliminated. Consider carefully what is really needed and consider all of the alternatives.

Study the Cost Over Time. It is imperative, as we have already noted, to look at the cost over time. Part of our consideration in a purchase should be the cost including lost interest from not saving the money. We have already noted the cable TV example earlier. Even without looking at the interest issue the actual cost should at least cause you to stop to think about it. Going back to the cable TV example, if I pay $50 a month for 50 years I will have spent $30,000. That alone should seem like a fairly significant amount to pay for the little material that comes from it that can be considered edifying for the Christian. If that were not enough when we figure in the interest if we saved the $50 a month the $30,000 lost now becomes almost $135,000. I cannot see how spending that kind of money can be of any value for the Christian in light of the paucity of the return from the cable TV companies. This is just one example. Every expense should be considered in light of its long-term cost.

If after considering these various questions we find an expense warranted then we should then undertake an analysis to determine which actual product or service will be purchased. In the next section we briefly discuss some ways to reduce the cost of an item.

Reducing the Cost of an Item

There are many ways of reducing the actual outlay of funds for a particular product or service. In this section we try to touch on some of the key ones which certainly do not exhaust the possibilities.

Coupons. Manufacturers print billions of coupons each year to encourage folks to purchase their products. It is worthwhile to cut and save coupons for future use. They can be especially useful for groceries where some stores will double or sometimes even triple the value of the coupon up to a certain amount. Wal-mart and other large retailers will also accept coupons. You can save hundreds of dollars a year by using coupons when shopping. If you were able to save $300 a year over 30 years at 6% interest you would have almost $24,000. When one sees this kind of number the benefit of using coupons is clear There are some important points to keep in mind when using coupons:

Organize your coupons otherwise you will lose track of some savings opportunities, or worse, get frustrated and scrap the whole effort as too much work.

Don't use coupons just for the sake of using one. Use them for items that as a good steward you would normally buy. Manufacturers often use coupons to steer consumers to new products or those where there is more profit for the company.

Look for items that you have coupons for that are on sale at a store. The combined savings may make it worth buying as an alternative to another product.

Be careful of expiration dates and restrictions for coupons. Manufacturers are making the coupons more complex by requiring multiple items or different items, some of which you will never use. Going with some members of the church may make this easier since items you would not use another might. Most coupons today have relatively short expirations. This is another effort by the manufacturers to get you to buy more often and on a whim. Be careful. Some have also restricted their coupons so they cannot be doubled or tripled in value by the store.

Be on the look out for store coupons as well. Many grocery and pharmacy stores offer coupons and many are quite good such as "buy 1 get 1 free." If you don't need two shop with someone and split the cost. Some department stores also print coupons but quite often have a load of restrictions on them so be careful. Some real deals can be found. When my wife and I were visiting our son and his wife in Texas we saw an add for Coca-Cola at 2 for $5.00 which is at this time still a good price for 12-packs of 12 ounce cans. In addition, it was a grand opening with a coupon for $10 off on any purchase. Since there was little else we were interested in we bought 4 cartons of Coke for free.

Save restaurant coupons so that you can save when you eat out. My wife keeps them in the glove compartment of the car so that if we are on the road we can use them to reduce the costs of meals. We rarely spend over $10 for a lunch for two on the road as a result.

You can find many coupons on the Internet as well, although you should be careful of scams. The scams usually involve you purchasing coupons. You should not need to do this. There are some sites dedicated to keeping track of discounts and coupons being offered by stores. Use the keyword "coupons" in a search engine to locate some of these.

ⓘ **Shop Around**. If you have several grocery and/or pharmacy stores close by then make a list and shop at each buying an item at the lowest cost among them. Take someone else along from the church as well so you can work together and share the costs. For larger items call around to various stores and get prices. You can also check on the Internet for pricing at many of the larger stores.

Coupon Books. There are many coupon guides that are published throughout the country. The Entertainment Guide is one of the best known and offers discounts on hotels, restaurants, recreation, and other services. There are others such as the one for the Nashville area called "CityPass." These books generally cost from $10-$20. Before you buy one be sure to check that it will have coupons for services that you would, as a good steward, normally use. The intent for the vendors is to create new and repeat business. Giving a discount is to try to get you in the door to try it and hopefully you will return next time without a coupon. Of course, our goal would be to find another coupon if we returned.

ⓘ **Shop the Web**. There are many search engines available to perform price comparisons for products. You may find something you are looking for cheaper on the web. Keep in mind the cost of shipping when buying something off the web and you may still need to pay sales or use tax on what you buy off the web even though there is currently no tax on web purchases in general. Sometimes it is cheaper to go to a local store after taking into account shipping especially for larger items. Also be aware that many organizations overcharge on shipping in order to reduce their product price to make it look more attractive. I have seen some shipping costs that are ten times what it would cost to ship the item. Online auctions can also prove fruitful but the same caveats apply and you need to read the terms carefully since a bid is a binding contract to buy. I have seen many people overbid for an item because they were not aware that they could buy it cheaper elsewhere on the web.

Auctions and Sales. Auctions and garage sales (sometimes called yard sales or tag sales) can be great places to find bargains, if you don't mind buying something that has been used. Occasionally you can also find items that are new. Again, knowledge is important so know what you should pay for an item before making an offer or bid. Also consider the tradeoffs of cost, quality, condition, and future plans. Also, it never hurts to offer less or ask for a discount. The worst case is that they say "no." My recently married son and his wife needed a dining room table and chairs in order to have a place to eat as well as for other functional uses. Together we investigated a number of possibilities but each had drawbacks. In going to a thrift store the prices were from $70 for a table that needed repair with no chairs to over $300 for a complete used, but functional set. If we went to Wal-Mart a small table with 4 chairs could be had for around $100 but they were not made for long-term constant use in a home and would likely need to be replaced in the future. In going to a retail furniture store you could get nice dining sets that would likely last a lifetime but could run anywhere from $500 into the thousands of dollars. We did see one set at a discount furniture store that seemed to be a quality set (wood butcher block) and had good chairs but one was missing. The cost for the set would be $250. As you can see it can be time consuming to look around and weigh the various factors based on their situation and their likely future needs in this area.

We finally went to an estate sale where they had a high quality dining set (Ficks & Reed) in rattan and with a glass top and cushioned chairs. There were a few small scratches on the glass and one of the chairs had a little of the rattan missing where someone had picked it but this could be easily repaired. The asking price was $1200, which for a set such as this might be considered reasonable since new they can run to over $4000. Yet, being a good steward it didn't make sense to spend too much for the higher quality. That is, the extreme quality of the product was reflected in the price but was not enough to warrant the amount. The manufacturer's name and the original price new were also making the price higher than made sense for my son and his wife. But, at a much lower price the set would be a great addition and could last them a lifetime. I asked the seller if she would be willing to record an offer to consider, if the set did not sell by the end of the sale. She agreed and I left an offer of $350 and said I would stop by at the end of the sale to see if it was still available. That offer was 71 percent less then what the seller was looking for but believed it was a fair price based on what could be afforded and keeping in mind what we would spend if we were to take any of the other options with their various drawbacks. If the offer were accepted they would have a beautiful dining set that could be used in many types of rooms such as a sunroom in the future and last them a lifetime. In addition, they would have purchased something that they likely would never be able to afford at retail and would have been much less than other sets of lesser quality at a furniture store. On returning to the sale the seller accepted our offer and now my son and his wife have a great dining room set for many years to come at a small fraction (likely much less than 20%) of its original cost.

The key in dealing with sales and auctions is to be patient, be willing to make offers, and be willing to take a "no" and walk away when the price isn't what you need it to be. Do not let your emotions get the best of you. We knew that if we received a "no" on our offer for the dining set that there would be many other opportunities available in the future. It does not make sense to pay more than you are able. In fact, when we returned to the sale we made an offer of $25 for two stools (priced at $150) that matched the dining set but the owner wanted $50. We walked away from it because we did not want to spend more than what we felt we could offer for them and based on the other factors we have noted.

Church Community. Another way to reduce the cost of items is by sharing together as a church community. This may include buying items in bulk together or working together to accomplish various tasks. For example, we have already noted having a car repair day where those in the local church who are experienced in car repair invite the brothers and sisters to bring their vehicles to them for auto maintenance or repair at a reduced cost or for the cost of materials. The same could be done for cleaning, painting, home repair, and the like. In order for this kind of thing to be successful individuals must be willing to communicate about their needs so that the appropriate efforts are made.

Along the same line is renting items together for major projects and splitting the cost. Quite often it is more economical to rent power washers, compressors, log splitters, and the like rather than buying them. Perhaps more than one church member has the same need and they can share the cost of renting the equipment.

Thrift Stores. Don't forget the savings available by shopping at thrift stores. In addition, these often use the proceeds of their sales to help individuals in the community. Examples include the Salvation Army, Goodwill, and Habitat for Humanity. You can often secure furniture and household goods in very good condition from these stores at a deeply discounted price.

There are many ways of reducing the cost of goods purchased but it is important that you make an effort to consider how that can be done each time you purchase something. You will be amazed at the savings you will find if you total the savings on each item you purchase. Those savings can then be used to build your assets that can produce income in the future.

Managing Outflows to Liabilities and Others

Loan and Debt Payments

Today we are inundated with offers to reduce our "monthly" payments. As long as we continue to think from a "monthly" perspective we will not understand the true cost of what we are buying. Occasionally you may hear of the amount per "day" that you either pay or spend depending on the objective. As will be discussed in detail in the next chapter, we should be eliminating outflows for debt. The more you are paying out for liabilities the more difficult it is to give, save, and support your family. It has gotten to the point where some have to borrow from one credit card to pay another all the while increasing the burden.

It is difficult to get rid of all liabilities. For instance, annual tax bills are still something that must be paid. Outside of that type of liability (which can be seen as an annual expense) all debt and loans should be paid off as quickly as possible. I realize there will be arguments related to the low interest rates and the tax benefits of home equity loans and the like. Forget them. Get your debt paid off. There is more than just the interest rate and taxes involved in most financial decisions. We will discuss the Christian's view of taxes later in this chapter. Your goal is to have your funds, as a steward flowing into the asset column, not the liability column. Assets can generate additional income, liabilities do not.

The Home and Car as Liabilities

As we have already noted in the text, the home and car are viewed as assets from an accountant's perspective. From a steward's perspective we need to view them differently. That is, for the steward they become liabilities. Our thinking has been colored by the world's view. It sees houses and sometimes cars as investments that appreciate in value. In reality, homes can, and cars will, depreciate in value. In addition, the cost of maintaining these purchases is huge and thus, any idea that they are an investment is lost. How many of us would be willing to spend an amount maintaining an investment portfolio equal to what we spend on maintaining our homes or cars? Few would take up the idea.

Assets generate income and this is why in chapter two we emphasized the steward moving the home and car from the asset column to the liability column. Homes and cars are not investments because they don't generate any income. Now you may raise a flag and say, "wait a minute, the value of my house has gone way up so it should be seen as an investment!" Is the purpose of your home to generate that value or for a place to live? That is, any value created by owning a home is secondary to the purpose of having the home – a place to live. In fact, it should not matter whether it goes up or down in value since its purpose is not for investment but for living in. To see a home as an investment we must be willing to relinquish it at any time. Let's say to tap the value of your home you take out a loan and invest the proceeds. You use the income from the investment to help pay the new loan. What happens if the market tumbles and you lose most of the value of your investment or at least enough to make it so that you are unable to repay the loan? Now what will you do? If you don't find a way to keep up the payments the bank will foreclose on your "investment." Where will you live then? See, the world has us thinking the wrong way, and from a Biblical perspective we need to be good stewards and provide for our families. The world's thinking is don't worry about being a steward you deserve all that you can get and if you lose it then others (such as the government) should provide for you and your family.

Although we will continue, for accounting purposes, to keep our cars and homes in the asset column let's continue to view them as liabilities. As a result our goal is to pay them off and keep the expenses to maintain them to a minimum so that we are able to keep them for what they are intended – a place to live and a way to get from one place to another. The stories are numerous of those who have seen them as investments and as a result lost them as an investment and had no place to live or a way of getting from one place to another. Commit now not to put you or your loved ones in that situation.

Gifts

We have already noted that Christmas gift buying is quite often a silent budget buster. Because of the excitement and fanfare of this time of year as well as our natural desire to show love for those in our family we likely will overspend. As with other areas of spending we need to have a plan or list of what gifts will be purchased for whom. We need also to keep in mind our list of questions when considering such an expense especially whether there is a way of reducing the cost.

In addition to Christmas, there are many other events throughout the year that will occur that may result in the spending of resources for gifts. These include birthdays, anniversaries, weddings, and the like. You need to plan these ahead and see if there are ways of reducing the cost such as by making your own gifts or using some of the other savings ideas noted in this book. It truly is the thought that counts and the goal should be to express that love without overspending or going into debt.

Keep in mind there are often collections at work for various individuals when they retire, have birthdays or leave for a new position. Although you may want to help, be careful to budget wisely. If you cannot afford to give then make a little something and create a card by hand to give rather than giving cash as others do.

The point to note here is that many individuals and families do not realize how much they end up spending on gifts and cards until they begin to keep track of it. After they do they are amazed by the sum they have spent. This is because the giving occurs throughout the year and thus is spread out in small amounts. When they are added together they become very large.

Managing and Reducing Taxes

The Biblical View of Taxes

Another issue related to the outflow of financial resources is in the area of taxes. Views from Christians run the gamut on the issue of taxes. Some go as far as to say that we should not pay them. Although this will not be an entire treatise on the issue we should at least understand the basic views from a Biblical basis.

On one end of the spectrum we have those who believe that as Christians we should pay taxes because not to do so would be illegal. For Christians doing something illegal would not be a viable option unless the request of the government was not Biblical. For instance if the government passed a law that required us to steal from our neighbors we would not obey it since the Bible clearly is against stealing. Most folks who take this perspective use Matthew 22:15-22 as a basis for paying taxes to authorities. This is the section where Jesus answered the Pharisees concerning tribute to Caesar by replying "render unto Caesar what is Caesar's and unto God what is God's". This verse seems to point out not just that taxes would be paid but that in reality such authority to collect taxes in reality comes from God. That is why he adds "render unto God what is God's."

There are other verses that clearly show that by God's permission other kings and/or governments taxed the inhabitants. Jehoiakim taxed the land so he could pay Pharoah (2 Kings 23:35). Daniel 11:20 speaks of a raiser of taxes being on the throne for a short while which was fulfilled by Philopator (Seleucus IV) who evidently raised taxes to pay a war-tax to Rome. 1 Samuel 8 makes it clear that if the people would have a king over them that he would have the authority to exact taxes. Despite this the people wanted the king. Even in Matthew 17:24-27 where it is clear that it is the strangers of the land that are normally taxed the Lord still pays the tax so as not to offend those who expect it.

The one difficulty for those who do pay taxes may be what the government does with the funds. Even the taxes the Lord paid when on earth I am sure were not necessarily used for what He would have them used for, but God has given the earthly authority into the hands of those in leadership in the nations. Thus, taxes you pay could end up paying for that which you believe is unscriptural. It appears the Lord's example of paying taxes should be enough to quiet our hearts on this and recognize that we are not making the decision of how the government spends the funds. Your contributing taxes does not appear to be viewed in the Bible as in any way wrong from what I can see there.

Another school of thought is that taxes are unbiblical and seen as the government stealing from the people. Since the Bible is against stealing it is thought that we should not pay taxes. Another argument is that God is sovereign and since the U. S. government is a republic and does not have a king, sovereignty to collect taxes has not been conveyed to it so it is wrong for them to collect them. Others suggest that if a government takes more than a tithe or ten percent that it is wrong or if the tax is progressive it is wrong. Most of these concerns are based on a misunderstanding of Scripture or by applying that which applies to Israel to the Christian. As we have already noted under the topic of giving, tithing was far more than ten percent and in reality was a 22-25 percent tax to fund the government of Israel from the people themselves. Keep in mind there was no king at that time. Other than the concern about how the funds are used there is little if any Biblical support for not paying taxes that are due. Interestingly, the tax by Jehoiakim could be read as being progressive – "he exacted…everyone according to his estimation" (2 Kings 23:35). Most of these folks who support not paying taxes are well meaning but not well read in the Scriptures. Most of the arguments are in man's wisdom dealing with history or logic rather than with the Word of God.

Interestingly, both groups of people use the verse from Romans 13 to emphasize that God works through rulers in the nations. Those who support paying the taxes emphasize Romans 13:6-7 where it twice says to pay tribute. Those against taxes emphasize Romans 13:3-4 that speak of the rulers' purpose of avenging evil. Thus they would limit the government's work to that area. That is, no road building, no helping the poor, no space exploration, and the like since they are not specifically mentioned in Scripture. Unfortunately, it is clear from the Bible that governments can collect taxes and that they become the stewards of those funds and the ones who will give account. That is, our being Biblically disobedient because the government is being Biblically disobedient and improperly spending money is wrong. The old saying "two wrongs don't make a right" is true. We cannot be held responsible for what another does when we have done the right thing and have been obedient to the Scripture and paid the taxes. Just because the government misspends or occasionally funds that which would be objectionable to us as Christians based on a Biblical perspective does not seem to be a strong enough reason for being disobedient to a direct command to us to pay tribute to whom it is due.

Based on a review of the applicable Scriptures it would seem that Christians should be obedient and pay their taxes especially since the Christian's particular payments are in no way earmarked for a particularly unbiblical support area. That being said, Christians should certainly make efforts, where appropriate and Biblical, to reduce the amount of the funds spent in this area. Just like with other expenses and liabilities, saving here will allow us to do more in the future. Being a Christian does not mean we have to overpay the government but we should be honest in our tax dealings as well.

Income Tax Basics

Income tax, as the term implies, is a tax on your income. Citizens of the United States are subject to what is called a "federal income tax." Many states impose an additional "state income tax" on income. In addition, some cities such as New York City have a "city income tax." Most of these taxes are what is called "progressive" in nature. That is, the rates are higher as the income goes up. These rates are usually applied in some way to a division of the income into brackets. Thus, we get the term tax brackets. Although the income tax is a huge part of most states' income, many government entities raise taxes or levies by other means such as on sales, personal property, corporate and business income, real estate, inheritance, and cars, among many others. Although it is proper for Christians to pay their taxes it behooves them to minimize as best they can their total tax burden so that more is available for other areas. For the non-income taxes usually the rule is the more you spend the more you pay in taxes. These non-income taxes don't usually apply when you give or save. There are also some additional taxes (although they may not always be called taxes) that fund the social welfare system and retirement. These are the social security taxes that are often noted as FICA (Federal Insurance Contributions Act) and include the Medicare taxes. These are sometimes lumped together but they have differing amounts and ranges to which they apply. Let's take a look at a few of these key taxes in more detail since you either have seen or will soon see them on your pay stub.

? Tax Bracket

The Social Security tax is used to fund income for your retirement or for you and/or your family if you should become disabled or die. There are various formulas for determining the amount that you are entitled to but is subject to age, number of years giving to the system, amount earned, and other criteria. Currently, Social Security taxes take 6.20 percent of your salary. These taxes apply to earned income of up to $89,000 (90,000 in 2005). This income level has been regularly increased by congress so you will need to check if it will change in the future so you can plan ahead. For every $1,000 the level is raised, and that falls in your earnings range, an additional $62 in taxes is paid by you.

? Social Security

The Medicare tax, which is sometimes combined with Social Security taxes and called FICA funds the government healthcare program for retirees. Currently the tax rate for Medicare is 1.45 percent of earned income regardless of the amount. So, unlike Social Security that has a cap, Medicare does not.

? Medicare

For both taxes the employer also pays the same amount on your behalf. So your employer also pays 6.2% of your salary up to $89,000 and an additional 1.45% of you entire income to the government. Thus, between you and your company the taxes are the equivalent of 15.3%. The reason we mention this here is that if you decide to have your own business you will need to pay both portions to the government, part from the business (a business expense and tax deductible) and part from your income.

Our focus here will be on a brief review of the federal income tax. Keep in mind that the rules for filing federal income tax statements changes every year so be sure to check the www.irs.gov website for the most current information. It is the Internal Revenue Service (IRS) that is responsible for implementing the tax system that has been legislated by congress. That is, the IRS does not make the tax laws but implements the laws that have been passed by the legislature.

Marital Status	Age	Minimum Gross Income
Single	under 65	7,950
	65 or older	9,150
Married living together-joint return	both under 65	15,900
	one 65 or older	16,850
	both 65 or older	17,800
Married living together or apart-separate returns	any age	3,100
Head of Household*	under 65	10,250
	65 or older	11,450
Widowed*	under 65	12,800
	65 or older	13,750
Single dependent**	under 65	4,850
	65 or older	6,050
Married dependent	Under 65	4,850
	65 or over	5,800

* Have a dependent
** Students may also have to file even if they are claimed as a dependent by their parents.

Even if you do not qualify to file using the above criteria you may also be required to file for other reasons such as paying self-employment tax. You may also wish to file if you are due a refund. Your qualifying income may also be different based on other characteristics such as being blind. For a complete discussion of all the possibilities see IRS Publication 501 at www.irs.gov/publications/p501/index.html which is the source of this information.

Exhibit 4-2. Income Tax Filer Determination for 2004.

Who should file a tax return? The determination of who must file depends on age, marital status, and gross income. Gross income as defined by the IRS would be all income that is not exempt from taxes. For instance, some interest and life insurance proceeds are exempt. Exhibit 4-2 shows the basic tests of whether you must file as of 2004.

What are the tax rates? There are now six tax rates at which your income can be taxed: 10, 15, 25, 28, 33, and 35%. The income range for each is different based on your filing status. That is, whether you are filing as a single, married filing jointly, married filing separately, or filing as a head of household. Exhibit 4-3 shows the tax brackets for 2004. One important thing that is often misunderstood is that your income is taxed in stages. There is no need to worry

Taxable Income				Tax Rate
Single	Joint/ Widowed	Separate	Head of House	
1-7,150	1-14,300	1-7,150	1-10,200	10%
7,150-29,050	14,300-58,100	7,150-29,050	10,200-38,900	15%
29,050-70,350	58,100-117,250	29,050-58,625	38,900-100,500	25%
70,350-146,750	117,250-178,650	58,625-89,325	100,500-162,700	28%
146,750-319,100	178,650-319,100	89,325-159,550	162,500-319,100	33%
319,100+	319,100+	159,550+	319,100+	35%

Exhibit 4-3. 2004 Marginal tax Rates.

if your income causes you to go into the next bracket by $10. Only that $10 is taxed at the higher rate. So in Exhibit 4-3 it shows that for a single person the first $7,149 of taxable income is taxed at 10%. The next $21,900 (7,150-29,050) is taxed at 15%. The grand schemes for trying to get into a lower tax bracket do not have nearly the effect that you might expect. For instance, if your income of $58,140 while filing jointly (which is in the 25% bracket) were reduced to $57,990 (which is in the 15% bracket) your tax savings would be $10, of which only $2 is a saving due to the tax rate change while $8 is a saving from having a slightly lower income to be taxed in the first place. The bracket that your income is currently being taxed in is called the marginal tax bracket. This means that any additional or marginal income will be taxed at the bracket rate you are currently at until you reach its maximum and then you will enter a

Mindy has filled out the tax return for her and her husband and has calculated that their taxable income is $121,345. She calculates her taxes using the brackets in Exhibit 4-3.

First $14,300 taxed at 10% =	$ 1,430.00
Next $43,800 (7,150-58,100) taxed at 15% =	6,570.00
Next $59,150 (58,100-117,250) taxed at 25% =	14,787.50
Next $4,095 (121,345-117,250) taxed at 28% =	1,146.60
Total Tax Due:	$23,934.10
Actual Tax Rate = 23,934.10/121,345.00 =	19.72%

Exhibit 4-4. Tax Calculation Example.

new marginal tax bracket at which any additional income will be taxed. Exhibit 4-4 gives an example of how this works. Based on this example it is clear that even though Mindy is currently in the 28% marginal tax bracket her actual tax liability amounts to less than 20% percent of her income.

Form **1040** Department of the Treasury—Internal Revenue Service
U.S. Individual Income Tax Return **2004** (99) IRS Use Only—Do not write or staple in this space.

For the year Jan. 1–Dec. 31, 2004, or other tax year beginning , 2004, ending , 20 OMB No. 1545-0074

Label (See instructions on page 16.) **Use the IRS label.** Otherwise, please print or type. LABEL HERE

Your first name and initial | Last name | **Your social security number**

If a joint return, spouse's first name and initial | Last name | **Spouse's social security number**

Home address (number and street). If you have a P.O. box, see page 16. | Apt. no.

City, town or post office, state, and ZIP code. If you have a foreign address, see page 16.

▲ **Important!** ▲ You must enter your SSN(s) above.

Presidential Election Campaign (See page 16.) **Note.** Checking "Yes" will not change your tax or reduce your refund. Do you, or your spouse if filing a joint return, want $3 to go to this fund? ▶ You ☐ Yes ☐ No Spouse ☐ Yes ☐ No

Filing Status Check only one box.
1 ☐ Single
2 ☐ Married filing jointly (even if only one had income)
3 ☐ Married filing separately. Enter spouse's SSN above and full name here. ▶
4 ☐ Head of household (with qualifying person). (See page 17.) If the qualifying person is a child but not your dependent, enter this child's name here. ▶
5 ☐ Qualifying widow(er) with dependent child (see page 17)

Exemptions
6a ☐ **Yourself.** If someone can claim you as a dependent, do not check box 6a
b ☐ **Spouse**
c **Dependents:** (1) First name Last name | (2) Dependent's social security number | (3) Dependent's relationship to you | (4) ✓ if qualifying child for child tax credit (see page 18)
If more than four dependents, see page 18.
d Total number of exemptions claimed
Boxes checked on 6a and 6b
No. of children on 6c who: • lived with you • did not live with you due to divorce or separation (see page 18)
Dependents on 6c not entered above
Add numbers on lines above ▶

Income
Attach Form(s) W-2 here. Also attach Forms W-2G and 1099-R if tax was withheld.
If you did not get a W-2, see page 19.
Enclose, but do not attach, any payment. Also, please use Form 1040-V.

7 Wages, salaries, tips, etc. Attach Form(s) W-2 — 7
8a **Taxable** interest. Attach Schedule B if required — 8a
b **Tax-exempt** interest. **Do not** include on line 8a — 8b
9a Ordinary dividends. Attach Schedule B if required — 9a
b Qualified dividends (see page 20) — 9b
10 Taxable refunds, credits, or offsets of state and local income taxes (see page 20) — 10
11 Alimony received — 11
12 Business income or (loss). Attach Schedule C or C-EZ — 12
13 Capital gain or (loss). Attach Schedule D if required. If not required, check here ▶ ☐ — 13
14 Other gains or (losses). Attach Form 4797 — 14
15a IRA distributions 15a — b Taxable amount (see page 22) — 15b
16a Pensions and annuities 16a — b Taxable amount (see page 22) — 16b
17 Rental real estate, royalties, partnerships, S corporations, trusts, etc. Attach Schedule E — 17
18 Farm income or (loss). Attach Schedule F — 18
19 Unemployment compensation — 19
20a Social security benefits 20a — b Taxable amount (see page 24) — 20b
21 Other income. List type and amount (see page 24) — 21
22 Add the amounts in the far right column for lines 7 through 21. This is your **total income** ▶ — 22

Adjusted Gross Income
23 Educator expenses (see page 26) — 23
24 Certain business expenses of reservists, performing artists, and fee-basis government officials. Attach Form 2106 or 2106-EZ — 24
25 IRA deduction (see page 26) — 25
26 Student loan interest deduction (see page 28) — 26
27 Tuition and fees deduction (see page 29) — 27
28 Health savings account deduction. Attach Form 8889 — 28
29 Moving expenses. Attach Form 3903 — 29
30 One-half of self-employment tax. Attach Schedule SE — 30
31 Self-employed health insurance deduction (see page 30) — 31
32 Self-employed SEP, SIMPLE, and qualified plans — 32
33 Penalty on early withdrawal of savings — 33
34a Alimony paid b Recipient's SSN ▶ — 34a
35 Add lines 23 through 34a — 35
36 Subtract line 35 from line 22. This is your **adjusted gross income** ▶ — 36

For Disclosure, Privacy Act, and Paperwork Reduction Act Notice, see page 75. Cat. No. 11320B Form **1040** (2004)

Source: http://www.irs.gov/pub/irs-pdf/f1040.pdf

Exhibit 4-5. Form 1040 – Front Side.

Exhibits 4-5 and 4-6 show a sample of the standard Form 1040 that you can reference as we discuss the key aspects of the income tax process. For a more detailed discussion on taxes and all of the entries on the form consider one of the many tax guides that are published toward the end of each year. J. K. Lasser's *Your Income Tax* is quite popular and I have found it to be quite helpful. These guides can also help you determine which form you should use to file. In addition to Form 1040 there are Forms 1040A and 1040EZ. Generally 1040EZ is for those whose income is limited to wages and interest (up to $1500) that totals less than $100,000 and have no other itemized deductions or tax credits to take. The 1040A will allow most types of income and tax credits but does not allow for itemized deductions. Itemized deductions are those deductions that you list that are allowed by the IRS to reduce the gross income that is taxed. Examples include mortgage interest, real estate taxes, and charitable contributions.

The first half of the Form 1040 front page is for demographic data concerning your mailing address, who you and your family members are, filing status and of course your social security numbers by which data concerning you is tracked. The second portion describes your income. Just about any type of income is recorded here. For wages earned you will receive a W-2 form from your employer which you should receive by January 31 and identifies the amount you earned. For interest, dividends, retirement fund distributions, tax refunds, and others you will receive 1099 forms usually suffixed with one or more letters. These all identify anything that was reported to the IRS as income. Be sure that what you report matches what is on the forms you receive otherwise your return will likely be flagged and more carefully scrutinized and perhaps audited. You may need to report some income in more detail on other forms that you will file with Form 1040. For interest or dividends that exceed $1500 you must complete and file Schedule B. For business income you must complete and file either Schedule C or Schedule C-EZ. For income or losses from investing you file Schedule D. Rental income, royalties, trust income, as well as other forms of income are reported on Schedule E. Farm income is reported on Schedule F.

The last part of the front of Form 1040 allows you the opportunity to reduce your income that will be taxed by adjusting for various expenses approved by congress. These include education expenses, IRA deductions, moving expenses, and self-employment taxes among others. Subtracting these items provides you with your adjusted gross income or AGI.

Your adjusted gross income is not your taxable income. On the back of Form 1040, shown in Exhibit 4-6 we can make some additional adjustments that usually reduce the tax owed. You have the choice of itemizing allowed deductions on Schedule A and reducing your income by that amount or taking the standard deduction that is allowed. You will want to take whichever is greater. The standard deduction has gone up significantly recently so fewer find it helpful to itemize deductions. Currently the standard deduction for a couple filing jointly is $9,700. There are additional deductions allowed for those over 65 or who are blind. In addition to the standard deduction, there is a standard amount of income that is exempt per individual in the household. In 2004 that was $3,100 a person. Thus, for every dependent person in the home income can be reduced by an additional $3,100. Once your income has been reduced by the appropriate amounts you are left with your taxable income. You can either calculate the tax owed or look up your tax in a tax table in the guides that are available or by checking the IRS website at www.irs.gov.

Form 1040 (2004) Page **2**

Tax and Credits

37 Amount from line 36 (adjusted gross income) . . . 37

38a Check if: ☐ **You** were born before January 2, 1940, ☐ Blind. ☐ **Spouse** was born before January 2, 1940, ☐ Blind. } **Total boxes checked ▶ 38a** ☐

b If your spouse itemizes on a separate return or you were a dual-status alien, see page 31 and check here ▶ 38b ☐

Standard Deduction for—

- People who checked any box on line 38a or 38b **or** who can be claimed as a dependent, see page 31.
- All others:

Single or Married filing separately, $4,850

Married filing jointly or Qualifying widow(er), $9,700

Head of household, $7,150

39 **Itemized deductions** (from Schedule A) **or** your **standard deduction** (see left margin) . . 39

40 Subtract line 39 from line 37 . . . 40

41 If line 37 is $107,025 or less, multiply $3,100 by the total number of exemptions claimed on line 6d. If line 37 is over $107,025, see the worksheet on page 33 . . . 41

42 **Taxable income.** Subtract line 41 from line 40. If line 41 is more than line 40, enter -0- . 42

43 Tax (see page 33). Check if any tax is from: a ☐ Form(s) 8814 b ☐ Form 4972 . . . 43

44 **Alternative minimum tax** (see page 35). Attach Form 6251 . . . 44

45 Add lines 43 and 44 . . . ▶ 45

46 Foreign tax credit. Attach Form 1116 if required . . . 46

47 Credit for child and dependent care expenses. Attach Form 2441 47

48 Credit for the elderly or the disabled. Attach Schedule R . . 48

49 Education credits. Attach Form 8863 . . . 49

50 Retirement savings contributions credit. Attach Form 8880 . . 50

51 Child tax credit (see page 37) . . . 51

52 Adoption credit. Attach Form 8839 . . . 52

53 Credits from: a ☐ Form 8396 b ☐ Form 8859 . . . 53

54 Other credits. Check applicable box(es): a ☐ Form 3800 b ☐ Form 8801 c ☐ Specify ______ . . 54

55 Add lines 46 through 54. These are your **total credits** . . . 55

56 Subtract line 55 from line 45. If line 55 is more than line 45, enter -0- . . . ▶ 56

Other Taxes

57 Self-employment tax. Attach Schedule SE . . . 57

58 Social security and Medicare tax on tip income not reported to employer. Attach Form 4137 . . 58

59 Additional tax on IRAs, other qualified retirement plans, etc. Attach Form 5329 if required . 59

60 Advance earned income credit payments from Form(s) W-2 . . . 60

61 Household employment taxes. Attach Schedule H . . . 61

62 Add lines 56 through 61. This is your **total tax** . . . ▶ 62

Payments

63 Federal income tax withheld from Forms W-2 and 1099 . . 63

64 2004 estimated tax payments and amount applied from 2003 return 64

If you have a qualifying child, attach Schedule EIC.

65a **Earned income credit (EIC)** . . . 65a

b Nontaxable combat pay election ▶ 65b

66 Excess social security and tier 1 RRTA tax withheld (see page 54) 66

67 Additional child tax credit. Attach Form 8812 . . . 67

68 Amount paid with request for extension to file (see page 54) 68

69 Other payments from: a ☐ Form 2439 b ☐ Form 4136 c ☐ Form 8885 . 69

70 Add lines 63, 64, 65a, and 66 through 69. These are your **total payments** . . . ▶ 70

Refund

Direct deposit? See page 54 and fill in 72b, 72c, and 72d.

71 If line 70 is more than line 62, subtract line 62 from line 70. This is the amount you **overpaid** 71

72a Amount of line 71 you want **refunded to you** . . . ▶ 72a

▶ b Routing number ▶ c Type: ☐ Checking ☐ Savings

▶ d Account number

73 Amount of line 71 you want **applied to your 2005 estimated tax** ▶ 73

Amount You Owe

74 **Amount you owe.** Subtract line 70 from line 62. For details on how to pay, see page 55 ▶ 74

75 Estimated tax penalty (see page 55) . . . 75

Third Party Designee

Do you want to allow another person to discuss this return with the IRS (see page 56)? ☐ **Yes.** Complete the following. ☐ **No**

Designee's name ▶ Phone no. ▶ ( ) Personal identification number (PIN) ▶

Sign Here

Joint return? See page 17. Keep a copy for your records.

Under penalties of perjury, I declare that I have examined this return and accompanying schedules and statements, and to the best of my knowledge and belief, they are true, correct, and complete. Declaration of preparer (other than taxpayer) is based on all information of which preparer has any knowledge.

Your signature | Date | Your occupation | Daytime phone number ( )

Spouse's signature. If a joint return, both must sign. | Date | Spouse's occupation

Paid Preparer's Use Only

Preparer's signature ▶ | Date | Check if self-employed ☐ | Preparer's SSN or PTIN

Firm's name (or yours if self-employed), address, and ZIP code ▶ | EIN | Phone no. ( )

Form **1040** (2004)

Source: http://www.irs.gov/pub/irs-pdf/f1040.pdf

Exhibit 4-6. Form 1040 – Back Side.

Once the tax you owe is determined there are additional adjustments that can be made to the tax itself. These adjustment are far more important since they increase or decrease the tax directly rather than the income that determines the tax. A $1000 increase in income may raise your taxes anywhere from $100-$350 dollars but a $1000 increase in your taxes is just that – a $1000 increase. The back of Form 1040 allows adjustments for the reduction of taxes by use of tax credits. These might include credits enacted by congress such as the adoption credit, credit for foreign taxes, and credits for buying alternative fuel vehicles, among many others. The addition of other taxes such as self-employment tax or social security taxes on tip income not reported to your employer is also included following the adjustment for credits. These of course will raise the amount of tax due.

Once the total tax due is figured you can reduce it by any payments you have made during the year either through payroll deductions, quarterly payments to the IRS, or overpayment of social security taxes because you earned income from more than one job. The final result is either what you owe or what you are due. If you find that you have a substantial refund due you may want to file a new W-4 form with your employer to reduce the amount of withholding so you get more of it back during the year. This way you can invest it and get additional income rather than letting the government use it for free. Of course if you owe a substantial amount you may also want to have more taken out so that you don't get a penalty for underpaying your taxes.

To summarize then, taxes are calculated by using the model shown in Exhibit 4-7. There are appropriate ways to reduce the total tax owed but these must be carefully thought through. This topic is discussed in more detail in the next section.

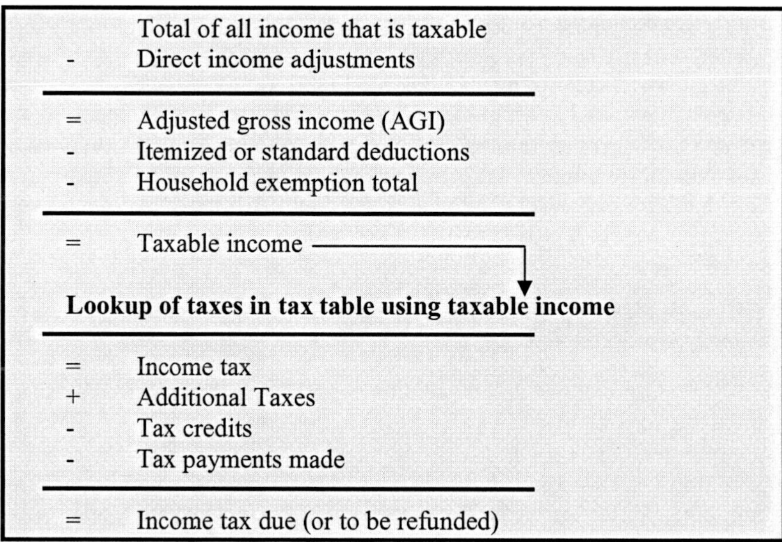

	Total of all income that is taxable
-	Direct income adjustments
=	Adjusted gross income (AGI)
-	Itemized or standard deductions
-	Household exemption total
=	Taxable income
	Lookup of taxes in tax table using taxable income
=	Income tax
+	Additional Taxes
-	Tax credits
-	Tax payments made
=	Income tax due (or to be refunded)

Exhibit 4-7. Tax Calculation Model.

Tax Planning to Save, Not Spend

Before discussing some ways to reduce your taxes it is important for us to discuss the purpose of tax planning. Our purpose in reducing taxes is to create more assets that can generate income. Now, you may say, "well, that is obvious," but there are two modes of thinking concerning taxes that folks use that will create problems rather than benefits. First, they seek to save on taxes so they can spend it in some other way. Usually these other things are not needs and then the net effect is that it is just a different expense rather than really providing any benefit to the family.

A second mode of thinking that is not good is "that we should reduce taxes by all means." This comes from the world's marketers trying to sell you mortgages, home equity loans, and other lines of credit that will help you to reduce your taxes. Families will sometimes mortgage a debt free house so they can reduce their taxes. As we have already noted from a stewardship perspective this does not make sense unless you would not mind possibly losing your home at some point. Secondly, it costs more to pay the bank the interest on the loan than the tax savings you receive. For instance if you are in the 28% marginal tax bracket you save 28 cents for every dollar you pay to the bank. Or, in other words, you are paying the bank $1 for the privilege of being able to save 28 cents on your taxes. So the cost for this benefit is $3.60 cents for every dollar saved in taxes (72 cents for every 28 cents saved). It is certainly something to avoid writing home about. Some will argue that they can invest what is borrowed at a greater rate thus creating income. Perhaps, but as we have noted this is not guaranteed and your home should not be viewed as an investment vehicle. What happens if the investment returns less than the mortgage rate or worse yet you lose a substantial part of the principal?

The motto of the above is we do not want to spend more in order to save on taxes. Almost inevitably the increased spending outpaces any tax benefit. Many are the stories of rich people who have sought every tax shelter possible for their money only to find that they would have substantially more if they had invested wisely and paid their taxes. This happens because of the salesmanship of the world.

How to Reduce Your Taxes

Although we do not want to spend more just for the sake of reducing taxes we do want to make every effort to be careful that we only pay what we are required to pay. First, we would unequivocally state that we want to be honest in what we report to the IRS. As Christians we want to avoid any improprieties that tarnish our testimony for Christ. We should also note that the tax law is voluminous and honest mistakes will be made by even the most well-meaning people because they are not aware of all that the law contains or may have been misinformed by another on some point. Some of these will be caught by the IRS and will need to be corrected. At other times it may not be an issue of a mistake but perhaps you receive a letter asking for verification of a deduction and you find that you have misplaced the receipt or discarded it by accident. Unfortunately, these things happen and as a result we may end up having to pay additional tax (sometimes a mistake results in a refund). It is a reminder that we should be vigilant in keeping copies of our tax returns and any documentation that supports anything reported as well as anything that we are taking a deduction for.

I mention the above because at times in our zeal to reduce our taxes we may forget to put together the appropriate documentation or we may take a tip from someone that seems to know about reducing taxes without truly understanding what it entails. That being said, there are many legitimate ways of reducing your taxes by taking a thoughtful and careful approach to your financial plan and to your tax plan. Here are some to consider:

Start early. The filing deadline is April 15th unless you have filed for an extension by that date. By waiting to the last minute you are likely to make mistakes and well may cost yourself money by overpaying your taxes or make a careless mistake that makes them lower than they should be and if caught will cause more stress to get rectified. Start in January to get your receipts and other materials together. Install tax software if you use it or download the latest forms from the IRS website. Even if you wait to mail in your return you should have it completed by March 1.

Keep your receipts and records straight. Keep all your receipts throughout the year so that they will all be in one place when you need them in January. I use a large box for receipts and all receipts end up in that box whether they will be used for tax purposes or not. By doing this you can avoid missing valuable deductions that you could forget about. It is also great for when you want to return an item to the store or need a receipt for warranty purposes. You will know right away where to go.

Consider the computer. If you have a computer at home consider keeping track of your financial matters (including taxes) by using it. There are plenty of software packages available to help with this task. Products such as Quicken by Intuit and *MS Money* by Microsoft are two of the most popular. Perhaps the simplest and best I have seen for its cost was *MoneyCounts* by Parsons Technology. Intuit bought it and then as you might expect it died. These software packages will also keep track of tax related items to make it easier at tax time and you can also import data into the tax software from the financial package. The more popular tax software packages include *TurboTax* by Intuit, and *TaxCut* by H & R Block. You will also find specialized tax packages to help you maximize your deductions. One that is growing in popularity is *It's Deductible* from Intuit. It appears to be quite helpful in tracking and valuing household items that you give to charity. Generally people way over or under estimate the value of items they give to charity.

Take all exemptions. Be sure to include all dependent children and others you support that meet the IRS guidelines for those considered dependents. For each dependent there is currently a $3,000 exemption, which is significant. If you share the support of a dependent then you may be able to take turns in claiming the individual as a dependent.

Contribute to a tax-deferred retirement plan. Taxes can also be reduced by legally reducing income. One of the most popular ways is by contributing to an IRA, or an employer sponsored 401K or 403B (non-profit, government). The amount you can put in and deduct is subject to various limitations based on age and income so you will want to do some research on it. Keep in mind that these funds will be taxed when they are withdrawn. We discuss these in more detail in the chapter on tax-advantaged investing.

Generate tax-exempt income. Another mechanism that can be used as part of your tax planning for the future is to invest in instruments whose return is tax-free, and thus, does not need to be included in you taxable income. These might include a Roth IRA or municipal bonds. These are also covered later in our tax-advantaged investing chapter along with tax-free employer benefits.

Generate capital gains income. A capital gain is the amount realized on sale of an asset such as stocks, bonds, or real estate that exceeds the original purchase price. This income (sale price – purchase price) is taxed at a much lower rate than standard income. Depending on standard income you pay capitals gains tax at the rate of 8-20%. This is significantly less than the 10%-35% you would pay on normal income. Another nice thing about this is you can decide when it would be best to sell and take the gain (or loss if it has lost value).

Give your money to others. You can give up to $11,000 to as many people as you care to without encountering any tax consequences. The person receiving the gift does not have to pay taxes on the gift either. What is nice about this option, as well, is if the individual receiving the gift is in a lower marginal tax bracket then any income he earns will be taxed at a lower rate than if you had been taxed on the income. This in particular is a nice way for relatives and brethren in Christ to share the wealth.

Outcomes and Chapter Summary

In this chapter we focused on the major components dealing with the inflows and outflows of a spending plan with a special emphasis on ways of reducing the outflows to allow more funds for building assets. We also learned about the importance of education in developing skills that will allow us to earn more over time. We finally looked at the issue of taxes from a Biblical perspective and briefly looked at how the American income taxes are assessed.

Learning Objective 1. **Identify and describe various sources of income, and identify the tradeoffs and determine the efficacy of both parents working.**

A majority of our income will come from our career related pursuits. As a result it is imperative that we procure education and develop our skills in order to have the best return for the use of our time. This development includes setting career goals, working diligently, and learning to network. The other sources of income include the return on our assets and gifts or inheritances from others.

Learning Objective 2. **Be able to develop and analyze spending plans to find ways of reducing spending and meeting financial goals**

The key to reducing outflows is identifying whether expenses are really necessary. Being prepared for large expenses can help to keep the spending plan intact. There are also many smaller, perhaps monthly expenses that, over time, can quietly destroy the spending plan or reduce the funds available for saving. These include eating out, entertainment, communication services, gifts, pets, and the like. Ways of saving in this area include using the church as a community and getting an item at a reduced cost.

Learning Objective 3. **Understand the effect of outflows to liabilities on the spending plan and net worth.**

For each dollar that is spent there is a dollar lost in net worth. We recognize based on what has been discussed that the home and cars should be seen as liabilities because of the large maintenance expenses they generate. Three very large areas of cash outflow are loan and debt payments, homes and cars, and gifts.

Learning Objective 4. **Understand and explain the basics of the American tax system and be able to differentiate good and poor tax planning strategies.**

We looked at the Biblical basis of taxes and found that the payment of taxes is valid and evident throughout the Bible. The United States has a tiered income tax system where the income earned is taxed at a progressively higher level. Each tax bracket is a marginal bracket which means only the income that falls into that bracket is taxed at that rate. A variety of tax forms are used to report and calculate taxes and we looked at Form 1040 that is commonly used.

Bible Texts Referenced

Genesis 2:18	Genesis 41	1 Samuel 8	2 Kings 23:35
Proverbs 31:10-31	Proverbs 31:24	Daniel 11:20	Matthew 6:19-21
Matthew 17:24-27	Matthew 22.15-22	Matthew 25:14-30	Luke 15: 11-24
Luke 16:1-8	Luke 22:15	Romans 13:3-4	Romans 13:6-7
1 Corinthians 11:2	Ephesians 5:21-24	Colossians 3:23	1 Timothy 3:4-5
2 Timothy 2:15			

Exercises and Research Activities

1. Develop a list of career goals and then prioritize them based on what you have learned in this chapter.

2. Find an article about hunting for a job and create an annotated abstract of what you learned and share it with your group or class.

3. Visit a human resource manager or an employment agency manager for an informational interview and find out what he believes are important requirements for individuals in your field of interest. Create a report about your findings and share what you found with others in the class.

4. Assume you are married and you and your spouse have both decided to work. Make a list of the additional costs you may have to deal with as a result of the second person working.

5. Take a month to record every penny that you spend. After the month is up analyze the results and identify at least 3 ways that you can reduce your expenses. Write a short report that summarizes your findings and discuss your reactions to what you found.

6. You have decided to purchase a cell phone plan for $40 a month. Assuming no inflation and an interest rate of 7% how much will the phone have cost you after 40 years?

7. You have decided to buy a new 5 mega-pixel digital camera. Do some research and find the lowest price you can for it. Write a report that identifies where you checked and the steps you took in trying to reduce the price to the absolute minimum.

8. Visit an auction and just watch what occurs. Create a brief report on what ways you thought individuals were doing well and ways in which they overspent and why.

9. Create a complete list of all the gifts and cards you usually buy in a year. Include all friends, relatives, fellow-workers, and your church community. Try to identify how much you would spend over the year and then comment on the results.

10. You currently own your home debt free but a buddy has just heard about a great deal on a home equity loan that will give you cash for a vacation and the interest on the loan is tax deductible. What would you do and why?

References and Resources

Web Sites:

Education Pays. www.educationpays.org.

Internal Revenue Service. www.irs.gov.

Forms:

Form 1040. http://www.irs.gov/pub/irs-pdf/f1040.pdf

Publication 501. www.irs.gov/publications/p501/index.html

CHAPTER 5

Managing Credit, Borrowing, and Debt

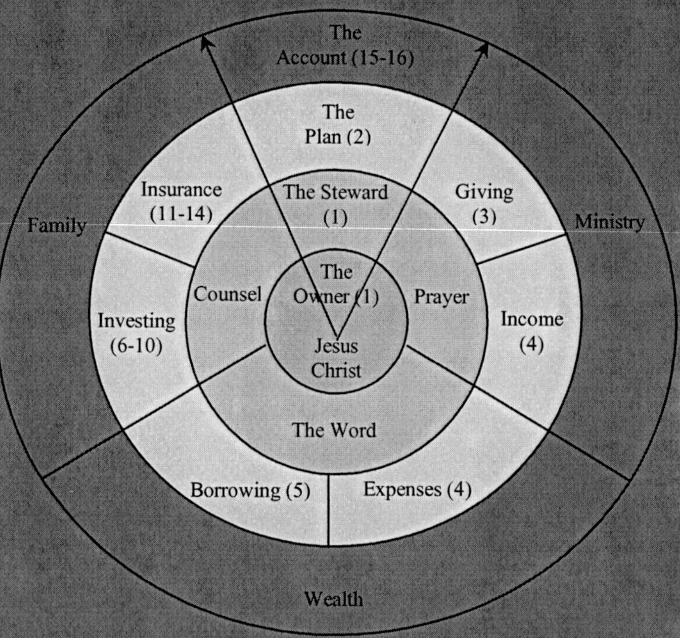

Learning Objectives

1. Understand and explain the beginnings of credit and be able to describe what is included in a credit report as well as secure a copy of one.
2. Explain the Biblical perspective on borrowing, debt, and surety and how they differ.
3. Describe the various sources of credit and be able to select an appropriate scenario for a given credit situation.
4. Explain the Biblical view of bankruptcy and the bankruptcy process in America.
5. Identify major purchase needs and be able to research and make appropriate major purchases.

Lord, I commit to being debt-free.

Lord, I know you are able to provide for my needs. Help me to not rush into large purchases that will cause me to have a different ruler other than you in my life. I commit now to become and stay debt-free. By your Spirit guide me in taking the right steps to eliminate any debt I currently owe and to begin to build assets that I can use to make the major purchases that may be necessary in the future. It is only with your help that I can make this a reality so I put my confidence in you.

The Beginnings of Credit

The Basics of Credit

? Credit

Credit comes from the Latin "credere" meaning to trust, loan, believe. The idea being that one could be trusted to return or repay that which they have borrowed. Today we see it as the ability to borrow based on our ability to repay. That is, we are deemed trustworthy and able to repay. If I have no source of income and wish to borrow money the bank will not lend it since they do not trust that I can repay it. Even if I have the ability to repay the funds, if the bank finds that I have gone bankrupt or have not been consistent in paying my bills they will not consider me to be "trustworthy" and may deny me the ability to borrow.

Where did the idea of credit come from in the first place? Credit likely started as a small thing but has mushroomed into a multi-billion dollar business for banks. The parable of the talents shows that even in New Testament times there were bankers who could take your money at interest (Matthew 25:27). It was likely that they would then trade with the money in hopes of making a profit on it greater than the amount that they had to pay out in interest.

Credit likely was born out of the economic process. Let's see how that might have occurred. Larry Burkett, in his book *Your Finances in Changing Times* gives an excellent example how this may have developed and I will paraphrase the idea here using corn instead of nails as he does. Let's say I grow corn to swap for goods or sell for money. The recipients of my payment of corn may not need it right now so they ask me to keep it for them. This works fine for a while and I actually end up with a surplus owned by others because they have paid for it but they don't have the room to store all of it. As they need some corn they can come and get it. Others continue to buy it as needed. One day someone comes and wants to buy some corn but cannot pay until their next paycheck comes in. This gives me a great idea. I can lend some of the corn others have left with me to the individual and charge a little extra (interest) for the risk that I am taking. So, easily, the economy has now begun to work on credit. In fact, word gets around to others that I am willing to help in this way and pretty soon I have become a corn banker. As long as I have enough corn to cover the amounts requested by those who own it, the system works fine.

What happens if someone comes and wants all of his corn and I don't have enough to cover the request until I buy some elsewhere or until the next harvest? Just as fast as the word got around about my willingness to lend, the word gets around that I cannot pay back what is owed. Individuals quickly lose confidence in me and soon I am forced to close my operation in bankruptcy. What happened? Credit seemed to be so attractive and it helped others but eventually led to the downfall of the business. The problem is that credit looks and behaves like money. You can save it, divide it, sell it, and give it to others and yet it lacks one key thing – it has no tangible value. That is, we can create credit without it costing us anything. See, it goes back to our definition – the ability to borrow or to be trusted to repay. In the credit scenario no additional value is attached. We are just lending what belongs to another. We can store what belongs to another and we can divide it into portions and give it to others, and we can sell what belongs to another but that does not change the fact that it costs you nothing to do so. Another way of looking at it is that there is no corresponding component created that backs up the "corn" that was lent so when the individual that owns the corn wants it, you must get it from another or create more.

Similarly in our banking system today we have money instead of corn. Many individuals put funds in the bank for safekeeping. As individuals need access to their funds the bank gives it to them. Now in this scenario the bank desires that you deposit funds with them so they do give you interest on your funds. Thus, there is some cost related to banking as we know it but this is more than recouped by the bank in lending out your funds to others at higher interest. That is, just like with the corn. The bank does not keep all of your money in one place doing nothing. It uses it to generate revenue through interest on the funds it lends to others. The system is fine as long as everyone doesn't request their money all at once. Why? Because the credit does not create any additional value in terms of real money. Knowing that money deposited in the bank is usually more than is requested from the bank allows the bank to lend much more than they receive. Thus, the money you deposit at the bank is not really there, it is "virtual." When you want it the bank will either take it out of what cash reserves it does have or borrow it. To you it is no different than if it were your money specifically, as long as you get the money when you request it. It is when a request is denied that panic sets in and confidence in the system causes it to collapse much like it did around 1930.

What many don't realize is that credit (the ability to borrow) has also made the value of some items quite expensive. Homes for instance would likely be much less expensive if credit was not available. I remember my grandfather bought his house in 1945 for $4500. At the time 10-year mortgages were the standard. As banks changed the standard to allow longer borrowing periods the number of individuals who could afford a home increased. This, of course, increased competition for the supply of houses and that caused the values to go up. Now mortgages are available for up to forty years and few people ever pay their home off. The same has occurred with automobiles. Loans that at one time would be for a year or two now are for seven years or more. Few people ever pay off their cars before getting another.

In summary, credit is the ability to borrow, and implied in that word is the confidence that you can repay what is owed. It allows an individual to buy that, which currently would financially be out of reach. In the American economy credit started out as a way of helping folks who had real needs and could be trusted to repay but quickly mushroomed into a way of getting money for most any purpose and for extremely long periods of time. As a result many borrowed to speculate with investments and unfortunately many have lost

(1930s) and continue to lose all that they have. An important lesson in credit is that we need to have the ability to repay. Credit can be helpful in buying expensive items such as homes but it must be carefully considered in light of the entire financial plan.

Establishing Credit and Credit Reporting

Now that we understand that credit is the ability to borrow the question becomes how does one establish this ability? First we will assume that you may have some future need for credit. If you make a decision to live without using credit then there will be no need to concern yourself with establishing credit. By the way, it is fine to make such a decision and quite often it has huge benefits in controlling spending and carefully establishing a spending plan. Although rare, in our country there are those who will not purchase something until they have the funds to do so.

Assuming you may have the opportunity to use credit in the future it is a good idea to establish it. What we mean by that is that we establish that we are trustworthy. The key things a lender will look at are the income you have to repay and whether you have demonstrated that you can be trusted to do so. There are some other factors as well and we will touch on these when we discuss how credit ratings are determined later in this section. For the first concern, dealing with income, the bank will look at your income and current recurring obligations such as loans, mortgage or rent, credit card payments, etc. That is, they will be looking to see if you have adequate income not only to cover what you are requesting but that you can cover the loan you are requesting in addition to your other obligations. It is rare to find a lender who will let you commit more than forty percent of your income to payments for these types of items. They will also want to confirm that the income is steady and will be expected to continue. This is why they will look at how long you have been in a job as well as a particular industry. Income to repay is important so factors relating to it are analyzed as well.

The other key factor is your demonstrated trustworthiness to repay. For those who have had loans before and have properly repaid them, they have a demonstrated track record of being able to repay a loan. That is, they have demonstrated by sending in payments on time without missing them that they can be trusted to give money back that they borrow. The difficulty is for those who are young or just married who have no such record. What should they do? Quite often, to deal with this short-coming many will encourage young people to obtain and use credit cards in order to establish their credit. This I believe is not necessary and often will put folks in a very tempting situation of using the cards on items that are unnecessary just because they are available. Many college students thinking they would establish their credit with a credit card find it too easy just to charge whatever they need and then as they graduate they are stuck with thousands of dollars in credit card balances to repay. Using a credit card and paying the balance each month can be one way of showing your trustworthiness but certainly is not the only or best way. If you rent an apartment, keep accurate records showing your regular and timely payments of the rent. A lender can contact the landlord to verify that you have demonstrated an ability to pay the rent. If you need to make a purchase and have the cash in the bank you could take a small loan secured by the savings account that will cost much less since the bank will have little risk that you will not pay it since they can always make sure there is enough in the account to repay the loan. What is nice, of course, is that you can make regularly, timely payments on the small loan to demonstrate that you are capable of doing so. Some banks will allow you to set up a credit card secured by your bank account as well which will keep you from overspending on the credit card since the line of credit on the card is tied to a balance in the savings account.

Another avenue that was used heavily in times past is the lay away plan. I remember buying my first baseball glove (Carl Yazstremski) this way. I think at the time I was a young teenager and put the glove on lay away at a local department store. Each week I would take a little money from the profits on my paper route and pay off part of the price of the glove. After the last payment was made the store would then give me the glove. It was exciting to get the glove but little did I realize I was also demonstrating my ability to make regular timely payments for an item. What we are trying to point out here is that there are ways of demonstrating your trustworthiness without putting yourself into debt or in a position that will lead to it.

Credit Ratings and Reporting. Most lenders and other organizations that give you goods and services on credit will report your history to a credit-reporting agency. In addition to banks, credit card providers, and other financial institutions, you will find that landlords, utilities (electric, telephone, gas, etc.), and the like that provide you goods or services with the expectation that you will pay them when billed will also use these reporting agencies.

There are three main credit-reporting agencies in the United States. They are Trans Union, Equifax, and Experian (formerly TRW). These organizations track only that which relates to your financial dealings usually along the lines of the items we have mentioned in this section. In addition they will track employment information and basic demographic information such as your age and address. Exhibit 5-1 identifies the key components of what these organizations track about you. The credit reporting web sites provide a sample copy of a credit report. It should give you a good idea of what detail the credit bureaus use in their credit reports.

1. Demographic information: This includes your name, social security number, address (current and previous), and age.

2. Employment information: Generally this will be information about your current and previous employer as well as your vocation.

3. Credit History: This section will contain information on what credit has been extended to you including credit cards, utilities, and the like. Information will include the amount owed, the amount past due, how often past due, as well as a two year record of your payment history on each account.

4. Public Financial History: Here will be included any court related proceeding such as bankruptcies, liens, convictions, and judgments against you by creditors, among others.

5. Inquiries: This will include a two-year history of everyone who has requested a copy of your report. The greater the number of recent inquiries the more careful the bank will be in giving you credit

Exhibit 5-1. Credit Reporting Features.

? FICO

Some credit reports also contain a credit score sometimes known as the "FICO" score. It is named after the company, Fair Isaac Corporation, that developed the analytical models for evaluating credit. All three of the major credit bureaus we have noted also have their own FICO scoring mechanisms. These scores are not stored with your credit information but are calculated each time a request is made for credit either by the credit-reporting agency or by the lender. This score is calculated by assigning numeric values and weights to various questions that are asked on a loan application as well as some components of the credit report. The scoring usually involves anywhere from 15 to 30 factors depending on the institution. For instance a bankruptcy will result in a negative number of points in the score while if you have lived in your current residence for over ten years you will receive a strong positive score. Keep in mind though that not all types of data are used by all models. The credit bureaus usually stick with the financially related items while lenders may take into account other factors such as employment history and residency. Also, keep in mind that the computer can calculate a score very efficiently but does not take into account unique situations or life events that common sense would say should not affect the score. For instance, a fire destroys your home along with the bills you have received so it took a few months to get things back in order which means you were late paying some bills, you had to move, and there were additional inquiries on your account as you sought some initial relief from the fire by doing some additional borrowing. A computer might look at that and lower your credit score while a banker might look at the situation and see that you are credit worthy because he can dismiss the one-time fire event. Keep in mind that credit scoring formulas are computer models that are based on research on millions of consumers and their actual credit histories.

Exhibit 5-2 features some of the key areas that the various models may take into account. Financial institutions may use their own credit formulas or reports that either modify this credit information or credit scores or use it as a

1. Payment History – have you demonstrated that you can make on time payments as agreed to. The frequency, newness, and severity of delinquencies have a significant impact on your score.

2. Outstanding Debt. The number and total balances of outstanding debts are important. If you have more debt than you can already afford you are not likely to be approved.

3. Credit history. This categorizes how long you have had credit and the age of the credit accounts that you have. If you just opened five other credit accounts it may raise a flag.

4. Credit Pursuit. This usually considers the number of inquiries against your credit report as well as the number of accounts opened in the past year. If you appear to pursuing many credit accounts at once questions will be raised.

5. Credit Type. As you might expect the number and types of credit can influence your score. Most reports look at the numbers of each type of account such as credit cards, installment loans, and mortgages.

6. Employment. Even if not included in the credit score, lenders consider your employment history, including income, length of service, and type of position, in their decision-making process.

7. Residence. This is another category that may not always be reflected in the credit score but is considered by the lender or the lender's model. This would include the housing type (rent, own) and your residence history.

8. Public Records. Credit scores will take into account any financial difficulties that are on the public record including bankruptcies, judgments, liens, and the like.

Exhibit 5-2. Sample Credit Criteria.

weighted factor in their own formula. Keep in mind that factors on your credit application to the lender may also be used in determining your credit rating. The Fair Credit and Reporting Act (FCRA) prevents lenders and reporting agencies from using age, public assistance use, the exercise of rights under the FCRA, interest rates on debt, child support, rental agreements, or certain types of credit report requests such as your own requests for review purposes in making their determinations.

Factors that go into a credit score may include the number and types of credit accounts, the total debt outstanding, the percentage of your debt limit that you have used, the age of your credit accounts (have you just recently opened five other credit accounts?), and whether they are past due. Remember that all types of credit may be tracked including credit cards (revolving credit), charge cards (paid in full each month), service credit (home utilities), and installment credit (loans). If you are refused credit you are entitled to receive from the lender a list of the key scoring factors that affected your score.

You often hear about "fixing" bad credit and you will often get advertisements helping to fix bad credit. Beware of these offers. Unless an error has been made on your report there are no quick fixes for credit. You can get a copy of your credit report from the key agencies already noted and report discrepancies so they can be fixed. Truthful negative credit entries cannot be removed by "fixing." The best way to fix such credit is to pay your bills on time. Over time old items will be removed from your report including negative items. Some have tried to correct credit problems by challenging a negative item even if it is correct to see if it can be verified. If it cannot be verified it will be removed. As a Christian if there are specific entries that should be corrected then it is a good idea to challenge them with the reporting company and have them corrected. Most negative items will be deleted from your credit history after seven years. Bankruptcies can take 7-10 years and tax liens up to 15 years. Tracked inquiries for your credit report usually disappear after two years. As you can see, in addition to paying your bills on time and not overextending yourself, time is the key factor in "fixing" credit.

The Biblical Perspective on Credit

The Biblical View of Borrowing and Debt

Now that we have defined credit and how it is tracked in our society the question becomes whether the Christian should borrow or be in debt. Well, for an answer to this question we most go to the Bible. As we look at the Scriptures in their entirety we find first that borrowing is a valid Biblical principle and second that it is different from debt. Starting in the Old Testament we see borrowing first noted in Exodus 22:14. "If a man borrows anything from his neighbor and it is injured or dies while its owner is not with it he shall make full

restitution." We learn two things from this verse, first, that borrowing is allowed and second that it must be repaid. Whether its animals, equipment, or money we are to repay anything we borrow – that is the biblical principle. Psalm 37:21 reinforces this point "The wicked borrows and does not repay."

Often I will be asked about the verse in Romans 13:8 that states to "owe no man anything." Does this mean we cannot borrow? As we have already noted it is clear that borrowing is allowed but what is often missed is what is meant by "owe." That is debt is different from borrowing. In English our term "owe" is quite broad and includes those who regularly repay what they have borrowed. From a biblical perspective one is not considered to be in debt or "owing" until he has not met his obligation to pay. That is, he is not in debt until he breaks the vow to repay at the appointed time in the appointed manner. So in Romans 13 it is showing that our love will be constrained by priorities to others we have broken vows to. If we are repaying what we have vowed to repay then we are free to love. He who does not repay his vow enters a state of being in debt and is focused on that position rather than that of being able to love. The owing becomes one of not having paid what is supposed to be paid rather than the issue of borrowing. Thus, biblical debt and borrowing are different things.

So far then, we have seen that borrowing was allowed by the Bible and that one is not in a state of debt or owing, biblically speaking, until they have missed paying as agreed. On the other hand we need to note that generally borrowing is not seen as a positive thing in the Bible. That is, although the Bible allows borrowing, it never encourages it. Rather, often the comments concerning borrowing discourage the practice. Proverbs notes that "the rich ruleth over the poor, and the borrower is servant to the lender" (22:7, KJV). Concerning Israel the Lord said "thou shalt lend to many nations, but thou shalt not borrow, and thou shalt reign over many nations, but they shall not reign over thee" Deuteronomy 15:6, KJV). What the Bible shows us about borrowing is that the position that is assumed by the borrower is not good. Time and time again experience proves the Bible's correctness on this point. The borrower is put into a place of bondage. The terms are always in the lender's favor so that they will be assured of being repaid. This puts the borrower in the position of submission to whatever the whims of the lender might be. In many ways the amount of borrowing becomes a hindrance to what you would really like to do in life – even if it is something that God would want you to do. In a sense borrowing makes you a slave until you have repaid the borrowed amount. Isn't it interesting that we often look at those who have paid all their debts as those who are "free."

To summarize, then, the question of whether to borrow is not a question of whether it is Biblical (it is allowed) but what will be your state once undertaken, and for how long will that state remain. We should avoid borrowing, if at all possible, since borrowing often leads to debt (owing) and debt leads to slavery to the lender. We are to be bondservants of Christ and not to a worldly lender. Make a commitment now to avoid the world's ways of living off other people's money by borrowing. The world views this as smart finance and a way to freedom, but the Bible views it as foolishness that leads to bondage. This does not mean that you won't find a few in this world that become financially rich off of such tactics. The issue is not one of whether it works or feels right but whether it is Biblical. Commit to taking the Biblical road.

The Biblical View of Surety

Perhaps you have not heard of the word "surety" before. It means to pledge to repay that which you have no certain way of repaying. Often this means pledging to repay on behalf of another. This includes the common practice of co-signing for another. Let's look at what the Bible has to say about it:

> "*My son, if you have become surety for your neighbor, have given a pledge for a stranger, if you have been snared with the words of your mouth, have been caught with the words of your mouth, do this then, my son, and deliver yourself*" (Proverbs 6:1-2, KJV).
>
> "*He who is surety for a stranger will surely suffer for it, but he who hates going surety is safe*" (Proverbs 11:15, KJV).
>
> "*A man lacking in sense pledges, and becomes surety in the presence of his neighbor*" (Proverbs 17:18, KJV).
>
> "*Do not be among those who give pledges, among those who become sureties for debts. If you have nothing with which to pay, why should he take your bed from under you?*" (Proverbs 22:26-27, KJV).

Any questions? This should make it quite clear that any idea of pledging on behalf of others, or for borrowing that which we have no way of repaying, is not Biblical. I believe that this includes pledging for family members as well. The only viable way of borrowing is to borrow on collateral. That is, if you are unable to pay, the creditor receives the item that you put up as collateral and the obligation ends. Collateral is what you pledge as payment if you are unable to repay. Often this is done with homes and cars. So, if you are unable to make the payments the creditor receives the home or car as payment and the debtor is considered free of the obligation. Be aware that some loans now also require you to pay the difference between what the bank gets in selling the collateral and what you had owed the bank. In order to stay clear of surety in these situations work with a lender who will give you a strictly collateralized loan or be sure that the value of the collateral is worth more than the amount owed on the loan. This may mean making a larger down payment on an item.

It is perhaps needless to say that many have experienced much heartache from eschewing the biblical mandate against surety. Countless, are the sad events that have surrounded family members and friends who have pledged to pay for one another's loans only to find the family member or friend unable to pay and then finding themselves fully responsible for the debt incurred by the other. In addition, the repaying of that debt quite often has no return for the pledger since the item purchased is often of little value or has been repossessed. The legacy of broken families and friendships that have resulted from apparent well-meaning help in reality demonstrates that to pledge for another is no help at all and often robs the ones being pledged for the opportunity to use sound financial planning, careful seeking of God's will, and discipline in reaching goals. Keep in mind that 50% of all co-signed arrangements fail. There is a reason that the bank wants a cosigner – because they have a concern that the borrowers will not be able to repay. If the bank is unwilling to take a risk why should you?

Our lesson in this section shows us that although borrowing is biblical it puts the borrower in a poor position of being a slave to the lender when he is unable to repay. Our common practice today of pledging or cosigning for others for the most part encourages unscriptural borrowing and puts the Christian in a bondman's position until the loan has been paid. Biblical borrowing always involves having a way of repaying which means using proper loan instruments, worthwhile collateral, and appropriate down payments. Having nothing borrowed truly makes you free to serve the Lord.

The Sources of Credit

In this section we will explore the various sources of credit and the benefits and disadvantages they bring. We need to keep in mind the biblical perspective on borrowing as we consider these sources and whether to use them in our personal financial planning. Just because the world makes them available does not mean we need to use them. Also keep in mind that as with any financial planning aspect we want to be good stewards of what we have and this also applies to the use of credit.

The Use and Abuse of Credit Cards

Today financial institutions provide a variety of credit vehicles using cards. These can be divided into three main groups. The most common are credit cards. These have a "line of credit" pre-established based on your credit worthiness. Credit cards are often called revolving credit accounts because the credit line cycles up and down based on what you charge or pay. Thus, a $50 payment will in a sense revolve to $50 more (minus interest and fees) available on your credit limit. These accounts require a minimum monthly payment, which is usually a small portion of the outstanding balance on the account. A second type of card is a "charge card." This type of card may or may not have a credit limit although most theoretically do even if there is none stated. The key difference is that the full balance of the account is due each month. Thus, the funds are usually borrowed for brief periods until the next billing statement comes and the payment is made. A third type of card is the "debit card." These cards usually deduct money directly from your bank account as if you were paying cash. Although they are not usually sources of credit, many debit cards can also function as credit cards thus creating a ready source of credit. Using the card for this purpose is the same as using a standard credit card. ATM Cards at times can function as credit or debit cards.

The question will be raised as to whether it is necessary in today's society to have a credit card, perhaps for emergencies or for places that do not accept cash or checks. The answer is generally no, it is not necessary. With careful planning one can avoid having to use credit cards. I am not saying that they are not convenient but that does not mean they are necessary. There are some companies such as certain rental car companies that require a credit card. So without credit cards your rental car choices would be more limited but it would not stop you from being able to rent a car.

Exhibit 5-3 shows a list of advantages and disadvantages of credit cards with the key ones being detailed in the following discussion. There are some advantages to using credit cards judiciously. First, as noted they are quite convenient. They are easy to carry and use and can be handy in an emergency

Credit Cards	
Advantages	**Disadvantages**
Convenience	Overspending
Discount/reward programs	Habit leading to debt
Safety	Finance charges/fees
Merchant transaction liability	Terms favor the lender

Exhibit 5-3. Advantages and Disadvantages of Credit Cards.

situation. Of course using a check of some kind is only slightly less convenient but a debit card is another convenient way of having this benefit. Second they can be better than carrying large amounts of cash. Of course, careful planning and the use of debit cards, checks, or money orders can mitigate this advantage. They sometimes extend the warranty on purchases made with the card. This can be helpful for some purchases such as laptop computers where a repair might be more likely but records show that few of these warranties are ever used – that's why the company offers it as a free feature and yet few consumers will even remember that the warranty was extended even if they needed it. Unless you carefully record the information about warranties and the extension date it is likely to be forgotten. One benefit that can be quite good is that if there is any problem with the product most credit card companies will credit your account for the amount and deal with the vendor on your behalf. I remember purchasing a nice sofa at a great price a week before a company went bankrupt. Of course, they had not delivered my sofa and I had no way of getting it since it was in bankruptcy. Since I had used a credit card I was able to get a full refund of the purchase price from the credit card company. The last benefit often noted is the reward programs and the "points" you can accrue toward free or reduced price goods and services. Many cards will give you a point for every dollar (perhaps more in certain cases) you spend using the card. Keep in mind that these programs are created to encourage you to spend more and as a result keep a nice balance on the card so companies can profit off you. If you are able to restrict your use of such a card to only items that you would have purchased with cash and pay it off each month then the point programs can be a benefit. In addition, by paying the balance each month you get interest-free borrowing for your purchases for a month. The individuals are few that can do it without overspending or keeping a balance on the account.

In summary, then, the biggest benefit of credit cards that cannot be replicated by using cash is the protection offered the purchaser when a product or service is not as promised or is never delivered. Otherwise the other benefits of credit cards are only effective for those who are extremely conservative in their use and can use them as if they were cash.

There are also some disadvantages to credit cards and these are usually more than enough to offset any advantage gained from them for the average person. First, credit card users spend more because the cards usually represent more than is available with cash and there are more of them. The average American who uses credit cards has 3-4 credit cards which means the average couple has 6-8 credit cards. That is far more than is necessary for any type of emergency. The motto should be the fewer the credit cards the better. What many don't realize is that those who use credit cards are not only more likely to buy something they don't need, but will spend 30% more on items they do need than those who use cash. Those who commit to using cash will almost always spend less because when there is no more cash they have to stop spending, so they are more likely to conserve it. Using cash is a great way of getting your spending under control. Even National Bankcard Systems which supports merchants using credit cards emphasizes the advantages to the merchant of the consumer's use of credit cards. Exhibit 5-4 itemizes several of their points and should give us pause to consider whether we use credit cards appropriately.

Credit Cards
Advantages to Business of Consumer Use
Credit card customers spend 2.5 times more than those carrying cash
Credit cards give customers freedom to spend on unplanned purchases
Credit cards entice consumers to purchase more expensive items than they planned on buying
Credit card customers are often less conscience of slight price differences

Source: National Bankcard Systems at http://www.enbs.com/html/statistics.html.

Exhibit 5-4. Credit Card Benefits for Merchants.

Another disadvantage is that credit cards can be habit forming and quickly get you into debt. I have counseled individuals who in a short time have accrued $50,000 or more in credit card debt because they were unable to control themselves. The problem is that using credit cards can put you in such a situation very quickly but it can take many years to get out of it. According to CardTrak the average American who possesses a credit card has credit card debt of $3,632. The average household has about $8,000 in credit card debt. The reason many don't see the problem developing is that the financial institutions have made it seem so easy with the "low monthly payment." What many do not see is that low monthly payment on 5 to 8 credit cards adds up to a very large amount. In addition, as soon as you have made that low monthly payment you likely have used the card to purchase more goods that add that amount back on the balance. Keep in mind only 60 percent of the over $100 billion charged each month on credit cards is paid back. Which means American's credit card debt is growing at over $40 billion a month. Only about 35% of individuals pay off the balance in full each month.

Another disadvantage is the generally exorbitant fees, and interest that are charged; especially to those who keep a balance, are late paying, or go over their credit limit. Fees can range as high as 27% on credit card balances. That is, it costs you $27 a year to borrow $100. Only the bank makes out in this scenario. Most institutions charge $30 for being late with a payment or over the credit limit even though it costs the bank little if anything to let you be late or go over the limit. Remember, financial institutions are in the credit card business to make money – and that they do very well. In fact, the credit card industry made approximately $30 billion in profit in 2004.

Another important disadvantage is that the fine print is always in the bank's favor. How many of you as readers of this book and have a credit card have actually read the entire credit card agreement that you received with the card? Few do. It would behoove each reader to keep abreast of the constant changes to the agreements. They include clauses to increase the interest rate if you are late on a payment or have a fee to close the account. Some are changing how they calculate the interest, instituting minimum finance charges, or changing how they apply payments you have made, all of which are benefiting the financial institution and not you.

Looking for a Credit Card

If after what we have discussed so far you believe it would be of benefit to have a credit card then there are some things to take into consideration when looking to acquire one. Remember, it is not unbiblical to have a credit card but as a steward you need to be able to use it wisely. If you do decide to get a card because of some of the advantages noted be sure to track your use of it carefully to make certain that the "benefits" of using the card are not actually costing more than the benefits are worth. You can use web sites such as www.cardweb.com and www.bankrate.com to compare credit cards.

In selecting a credit card provider you need to keep many factors in mind including the following:

No Annual Fee. Be sure whatever credit card you select that there is no annual fee associated with it. Annual fees can run from $15 to over $100. Some of these try to include enticing awards program benefits. I recently received one that touted an accrual of 5 points for every dollar spent. In the fine print the annual fee was $50. No doubt they likely also made the number of points necessary to acquire one of the rewards higher than they normally might. If something appears to be too good to be true, it likely is. So point number one is get a card with no fees attached for just carrying it.

? Grace Period

Grace Period. The grace period is the number of days you have to make a payment before your payment is considered late. Look for a card with a 25-day grace period. Some cards are changing their agreements to reduce the number of days that you have. American Express a while back reduced the time to 20 days from the time they closed the monthly cycle to when they receive your payment. This is not much time. It usually takes 5-7 days for the company to process and mail the statement and for you to have it. In addition, you need to allow time for your payment to be received and recorded at the company. In reality, you have 7-10 days to make a payment with a 20-day grace period. If you have a vacation planned during that time, plan ahead. Tiogo State Bank on the other hand is quite generous and has a 30-day grace period from the closing of the cycle to the receipt of your payment for both its Visa and MasterCard. Remember the shorter the period the more likely you will get hit with a late fee.

Interest Rate. Although you don't want to keep a balance on your card it is a good idea to have a card that has a low annual interest rate. This way if you are late with a payment or decide to carry a balance for a brief time you will have reasonable finance charges. Be careful, some cards have tiered interest rates based on various factors such as payment history or amount of balance. To encourage you to keep a larger balance they may reduce your interest rate slightly. Don't be fooled by these types of teasers. Also beware of variable rate cards or cards that have a low starting interest rate for a few months and then go up substantially. Get a card that always has a low fixed rate.

Credit Card Pointers

In this brief section we will note some additional pointers to help you deal with credit card companies and to make sure you get on the right track when it comes to selecting and using a credit card.

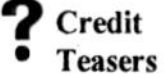

Credit Card Teasers. Each year millions of offers are mailed to families across America to entice them to acquire a credit card from a particular company. On average you will likely receive about 30 of these a year. You may also receive many more by phone. The better your credit score the more offers you will receive. All of these offers from credit card companies are trying to hit a nerve in you by offering something that is difficult to say no to that will make you jump at the offer. These offerings are often called teasers. The goal is to get you hooked on that card realizing that once you have it you are not likely to get rid of it no matter what happens after the offer ends. These offers need to be scrutinized very carefully, especially the fine print. These are the most common teasers:

? Premium Cards

Premium Cards. These cards usually come with an annual fee but they tout their status as "gold" or "platinum" cards. Quite often they offer a variety of additional benefits over a standard card. They are also sometimes marketed by emphasizing a larger reward program than normally found with a credit card. For the steward, status in the world is unimportant. Those who have the cards rarely use the additional benefits. Premium cards are moneymaking machines for the companies and should be avoided by the wise steward.

? Affinity Cards

Affinity Cards. Another way to entice you to acquire a particular card is by associating the card with a particular cause or organization. These are called affinity cards. That is, they have an affinity to a particular group. These are cards that bare the logo or design of a university, sports team, or charitable organization. A portion of the annual fee and/or interest charges goes to the organization on the card. Be aware that it is usually a very small portion of the fees that go to the organization and that many of these cards do have annual fees and higher interest rates. Much more of it goes to the bank. In addition, you lose the possible tax advantage of claiming the donation yourself. You are better off finding a basic credit card with no fee and a low interest rate.

Low-ball Offers. Basic cards are harder to make sound great since they lack the name recognition and status of the cards noted above. As a result, banks will often have ridiculously low "teaser rates" which today are between 0% and 3.9%. The catch, of course, is that the rates only last for a brief time although on occasion you may see they last as long as a year. Don't worry, the banks aren't losing money. They know that most people taking them up on the offer will have large balances to transfer and when the low rate period expires they will get a nice amount of interest on that balance. Those with little or no balance really have no need to look at these types of offers. Also, be careful of any fees that may be charged for transferring balances from another card. Sometimes there can be a minimum $50 fee for each of these types of transactions which can quickly eat away at any savings in interest. The modus operandi here is to be careful and check all the details of the offer. If there are no fees involved and a low rate for a substantial period, with a reasonable rate after the introductory period they might be useful as part of an overall debt reduction plan, otherwise pass on them. Also, keep in mind that when you make payments companies almost invariably will allocate your payment in a way that is best for them and not you. That means they will likely pay off any low-interest portions first so that your balance will accrue more interest to be paid. This can be painful, as some have found out, because they may think that they can keep the 0% interest balance and pay it later but if they use the card for other purchases then they will likely be in for a finance charge since any payment on the purchases will be applied to the 0% interest balance. The lesson here is to be careful of the low-interest introductory offers.

Cash Advances. As with the low-interest offers for new cards, current card owners will often get checks to use for purchases, cash advances, or balance transfers that have low rates associated with them. These are rarely worthwhile for several reasons. More often than not using the checks carries a substantial transaction fee that could eliminate some of the savings. Read the fine print carefully on the offer or on the back of the check. Secondly, any payments you make on your account are usually used to pay off the balance with the lowest rate first, based on your card-member agreement. If you do not use the card for anything else that may be fine but if you use the card for other transactions they will incur the higher rate and your payments will be applied to them last. Cash advances and the like are usually very expensive forms of borrowing – forget it.

It Does Not Hurt to Ask. The last key point to make about credit cards is that if you are not sure about something or something does not look right – ask. If you think the late fee you received was because of slow mail or you think your interest rate is too high in relation to others you see, call the card company. The worst they can say is "no" to your request, but more often than not, they will reduce your rate or refund the fee or finance charges. This is especially true if you have a good payment history with the company. On several occasions over the years I have been able to reverse late payment and finance charges because a check was posted a day or two late on the account. Most companies desire to keep good customers and it is cheaper to keep an existing customer than to try to find a new one.

Debt Consolidation Loans

Whether you are still in school or well into your career you will likely receive many solicitations for debt consolidation loans. Usually the intent is to combine your various debt payments that usually involve several sources into a single monthly loan payment that you pay to a single source. Of course the purveyors of these loans make it appear that they are trying to help you to reduce the amount you are spending. In reality, in almost all cases you will end up paying more for these loans over the long run. There are usually three key benefits touted by those who market these loans that you need to carefully weigh before using them.

? **Debt Consolidation**

The Financial Benefit. All of the loan advertisements will emphasize that you will pay less each month. As with most credit today the emphasis is on the "monthly payment" with little regard to the overall cost of the entire loan. Usually the emphasis will include the reduced interest rate you will pay on the loan. Most consolidation loans are used against the home so they are more secure for the bank and thus they can offer a lower interest rate because of the reduced risk. Some credit cards will tout their transfer capabilities as a way of consolidating debt as well. In relation to any financial benefits you need to look at three questions:

What is the total cost of the debt consolidation until the loan is paid off including any fees to initiate the loan? Most of these debt consolidation loans do not make sense in the long run as you will be paying interest on the balance for a much longer period. Second, have you dealt with the issue that got you into the current state? Many folks find it difficult to control their spending so they need to keep borrowing via credit cards. Once the payments get to be too much they consolidate them, which leaves the monthly payment lower but then they continue to use the credit cards to rack up more debt. Before undertaking any debt consolidation the root problem of spending must be dealt with first. Third, what is the interest rate? Look at the details of the offer carefully. Many times the interest rate is a very low fixed rate for an introductory period and then increases or the rate is variable based on some index that is based on the prime rate.

The Tax Benefit. Often debt consolidation loans are secured by a lien on you home. That is, they basically become a mortgage on your home. As a result the interest from the loan is considered tax deductible in many cases (although you should check to be certain). Even if the interest is deductible you may still end up paying more by taking the debt consolidation approach than by consistently paying off your debt based on a firm plan. Also, as we have noted under taxes, the standard deduction for taxes has been increasing each year making it more difficult for individuals and families to meet the threshold where itemized deductions help. If you don't have enough deductions to itemize them then the interest you pay will not be tax deductible and the benefit is useless. Also, if the loan is not secured by the home then the interest is not deductible at all.

Ease of Payment. A third benefit often touted is the ease of making a single monthly payment rather than incurring costs and taking valuable time related to mailing payments to a multitude of companies. Again there is some truth to this but the question becomes how much will the benefit cost over the long run? If you can pay your bills online for free then the savings is minimal at best and likely not enough to justify debt consolidation.

In summary, debt consolidation may occasionally be of benefit but only in very specific situations where the root problem has been dealt with and the reduced costs are demonstrable over the long term. They are normally not a benefit for those using them and usually cost much more than expected. Carefully consider other alternatives before turning to a debt consolidation loan.

Secured and Unsecured Loans

? **Secured Loan**

? **Collateral**

Perhaps at this point it might be good to note the difference between secured and unsecured loans. The issue is one of collateral. That is, if the loan has something that is pledged against it, then it is considered secured. The collateral is the item that is given in pledge that you will repay the debt. For instance, if you borrow funds to buy a car the loan will be secured by the car so that if you fail to make the payments the bank may then come and take (repossess) the car. The bank can then resell the car in order to recoup the money that they gave you to help purchase the car. Keep in mind that depending on the type of loan you signed you may still have to pay any balance left after the bank sells the car. You want to avoid that kind of debt. Banks like secured loans because they reduce the risk that they will lose their money. The most common secured loans are homes, cars, and major purchases such as appliances.

Unsecured loans involve borrowing based on your promise to repay without any collateral other than the promise itself. Banks, based on your credit rating, may let you borrow small amounts in an unsecured fashion. For larger amounts there may be a requirement to secure the loan with some collateral such as a bank account or other valuable item that you own. Credit cards are for the most part unsecured. As a result they are much riskier and carry much higher interest rates. That is, there is a greater likelihood that the financial institution may not get its funds back. If you default on the payment and there is no collateral the bank has nothing to sell to recoup its funds.

? **Unsecured Loan**

The Christian, whether the loan is secured or not, according to the biblical standard is to repay the debt based on the terms that he has agreed to. Thus, it behooves the Christian to be sure that a loan is fully collateralized. That is, if you are unable to make payments the bank agrees to take the collateral as payment and you owe nothing more. Avoid situations where this is not the case. Otherwise you are presuming that you will have funds in the future that you may not have. This puts you in a state of surety which is unbiblical.

Credit Lines

A final form of borrowing is through what are often referred to as credit or borrowing lines. These are similar to loans with the exception that you access the funds over a period of time rather than receiving a set amount up front. These can be secured or unsecured. For individuals the lines are usually secured against a home. As a result they are often called home equity credit lines and tap the equity that has built up on a home over time. These are not home equity loans, which are more like mortgages. Although parameters may vary widely, most credits lines allow the signer to withdraw funds using checks for a predetermined amount of time after which they must begin paying back whatever has been borrowed. Credit line interest rates are almost always variable so this is usually not a good choice for borrowing funds. Also, check the fine print so that you don't get into a bind if you are unable to repay. Some credit lines have clauses that allow the bank to call the total amount owed at any time.

? **Credit Line**

Financial Problems

Since most financial problems result from poor planning and use of credit we will discuss some of the key ways that individuals use to deal with financial problems and emphasize the ones that make the most sense for the Christian. Keep in mind that it can take a great deal of time to get yourself out of financial difficulties and so you will need to be committed to making it happen if you are to be successful.

Credit Counselors

Although most people might consider resolving financial problems though bankruptcy another alternative is to seek out a financial counselor who can counsel you concerning your debt. Be very careful though how you choose your counselor. There are hundreds of credit-counseling companies springing up that purportedly desire to help you but whose only goal is to make money off you. Companies whose intent is to fix your credit or only deal with your debt and not with your entire spending plan are not worth looking at. Consider checking with your local church to see if there is someone who is qualified to give good Christian counsel concerning finances. Whoever you work with should be a Christian grounded in the Word of God. You need to have a biblical perspective of finance and most of the organizations in this world will not provide that. Another possibility is to contact an organization such as Crown Financial Ministries. They keep track of trained Christian financial counselors who can be of help.

Keep in mind that even with Christian counselors there may be some fee involved. Be sure to ask what, if any fees there are. It is not wrong for the counselor to charge a fee but it should not be exorbitant and should be within your ability to pay. Anyone requiring a large up front fee should be avoided.

The Biblical View of Bankruptcy

Since we are dealing with credit and borrowing in this chapter it seems appropriate to take a moment here to cover the topic of bankruptcy. The term bankruptcy means that an individual is in a state where he is unable to meet his financial obligations or the legitimate claims against him. Often the term "insolvency" is applied which means the inability to pay just debts. Federal law has made it almost appear that bankruptcy is a normal part of life and many see it as a viable way of freeing oneself from financial debts that were the result of poor decisions. Americans have taken advantage of this to file record numbers of bankruptcies in an effort to easily get rid of debt. Is this the biblical perspective? Interestingly, the government now recognizes that many have abused the law and bankruptcy law was recently updated to make it more difficult to get rid of debt without paying it. These changes take effect in October, 2005.

It is a sad commentary to note the number of Christians taking advantage of the bankruptcy law today. Just because something is legal does not mean it is biblical. Prostitution may be legal in some states but it does not make it biblical. The biblical mandate is to repay what you owe. It is clear that those who borrow and do not repay are counted among the wicked (Psalm 37:21). How is it that Christians are so quick to be numbered with the wicked? The key is man's wisdom. That is, Christians rationalize that bankruptcy is a legal way that God has provided through the government to deal with a difficult situation and perhaps will go as far as to say that it provides a blessing to have it available. See how far rationalization will take you? To see something that is wicked as a blessing? See, human logic tries to find ways around the position that we have put ourselves in by poor financial planning.

The biblical perspective of bankruptcy is that we repay our just debts. It is important here to note "just" debts. These are debts that you have promised to repay for which the borrower has not accepted some form of payment. If you can meet with your lenders and get them to reduce your payments, interest rates, or to take something less or different than what was agreed on, then that is biblical. As long you and the lender can work out an agreement then you are abiding by the biblical standard. Luke 12:58-59 notes: "*for as thou goest with thine adverse party before a magistrate, strive in the way to be reconciled with him, lest he drag thee away to the judge, and the judge shall deliver thee to the officer, and the officer cast thee into prison. I say unto thee, thou shalt in no wise come out thence until thou hast paid the very last mite*" (JND).

It is possible that your creditors will force you into bankruptcy. That is something that they, by law, can do. By doing so they are accepting as payment whatever the court allows. The Christian does not initiate the bankruptcy because of financial mismanagement but seeks in every way to repay what is owed by working with the lenders. Once the lender takes action by law to accept whatever the court gives as payment then the Christian is no longer obligated to pay anything since the lender has agreed to accept what the court gives as payment in full for the outstanding debt. The problem is when the Christian initiates the bankruptcy. This forces the lender to accept as payment what the court gives and does not "biblically" absolve you of the need to repay the difference. Remember, when borrowing the lender becomes the master and must be the one that chooses whether an alternative payment is acceptable. Your forcing an unacceptable payment through bankruptcy does not free you from making up the difference to the lender so that the payment is acceptable.

It is possible with our litigious age in this country that you may be served with an unjust financial judgment. There are many in society who make a living by finding ways of suing another or who look for any way of making a financial gain of the smallest accident. This could be a financial award to another party for something that you had no involvement in or an award that far exceeds the repayment of whatever injury you caused. In these types of rare situations the Christian may have no other choice but to file for bankruptcy in order to lessen the burden of the unjust judgment. This is the only reason (an unjust debt) that I can think of, currently, that would provide the Christian a basis for filing for bankruptcy.

The Issues Related to Bankruptcy

It is likely that you have heard of various types of bankruptcies and their effect on a family who undertakes them. Here we will briefly note the various types of bankruptcy you might encounter, and the result and impact of taking a particular approach. Bankruptcy laws have changed recently and it would not be surprising to see them change again, so keep that in mind as you read concerning these options. Also state regulations may be different from state to state. All bankruptcy options have similar drawbacks. These include:

1. Court costs. There are costs related to filing a request with the court.

2. Attorney Fees. Fees are incurred to represent you before the court.

3. A blotch on your credit rating for 7-10 years. Bankruptcy usually makes it much more difficult to secure credit.

4. Possible loss of some assets. Some forms of bankruptcy limit what assets you can keep.

5. Approval of creditors is usually required.

Currently there are four options for individuals and families who determine they should file for bankruptcy:

Chapter 13. Sometimes called the 'wage earner plan" is used in about 30% of bankruptcy cases. It is available to those who have a current, steady income and have a good chance of paying off their debts in a reasonable period of time. It allows the debtor to restructure his debt in order to repay it. There are restrictions on how much debt you can have to enter this form of bankruptcy. Currently the limits are $750,000 for secured debt and $250,000 for unsecured debt. The key benefits of Chapter 13 include:

1. Waiver of late fees and interest payments throughout the payment period.

2. A single regular payment is made to the court, which in turn distributes funds to the creditors.

3. Title to all goods and assets is retained

4. Credit rating not usually as badly tarnished as other forms of bankruptcy.

Chapter 7. Sometimes called "straight bankruptcy" is used in 70% of bankruptcy cases. It is different than Chapter 13 in that rather than attempt a repayment plan it wipes out most debts and the individual starts with a "clean slate." Tax payments, student loans, alimony, and child support are not removed. There are restrictions on what assets can be retained and the limits may differ based on state law. The primary benefits of Chapter 7 include:

1. Most debts are eliminated.

2. Title to some assets can be retained.

Chapter 11. In the past known as "business bankruptcy," can now be used for personal bankruptcies as well. Less than 1% of personal bankruptcies take this form. This can be used if the restrictions and limits imposed by Chapter 13 are not met. It also allows for the restructuring of some or all of the debt with repayment over time. Usually this process is much longer and more expensive to pursue.

Chapter 20. Really this is a bankruptcy procedure rather than part of the code. It is called chapter 20 because it combines portions of Chapter 13 and Chapter 7. Usually this procedure allows the debtor to remove all unsecured debt as would usually occur in Chapter 7 and restructure secured debt as would be found in Chapter 13.

New Law. The Bankruptcy Abuse Prevention and Consumer Protection Act of 2005 still allows for the above bankruptcy proceedings. As the title of the acts implies the law undertakes to reduce the abuse of the proceedings that are available and forces consumers and attorneys to take greater responsibility for the their part in the case. Although there are many changes in the bankruptcy law the basic new tenets include:

- Income limit restrictions based on the state of residence.

- Restrictions on the determination of the state of residence.

- Emphasis on more accurate and significant supporting documentation.

- Restrictions that increase how much time must expire between filings.

- Required education and financial counseling for filers.

- Some additional restrictions on what debts can be discharged.

- Emphasis on proper attorney counsel and verification of facts.

- Restrictions on the use of automatic stays (where the creditor could not pursue payment of amounts owed).

- New criteria for determining presumption of abuse or fraud by a debtor (for example, how much was charged on credit cards recently, or filing when there is enough income to support paying debt).

- Restrictions to reduce the assets not subject to recovery.

As you can see, the emphasis of the new law is to reign in the abuse of the old law and make individuals take more responsibility for their financial decisions. Critics are concerned that these new regulations will negatively impact the uninsured that have financial difficulties because of large medical bills that cannot be repaid. The results of the new law will not be known until sometime after the law takes effect in October, 2005.

As a reminder for the Christian these options would only be important if they were forced into bankruptcy by creditors or if served with an unjust judgment.

Making Major Purchase Decisions

Since credit is quite often used to make major purchases we now take this next section to look at likely major purchases you will make in your lifetime. We discuss how to provide for those purchases and the role that credit should play in them.

Providing a Shelter

The Keys to Finding a Shelter

For the Christian renting or purchasing a home should be carefully considered as with any purchase decision. The first key is identifying the need. Most families now buy homes much larger than they need. The average poor person in the United States has a larger shelter than the average person or family in Paris or London. Quite often our decisions for homes are not based on need but rather a host of other less important items such as the appearance, how many garages, whether it has a recreation room, a separate bedroom for every child, and the like. Some items to consider in the home purchase or apartment rental that relate to need:

Location. There are a good number of cost issues related to location. There are two perspectives when looking at location, the national one dealing with where in the country we will live and then the local one once we have selected the state. When looking at the local choice we might look at issues such as: Where is work located in relation to the home? The further from work the more resources required to travel to and from it. How close is it to shopping and other services you need on a regular basis? Do you drive your children to school? If so, the home location will affect the cost. Often we like to choose the nicest neighborhoods with the best schools. These are often the most expensive neighborhoods with the highest taxes. Remember, supply and demand does have an effect. Perhaps finding a clean neighborhood with good schools will suffice. Perhaps you can find another Christian who would help with home schooling in a different neighborhood. Keep in mind that location will also influence the cost of your car insurance.

When looking at the issue of what state to live in just about everything related to costs is affected by it. Some states, such as Tennessee, Texas, and Florida, have no or limited income taxes, which can be a big plus. On the other hand other taxes may be higher such as sales or property taxes. Costs of goods will also vary. Gas in Connecticut for instance can be up to 30 cents a gallon higher than Tennessee. Depending on how many gallons a year you use that can be a large sum. If you use 20 gallons a week that would amount to a difference of over $300 a year. Of course this deals with the whole issue of cost of living. This is sometimes reflected in the higher salaries that are available in these states. Salaries are higher in Connecticut than Tennessee. The question is whether the higher salaries offset the additional cost. This can be determined by using a cost of living calculator to determine the difference between two locations. Several sites have such calculators including www.erieri.com.

Size. Be careful here. As with location there are cost issues related to the size of a home regardless of location. The larger the home the more you will pay for utilities such as electricity, and oil or gas for heating. The larger the home the more the insurance will cost and the greater the taxes will be (if you are buying). Keep the square footage for your home reasonable to reduce these costs.

Access. Keep in mind any special requirements such as ramps necessary for wheel chair access. Usually these are cheaper if already part of a home being purchased or rented. Making such changes after the selection can be expensive, although, you may be able to find some Christian brothers and sisters willing to help you with the modifications at a reasonable cost.

Remember the key in finding a shelter is "identify your need." Try to keep the desires and wants in check, as they will always have you purchase more than you need. Remember many other costs are influenced by your decision of home selection.

The Apartment Rental Process

Although many people own homes there is nothing wrong with renting an apartment or home if that is more affordable. Overextending yourself to purchase a home you cannot afford will likely lead to disaster including the loss of any funds you put into the home purchase. This is especially important for individuals or couples just getting started. Here are some of the steps involved in a property rental:

Need. Establish the criteria for selecting a rental home based on the notes above concerning what is actually needed. Once you have established what you are looking for you can investigate rental availabilities through various means including the classified section of a newspaper, friends, and real estate agents. A real estate agent can be helpful if you are new to the area.

Rental Application. Almost all owners of rental properties (sometimes called landlords) will require the completion of a rental application in order to be considered for filling a vacancy. The application will require personal information and information about past rentals, employment, and references. Many forms also include permission to secure your credit report from a credit reporting agency. The goal of the landlord is to make sure whoever he rents to will keep up the premises and pay the rent on time. The rental application may also include an application fee, especially if there is competition for the vacant living units. Sometimes application fees will ferret out those who are not serious about a vacancy or who would attempt to get away without paying rent.

Rental Security and Deposit. The landlord will check your application, and will likely check your credit report and references to make sure that you are a strong candidate for the vacancy. If you are selected for a vacant unit you will be likely asked to supply a rental security deposit. This can be anywhere from 1 to 3 months rent. This is put into a contingency fund to protect the landlord in case you damage the premises. By law the landlord must keep this separate and pay interest on the account. In addition, some will require you to pay the first and last month's rent up front. This protects the landlord in case you take off before the lease is up. You may also be assessed a pet deposit or fee as well. Some of these may be nonrefundable. Some also charge "pet rent" so be careful to check the terms. Be sure to get receipts for your deposits and rent you give.

Rental Lease. When you make your security and rent deposits you will likely be required to sign a lease for the rental unit. Keep in mind that these are written to protect the landlord and not you. It covers all of the rules regarding how you can use the unit and associated grounds as well as the steps that will be taken if there is a disagreement or non-payment of rent, and the like. You may want to request time to review it and in consultation with the landlord change any terms you do not agree with. When my son attended college I was required to sign a lease for his apartment and after reading it changed some of the terms to limit my liability. The property management had no problem with it. It does not hurt to ask about or clarify the terms. Use an attorney if you don't know what to look for. Remember, it is a legal document you are signing.

The Inspection. Normally there will be a thorough inspection of the apartment completed by you and the landlord so that any imperfections can be noted as existing in the apartment before you lease it. You and the landlord will sign the form as well. Be sure that this is done and that you receive a copy. Be sure everything that you see as an imperfection in the apartment or home is listed. Examples might include, peeling paint, stained countertops or floors, any chips, holes, or cracks in woodwork or walls, anything that is not working properly at move in, any faded or worn flooring, carpet, and tile, and the like. Remember if it is not listed you are assuming responsibility to fix it before giving up the apartment, otherwise the landlord can use your security deposit to fix it.

Rent Payments. Once you are in your living unit be sure to take care of it so that when you leave you can get your security deposit back. Be sure to pay your rent on time each month. Your payment history may become part of your credit history and will provide a means to demonstrate your ability to make a timely regular payment.

The Home Buying Process

Most of you reading this text at some point in your life will seek to purchase a home of your own. Let's look together at the key steps in the home buying process and what you can expect as you go through them. These should serve as a reasonable guide for you when you decide to undertake the process.

Need. As with rentals we need to first establish what it is we need to look for. We can again follow the guidelines noted earlier in this section dealing with identifying what is really needed.

Funding. Consider carefully how you will fund your home. We will look at the funding options in the next section but at this point it is important to have arranged any funding you need. Good home deals can be lost because you have a funding contingency (such as selling your current home) that another buyer does not have. Most people at this point either become pre-qualified or pre-approved. Becoming pre-approved is the much stronger of the two. Pre-qualification means that you qualify for funding based on the information you gave the lending institution while pre-approved means the financial institution has checked everything and has approved you for a loan. Pre-qualification does not guarantee approval. If you plan on funding the home using your own investments (a great idea) then make sure the funds are readily accessible. You'll likely need them within 30 days or so of signing a contract to buy a home.

Attorney. Be sure you have lined up an attorney that you can use to quickly review contracts or other paperwork related to buying a home as well as for the closing when it is time to take possession of it. It is best to find your own attorney through friends or through the church. As always it is best to find a trusted Christian brother or sister in the field to handle these things.

Real Estate Agent. Once you have the need, funding, and attorney established you are ready to touch base with a qualified real estate agent to help in your search. It is best to work with an exclusive buyers agency. That means that the company and the realtor only work for buyers and do not sell real estate. Be careful, there are many buyers agents that work for companies that sell real estate. This still can be a conflict of interest if it is not carefully handled. Do not work with a "dual agency" set up. By law selling agencies must represent the sellers and not the buyers. You want someone to look out for your best interest. Whatever you do be sure to seek appropriate assistance before signing documents. The buyer's agent fee should come from selling the real estate and not from you. That is, the fee that the seller pays to his agent for selling the home is split between the seller's agent and the buyer's.

The Contract. Once you have located a property you are interested in making an offer on the agent will help you fill out a standard real estate contract for purchase and give a deposit. It is better to have this reviewed by your attorney before signing it although many do not because of the standard nature of the contract. This of course is up to you. Just because the contract is standard does not mean you cannot modify it for your benefit. Be sure to include any contingencies that you must take care of before buying the property. This might include selling your current home or securing funding (although at this point you should have already secured the funding). An inspection contingency is very common and should be included. This usually gives you ten days to have the property professionally inspected and to notify the seller of any deficiencies. If you want to get another individual to review the property and approve it, such as a contractor, friend, or relative be sure to note a contingency that gives you a few days to receive his approval. It also gives you a way out if after a few days you have second thoughts about the property.

The Deposit. When you make an offer on the property you will submit a deposit that will be applied to the purchase price when you buy the house. You will receive your deposit back if the contract contingencies cannot be fulfilled by you or the buyer. If the contingencies are fulfilled by both you and the buyer then you are obligated to purchase the property or lose your deposit.

The deposit, contrary to popular belief does not have to be a huge amount. The thinking is that the larger the amount of the deposit the more likely you are to go through with the purchase. In reality most people once they put a deposit down go through with the purchase regardless of the size of the deposit. That is, undertaking this effort is no small matter and people have no interest in losing any deposit. That being said, if folks had to walk away from a deal for some reason they would rather lose a small amount of money rather than a large amount. The key is that the deposit becomes a payment to the seller if you are unable to complete the sale. It pays the seller for the time he has lost in having his property tied up by you. The deposit should be based on the cost of keeping the home tied up for a brief period rather than a percentage of the purchase price. If you expect the seller to tie up his house for three months while you sell yours without any way for him to sell it to a higher bidder then the deposit should be a bit more. If you are doing a standard closing within 30 days a $1000 deposit should be plenty. We have used that kind of deposit when purchasing a home of over $200,000 with no problem.

The Inspection. When you agree to purchase a home you will usually have ten days to have it professionally inspected. This is extremely important. You want to make sure you are not going to end up purchasing major headaches that will cost thousands of dollars to repair. We have found it difficult to find a good inspector. We have only seen one very good home inspector in all of our years of using them (and he was inspecting for the buyer of our home) and even he missed seeing termites the first time through. Be sure the inspector has building experience and is reputable. Also check their policy if they miss something that should have been caught. Many companies write the inspection contract in such a way that anything that was missed is excluded. You can also request a home warranty from the seller as a safety measure against the malfunction of a major component within the first year.

If the inspection uncovers problems that you want the seller to fix you usually have a few days (based on the sales contract) to present them to the seller. The seller can agree to fix them and the contract stays in force, refuse to fix them and give you a reduction in the sales price so you can fix them, or refuse to fix them and give you your deposit back if you don't want to continue with the purchase. Usually something can be worked out by you and the seller that will be acceptable to both parties. As a result of this negotiation the contract may need to be modified.

Insurance. You will need to secure insurance for the home if you plan on using funding from a third-party such as a bank. Even if you are paying cash it is a good idea to insure your home against loss due to fire or natural disaster. We discuss insurance in more detail later in the text.

? Closing

The Closing. This is the event at which the home is actually transferred to you. Once all of the contingencies have been satisfied a closing date is arranged within the time frame specified in the sales contract. There will be a plethora of forms and documents you will need to sign at the closing especially if you are using a financial institution to fund a mortgage on the home. It is at the closing where you actually receive the keys to the home. Be sure your attorney is with you and explains any documents you do not understand. It is not unusual to have several dozen documents to sign as part of the closing.

The Mortgage Payment. If you rent, your rental payments are due at the beginning of the period (usually the beginning of the month) for which you are renting. With a mortgage the payment is due at the end of the period (in arrears). That is, you are going to pay for borrowing money from the bank for the period (usually a month). Be sure to pay your mortgage payment on time. You usually have a 15 day grace period to pay it before a late fee will be assessed. Be careful, late fees can be substantial, such as 5% of the late amount. So if you have a $1200 mortgage payment you could be assessed a $60 late fee each month.

The Funding for the Home Purchase

The home purchase is often the largest purchase a family will make. The question will arise as to how such a large purchase should be funded? Keep in mind when purchasing a home there are many additional costs that are not funded by a financial institution that are paid by you. The key housing components to be funded include:

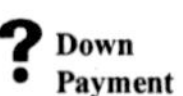

The Down Payment (one time payment). This is the amount your provide in cash toward the purchase of the home.

The Loan (one time amount). This is the amount provided by a third party to you so you can pay the amount left after your down payment. This must be repaid to the bank over a predetermined period from your own funds (usually on a monthly basis).

Home Purchase Costs	
Item	**Fee**
Origination Fee	0-2%
Loan Discount Fee (Points)	0-4%
Attorney Fees	$300-$750
Transfer Tax	.5-2%
Documentation Fees	$50-$300
Underwriting Fees	$200-$400
Delivery Fees	$20-$75
Title Insurance (Bank)	$250-$500
Title Insurance (Owner)	$250-$500
Home Inspection Fees	$200-$600
Real Estate Commissions	4-7%
Real Estate Taxes	Varies
Tax Service Fee	$50-$150
Utility Adjustments	Varies
Home Insurance	$600-$1200
Recording Fees	$25-200
Survey Fees	$650-$1000
Home Warranty	$350-$600
Flood Certification Fee	$15-$25
Pre-paid Interest	.005-.10%
Appraisal Fee	$100-$400
Credit Report	$15-$50
These fees can vary based on whether you are buying or selling and what has been agreed to in the sales contract for the home. Adjustment items will vary based on when the home is sold or purchased. If you are buying and there is no loan then some of these fees would not apply. The fees will also vary by geographic location.	

Exhibit 5-5. Estimated Home Purchase Costs.

Closing and Loan Fees (one time payment). The costs associated with purchasing and financing a home. These can run anywhere from 0-5% of the loan amount. The lower the fees the higher the interest rate on the loan involved. If there is no loan involved then the amount will be only for closing related costs. Exhibit 5-5 gives a listing of possible fees that you may incur when purchasing or selling a home. As you can see there can be many costs involved and the purchase or sale should not be undertaken lightly.

Principal (monthly payment). An amount you pay each month that reduces the amount owed to the bank.

? **Principal**

Interest (monthly payment). Usually the largest part of you monthly payment is the interest you owe in exchange for the amount you have currently borrowed from the bank. Basically, interest is payment for the use of funds.

? **Interest**

Pre-payment Penalties. Be sure if you fund your home with a loan that there are no prepayment penalties for paying it off early. As a Christian you want to pay it off as soon as possible and pre-payment penalties are just a way of the bank getting some additional funds they will lose because of the risk associated with you paying one rate and then when they re-lend the funds they may receive a lower rate than if you have gone the full term of your loan. Remember the financial institution is looking out for its welfare not yours.

Escrow (monthly payment). If you have borrowed funds from a financial institution they may also require you to deposit a portion of your annual taxes and/or insurance (sometimes called hazard insurance) in an escrow account so there will be sufficient funds when they come due. The bank will pay these directly. Even if you paid cash for the home you will need to set these amounts aside for when they come due.

? **Escrow**

PMI (monthly payment). Private mortgage insurance is usually required if the amount you are borrowing is more than 80% of the value of the home. This protects the bank in case you are unable to repay the mortgage and they cannot get their money back on reselling the home. It is very expensive insurance and should be avoided if at all possible. Financial institutions do have some creative ways of avoiding PMI using second mortgages, but it may also increase your interest rate on at least the part borrowed above 80%.

? **PMI**

Utilities and Home Repairs. Unless you are moving from a larger home to a smaller one you will need to budget for the increased costs of utilities for the larger home. Also, you will need to put aside funds for unexpected repairs such as a new water heater or dishwasher.

These are the key budgetary items to consider when buying a home. They can be substantial and so should not be taken lightly. Now, let's discuss some of the key ways we can fund a home purchase and identify the best approaches.

Savings. I realize that this may seem like a novel, if not impossible, idea for the reader, but individuals who start early can save enough funds to buy a home without having to borrow for it. This takes careful planning and restraint in spending but it can be done and is the best way of purchasing a home. A nice home can still be purchased in some parts of the country in the $60,000-$100,000 range. As long as you don't try to purchase in the nice areas of major metropolitan cities you probably can find some thing affordable in a good location. That means cities like New York, Boston, San Francisco, and the like probably won't be on the list. Of course you can buy a million dollar house in most any city where the housing prices are relatively reasonable but that is not our goal here. Remember, you will not likely duplicate what your parents acquired over a period of 30 years or more in just one or two years. It does take time – a tough sell in our instant gratification culture. Don't let the culture rule you, rather, let Christ rule in your heart and you will do the right thing.

Let's assume you and your wife just married and would like to have $100,000 to buy a home in 8 years. How much would you need to set aside assuming you could get 8% on your investment? Remember our sinking fund formula earlier in the text? That is, what would I need to save per period now to have the amount in the future? We are bringing the future to the present, in a sense. If we used a basic table such as the one in Appendix A we would find that for every dollar we need we must set aside .007470 dollars per month. If we multiply that by 100,000 we get $747 a month. If you can find a way of saving $747 a month for 8 years at the rate of 8% you will be able to buy a home with cash in 8 years. Of course if you save more you can do it sooner or have more to spend and the same is true if the interest earned is higher. If you only can save $500 a month then you could use the future value formula to see how much you would have in eight years.

The key here is to realize that most people could actually own their homes debt-free by the time they are 40-45 if they were to carefully save for them. If you start at age 20-25 that gives you 20 years to save for a home. The problem is that many of us do not want to wait that long. If you wish to shorten the time frame then you must increase the amount saved, reduce the amount spent on a home, or increase the interest earned on your savings.

Borrowing for Your Home. As we have already noted it is not unbiblical to borrow and in some areas of the country it is almost necessary because of the disparity between salaries and housing prices. If you do decide to borrow be sure that you do not put yourself into a poor or unbiblical position regarding borrowing. You want to:

Repay what you borrow. Avoid putting yourself in a position where you can not afford to repay your obligation. A larger down payment can help to avoid this scenario. Thus, if you had to quickly sell the home and repay the debt you would be able to. If your down payment is too small you may not be able to sell it at a price that allows you to repay the debt. The world will say use other people's money to buy your home with 0% down schemes, but Christians should avoid putting themselves in such situations where they are likely, as a result, to be in a "debt" laden situation that presents the very possibility that they would be unable to pay the borrowed funds if they had to.

Use a Fully Collateralized Loan. That is, make sure that if you must give the home back to the bank that it is the extent of your liability. The return of the home to the bank is full payment for the outstanding loan. Be sure this is the case even if they were to foreclose on the home. Foreclosure is the process by which the bank forces you to give up the home so they can resell it to pay the outstanding loan. The parameters that determine when such a proceeding starts are spelled out in the loan papers you sign at closing. Whether you give it up voluntarily or through foreclosure (which should be avoided) you want your liability to end when the home is returned to the bank. Many banks today also make you responsible for any amount left on the loan after reselling the home and applying the proceeds from the sale to the loan. Of course, if the home is worth more than what is left on the loan it would make more sense for you to sell it rather than giving it to the bank even if there is a clause that states the bank will give you any proceeds that exceed the amount left on the loan. The problem is that bank-owned property may not fetch the same value that you could get if you sold it first on the market and the foreclosure will also show up on your credit report.

Avoid Private Mortgage Insurance (PMI). Make every effort to avoid PMI payments on a loan. They are excessively expensive and only protect the bank and line the pockets of insurance companies. PMI is often required on loans that are more than 80% of the value of the home. The insurance protects the lender in case you default on your loan. Be careful if you must borrow more than 80% as you might get yourself into a position where you can't afford to repay the loan if you needed to. If you currently have PMI the laws have changed that require the insurance to be removed when the amount of your loan is less than 80% of the value of the home. This will occur as you pay down the principal and as home values increase. You may be required to have an appraisal on your home in order to verify that PMI can be removed. This can cost $300-$400 so be pretty sure that an appraisal will show that your loan is less than 80% of the value of the home.

Avoid an Adjustable Rate Mortgage (ARM). There are many adjustable rate mortgage products available but rarely do they make sense for the Christian who is following the biblical perspective on borrowing and debt. These types of mortgages usually have a fixed interest rate for an introductory period usually of 1, 3, 5, 7, or 10 years and then the rate varies based on some financial index that is published in a national newspaper. The rate is usually capped so that it cannot increase or decrease more than 2% a year and not more than 6% over the life of the loan. The loan is usually considered a 30-year loan. The benefit of course is the low initial rate, especially for those loans with a low introductory interest rate period and the possibility that the rate could go down in the future. With rates as low as they are this is unlikely to be of much benefit since the rates are currently near record lows. These types of loans are enticing because they allow someone to qualify to buy a home, at the low starting rate, for which they otherwise would not qualify. As a result though it presumes that you will be able to afford the increased payments in the future if the rates go up (which they almost always do since the introductory rate is artificially low). In addition, many who use these loans also have small down payments increasing the odds they will not be able to sustain the home.

? **Variable Rate**

ARMs are also used as a tool by those who only expect to be in a location for a short period of time. For instance if you will be moving in 3 years based on the plans of the military or your company some will recommend taking an ARM to take advantage of the initial low rate and then resell the home before the rates increase dramatically. This again presumes a great deal and should not be entered into lightly. What happens if the company decides not to move you? What if rates rise faster than expected? What if you cannot qualify to refinance to a fixed-rate loan when you need to?

Too many questions are left unanswered when pursuing an ARM. If you do choose to use an ARM because of one the noted benefits, be sure to make a significant down payment to avoid PMI and keep yourself out of surety where you have no certain way to repay. At least with a good down payment you would be able to resell the home and pay the loan. One other possible use of the ARM is if you want to really have a 5-10 year mortgage payoff. If the rates are significantly lower for the 5, 7, or 10 year ARM than a 15, 20, or 30 year fixed-rate mortgage then it might make sense to use one of those ARMs and then pay it as if you were going to have it paid off by the time the introductory rate expires. Thus, if you decided to use a 10-year ARM you could create a 10 year payment schedule that would have the entire loan paid in ten years at the lower rate. Often though, 15 year fixed rate mortgages have lower rates than 10-year ARMs. This is because there is risk on the bank's part that the rates could go down after the ten years. Beyond these possibilities, there are too many risks in taking on such a loan.

? **Conventional Loan**

? **Fixed Rate**

Fixed Rate Mortgages. The most popular and predictable loan for homes are the fixed rate type (sometimes referred to as conventional loans). If you are going to borrow for your home then for the Christian this will likely make the most sense. The benefit here is that the interest rate does not change and the payment schedule is fixed and known in advance. This can be very helpful when trying to create a spending plan. Although most fixed-rate loans are for 30 years you can also find 15 and 20 year fixed rate loans. The 15-year fixed rate loans have become more popular now that rates are at record lows. The benefits of a shorter period are that you will receive a lower rate and second you will pay substantially less interest over the life of the loan. Of course the tradeoff is that you must make larger payments each month to the bank. If you are not sure if you can sustain the 15 year monthly payments you can go with a 30-year fixed rate which will mean a slightly higher interest rate but will allow you to pay at the 15-year rate if you choose or revert to the 30-year payment amount. That is, there is nothing wrong with paying a loan faster by using larger payments. It will decrease the length of the loan and save significant amounts in interest expense. Be sure there are no prepayment penalties that kick in for paying off too much of the loan in a year.

Interest-only loans. Another hot loan instrument lately is the interest-only loan. As with the ARM it allows the individual to qualify to purchase a home they normally would not be able to purchase. This is because for the first several years of the loan the borrower only needs to make interest payments on the loan. As a result, the payments are lower. The problems are similar to those of the ARM. There is an assumption made that you will be able to afford the higher payments when the principal payments come due. In addition, many who take on these loans live in areas where property values have escalated quickly. If the real estate encounters a correction like it did in the late 1980s these folks will lose their homes and will likely still owe money on any outstanding balance after the sale of the home. As many as 50 percent of home loans in the San Francisco area are of this type. What many don't realize is that the use of this instrument has driven the price of houses up even further since it allows more buyers to compete for the homes that come on the market. This type of loan should be avoided by the Christian.

Gifts. Often family members desire to help a young couple who are buying there first home. Banks are becoming sticklers on this and usually require a letter and perhaps documentation showing that they have the gift funds available. If you decide to help (or receive help) in this area be sure it is clear that it is a gift. Much heartache and family disunity can be avoided if it is understood up front what the intentions are. If you are going to lend (or borrow) funds at no interest then that should be made clear. Keep in mind it would be better to make a gift if you know that the individual would never be able to repay you.

Lending. You may find a brother or sister who is willing to lend you some funds you need to purchase your home. The purpose of course is the help one another as a testimony to the world. Although the New Testament says little about lending between believers, the Old Testament emphasized not charging each other interest (Exodus 22:25; Deuteronomy 23:19-20; Psalm 15:5; Ezekiel 18:12-13). Thus, if you desire to help some believers purchase a home then you should not expect interest in return but repayment of the amount borrowed is expected.

As with other purchases, seek to be a wise steward when making a shelter determination. Keep in mind that it takes time to acquire the assets necessary to afford owning a home. Don't try to do too much all at once. It is better to build your savings and prepare for the time that you will be ready to purchase a home.

Providing Transportation

The Keys to Acquiring Transportation

If there is one area that Christians have followed the world's lead, it is in how they buy cars. American's rather than looking at the automobile as a form of transportation now view it as a status symbol or as a home on wheels. By viewing the car from this perspective we also view the amount we spend differently. If we see it as a home on wheels we certainly can't go without individually controlled, comfortable leather sets, or without the state of the art surround sound system, oh, and don't forget the DVD system for the kids and while you are at it you might want to install a refrigerator for those drinks and snacks you might need. See, before you know it you can rationalize spending thousands more on a vehicle just by how we view it. For the Christian the issues of having a car for a status symbol should never come to mind since we are not of this world. So the idea that a Christian needs a Mercedes, or Lexus to show God's blessing is ludicrous (though many preachers of the gospel drive them, sadly to say). The Christian recognizes that his blessings are spiritual, as he is seated in the heveanlies with Christ. Even if you spend many hours in your vehicle are all of the accoutrements that dealers try to sell necessary? Probably not.

With that as an introduction the keys to buying a car are as follows:

Establish the Need. As with purchasing a home it is easy to let wants and desires to influence your buying decision. Usually the result is a more expensive car than is required for our needs. We assume you have determined that public transportation will not due for your need but it is something to be considered, especially if you are looking at buying a second car. If public transportation is available consider the tradeoffs of cost, time, and convenience of using that mode of transportation. Based on those tradeoffs if you determine that you need to buy a car then make sure you list what you need in a vehicle. Will you need to carry goods or many passengers? Do you need to be able to tow a trailer? Will it be used for work, and if so, what type? Answering any questions like these will help you to identify the type of vehicle you will need.

The American public has been brainwashed into the idea that it is a good idea to get a new car every two to three years. This is great for the dealers and manufacturers but of little value to the people buying them. Purchase a good vehicle and plan on sticking with it for as long as it meets your needs, is safe to drive, and is less expensive to maintain than replacing it. A car almost always costs less in the long run to repair than to replace. We owned our last car for ten years and had replaced the engine and had the transmission rebuilt, but we have spent much less than if we had replaced our car in either case.

Funding. Carefully consider how you will fund your purchase. If at all possible pay cash for your purchase. When borrowing people generally buy more vehicle than they need and as a result also pay more in recurring costs to maintain the vehicle. If you decide to pay cash you are much more likely to be careful to conserve it because you already have it and might want to use some of it for other things. Consider beginning to save now for purchasing a vehicle in the future. If you currently have no car payment, consider making the equivalent of a car payment to a savings instrument so that so you will have cash to pay when you are ready to purchase your next vehicle. We discuss the funding issue in more detail later in this section.

Research. Unlike real estate where you can use a buyer's agent that works exclusively for you, purchasing a car involves primarily you. This means you must research the market carefully to see what ways would be best to fill your need. Whether you decide to buy a new or used car you need to perform research, visit car dealers, and test and evaluate vehicles. Exhibit 5-6 provides a list of sites that can be helpful in evaluating you alternatives. Consumer Reports is available at most libraries and they put out an annual car issue each

Automobile Research Sites
www.consumerreports.org
www.kbb.com
www.edmunds.com
www.nada.com
www.carfax.com
www.autocheck.com
auto.consumerguide.com
www.carsmart.com
www.theautochannel.com
www.trustmymechanic.com

Exhibit 5-6. Automobile Research Sites on the Web.

April that discusses all of the ins and outs of various vehicles, the best used cars, and the repair records of most vehicles. They also offer a paid service that will provide a detailed analysis of the vehicle costs for new vehicles so you will have an idea of how much to offer for a vehicle. See Consumer Reports web site for a sample of what the report looks like. The internet can also be a great tool and a number of web sites are noted in the table. Carfax and similar services can be quite valuable for weeding out cars that have been in accidents or natural disasters. They keep track of vehicle histories based on information from a variety of public sources. A sample of a report can be viewed on the Carfax web site at www.carfax.com. Although helpful, do not assume all vehicle-related issues have been reported to these services.

Insurance and taxes. As you look for a vehicle you need to keep in mind that the vehicle selected can significantly influence your insurance and taxes. Some states have personal property taxes on motor vehicles based on the value of the car. The newer the vehicle the more taxes you pay. An older vehicle no matter how great the car is will pay less tax. Insurance premiums can be much higher for vehicles that are more prone to being stolen. You can find out information on this likelihood at www.cars.com or the Insurance Institute for Highway Safety at www.hwysafety.org/vehicle%5Fratings/ictl/ictl.htm. Premiums also run higher for newer vehicles because of their greater value to replace in a collision. Also, where you garage the vehicle can also influence the rate you pay. Rates are higher in locations where car theft is higher. Keep in mind, as we have noted previously, that risk is the key factor that the insurance companies must consider so that it does not end up paying out more in claims than it takes in via premiums.

Mileage. Americans are buying huge numbers of vehicles that are much larger than they need and also use far more gas than smaller vehicles. The number of trucks, SUVs, and mini-vans on the road has grown dramatically over the last ten years. Many of the younger buyers have not experienced the costs related to the oil shortage back in the early 1970s when there was the impetus to create cars that used gas very efficiently. As is the case with supply and demand, once the shortage passed, people started to buy big again, most of the time not based on need. This is now beginning to hurt some as prices have now soared to $2.00 a gallon or more in many parts of the country due to various events or perceptions of events around the world. If the trend continues you will see a trend back to the efficient vehicles in order to reduce overall costs. For the Christian it is a good idea to count this cost up front and as a good steward to purchase a vehicle that produces good gas mileage. Unless there is an absolute need because of work, family size, or location to have one of the big three (truck, SUV, or mini-van) avoid them.

The Car Buying Process

Assuming you have evaluated your need, identified your funding source, and done your research you are ready to go through the actual buying process. The process basically involves locating a vehicle, evaluating it based on the predefined needs and research, buying it, and then maintaining it. Before tackling those steps the question is bound to arise based on dealer marketing whether one should buy used or new and whether a lease is a viable option.

New versus used. If you already own a car you may also have the option of repair. That is, some people who start looking for a car do so because their current vehicle requires some type of repair. Although each situation is unique the following general conclusions can be drawn. It is almost always cheaper to repair a car than buy a new one (unless you have loved one who owns the dealership or something of that nature). In a vast number of cases it is cheaper to repair than to buy a used car. It is almost always cheaper to buy a used car than a new car. New cars are rarely a wise choice unless you plan on keeping them for many years.

With these general points in mind the Christian, as a good steward of the resources that God has given will only consider a new car as a long term purchase that will last many years; normally ten years or more. With that in mind, if you expect, due to family changes (e.g. addition of children) to need to change vehicles in a shorter time frame a new car should be avoided. Most new cars loose a significant amount of value just by their being purchased and driven off of the dealer lot (sometimes as much as 25%). It makes no financial sense to be buying new cars every two or three years no matter how great the world portrays that scenario. If you do purchase a new vehicle and maintain it well for ten or more years then the per-year cost can be quite low.

To Repair or not to Repair, that is the Question	
Scenario: Barbara has a 1995 Saturn SW2 with 188,000 miles on it that needs a new transmission. The engine was replaced at 150,000 miles. What should she do?	
Alternative 1	Get the transmission fixed for $2700.
Alternative 2	Buy a new car that has a 3 year, 100,000 mile bumper to bumper warranty for $22,000 with $2700 down and 6 years at 5%.
Alternative 3	Buy a 2002 used car that has 63,000 miles on it for $13,000 with $2700 down and 6 years at 9%.

Exhibit 5-7. Car Repair Scenario.

Exhibit 5-7 gives an example of a scenario my wife and I had to make a decision on as regards whether to repair our vehicle. As you can see even though we were discussing a major repair bill the cost of the repair still was significantly less than buying another vehicle whether used or new unless we purchased a used vehicle that also had significant mileage on it. The key reasons for not repairing a vehicle or for deciding to seek a different vehicle really boil down to three things: 1) the vehicle no longer meets the needs of the family, 2) the car can not be made safe to drive, or 3) the cost of repair is beyond the cost of purchasing a used car of similar characteristics that needs no repair. We went with the repair. Beyond purchasing a new car as a long-term purchase, if a replacement vehicle is needed the used car is the way to go. Exhibit 5-8 shows that a new car purchase is only good long-term.

Buy versus lease. Another question often raised in the buying process is whether one should buy or lease the vehicle whether new or used. The answer is simply that it never makes financial sense for an individual or family to lease a car for personal use. There may be some tax benefits for businesses that lease vehicles but those benefits do not accrue to individuals and there are few benefits to leasing and we repeat NO LONG-TERM FINANCIAL ADVANTAGES. Considering there are no long-term financial advantages and there are many possible disadvantages the recommendation to Christians is to avoid leasing. When you lease you are basically renting the vehicle. Here are some of the key issues:

? Lease

1. You do not own the car. At the end of the lease you must return it. This puts you right where the dealer wants you – replacing your vehicle every three years on average. There is usually an option to purchase the vehicle at the end of the lease but such a combination of a lease followed by a purchase does not create financial benefit and often costs more. There is the slight benefit that you get to try the car before buying it at the end of the least but it seems like an expensive way of getting to know a car.

Buy versus Repair of Car (6 year cost)						
Item	**Repair**		**Used**		**New**	
Value	1500.00		13000.00		22000.00	
Price	2700.00		13000.00		22000.00	
Down Payment	2700.00		2700.00		2700.00	
Car Payment (Monthly/Total)	0.00	0.00	185.67	13368.24	310.83	22379.76
Depreciation	1000.00		8000.00		13000.00	
Insurance	2070.00		3360.00		4740.00	
Fees and Taxes (10%)	270.00		1300.00		2200.00	
2% Property Tax (Annual/Total)	54.00	324.00	260.00	1560.00	440.00	2640.00
Fuel	810.00		810.00		810.00	
Maintenance	12000.00		6000.00		3000.00	
Total Cost (Monthly/Total)	252.42	18174.00	404.14	29098.24	534.30	38469.76
Value of Car	500.00		5000.00		9000.00	
Value of Savings (5% Interest)	23611.50		10902.76		0.00	
Total Value	24111.50		15902.76		9000.00	
Actual Cost (Total Value-Actual Cost)	**-5937.50**		**13195.48**		**29469.76**	

Exhibit 5-8. New Car Purchase Scenario.

2. End of lease fees. Many leases pile on the fees at the end of the lease period. Inevitably there is a clause that says you will pay for excessive wear and tear. Of course, that wear and tear is determined by the dealer. In addition, most leases require you to pay more at the end of the lease for each mile that you use the vehicle beyond what has been agreed to.

3. Overpayment. Many lessees, especially older couples, return their vehicle having paid more for the use of the vehicle than they needed to, based on its usage. That is, they paid for up to 12,000 miles but only used it for a few thousand miles. This is great for the dealer since it can resell the car for more at the end of the lease, but the lessee loses.

4. You are still responsible for maintenance and repairs. Some folks are surprised to find that although they do not own the vehicle they are still financially responsible for maintaining and repairing it as if it were their own. This can be less problematic if it is a new car with an excellent warranty but for

items not covered by a warranty or for vehicles whose warranty has expired and are still on lease it can be very expensive. Basically you are paying to maintain someone else's car for the privilege of borrowing it for a payment. Wow!! You can only be a loser in this scenario.

Do you get the picture? Leasing just does not make long-term financial sense for a family. You are basically paying for the use of a vehicle which normally results in a lower monthly payment but over time you will almost always pay more and may not even end up owning anything at the end. Look at buying a used car; you'll be better off. If you still want more information on leasing see the resources noted in Exhibit 5-9. These will explore some of the benefits of leasing in more detail but the benefits from the perspective of the believer are less than those that might apply to those in the world. For instance, leasing might be quite beneficial if you desire to be always driving a new car. Is that a particular good desire for the Christian in light of the long-term financial cost that it entails? Do not be sold into the world's thinking.

Automobile Leasing Resources
www.consumerreports.org
www.leaseguide.com
www.leasecompare.com
www.leasetips.com
www.carbuyingtips.com/lease.htm

Exhibit 5-9. Car Leasing Information Sites on the Web.

The Trade-In. Quite often folks who purchase a vehicle desire to trade in their old one. Normally you should keep the trade-in discussion aside until you have agreed on a price for the vehicle you wish to purchase. The dealer will make every effort to include the trade-in as part of the negotiations so that it can manipulate the numbers in such a way to make it look good to you. This usually does not work in your favor. The trade-in value of your car will usually be less than if you sold it yourself unless the car is worth little. If a car is only worth a few hundred dollars a dealer might be able to give you $1000 (if you are buying another vehicle from the dealer) and then use the vehicle for parts to get its money back or may be able to fix it up and sell it for a little more. Otherwise, do not discuss the trade-in until you have the price you want on the car you are purchasing. Once that is complete discuss the trade-in. The trade-in value of your vehicle can be easily determined by looking at www.kbb.com, www.edmonds.com, or www.nada.com. These should give you a range to work with. If the dealer can't give you a fair trade-in value for your car then go elsewhere. CarMax is a company that will buy your car regardless of whether you buy from them. Compare its offer for your car to the market value from the sites above. You may get more from them than the dealer you are buying your next car from.

The Extras. Dealers are in business to make money and they make every attempt to get as much as they can when you are buying a car. They do this because they know that you are more likely to splurge for the extras since you are already spending a significant amount of money and the extras may not seem like all that much when compared to the total cost of your vehicle. Avoid buying the extras that a dealer will try to offer you as part of your car transaction. These include offers of rust-proofing, sealants, fabric protectors, extended warranties, service contracts, and the like. If the car is new or has been well maintained these should be unnecessary. These are great money makers for the dealers and few consumers can actually take advantage of them due to the exclusions that go with them. For the most part these are just costly extras. You would be better off investing the funds you would have spent on these so that you would have a repair fund in case you needed it. The dealer knows that if you don't buy the extras when you buy the car they will have lost the opportunity to improve its profits.

The Funding for Your Vehicle

We have already noted the basic guidelines for borrowing by Christians and those guidelines also apply to the purchase of a vehicle. The preferable way to purchase a car is, of course, cash that has been set aside for that purpose. Assuming you have decided to borrow funds for a vehicle there are a few key points to consider.

The Monthly Payment. The dealer's greatest marketing tool today is the "monthly payment." If the dealer can get you thinking about the monthly amount then he can extract the retail price or better from you because that is not your focus. The Christian must be vigilant and look at the total cost of all alternatives based on actual numbers that the dealer gives in answer to your questions of various options available. Use your research into actual dealer costs to make sure you are not overpaying for a vehicle. You should expect a dealer to make a small profit so it can stay in business but you don't need to enrich them by being a poor steward.

Zero Percent Down. Dealers will often entice purchasers by emphasizing zero percent down deals. This requires the purchaser to finance the entire purchase price of the vehicle. This would immediately put the individual in a situation of being unable to pay off his debts if necessary since reselling the vehicle would not fetch the amount owed on the loan. The caveat is that some may have the funds earning interest in the bank at a rate greater than the loan for the vehicle. So taking advantage of the zero percent down offer seems to make sense and if they had to they could still repay the loan. This may work but it should be carefully considered in light of other alternatives. That is, usually zero-percent down deals have higher price tags or interest rates than cash or other types of deals. Thus, to take advantage of the zero down deal sometimes requires paying a higher price for the car. The key here is to be careful that you don't pay more for the car because of the deal for zero down and be sure you would be able to repay all you have promised if necessary.

Zero or Low Interest Loans. Dealers also often entice purchasers by touting their low interest rates. As with the zero down inducement there is usually a catch and that is in the price. That is, you will end up paying closer to the retail price of the car to get a low or no interest deal. Thus, the apparent benefit may be a small one or no benefit at all, if you could have had a substantially reduced price on the car.

Funding Source. Many new car manufacturers have their own financing subsidiaries that offer rates significantly lower than other financial institutions. Keep in mind that they may also be adjusting the price to compensate for that. Check other financial institutions' rates and see if providing your own funding from another source makes the overall cost of the deal cheaper.

Finalizing the Purchase. Be sure there are no other hidden costs related to the borrowing of funds for the purchase. Remember that you will be signing a binding loan document. Have an attorney check it if you are not sure what you are signing. Also verify that it is fully collateralized if at all possible or that you have sufficient funds to cover the difference if the car must be sold. You do not want to be in a situation where you must repay that which you cannot.

Providing Education

Education is the one non-investment instrument that might be called an investment. That is, it is funded with a large initial payment over 4 or more years in hopes that the return on that investment in the form of a better career will produce a much larger return than if it was not undertaken. For some types of professions such as law or accounting there may be ongoing expenses associated with maintaining a licensure. But some consider this no different than the expenses related to managing an investment.

Research does show that on average investing in education proves quite valuable and provides increasing returns based on the level of education attained. Exhibit 4-1, shown earlier in the text shows the correlation between education and average lifetime earnings. An associate's degree will lead to an additional half million dollars of lifetime income compared with those who don't have a college degree. Attaining a bachelor's degree adds another $650,000 of income making such a degree worth about a million dollars more than not having a college degree. Adding a master's or doctorate degree also leads to higher earnings than the bachelor's degree. Keep in mind that these are average earnings and are influenced by the current employment market and the career specialty entered.

It would seem clear, then, that it behooves stewards to prayerfully and seriously consider what career God would have them to enter. Keep in mind that God does not have all to attain college degrees and money should not be the focus of our desire in this world. What we learn here is that God may have some to develop certain talents and skills that will lead to greater capacities to support others. He may lead others to minister as a Bible teacher or evangelist.

These, of course require a spiritual gift rather than formal education. This is why many of those who taught in the New Testament were able to do so without an education. This does not mean that a Bible teacher cannot have an education but that it is not a requirement for ministering for God. The key here, as in other decisions we make, is taking a biblical approach to our decisions seeking guidance from His Word, through prayer, and the Godly counsel of others.

The School Selection Process

Although in a text such as this we can only touch briefly on some of the key points in the university selection process it is important that regardless of the training or degree you wish to pursuit you will need to go well beyond the thoughts here in your research. Some general points in pursuing an education include:

Commitment. As with everything relating to stewardship, education requires you to make a commitment. This means doing well in your education activities before entering college. There is much to distract young people in this world today in the form of entertainment that pleases the flesh and as a result is more enticing than the time and commitment it takes to do well in educational studies. Determine now that you will commit to doing well in whatever educational endeavor that you, by God's grace, are put into. Of course, the benefit of this can be seen in better knowledge and understanding, and improved scholarship opportunities in the future.

Perspective. Keep in mind that as a Christian you seek to find an educational opportunity that will provide you with the education and experiences necessary to succeed in your chosen field and provide an environment in which your faith can be expressed and grow. Choosing a school because it is easy or has the most activities is not likely to help you accomplish any career goals you have set. Christian schools should be given significant consideration in light of their opportunities for significant growth in the faith and the emphasis on a biblical basis for conduct.

Price. There is no question that for many the cost of schooling plays a significant role. Although the costs of higher education have increased significantly over that last two decades there are still many good values in the educational arena. Several guides are published related to schools with the best values. A few include: *Kiplinger's 100 Best Values in Public Education* at www.kiplinger.com/tools/colleges/ and U. S. News and World Report's America's Best Colleges 2005 at www.usnews.com. High price does not necessarily mean great education. Price often can be associated with the well known name of a school such as the Ivy League schools like Yale and Princeton or other schools such as MIT. Although some companies may look for a degree from a certain institution this rarely will be the only criteria used. Most companies look for a solid education with demonstrated work in the area of endeavor. Thus, internships, practicums, projects, and co-operative experiences play a far more important role than the school attended.

The Funding of the Education

Seeing that education is an important criterion for most fields of endeavor and that it can affect our earnings it is important that we find a way of funding that experience. Although we will cover some of the specific investment vehicles for education under the chapters on investing we will identify the key sources of funding here.

Savings. Saving regularly starting at a young age will help you to be able to fund your education or that of your children. The trend of saving in America is not good and yet this is one of the best options for being ready for the need.

Scholarships. Many organizations and universities offer grants or scholarships based on a variety of factors including need, ability, and a host of other demographic factors. The great benefit of these is that they do not need to be repaid. Be careful of scholarship scam services that claim they can get you thousands for just filling out a single form. There is a great deal involved in seeking and applying for scholarships. Check where you or your parents work as they may also provide these.

Tuition Reimbursement. Many employers provide tuition reimbursement for employees. If you plan on an advanced degree this may be of help. In fact you may want to seek an employer who offers such a benefit.

Student Loans and Grants. The federal government provides a number of programs designed to support those who have a financial need for college funds. These programs are available only to those who have filed the Free Application for Federal Student Aid (FAFSA) form with the federal government. If, based on the federal formula, you qualify for need-based assistance you can then apply for it. Grants by the government such as the Pell grant do not need to be repaid. Student loans are available from most banks and, if you qualify, are guaranteed by the federal government and there is no interest until 6 months after school is complete. Now that brings us to another concern. Biblically speaking we need to have a way to repay what we borrow. This is rarely the case for a student. What happens if for some reason you do not finish school? What happens if it takes you a year or two to find a good position? You end up with no way of being able to pay for the loan. Because of this I can not recommend students take out student loans unless they have a certain way of repaying them either by collateralizing them or having something of value that they could sell to repay them.

? **FAFSA**

? **Grant**

Student Employment. Most universities offer employment opportunities for students that allow them to pay their tuition or lead to a remission of tuition. Although tuition remission is more common for graduate level programs some undergraduate programs offer this for juniors or seniors.

Although we may view education as an investment we realize that we must still follow the biblical mandate of having a way of paying our just debts.

That is, borrowing for the purpose of "investing" in education is treated no differently than the other borrowing we have discussed. The best way of preparing for the reality of paying for education is to plan and start early. If you do not start early it can be difficult to afford the costs of education even with the various sources of help from state and federal governments as well as the schools themselves. Lack of funding is one of the primary reasons that students do not finish their college education.

Other Major Purchases

Well, we have tackled most of the major expenses that we are likely to encounter. Before we leave this area though there are few others that you are very likely to encounter but are not normally considered.

Appliances and Furnishings

Many folks don't give much thought to appliances until there is a need to replace one. By that time, quite often, one is pressed to make a quick purchase, which inevitably leads to making poor decisions and increasing costs. We should make every effort to carefully consider appliance purchases just as with other expenses. Some key points of insight regarding acquiring appliances include:

Never Rent Them. What I mean by appliances here are the ones you use regularly in the home. You should never rent or participate in a rent-to-own for washers, dryers, TVs, stoves, refrigerators, and the like. These are losing propositions for you and a great boon to the company. I have seen some of these rent-to-own stores sometimes charge as much as 600% interest on the life of a contract. Renting a large power tool for a single day may be fine (although better to borrow from a friend) but anything you use on a regular basis should be purchased.

Don't Borrow for Them. Appliances and furnishings need to be paid with cash. To borrow for an appliance will almost always put you into, biblically, a debtor's position which means if you had to sell the appliance and/or pay the balance remaining you would not be able to. Appliances depreciate extremely quickly. I have been at auctions where very good washers and dryers go for thirty dollars each even though they originally sold for many hundreds.

Be Diligent. The best way of finding good deals on furnishings and appliances is to be watching and know the market. Watch for classified ads in the paper, or for yard sales (tag sales), moving sales, auctions, and the like. Although some folks will overprice their goods most will be looking to get rid of the merchandise and will be willing to strike a deal. In reality you can probably furnish your entire home with quality items with out going to the store. My son recently got his leather living room set for $100 at a yard sale. Certainly sounds better than $1000 or more that it likely would cost new. I also remember a brother in the Lord purchasing a high-end sofa from Habitat for Humanity for $100. Deals can be found, it just takes patience and diligence in finding them.

Weddings

Although weddings should be joyful occasions, for many they are becoming a financial burden. Most of this is due to catering to what the world expects for a wedding celebration. The average American wedding now costs $22,000 excluding the honeymoon. This is an outrageous sum for parents or newlyweds to spend for a one-day celebration. If you must fund your own, or your child's, wedding go the simple route and carefully plan it to reduce costs yet provide a memorable time for all. My son recently married and it was great to see how he and his fiancé carefully planned with her parents to keep costs down. Instead of a big modern church the marriage was performed in a small historical church for a nominal fee. The reception was at a community hall that was rented for $50. The food was catered by Fazoli's, which provides a great Italian buffet for less than $10 per person. My son bought a suit that can be reused rather than a tuxedo and the list on money saving ways goes on. Although I don't know all the financial numbers I would estimate that it cost less than $2000 for the wedding and reception. By being careful they (and her parents) are in much better financial shape than would have been the case if they sought to put on a lavish spread. If you are a parent with children (especially girls in our culture) then suggest that for every $100 they save in wedding costs they receive $25.00. Just a little incentive can go a long way.

Funerals

Although sad to consider, there is no getting away from the fact that dying today is expensive. But, just like with weddings it is not necessary to spend inordinate amounts for services related to the final arrangements related to the deceased. The average American funeral is now $5,000-$6,000. Much of this though is related to lavish spending on monuments, caskets, vaults, and other accoutrements.

Again, planning ahead will help here. Consider where you would like to be buried and consider purchasing a burial plot ahead of time. Keep in mind if you move there will be expenses related to getting your body to the burial plot. Although, it may be possible for those remaining to sell the plot and buy another where you died. Also, some funeral homes have large enough networks that they can exchange or transfer plots for you. Keep the expenses to a minimum. A simple chapel service where all can come to rejoice in the believer's home-call is the best. In fact the body of the deceased is not even needed for the memorial service. Viewing hours, or wakes as they at times are called, are really optional and can reduce the cost considerably. Perhaps setting up a time for calling hours at a local church for fellowship and encouragement would be sufficient. When the body can be immediately buried the costs are substantially reduced. The viewing of the dead is not necessary so don't feel you have to plan for it. Much of what is done today takes place by tradition and has developed into a profit-making venture for many companies.

You can still provide for the burial of a loved one for a reasonable cost in the range of $2000. Interestingly, it is about the same as a carefully planned wedding. Don't be afraid to buck the popular trend and do that which any good steward would do. The key is to plan now so there is no rush later when you or your loved ones are likely to make poor decisions.

Outcomes and Chapter Summary

In this chapter we focused on the Biblical perspective of borrowing and debt. Although borrowing is not unbiblical it is never encouraged. The borrower ends up being a servant to the lender from a Biblical perspective. We explored the various sources of credit and which are the best alternatives. We considered the Biblical view of bankruptcy and how bankruptcy works in America. Finally, we learned about the keys steps to take when looking at major purchases such as homes and cars.

Learning Objective 1. **Understand and explain the beginnings of credit and be able to describe what is included in a credit report as well as secure a copy of one.**

We explored the history of credit to see its basis and then looked at how credit is established and what credit agencies track about you. Some of the components tracked include demographic information, employment information, credit history, public financial history, and inquiries against your credit file.

Learning Objective 2. **Explain the Biblical perspective on borrowing, debt, and surety and how they differ.**

The Bible does not encourage borrowing but does not forbid it. Biblical debt occurs when you do not pay obligations that you have committed to. Not being able to pay what is owed, through the sale of assets or savings, is a form of surety. The Biblical view of surety or pledging for another is not Biblical and is to be avoided.

Learning Objective 3. **Describe the various sources of credit and be able to select an appropriate scenario for a given credit situation.**

We have looked at the various sources of credit and they include credit cards, debt consolidation loans, secured loans, unsecured loans, and credit lines. We have also learned what to look for when reviewing credit offers.

Learning Objective 4. **Explain the Biblical view of bankruptcy and the bankruptcy process in America.**

We learned that bankruptcy for Christian should be avoided unless forced by a creditor or unjust judgment to do so. Christians must repay, as agreed to, what they have borrowed.

Learning Objective 5. **Identify major purchase needs and be able to research and make appropriate major purchases.**

We explored the details of major purchases that we are likely to make over the period of our earthly lives. These included home and car purchases, renting an apartment, purchasing an education, appliances and furniture, weddings, and funerals.

Bible Texts Referenced

Exodus 22:14	Deuteronomy 15:6	Psalm 37:21	Proverbs 6:1-2
Proverbs 11:15	Proverbs 17:18	Proverbs 22:7	Proverbs 22:26-27
Matthew 25:27	Luke 12:58-59	Romans 13:8	

Exercises and Research Activities

1. Secure a copy of your credit report and review it. Write a brief review and identify any errors in the report and the steps you will take to correct them. What can you do to improve your credit score if you so desired?

2. What does it mean in Romans when it speaks of "owing no man anything"?

3. Write a brief abstract on what surety is and its advantages and disadvantages. Explain why the Bible is so against it.

4. Research a story about the abuse of credit cards and the results of that abuse. Write a brief paper about the story and what we can learn from it.

5. You have just arrived in the area and would like to secure a credit card. Research the possibilities and choose a card based on all of the relevant characteristics of a credit card. Write a brief abstract that identifies your top two choices and how they are better than others. Include a table that compares the features you were looking at.

6. The bankruptcy laws have recently changed. Why is there a desire to change the laws and what are the pros and cons of making the changes?

7. You and your team have been assigned to find you a home. You have decided that you are willing to move anywhere in the 48 contiguous states and that you want to pay cash with a maximum $60,000 price plus $2,500 for closing costs. Using appropriate criteria find the best deal possible. Various factors should be researched and weighed including location, safety, general job availability, and the like. The home should have 3 bedrooms and two baths and be on at least .20 acre.

8. You have decided to borrow $80,000 for your $150,000 home in Dallas, Texas. Find the best financial deal that results in the least amount being spent in total costs to acquire and pay off the loan keeping in mind that you can not afford more than $600 a month.

9. Jae's car, a 2001, Honda Accord LX sedan, has just blown a head gasket. The mechanic suggests that it will cost $4,400 to have it fixed. He has about $6,000 in his emergency fund. Perform an analysis and create a report that shows any comparisons you undertake and identifies what you would do.

10. You and your fiancé plan on getting married soon and now need to create a budget for the big event. Create a detailed spending plan and identify ways that the cost could be reduced if necessary. Also create a spending plan based on only having $2,500 available for everything.

References and Resources

Web Sites:

AutoCheck. www.autocheck.com
Bankrate.com www.bankrate.com
CardWeb.com. www.cardweb.com
Carfax.com. www.carfax.com
Cars.com. www.cars.com
CarsMart. www.carsmart.com
Consumer Guide. auto.consumerguide.com
Consumer Reports. www.consumerreports.org
Edmunds. www.edmonds.com
Insurance Institute for Highway Safety. www.hwysafety.org
Kelley Blue Book. www.kbb.com
Kiplinger's. www.kiplinger.com/tools/colleges/
National Automobile Dealer Association. www.nada.com
National Bankcard Systems. http://www.enbs.com/html/statistics.html

The Auto Channel. www.theautochannel.com
TrustMyMechnic. www.trustmymechanic.com
U. S News. www.usnews.com

Lease Guides:

www.leaseguide.com
www.leasecompare.com
www.leasetips.com
www.carbuyingtips.com/lease.htm

Calculators

Cost of Living. www.erieri.com

PART THREE

Investing for the Future

Chapter 6
Introduction to Investing

Chapter 7
Using Tax Advantaged Investments

Chapter 8
Investing in Stocks

Chapter 9
Investing in Bonds

Chapter 10
Mutual Funds and Other Investment Vehicles

CHAPTER 6

Introduction to Investing

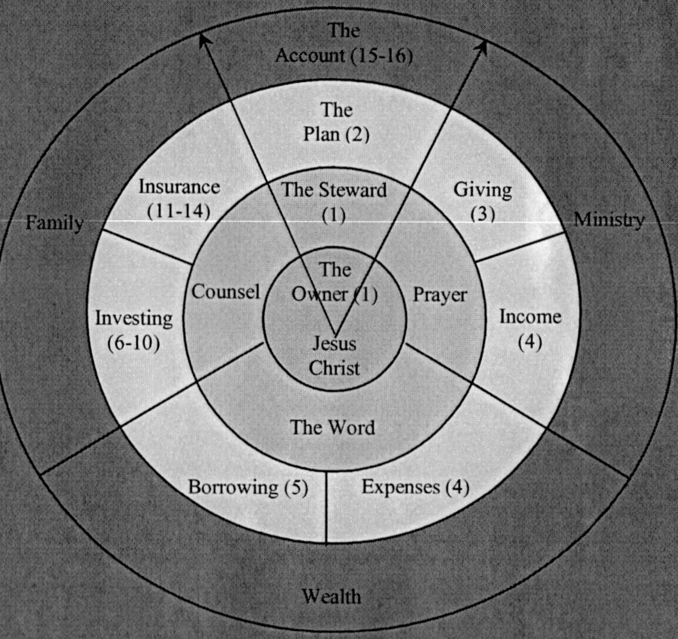

Learning Objectives

1. Understand and explain the basics of investing from a biblical perspective.

2. Identify and explain the basic investing issues such as funding, timing, risk and return, consistency, and compounding.

3. Define compounding and describe its effect on an investment. Be able to explain the role time plays in compounding.

4. Understand, identify, and select basic banking instruments such as checking, savings, and certificate of deposit accounts.

Lord, I commit to providing a return.

Lord, thank you for the financial resources you have provided to me while walking here below. I desire to use them for your glory and to provide you an abundant return. I commit to you now to use these resources in such a way that they will create a return that is pleasing to you. Give me wisdom as I seek to establish accounts that will be appropriate for the use of the resources you provide. Thank you for your continued strength as I learn more about investing for your glory.

The Biblical Perspective on Investing

? Investing

Investing deals with putting assets to use for a return in the future. There is no doubt that the Bible provides a multitude of examples of those who are wise, investing for the future. The perspective is both material and spiritual. That is, the Bible speaks of the importance of laying up for ourselves treasures in heaven as well as being a good steward on earth. The point of this is that the world has no way of taking those treasures that are in heaven. The Bible also speaks of being a good steward investing in the present so there will be plenty in the future. Joseph is an example of this in Genesis 41 where he, by God's will, saw the coming famine and stored up food in a time of plenty so there would be food available during the famine. One might question this example as an investment. Where is the return? The return was in the saved lives in Egypt as well as the price they received for the grain during the famine. The return was not immediate but it indeed was great.

The Spiritual Perspective-For the Master

The first point to be understood concerning investing for the future is that it must be of God and for Him and His glory. Many are the sad stories of well-intentioned Christians rushing into the "can't miss" opportunities only to find too late they have little or nothing left for their investment. Worse still, is that many Christians will focus on developing a financial portfolio with little thought to the heavenly one.

Let us note, then, that any investing must be done for the Master (laying up treasure in heaven) and not for ourselves. That is, we recognize that God allows us to invest what He has provided that He might provide for others and ourselves in the future. The key is that any return belongs to Him as well. It is when we recognize that the "treasure" and the return are His that we can be free in responsibly investing it.

We must also recognize that laying up spiritual treasure also involves investing in spiritual things. These include studying His Word, praying, and serving Him. Spiritual returns can only occur if these are also part of the "investment mix." Matthew 6:19-21 serves as a good reminder of this where it speaks of "treasures in heaven." The Bible reminds us on more than one occasion that our citizenship is not earthly but heavenly. Ephesians 2:19 emphasizes that the household of Christians is now of God and not the world. It states "*so then* ye *are no more strangers and foreigners, but ye are fellow-citizens of the saints, and of the household of God* (JND). Philippians 3:20 reminds us that "*our commonwealth has its existence in the heavens, from which also we await the Lord Jesus Christ as Savior* (JND). If we expect to have a spiritual return we must be investing in spiritual things. Remember that both literal and spiritual investing are for the Master, our Lord Jesus Christ.

The Spiritual Perspective-If God Will

The second key area in understanding the Biblical perspective of investing is to recognize that all must be done according to His will. You may ask how do I know His will? Well, this goes back to our first point-investing time in His Word and prayer. God has already made known to us His will through the Word. The difficulty lies in putting aside the enticements of the world to pursue what God has to say. For young people this can be extremely difficult because there are so many things clamoring for their time and attention. You cannot know the Lord's will in your life if you do not know Him, are not reading what He has said, and asking Him for guidance.

Seeking the Master's will is a great way to keep the "flesh" in check. Remember the "flesh" or old nature lusts after the things of the world and so physical riches can be very enticing. Paul notes in 1 Timothy 6:9 that "*those who desire to be rich fall into temptation and a snare, and many unwise and hurtful lusts, which plunge men into destruction and ruin*" (JND). In this verse we see the lust of the flesh at work that can ruin a man and his testimony. This becomes clear in verse 10 where it notes that some that have coveted after money have "*wandered from the faith, and pierced themselves through with many sorrows*" (JND).

See, anything financial including investing must be according to His will and Word. As regards making an investment gain James makes it very clear that it should be undertaken with –"if the Lord will." James 4:13-15 states "*go to now, ye who say, today or tomorrow will we go into such a city and spend a year there and traffic and make gain, ye who do not know what will be on the morrow, (for what is your life? It is even a vapor, appearing for a little while, and then disappearing,) instead of your saying, if the Lord should so will and we should live, we will also do this or that*" (JND). This makes it clear that the Bible has no problem with investing or trading and making gain. The question becomes is your heart right and are you taking steps-if the Lord should so will? Working outside of his will is bound to lead to much sorrow in the future.

The Spiritual Perspective-Effort is Required

Perhaps you have heard the saying "there is never a free lunch." Now, perhaps you have had an occasional free lunch from someone but the adage goes beyond the physical lunch. Have you ever received an email from Nigeria saying that you can have millions of dollars or a chain letter that asks you to send 20 dollars to five different people so you will get many thousands? These requests at times seem very real but whenever something sounds too good to be true, it likely is. The Nigerian email still makes its rounds and after the initial round some "investors" lost $20 million. These types of scams or "investments" prey on the flesh's desires and are basically a "get rich quick" scenario that entices that flesh within. The point here is that investing requires an effort over time. Get rich quick scenarios usually try to mitigate these factors by noting there is little for you to do and you can be enriched in a very short period of time. This is against the very nature of storing up or investing.

In Matthew 25:14-30 the Lord uses an investment related parable to describe the kingdom of heaven Not only does the parable teach us a spiritual lesson about using what God gives by the Spirit during this present age for a return for His glory but gives us a general lesson about investing our earthly goods for the Master's glory as well. There are several things to note about this parable. First God gives according to as a man is able. There is a choice on God's part of how much He will entrust to your care. Second, there is time (the Master is now in heaven until he comes for us) and effort involved (they went and traded). Third, as you are faithful in what has been given to you additional resources and responsibilities will then be given to you. It is important to note that we cannot feign being a servant of His. Many are those today who profess to know Christ and give the semblance of serving Him but are unprofitable. This was the case of the wicked servant in this parable. If he were a true servant he would have at least put the Master's money in the bank to receive interest. The true servant always has a return for the Master. In Matthew 7:22 the Lord notes that many will say "*Lord, Lord, have we not prophesied through thy name...*" and the Lord in the following verse says, "*I never knew you*" (JND). Be sure your motives in investing are right and in line with what the Lord would have. Don't use Him as a cover for trying to get physically rich in this present world as many do today who preach the "health and wealth gospel."

The Spiritual Perspective-Plan Before Action

There are numerous scriptures that deal with faithfulness in the use of our resources and emphasize the point we have been making. In addition, they point to the importance of planning before taking action. Proverbs 28:20 notes "*a faithful man shall abound with blessing, but he that maketh haste to be rich shall not be innocent*" (KJV). That is, the one who hastens to be rich will not go unpunished. Although there appears to be blessing the result in the end is not. The Bible is clear here that we are not to pursue the "get rich quick" schemes of the world. We have already noted several including chain letters, but this would also include lotteries, gambling, and high-stakes investing such as options, derivatives, and the like. The goal of all these is to get rich quickly. Almost invariably you loose in these situations either literally and/or spiritually. The godly woman of Proverbs 31 is an example of one who is careful and diligent in the use of her resources to build for her family's future. Verse 16 notes that she "*considereth a field, and buyeth it; with the fruit of her hands she planteth a vineyard*" (KJV). She is careful to use her mind to consider what she should do and actually invests several different ways. She plans before she acts. Proverbs 21:5 reminds us that "*the plans of the diligent lead surely to advantage, but everyone who is hasty comes surely to poverty*" (KJV). So too, we need to plan and consider what God would have us to do before we act in the area of investing as with the other areas of finance. Other verses to consider in relation to this include Proverbs 23:4-5, 24:3-4, 27:1, and 28:22.

The Basics of Investing

Now that we have reviewed investing from a Biblical perspective we are ready to look at the basics of investing. Earlier in the text we had looked at the importance of what is called the time value of money and the effect of compounding. These play an important role in both borrowing, and investing or saving. If you are borrowing, the benefit of compounding accrues to the bank whereas if you are saving, the benefit accrues to you. In this section we will briefly review these key points along with a few other basic issues related to investing.

The Issue of Funds

We noted in an earlier chapter that there are a number of tradeoffs we make in determining how we spend the funds we have available. These trade-offs are often related to what we call opportunity cost. That is, by making a decision to do one thing with our funds we are giving up the opportunity to do something else. Thus, there is always a cost related to our decisions-the opportunity to do what we decided against. With that in mind it is important that in order to invest we must have a positive cash flow. That is, our expenses must be less than our income. In order to take advantage of the saving opportunity we may be required to forgo other opportunities to use those funds. You may need to give up the cruise you were thinking about or reduce the number of times you eat outside the home. By going for these expenses we give up the opportunity of saving or investing for the future. So make a commitment now to reduce the expenses so that you can have the opportunity to be a blessing in the future to your family and to others.

The Issue of Risk and Return

We have previously discussed some influences on the value of an item such as inflation, perception, scarcity, risk, and time. These influences also relate to investing. The first component we want to look at is return. It is defined as what the investor expects to get in return for the use of the investor's money. Usually this is the original amount the investor supplied plus some additional amount that pays the investor for the use of the funds. Returns take many forms but usually are in the form of interest, dividends, or capital gains. Basically it is the amount that you earn for lending your money. We have already discussed interest (cash paid by the borrower) that is usually the return that is given for bank instruments such as CDs, and saving accounts and other instruments such as bonds. Dividends are a return of some of the profits a company creates, to the shareholders of the stock, either in cash or in additional stock. Capital gains are the amounts realized, from selling an investment such as a stock, above the original purchase price. Whatever the form of the return,

? Return

the percentage increase (or decrease) of your original investment is called the rate of return.

So, we all would like to have great returns on our investments whatever the form that return might take. As a result we might look for investments with the highest returns. Well, it is not quite that easy. There are many factors that can affect the rate of return. These factors comprise a second component that is known as risk. Risk is the uncertainty related to the investment's return. That is, there is no guarantee that you will earn anything on your investment or for that matter get the principal back. The more likely you are to receive your principal along with some earnings the lower the return. What factors influence risk? One factor is business risk. This deals with the level of uncertainty related to the company's ability to continue to operate profitably and meet its obligations. Companies that are struggling must pay higher returns to compensate investors for the greater risk of losing their money. Related to this factor is financial risk, which deals with the amount of debt the organization has on its balance sheet. Remember, just as individuals have problems with too much debt so do companies. The greater the debt load of the company the more risk that the company will experience difficulties, requiring them to pay investors a greater return to entice them to invest in the company.

? Risk

Another important factor that influences overall risk is market risk. This is the general risk of being associated with the market and the influence of various political, social, and economic factors that may have nothing to do with the particular company. This is sometimes called perception risk. The more a company is perceived as affected by external factors the more volatile will be the stock and thus, the return. Another factor related to this that we previously touched on is inflation risk. Inflation affects the return in two ways. One is the effect on the company and the costs it must incur to create a profit. The higher the costs, the lower the profits. Thus, there is a greater risk to investors. Also higher inflation reduces the buying power of consumers, which can limit a company's sales. Also related to this is interest rate risk. This is the risk associated with changing interest rates in the market.

Keep in mind there are other risks such as the ability to sell an investment at a reasonable price quickly. This is called liquidity risk. The less liquid, or the more difficult to sell an investment, the higher the return.. Real estate is generally less liquid than other investments and as a result its return can be influenced by how quickly it must be sold. Occasionally you may hear of another factor that influences risk called event risk. This is the effect of a sudden unexpected event that dramatically influences the investment. For instance recently Merck withdrew the drug Vioxx from the market based on a study that it increased the risk of heart problems. As a result the stock price plummeted from $45.07 to $33.00 in one day (September 30, 2004) and still has not recovered. Investors were not only worried about the lost revenue from selling Vioxx but from the possible lawsuits as well. The effect on other related stocks should not go unnoticed in these events. Stocks such as Pfizer with similar drugs took a large hit as well.

? Liquid

Another factor is the safety of the investment. The more secure or safe your investment is, the lower the rate of return. Saving accounts that are insured by the Federal Deposit Insurance Corporation (FDIC) is about as close as it gets to being guaranteed of getting your investment back. As a result the rates of return are almost negligible as of this writing with some banks offering as little as .25 percent (that is a quarter percent, not 25 percent). The length of an investment can also influence the return. Usually the longer you invest your funds the greater the rate of return. For instance bank CDs that require a five-year deposit will pay significantly more in return than those that are for six months. Sometimes the amount invested can influence the return as well. This again usually relates to bank instruments such as saving accounts and CDs. Fees can also influence returns. The greater the cost of investing, the lower the overall return. Sometimes there is a reduction in fees for investing more so there could be an improved rate of return for a greater investment.

? FDIC

A final factor that can influence return is taxes. There is a benefit to purchasing tax-free investments such as municipal bonds. Since normal investment income is taxed some portion of your investment earnings must go to pay those taxes. If the investment is tax free then you get to keep the funds you would have normally used to pay taxes. This increases your return on the investment. Of course you will need to compare carefully since some tax-free investments may not offer as high a return as taxable investments.

As you can see there are many factors that can influence the risk and return associated with an investment and thus the return that is offered to the investor. As an investor you will need to weigh the tradeoff between these two key components. The greater the risk, the greater the possible return, but also the greater the possible loss.

The Issue of Timing

Now that we have delved into the contrast between risk and return we want to tackle a few other basics related to investing. Another of these issues relates to timing and there are several aspects of it to be discussed. First, no doubt you have heard the term "market timing." The idea is that you time your investment to occur just before the price of an investment goes up and time the sale for just before the price goes down from its peak. The question naturally arises-how do I accomplish market timing? The answer is that you can't, at least not with consistency. Occasionally individuals will make an intelligent guess or throw a dart at a board of stocks and happen to get the right one just before it soars but that is the exception and not the norm. In reality market timing is another form of "get rich quick" and should be avoided.

? Market Timing

A second investing approach also deals with timing and that is "day trading." The goal of day trading is to quickly buy and sell stocks during a given day in order to gain small profits on the small changes in the stock price during the day. Thus, if you can buy 1000 shares at $10.40 and resell them at 10.49 an hour later you have made a profit of $90. Another goal of day trading

? Day Trading

is to get in the market in the morning and be out of the market by the time the market closes. The problem with this approach is that its foundation is still related to getting rich quick and timing the buy and sell within a single day. Many have lost all their savings trying to beat the market this way. There is no guarantee that a stock will go up in time for you to make a profit that day and there are heavy trading fees related to buying and selling constantly.

Another perspective on timing deals with the length of time one invests. As we have already noted there is value in time and the longer you invest and reinvest your earnings the larger your investment becomes. Regardless of age it is a good idea to invest appropriately but for those who are young, the benefits of starting now are astounding. Had this author known what he knows now back when he was twenty, concerning the Biblical principles of finance and investing, he would be in far better shape than he is today. Start investing today for the future. Don't put it off.

The Issue of Consistency

When we speak of consistency in investing we mean that we are regularly setting aside funds in an investment vehicle. Consistency in putting funds into investments makes your investment portfolio grow, usually regardless of the current market conditions. Yes, you may lose some value on some days and gain on others but over time your additions will make it grow and based on historical data the return will increase as well. The problem here is that most individuals are excited to get started and with zeal will invest for a brief time, but then allow the zeal to wane. Unfortunately, many find it difficult not to spend the amounts they have saved, deciding after a while that they now have enough for a vacation or newer car and the like. Thus, consistency of investing purpose is imperative to being successful in being a steward of the resources you have received, even if it is small amount set aside each month.

The Issue of Compounding

? Compounding

We discussed the issue of compounding earlier in the book but we revisit it here because it is such an important aspect of building your investment return and portfolio over time. Compounding is simply the act of combining, and from a financial perspective is the act of earning interest on the combined principal and interest thus far received. Thus we often hear the phrase earning interest on interest. As a review, if you have $100 and you earn 10% compounded annually on your money after the first year you would have $110 ($100 principal + $10 interest). During the second year you now have $110 earning interest. At the end of the second year you would have $121 ($110 + $11 interest). After a third year you would have $133.10 ($121 + $12.10 interest). You will notice that the amount of interest we earn each compounding period (in this case a year) continues to rise since we are combining it with the original principal. If we were to take the interest earned out of the investment and spend it we would lose the benefit of compounding and would earn the same amount of interest each year ($10). So, by leaving the interest in the investment the future interest payments will grow. Thus we see in this example that the payments would be $10, $11, $12.10, $13.31, etc.

Another important compounding aspect is its frequency. That is the more frequent the interest payments the greater the compounding. Thus, assuming the same simple annual rate, monthly compounding is better than annual compounding. This can be easily shown by using a table. The key is that the rate may be the same but the yield (the actual return including compounding) may be different and should be carefully considered.

Let's assume we invest $1000 at a 10 percent annual return and interest reinvested. Here are the results of the various compounding periods:

	Year 1	Year 5	Year 10
Annual Compounding	1100.00	1610.51	2593.74
Quarterly Compounding	1103.81	1638.61	2685.06
Monthly Compounding	1104.71	1645.31	2707.04
Daily Compounding	1105.16	1648.61	2717.91

As you can see from the table compounding frequency affects the total return on your investment. Although the difference may seem small using the $1000 example, the difference can be quite great when you are speaking of a larger sum and or speaking of a much longer period of time. As we have noted before, compounding is often referred to as the time value of money. Take advantage of that time value by starting today. The longer you have to compound the better.

Investing in Bank Instruments

There was a time, perhaps as late as the mid to late 1980s when just about every bank offered good rates on financial instruments. With market changes and bank deregulation came changes in these instruments and changes in the use of these instruments in the investment and banking portfolio. Here we review a few of the standard products offered by banks in relation to their suitability for investment.

Checking and Money Market Accounts

Using a checking account for its investment return is not likely to leave you enamored with it. Most financial institutions who offer interest bearing checking accounts are paying miniscule rates no matter what the type of account. Interest bearing checking accounts, also known as NOW accounts (Negotiable Order of Withdrawal) and money market accounts usually offer paltry rates. NOW or interest bearing checking accounts may have various restrictions on their use or a required minimum balance to earn interest. Money market checking accounts have a rate of interest tied to the market rates that change fairly frequently and usually pay a little higher than a standard NOW account. Current rates are as low as one-tenth of one percent (.10) for interest bearing checking accounts no matter what the flavor is.

The recommendation here would be to choose your checking account for its free services and low balance requirement. The main purpose of a checking account is to provide an easy way to access funds using a check. You should be able to do so without having to pay for it. Avoid choosing a checking account solely on its return. If you can find a checking account that has a low minimum balance and free check writing that offers interest then take it. Don't use checking accounts as investment vehicles. The rates currently offered are not worth keeping large sums in them.

Savings Accounts

It wasn't long ago that most banks offered a 5 to 5.5 percent fixed rate for their savings accounts. With the regulatory and market changes, that is history, and bank savings account rates have plummeted along with other interest rates. Some banks currently offer as little as .25 percent (one-quarter percent) on their savings account instruments. Like any investment you want to earn a maximum rate with significant safety. Although the safety of financial institution savings accounts is quite good their rates currently are mediocre. You may want to consider an online bank where savings rates are up to 10 times better than a local bank. Of course you will need to keep in mind the tradeoffs related to convenience.

You may want to consider using a savings account as a backup to your checking account so that if there is an overdraft in checking the penalty is smaller, usually a $10 fee versus a $30 fee. The liquidity of a savings account can be quite helpful for those who need funds availability. If you use a savings account for investing, compare carefully and look at online banks so that you get the highest return with the fewest restrictions. If liquidity is not an issue then keep a small savings for backup to checking or transferring funds to checking. Also, if you have direct deposit from work then you can also have that directed to the savings account so it immediately starts earning interest. Most people direct deposit to checking since that's where employers and banks steer people but you are allowed to direct deposit to savings. This way you earn some interest on the funds that the bank usually gets to use for free.

Certificates of Deposit

Another investment instrument offered by most financial banking institutions is the certificate of deposit (CD). As its name implies in exchange for a deposit you receive a document (certificate) that shows the amount

? CD

deposited and the agreed on terms of the deposit. Certificate of deposits usually offer higher interest rates but as a result also have some restrictions. Each CD has a specified rate of return and a stated term or length of time the bank will hold the deposit. These time periods usually run from six months to five years. So, in return for a higher rate you are agreeing not to take your money from the bank until the term is up. Thus, your investment is less liquid than a savings or checking account. If you decide to take your money out early you end up paying a penalty. This penalty can be a loss of a month's interest or more depending on the term. The longer the term the higher the rates offered and the greater the penalty for early withdrawal.

Shopping around will enable you to find good rates on CDs and the rates will be significantly higher than savings accounts with the same safety level. Be sure that the CD is FDIC insured by the bank. Some organizations offer CDs that have much higher rates to compensate for the fact that you could lose all your money. Keep in mind that you don't need to use a local bank for a CD. You often can find better rates elsewhere in the country and use the internet or mail to establish the investment. If you don't need your funds for a while and need significant safety in your investment then CDs can be a viable alternative, assuming you can get a good rate based on the market.

Bank instruments, then, are excellent for their security and liquidity. Unfortunately the tradeoff is their relatively lower interest rates. If you need liquidity for paying bills or for upcoming purchases then use bank instruments, otherwise it might be better to seek another avenue for investing your funds.

Outcomes and Chapter Summary

In this chapter we focused on the basics of investing with a special focus on the Biblical perspective of investing. We also explored the investing issues and the role compounding and time play in successful investing. We also discussed basic bank-related investment vehicles.

Learning Objective 1. **Understand and explain the basics of investing from a biblical perspective.**

We explored carefully the Biblical foundation for investing. We identified four key spiritual truths concerning investing. They included investing for the Master, investing according to God's will, investing with effort, and planning before investing.

Learning Objective 2. **Identify and explain the basic investing issues such as funding, timing, risk and return, consistency, and compounding.**

We explored the importance of having funds available to invest. Without funds to invest we can not build our assets. We reviewed the tradeoff between risk and return. We also looked at some basic approaches to investing.

Learning Objective 3. **Define compounding and describe its effect on an investment. Be able to explain the role time plays in compounding.**

We examined the role of compounding in investing and noted its effect over time. We also explored the different lengths of compounding periods and their effect on an investment.

Learning Objective 4. **Understand, identify, and select basic banking instruments such as checking, savings, and certificate of deposit accounts.**

Finally we explored the basic bank investment instruments and the tradeoffs they offer for the investor. We noted that most bank instruments are safer and thus have less risk but also have lower rates of return.

Bible Texts Referenced

Genesis 41	Proverbs 21:5	Proverbs 23:4-5	Proverbs 24:3-4,
Proverbs 27:1	Proverbs 28:20	Proverbs 28:22	Proverbs 31:16
Matthew 6:19-21	Matthew 7:22	Matthew 25:14-30	Ephesians 2:19
Philippians 3:20	1 Timothy 6:9-10	James 4:13-15	

Exercises and Research Activities

1. Choose a Bible passage that appears to deal with investing and explain the lessons it shows us.

2. There are many issues to be considered when investing. Briefly outline the major issues and how they influence the return on your investment.

3. What roll does compounding play in investing? Explain how the frequency of compounding is important.

4. What are the best investment vehicles that banks offer? Explain when they might be suitable for an investor.

5. Research an article that deals with some of the investing issues discussed in this chapter and write a brief annotation that outlines what you learned.

CHAPTER 7

Using Tax Advantaged Investments

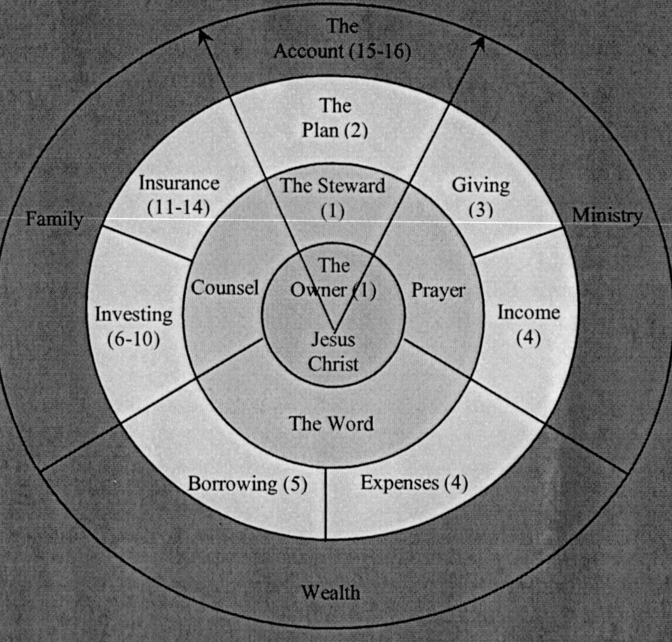

Learning Objectives

1. Identify and describe the types of pension plans offered by companies.
2. Identify the types and key advantages and disadvantages of Individual Retirement Accounts (IRAs).
3. Identify and describe the unique benefits of the education IRA and 529 Plans and be able to contrast them based on the benefits and drawbacks of using the instruments.
4. Describe the purpose of flexible spending accounts and how they can benefit the individual.
5. Identify and describe other tax advantaged investment vehicles such as municipal bonds.

Lord, I commit to keeping as much as possible for you.

Lord, thank you for the insights you have given me thus far related to the Biblical perspective of investing. I know there are many options available in this world for earning a return on the funds you have provided. I want to make sure I do what is right in your sight. I know that taxes are a part of providing for government in this world but help me understand how I might minimize as much as possible that which takes away from what could be used for your work here in this world. I commit now to be careful to conserve as much as possible for you and the work you have for me here.

The Tax Perspective of Investing

Before tackling the various tax-advantaged instruments it might be good to review how taxes, in general can be saved by using them. Usually there are two ways to reduce your taxes. You can reduce your taxable income or lower the tax itself. In the first scenario you can reduce your income by deferring it or by taking reductions against it for allowed expenses. If you are in the 15 percent tax bracket, for every dollar you reduce your income you save 15 cents. Of course if you are in a higher bracket you will save more. The second scenario is considered a tax credit. That is for every dollar of tax credit you find is a dollar you save. Most investment tax vehicles deal with the first scenario of reducing your income at least in the short term. We should also note here that there are also many tax-free work related benefits. These benefits such as life insurance would normally be considered additional income but when they are tax-free they are not included with your income thus keeping your taxable income to a minimum.

Taxable versus Tax-Free Benefits

Earlier when we discussed taxes and tax returns we had mentioned ways of reducing your taxes to allow you to have more to invest. One of the things we put off discussing was the difference between taxable and tax-free benefits. Taxable means that it is a form of income that can be taxed while tax-free means that it is form of income that is not taxed. Since we are dealing with tax advantages related to investing and saving this might be a good place to cover this topic though it may not be directly related to investing. It is indirectly related because of the difference in return on the benefit. Let's take an example to make it easier to understand. Let's say you have a choice of an additional $200 in salary to get a $50,000 life insurance policy or a $50,000 life insurance policy valued at $200 paid by the company. Which benefit is better?

? Taxable

Assuming all other factors are equal the company paid life insurance is a better benefit because it is tax-free. The comparison can be calculated two ways; either by looking at the cost of the taxable benefit after accounting for taxes or by adjusting the tax-free benefit to include the taxes. Assuming a 28% marginal tax bracket the following would be the result:

Scenario 1: $200 – (200 * .28) = $144

The taxable income is worth $56 less than the $200 life insurance policy.

Scenario 2: $200 / 1-.0.28) = $277.78

The tax-free life insurance policy is equivalent to a $277.78 taxable benefit.

So to make these two equivalent, would require a reduction in the tax-free benefit or an increase in the taxable benefit. What this shows us is that tax-free benefits are worth more than taxable benefits.

Tax-Deferred versus Tax-Exempt

Just as there is a distinction between taxable and tax-free income or benefits there is a difference between tax-deferred and tax-exempt income. Tax-deferred income means that taxable income is taxed at a later date than when it was first received. That is, taxes must still be paid when the money is used for a purpose other than that which allows a tax deferral. Tax-exempt on the other hand means that no taxes need to be paid on the income. All things being equal, tax-exempt income is better than tax-deferred income. That being said there are a number of tradeoffs that may make one better than the other. For instance if I can get a better rate of return on a taxable investment that would exceed the return of a tax-free benefit even after taking in account the tax-free benefit then the taxable investment would be better. How do you know which to choose? Well it takes some careful review and a few calculations based on the scenario that you find yourself confronted with.

? Tax Deferred

? Tax Exempt

Since every situation will have a variety of variables we can only provide an example or two to help you analyze your circumstances. Is it better to choose a tax-free return of 6% or a taxable rate of return of 7%? Assuming you are in the 28% marginal tax bracket: you would use the formula:

Tax-free rate / (1 – your tax rate)

$$6.0 / (1 - .28) = 8.3$$

A six percent tax free yield is the same as an 8.3 percent taxable yield. In this case the tax-free investment is a better deal. If the taxable investment had a rate of return greater than 8.3% then it would have been a better choice.

The comparison between benefits of tax-deferred investments versus taxable investments can involve a bit more work since they usually are over a long period of time and the future tax implications are not entirely known. For instance, what will the tax rates be in 20 years? Will they be lower or higher? If lower, then tax-deferral will likely be better; if higher, it may not be. It would be impossible to provide every possible scenario here but here is an example to give you an idea of what to look at. Let's assume the scenario is one where you will be putting aside $2000 a year in a tax-deferred instrument versus paying your taxes and investing the difference. Assume you have a $30,000 annual income. Let's assume a period of ten years and you receive the amount in a lump sum after ten years. The return rate is 6% compounded annually.

> Account 1: $2000 a year compounded annually in ten years = $26,361.59.
>
> You will receive 26,361.59 – (26,361.59 * 0.28) = $19,980.34

In addition, your reduced income from making the contribution would reduce your taxes by $300 each year. If that were saved at 6% interest for ten years as well you would have an additional $3,984.37 after paying taxes.

> Account 2: $2000 a year – 28 percent taxes compounded annually in ten years = 18980.34.
>
> You will receive 18980.34.

Assuming no differences in other variables such as taxes or return, a tax-deferred investment is better than a taxable one. If the other variables change such as the taxes went up after ten years then the result might be different. Of course taking a distribution over many years rather than as a lump sum could also reduce the taxes paid.

There are other variations of the tax issue to consider. For instance when we discuss Roth IRAs (which uses taxable income) later in this chapter we will look at a comparison of using it versus the deferred investment approach to see if it is better. This section should make it clear that the comparisons take a little work and are unique for your situation keeping in mind the various variables that can influence the outcome. These variables include the rate of return, the length of the investment, the speed of distribution, the current and future tax rates and the taxability of the earnings of the investment. Investment planning becomes essential as a good steward as you plan for the future.

Employer Pension Plans

Although pension plans are often covered under retirement planning by authors it would seem better suited to cover the topic here because of the changes that have occurred in these plans over the last twenty or so years so that they are seen more as savings plans funded by employees. In this chapter we will focus our discussion on the types of plans and their investment and tax perspectives and leave the issue of retirement planning for a later chapter.

The Key Types of Plans

There are two basic types of pension plans offered by employers for funding your future. They are defined-benefit plans and defined-contribution plans. For many years employers offered define-benefit pension plans. These plans specified the benefits that the employee would receive based on their age at retirement. Defined benefit plans were funded by employers based on the expected retirement age and projected funding needs to pay the retiree benefits. There was one fund for all employees and employees had little involvement in the process other than completing the required number of years of employment to be vested or to have access to the benefits of the plan at retirement. Vesting just indicates that the employee has secured the rights to access the benefits of the plan. These types of plans are becoming scarce and most companies are now moving to a defined-contribution plan that requires more participation on the employee's part and saves the companies substantial sums in future retiree liabilities.

? Defined Benefit

Defined-contribution plans are significantly different than the defined-benefit plans noted above. With this type of plan each employee has his or her own account. The key difference is that the plan identifies what the employer will contribute to the plan and does not identify the benefits you will receive. The benefit is what is in your account when you retire. In addition, many employers now require employees to help fund their own accounts or encourage them to do so by offering a matching contribution. Another type of plan similar to this is the cash-balance plan that has the added feature of portability so that if you leave before retirement you may take it with you to another qualifying plan. Most of these plans take the form of what is called a 401K, 403B, 457, Keogh, or SEPP. All provide tax-deferred savings for retirement but are implemented by different types of organizations based on various sections of the tax code. Section 401(k) of the tax code deals with 401K plans and is used by for-profit employers. Section 403(b) as you might guess deals with 403B plans. These are plans that are offered by non-profit institutions such as hospitals and universities. Section 457 deals with 457 plans, which are offered by governments. So, for each type of organization there is a section of the tax code to be followed in offering these plans. For those who are self-employed there are two pension plan options. The first, based on the Keogh Act of 1962, is called a Keogh plan, and the second, an easier to administer option for small businesses, with no employees, which is called a Simplified Employee Pension Plan (SEPP). All of these plans are often referred to as tax-sheltered annuities (TSA) plans. We will consider them again under retirement planning but note them here because of the tax advantages offered in relation to investing in them.

? Defined Contribution

? 401K

? 403B

? 457 Plan

? Keogh

? SEPP

? TSA

The Tax Advantages of Pension Plans

We bring up the issue of pension plans here because they are an investment that has tax advantages. Whether company funded, individually funded, or a combination of the two, contributions made to the pension fund are not taxable until withdrawn. There are some restrictions dealing with age and income level that can limit the amount that is tax-deferred and/or that can be contributed. Thus, it is possible that some funds in a retirement account may have already been taxed but the earnings from those funds are tax-deferred. We have already noted that deferring taxes can improve your investment result over paying taxes first on a contribution to an investment vehicle. This is because the balance earning interest is greater in the tax-deferred case.

When we looked at the comparison between taxed and tax-deferred investments we had noted that there was a factor of the initial savings on taxes by deferring the tax to later. So, in addition to earning more income on a larger investment balance, you can save some additional funds based on the reduced taxes you paid when you made the deferral. This is how this second part of the savings might look (using standard tax tables):

	Taxable Investment	Tax-Deferred Investment
Income	$30,000	$30,000
Tax-deferred contribution	0	- 2,000
Taxable income	$30,000	$28,000
Federal income taxes	- 3,804	- 3,504
Gross take home	$26,196	$24,496
After-tax contribution	- 2,000	0
Net take home	$24,196	$24,496
Increase from tax savings		**$ 300**

If your employer matches your contribution you then have even a greater return on your investment. It is extremely difficult to beat a 100% match by an employer on your pension plan so you should take advantage of it. Even though you will need to pay taxes on it when you withdraw the funds the return is hard to beat. Let's take an example where you can choose among the options of investing in your employer's plan, 5% of your salary matched at 100%, investing the 5% in your own tax-deferred investment with no match, or investing the 5% in a taxable investment. If we use the same parameters as in the previous example we come up with the following results after the first year (using standard tax tables):

	Taxable	Tax-Deferred	Matched Tax-Deferred
Income	$30,000	$30,000	$30,000
Tax-deferred contribution	0	- 1,500	- 1,500
Taxable income	$30,000	$28,500	$28,500
Federal income taxes	- 3,804	- 3,579	- 3,579
Gross take home	$26,196	$24,921	$24,931
After-tax contribution	- 1,500	0	0
Net take home	$24,696	$24,921	$24,921
Increase from tax savings	0	$ 225	$ 225
Employer Match	0	0	1,500
Pension Plan Amount	$ 1,500	$ 1,500	$ 3,000
6% return	90	103.50	193.50
Estimated taxes	13.50	240.53	- 512.78
Total Saved	**$ 1,576.50**	**$ 1,587.97**	**$ 2,905.72**

Assuming the amounts have been invested for one year earning a 6% return the matching contribution ends up with substantially more. The return after taxes for the first option is 5.1%; the return for the second option is 5.9% after taxes, and the third option has a return of 93.71%. Which would you choose? Even the tax-deferred option is slightly better than the first option. Keep in mind though that the second option could turn out worse if tax rates were to go up when you started taking the money out. As you can see careful calculations and consideration of your options can have a profound effect on your future financial balance. Keep in mind, then, that employer pension plan opportunities can be a great benefit including savings on taxes.

Individual Retirement Accounts

Up to this point we have looked at pension plans that are created as part of working for a company whether for-profit, governmental, non-profit, or self-employed. Beyond this, individuals also have an opportunity to invest in these types of plans on their own, even if their employer does not offer one. These accounts are often identified as Individual Retirement Accounts (IRA). Again, in this section we will only note the types of accounts and their tax advantages.

? **IRA**

The Key Types of Accounts

There are several types of individual retirement accounts available and are offered by most financial institutions who become the trustee of the account. The first type of account is the "traditional IRA." By traditional we mean it is tax deductible and tax-deferred just as with the employer-based plans we have discussed. The rules are very similar to those accounts although there are some restrictions on who is eligible to open one. Another type of account is the non-traditional IRA which can be opened by anyone and has similar features except that contributions to the plan are made after taxes have been paid on the income. So contributions made to the account are not tax deductible. All earnings on the account are tax-deferred as with the traditional IRA. A third type of account is the Roth IRA named after Norman Roth who sponsored the bill that made it a reality in 1998. Roth IRAs also have similar rules to the other two and like a non-traditional IRA contributions are not tax deductible. In addition, earnings from a Roth IRA are tax-free. That is, when withdrawn at an appropriate time there are no taxes on the earnings to pay.

? **Traditional IRA**

? **Non-Traditional IRA**

? **Roth IRA**

? **Tax-Free**

The Tax Advantages of IRA Accounts

The tax advantages of the three types of IRA accounts mentioned are similar in nature to those of the pension plans we have discussed. As with the pension plans there are differences in the final result and sometimes it is nearly impossible to know for sure what the future will hold. The same issues that affect the result of pension plan planning can also affect IRA planning. That is, changes in tax rates, laws, and rules can have a significant impact on our planning especially if enacted close to when your plan is about complete. With that caveat we will present a chart that shows a sample result of investing the same amounts in the three different IRAs and then briefly discuss the results. Our table assumes a $2,000 a year investment at 7% APR, and a 15% marginal tax rate for 10 years, for each of the IRA scenarios.

	Traditional	Non-Traditional	Roth
Contribution	$20,000	$20,000	$20,000
Compounded tax savings	+ 4,145	0	0
Earnings	+ 7,633	+ 7,633	+ 7,633
Total savings	31,778	27,633	27,633
Estimated taxes	- 4,767	- 1,145	0
Total Saved	**$ 27,011**	**$ 26,488**	**$ 27,633**

What we learn from this example is that tax-deductible contributions continue to provide a benefit over after-tax contributions just as with pension plans but Roth IRAs provide a significant advantage over either. That is, the tax-free earnings, given enough time, will beat tax-deductible contributions. As the time frame grows the difference becomes greater. If the above scenario was computed over 20 years the difference grows from $622 to $1845. Another point is that the higher the tax rate the greater the benefit of the Roth IRA. The same scenario above computed for a 28% tax bracket increases the difference from $622 to $2187. The only time the Roth IRA has no benefit over the other scenarios is when there is a 0% tax rate. Based on this information the only reason not to choose a Roth IRA would be to choose an employer plan that either is paid by the employer or which has matching of your funds. Employer matching will almost always beat a Roth IRA unless the match is extremely low.

Education Investment Vehicles

Another area of tax-advantaged investment is for education. There have been significant changes to the tax code to help parents deal with funding their children's rising education costs. In addition to several available tax credits that are now available for parents, several new investment instruments have been developed that encourage either saving or reducing the cost of education. Most instruments are based on the rules for an education IRA or a 529 Plan both of which are described in the next section.

The Education IRA and 529 Plans

At the time the Roth IRA was introduced in 1998 the education IRA was also introduced. It is now known as the Coverdell Education Savings Account (ESA) but is by most folks simply known as an education IRA even though, technically, it is not an IRA. It is really a trust or custodial account and not an IRA. The education IRA is very similar to the Roth IRA having the key feature of tax-free earnings. The basic rules of this type of IRA are:

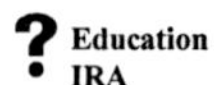

- Can be opened by anyone for a named beneficiary including the beneficiary.
- Anyone, including the beneficiary, can contribute to a child's account assuming the individual meets the income restrictions.
- There is no limit on the number of accounts that can be opened for a beneficiary.
- Contributors must meet income restrictions to make a full or partial contribution. For a full-contribution you must have an adjusted gross income of less than \$95,000 (\$190,000 for a couple). For a partial contribution adjusted gross income must be less than \$110,000 (\$220,000 for a couple).
- There is a maximum annual combined contribution of \$2000 to any one beneficiary regardless of the number of accounts or individuals contributing. Any funds received above that are assessed a 6% excise tax, payable by the beneficiary each year the additional funds (and the earnings on those funds) are in the account.
- Contributions must be made by the April 15th filing deadline of the tax year.
- No contributions are allowed before a child is born nor after the eighteenth birthday.
- All funds must be withdrawn by age 30 to avoid taxes and penalties. There is a 30-day grace period. If not, then they will be taxed as normal income and subject to a 10% penalty.
- All funds withdrawn in a particular year must be used for qualified education expenses to avoid taxes and penalties to the beneficiary. Education expenses can be for elementary, secondary, or post-secondary education (higher education - assuming it is a qualified institution under the program). It

does not matter what the student status is. That is, there is no requirement that a student be attending full-time.

- If funds are used for non-qualified expenses then the tax-free portion withdrawn from the account is taxable along with a 10% penalty, both payable by the beneficiary.

- Funds can be rolled over to another beneficiary's account in the same family. This includes almost anybody related to the beneficiary above (parents, grandparents, etc.) as well as below (to the first cousins) in the family tree. Spouses are also included except for first cousins.

? 529 Plan

Another more recent development for saving for education is the 529 plan or sometimes called a Qualified Tuition Plan (QTP). The name comes from section 529 of the tax code that makes permanent tax-free giving of money to a state (which is what got this whole thing started) that can then be distributed by the state back to a beneficiary without the beneficiary being taxed (which is the new part). In addition, any earnings withdrawn is not taxed unless the amount withdrawn exceeds the educational expenses for the year. The law, as of 2004, allows for the creation of private 529 plans as well that are tax-free. Before 2004 these plan's earnings were taxable but state plans were not. As of 2004 both state and private 529 plans operate the same. The basic instrument that accomplishes this is either a state sponsored savings plan or a college prepayment plan that is either state or school sponsored. Unlike an education IRA, 529 plans can only be used for higher education expenses. The basic rules (some may not apply to prepayment plans) that apply to a 529 plan are:

- A 529 plan is available to anyone.

- Unlike the Coverdell ESA there are no income limitations.

- Unlike the Coverdell ESA, there are no limits on the amount you can contribute to a 529 plan. Your contribution could be subject to gift tax if it exceeds the gift tax limits allowed for contributions to a 529 plan in a single year (currently $55,000 for singles and $100,00 for couples). Some states may have limitations on their individual plans.

- There are no state residency requirements. You can establish a plan with any state or school.

- Unlike the ESA, the 529 plan is controlled by the donor and not the beneficiary. As a result, the tax consequences by state and plan may vary.

- All funds withdrawn in a particular year must be used for qualified education expenses to avoid taxes and penalties.

- If funds are used for non-qualified expenses then the tax-free portion withdrawn from the account is taxable along with a 10% penalty.

- The beneficiary of a 529 plan can be changed to someone else in the family.

- Savings plans can be used for any school but pre-payment plans may have restrictions or penalties for going to another school. Be sure to check since some states offer prepayment plans that can be transferred to any school in the country.

Although the 529 savings plan may seem straightforward there will be differences from plan to plan including investment options and differences among states including whether earnings are tax-free for state taxes. The prepayment plans for specific colleges will vary greatly and you will need to plan and research carefully to make the right choices.

Prepayment plans can be particularly helpful since they usually involve purchasing tuition credits certificates that can be redeemed for education thus placing the cost of inflation on the school rather than you. Prepaying for a college now can save a great deal in the future especially if your child is quite young.

The Tax Advantages of Education Accounts

For the Coverdell ESA account the tax benefit accrues to the beneficiary and not the contributor (although there is no gift tax for the amount given by the contributor unless they exceed the annual gift limit for an individual). That is, the tax advantage of tax-free earnings helps the beneficiary reduce income for tax-reporting purposes. This may not seem like much if the amount is small over a brief period of time but at $2,000 over 18 years it can be a substantial amount of earnings each year that is sheltered from tax. Of course if you are trying to reduce the size of your estate to reduce estate taxes when you die then there is a benefit to the contributor as well.

The 529 plans have the same tax advantages of the ESA as long as the funds withdrawn are used for educational expenses. For many 529 plans, when funds are withdrawn and not used for education purposes the donor pays tax and a 10% penalty for the earnings portion of that withdrawal whereas for the ESA it is the beneficiary. Like the ESA, 529 plans provide a nice way to reduce an estate that may be taxed in the future. A 529, unlike the ESA will allow you to take full benefit of the gift tax in a single year by only contributing to the plan.

Unless we see a large deflationary period prepayment 529 plans seem like the most valuable education plan available since the tuition you pay now will not be increased in the future when you or your child goes to school. Also, it is an opportunity for you to set aside funds for graduate education in the future at a reduced rate. For non-higher education expenses an ESA is the way to go.

Other Tax Saving Vehicles

In this section we want to touch on a few other investment vehicles that can save taxes and put more of your money into funding the future. These are a few possibilities and a little research will likely turn up many others.

Flexible Spending Accounts

Flexible Spending Accounts (FSA) allow you to set aside funds before taxes through payroll deduction for qualified expenses such as childcare, medical expenses, and other insurance premiums. You then submit receipts for reimbursement from the account as they occur. This is all usually accomplished through a third party who administers the accounts for the employer. The key tax benefit for the employee is the fact that taxes do not have to be paid on the reduction that is put into the account. If you use the funds in the account by the end of the year you will have saved the equivalent of your marginal tax rate on the funds used. For instance if you spend $3000 a year on child care plus another $2000 on medical costs and deductibles you would plan on setting aside that amount via payroll deduction into an FSA. The amount would be divided equally among the number of pay periods your organization has. Here is the comparison between using post-tax funds versus the FSA assuming a 28% marginal tax bracket:

Post-tax In order to have $5000 from our paycheck after federal taxes requires us to start with a figure of $6,945. The formula would be 5000/ (1- .28) = 6945. In other words it normally requires us to earn $6,945 in order to have $5,000 in take home pay after federal taxes. Stated that way the formula would be 6945 – (6945 * .28) = 5000. So to pay for qualified expenses totaling $5,000 using the post tax dollars requires us to actually earn $6,945.

Pre-tax: since the money earned is deducted from your paycheck before federal taxes the amount you must earn, to have $5,000 available for qualified expenses, is $5,000.

Based on the marginal tax rate and the amount of annual qualified expenses there is an annual savings of $1,945 by using the FSA.

That kind of savings over a long period of time can be dramatic as you saw when doing the time value of money. As long as you are paying taxes and you use the funds in your account there is a benefit to using them. Most plans require you to forfeit any unused funds at the end of the benefit period which usually is the end of the plan year so be sure you plan carefully so you don't have any funds in the account at the end of the period.

Municipal Bonds

Municipal bonds are debt issues made by various political entities such as states, cities, counties, and school districts. We discuss bonds in more detail in a later chapter but note them here because of their tax benefit. That is, most municipal bonds earn income free of federal, state, and local taxes. Now if the bond rates are the same for both municipal and other bonds and both were held to maturity then the tax-free municipal bond would always be the bond of choice assuming you pay taxes. But, alas it is not always that easy. Municipal bonds often have a lower rate than other bonds so you need to figure if the tax benefit more than makes up for the lower yield. Of course the higher your tax bracket the more likely municipal bonds will be of benefit to you.

To compare the rate of a tax-free bond with that which is taxable you will need to make the following calculation.

Taxable yield = tax-free yield / (1-tax rate)

Once you have computed the tax equivalent yield for the municipal bond you can compare it to the taxable bond yield. If the equivalent yield from the municipal bond is greater, then that would be the one of choice. Keep in mind the tax rate should include your federal, state, and local taxes. If your federal rate is 15%, and your state rate is 7% then you have a rate of 22%. Also, keep in mind if you sell the bond before maturity at a profit the profit is still taxable. If you are in the 15% marginal tax bracket and you were to compare a 4% interest-bearing, taxable bond with a 3.5% interest-bearing, non-taxable bond, which would you select? Just use the formula to determine the equivalent table yield of the non-taxable bond.

Taxable yield = .035 / (1-.15)

Taxable yield = .035/.85 = .0412

The result makes it clear that the tax-exempt bond is a better deal since it has a taxable yield of 4.12% versus the other which has 4%. If the taxable yield were less than 4% then the taxable bond would be a better choice.

Outcomes and Chapter Summary

In this chapter we focused on the benefits of using tax-advantaged investment instruments. By carefully considering our investments we can find additional return that results from investing in instruments whose income is not taxed.

Learning Objective 1. Identify and describe the types of pension plans offered by companies.

We looked at the two basic types of pension plans offered by companies. In the past defined benefit plans were the primary pension vehicle which defined what one would receive from the plan at retirement. Today the defined contribution plan is the primary vehicle which defines how much you will put in. We also looked at the benefit of having tax-free benefits.

Learning Objective 2. Identify the types and key advantages and disadvantages of Individual Retirement Accounts (IRAs).

We contrasted and compared the three main types of IRA accounts including traditional, non-traditional, and Roth. The traditional IRA provides for tax-deductible contributions while the others do not. The earnings on both traditional and non-traditional IRAs are taxed while the earnings on a Roth IRA are tax free. The Roth IRA almost always will yield a better return.

Learning Objective 3. Identify and describe the unique benefits of the education IRA and 529 Plans and be able to contrast them based on the benefits and drawbacks of using the instruments.

We explored the Coverdell Education Savings Accounts (ESA) commonly misnamed as an education IRA. We also compared them to the 529 plans that are common from various states and colleges. One key benefit of the ESA is that it can be used for any level of education.

Learning Objective 4. Describe the purpose of flexible spending accounts and how they can benefit the individual.

We discussed flexible spending accounts which allow us to pay for qualified expenses with before tax dollars. They are often used for healthcare and child care expenses.

Learning Objective 5. Identify and describe other tax advantaged investment vehicles such as municipal bonds.

Municipal bonds provide an additional tax savings advantage since they are not usually taxed on any level including federal, state, and local.

Exercises and Research Activities

1. You have been offered a choice of two new benefits at your place of work. You may choose only one. The company, in order to keep employees available for emergencies, is offering free lunches each day during the 5-day business week. These would normally cost $7.50 a day. The other option is to take an annual cash bonus of $2,000. Which would you take and why?

2. You want to invest $2,000 a year in a tax-advantaged instrument such as an IRA. Currently your employer offers a 20% match for its 401K plan. Which should you choose: your employer's plan, another traditional IRA, a non-traditional IRA, or a Roth IRA?

3. You have a child that will likely be attending college in 12 years. Research the best education savings plan or 529 plan that you can find and write a brief report that shows your results.

4. Your employer has begun offering flexible spending accounts for healthcare. Assuming you spend $3,450 each year how much will you save by using the account if you are in the 15% marginal tax bracket?

CHAPTER 8

Investing in Stocks

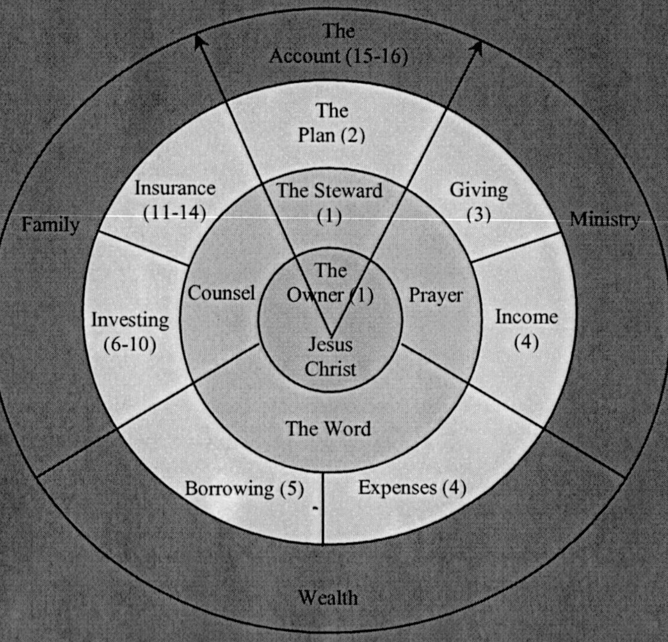

Learning Objectives

1. Define company stock from an investment perspective and identify types of stock that a company can offer. Describe the elements that influence stock pricing and what the expected returns from a stock investment can be.

2. Identify and locate organizational and stock information from a variety of sources. Identify and select a strategy for stock investing.

3. Identify and describe the vehicles available for purchasing and selling stocks as well as select a particular vehicle based on its particular benefits.

4. Be able to identify and select a stockbroker based on your investing needs and experience.

Lord, I commit to investing in assets.

Lord, I confess it is so easy to spend resources on things that will not last or have no return. Thank you for showing me the importance assets can play in providing for the future. I commit to investing wisely in assets that are likely to provide a solid return. I ask that you allow your Spirit to guide me as I seek to make the right decisions concerning which assets to invest in. May the return that accrues on them be an evidence of faithful stewardship and a delight to you.

Introduction to Stocks

We have already noted that as a good steward of the financial resources that God has given to us that He expects us to appropriately trade with them and have a return commensurate with the amount and insight He has given us. The parable in Matthew 25:14-30 is a good reminder of this. In the rest of this chapter we explore the various ways in which we can trade and earn a return from stocks, in this world for the Master.

What is Stock?

? Stock

? Share

Most individuals reading this book will have heard of the term stock but know little about the implications of investing in it. Corporations, like individuals, are legal entities that can buy and sell goods, loan and borrow money, and must obey the laws of the country including paying taxes. Who owns this legal entity? Initially it is the few who actually start the company. At that time the company is considered private and ownership is among relatively few people. Those in ownership are said to have "stock" in the company because it is highly likely they have invested time and money in making it successful. As part of that investment they of course expect their money to do well and earn a great return. To identify who these owners or "stockholders" are, a company issues "stock certificates" that identify how much of the company or what "share" is owned by the one holding the certificate. Today these are often maintained electronically. So stock represents a portion or number of shares of ownership in a corporation.

? IPO

Once a company grows and has shown that it is a viable or "going" operation others may be interested in investing in the firm by buying a portion of the ownership. Once established, firms will often make a "public" stock offering called an IPO or Initial Public Offering to attract investors to invest in and become part owners of the corporation. Of course the private owners of the company will still retain some stock in the corporation but will have less control since others from outside will also own some of the company. Once an IPO has occurred the company is considered a "public" company, that is, one whose stock is available to the general public. Although there may be many thousands of public owners of a corporation based on the IPO they obviously can not all run the company together, so the stockholders vote for a board of directors that is responsible for the running of the corporation. The stockholders will meet occasionally to vote on business of the corporation.

So once the IPO is complete and the owners of the company have been established how does one become part owner or acquire shares in a company if you do not already have stock? The answer is to buy somebody else's ownership piece. That is, you can go to a current owner and agree to buy all or a portion of his stock for a certain price. He in return would give you the stock certificates representing what you have purchased. You could then make sure that you are registered with the corporation as the new owner of those certificates. This of course works well until the number of companies, owners, and amount of stock becomes unmanageable by personal transactions. As the interest in stock ownership increased it became clear that there needed to be a clearinghouse to take in requests to sell as well as requests to buy and match them up and maintain records more easily. Out of this need was born the stock exchange. The totality of the entities that are involved in the exchange of stock is called the stock market. We will briefly discuss how the market operates later in the chapter.

Understanding the Return on a Stock Investment

Why would you want to be part owner or, in other words, buy stock or shares in a company? You obviously hope to get something in return for spending money to become part owner of a company. There are basically two types of return that you can look for in investing in the stock of a company. The first is any money the corporation pays to the owners from its profits. When organizations give some of the profits back to the owners they are giving what is called a dividend. The remaining profits of the organization are retained by the organization to grow the business and develop new products and services. This portion of the profits is called "retained earnings." The greater the dividend that the company pays to its owners the more attractive it is to investors. That is they will desire to become owners as well.

? **Dividend**

? **Retained Earnings**

The second key avenue of return to the investor occurs when he sells his ownership stake; that is, the increased value (hopefully) of the share of ownership over time. As companies grow and prosper they become more valuable. Thus, there is more interest in ownership by more investors, which creates competition, which in turn raises the price of a share of the company's ownership. Now there are many factors that affect the price of a share of ownership and we will get into that later in the chapter. Suffice to say here that one who invests at one price and sells at another either has gained or lost something from his original investment.

The return, then, on an investment in stock is composed of both the dividend and the net sum realized from the sale of the share. Keep in mind that many companies do not declare dividends so the return is only in the growth of the share price. Also note that there may be fees associated with purchasing and selling the shares that can affect how much your final return is.

With all of this in mind let's take a look at an example where all of these components exist. Let's assume you bought 500 shares of General Electric at $45.53 per share and they pay a 2.8% annual dividend. It costs you $9.99 to buy or sell the shares and you sell them for $51.11 after one year:

Initial outlay	500 * 45.53 + 9.99 = 22774.99
End of year 1 dividend	500 * 51.11 * .028 = 715.54 (3.1% return)
End of year 1 sale	500 * 51.11 = 25555.00 (12.2% return)
Total return	2789.01 + 715.54 – 9.99 = 3485.56 (15.3% return)

To annualize a rate of return for a calculation that covers more than 1 year just divide the calculated return by the number of years the investment was held. If the above return of 15.3% were for two years, you would divide 15.3 by 2 and get an annualized return of 7.65%.

Of course if we sold the stock for less, then it is possible that we would have had a loss on the investment unless the dividend was enough to make up for the difference in price. Also keep in mind that we have not included the issue of taxes here but these would need to be paid. The gain or loss realized on the sale of a stock is considered to be a capital gain or loss and is subject to different and quite often better tax treatment than normal income.

Determination of Stock Prices

Who determines the price of a stock in the first place? What makes the price of a stock share go up and down? These are good questions for which there are no easy answers but we do want to explore some the forces that influence stock prices. Normally a price would be based on the underlying value of the company. But, even value is subject to influence. When an IPO is made the company tries to set a price for the shares based on the demand for the stock by current non-owners, the amount of funding they wish to raise for the business, and the number of shares they wish to have the company divided into. This in a sense establishes the initial value of the company. So, although the company sets the initial price of the stock, it does so based on various market forces that it does not have control over. Even if the company has made good on the things it controls, such as being profitable, other forces such as other market entrants may influence the outcome. For instance, if you are a profitable technology company due to make an IPO next week and five other similar companies decide to also offer their IPOs the same week, what is the effect? It is likely that the initial demand for your company's IPO will be reduced because some of that demand will go to the other IPOs. This may reduce the number of shares you will be able to sell or force you to reduce your price. There are many forces such as this at work that can affect the stock price both when initially offered by the company and when available in the stock market. We will now look at some of these forces and begin to see why it can be difficult to know exactly what will happen to a stock. Later in the chapter we will explore ways of reducing this uncertainty when selecting stocks to purchase.

Supply. Economics shows us that the more there is of an item the lower the price will be in order to attract enough people to buy the supply. The more stock the company creates initially or adds later the lower the price of each share of the company (unless the change results in additional value being added to the company). This actually makes sense using the example of a pie. If the pie represents the whole company and each slice represents share ownership in the company then in order to create more shares what must happen? The pie will need to be cut into smaller pieces. If you already had owned one of those pieces that means your piece of the company becomes smaller. If your piece of the pie is smaller, then trying to sell it will fetch you less than what you could have received if you sold it when it was larger. That is if your piece of the company is smaller it obviously will not command as large a price when you sell it. Thus adding stock generally reduces the price of each share of it that already exists (unless the size of the pie has been increased by the addition of value to the company).

Companies add stock by authorizing the sale of more shares thus diluting the ones currently owned (making the current owners' pieces smaller) or by splitting the current shares owned. By splitting the ones currently owned the companies are executing a stock split. That is, all of the shares are equally divided by the same amount creating 2, 3, 4 etc. times the current number. The purpose usually is to reduce the price of the stock in order to attract investors who can not afford the current high price of the stock. When a stock split occurs the price is reduced by a corresponding amount. For instance, if Oracle is selling at $80.00 a share and they would like to get the price down to $40 a share they could approve a 2 for 1 split which means each share will become two shares worth half of the original whole. If they did a 4 for 1 split then each share would be worth $20.

? **Stock Split**

Up to this point we have been emphasizing how increasing the supply of shares reduces the price. We should note that the reverse is also true. A reduction in shares usually increases the price. This is usually accomplished in two ways. The first is when the company approves buying back shares off the market. By having fewer shares available those who own pieces of the company end up with larger pieces. These larger pieces are worth more when sold. The second way is to approve a "reverse" stock-split. That is, for every 2, 3, 4, etc. shares a single share is created. Taking the Oracle example again, if there were a 1 for 4 reverse split then for every 4 Oracle shares owned we would end up with 1 but the price of that share would also be 4 times the original or $80 ($20 times 4).

? **Buyback**

? **Reverse Stock Split**

Demand. Of course as supply has one effect "demand" has the opposite effect. That is the more demand for a share of stock the higher the price because people will be willing to outbid one another to get a piece of the company. The less demand the lower the price because there will be excess shares with no buyers. Perhaps you have seen examples of this in the retail world. Back in the 1980s the "Cabbage Patch" dolls came on the market. Each was unique in some way and had its own documentation. These would normally sell for around $30 but they became so popular that individuals were willing to spend hundreds of dollars to get one for their children for Christmas. There were just not enough of them available and as a result the demand drove up the price. As long as parents were willing to pay the price it would remain high.

Today though most are worth less than what was paid for them. The same kind of craze occurred with the Ty "Teenie Babies." They were hugely popular and the prices went extremely high, some into the hundreds of dollars. Today most of them can be had for a few cents on the dollar. Just as with these retail examples stock prices can be influenced by investor demand. As investor demand goes up so do the prices and as investor demand wanes they come back down.

Now, you may raise the questions as to whether demand is influenced by other factors and certainly the answer is, yes. That is, although there may be what we call an inherent demand based on an item being new, there are many factors that influence demand and as a result influence the price. Clearly, though, demand is a direct influence. Let us note here that supply and demand also deal with what is known as liquidity risk; that is, the ability to sell your stock quickly at a fair price. The fewer people there are to buy it the longer it takes to sell it or the less you will receive in exchange for it.

Sudden Events. Many types of sudden events, regardless of their source, can influence the prices of stocks. When the terrorist attacks of 9/11/2001 occurred most stock prices went down even though the value of most of the companies themselves were no different than the day before the attack. It is the uncertainty (or additional perceived risk) that causes such things to influence stock prices. That perceived risk gave the impetus for many to sell their stocks which made the supply of stock available for purchase greater forcing the prices down so they could be sold. So, any type of event that has a far reaching impact such as wars, rumors of wars, oil shortages, major storms, and the like can have profound influences on stock prices because they raise uncertainty.

Interest Rates. Generally, interest rate changes can influence stock prices. The problem is understanding which direction they will go based on an interest rate increase or decrease. Interest rate increases would normally be seen as bad for stocks because that means it will cost companies more to borrow money making it more expensive to do business. As a result they will not be as profitable, or they would need to raise prices to maintain profitability, which may lead to decreased demand for the company's goods thus reducing profits. Whatever the case higher interest rates are seen as a negative related to profitability. Also, higher interest rates also make other investment instruments that pay interest more attractive, which will lead some investors to sell their stock and invest in these other instruments. This movement of funds from the stock market to other markets can force stock prices down. Usually interest rate increases are a minus for stock prices and decreases are a positive.

Inflation. Related to interest rates, inflation acts in a similar fashion. Inflation basically means that prices are increasing. This usually has a negative effect on stock prices because it will cost a company more to secure goods and services it needs to produce and sell its product or service. In addition, employees may demand higher salaries in order to meet the increased prices they must pay for goods on the market. In both of these cases the profitability of the company will be affected in a negative way and the stock price will very likely decrease.

Regulations. Governments can also have a profound effect on stock prices. This may be the result of a new law or rule, or by approval or disapproval of some new product or service, a merger, new taxes, tariffs, or the like. Generally, higher taxes are negative for stock prices because they either reduce a company's available funds (for corporate tax increases) or consumer spending for individual tax increases. Drug approvals can lead to increased stock prices while disapprovals can have a substantial negative impact. New travel safety related rules have had profound effects on airline industry stocks recently. Basically, any government intervention that is seen as reducing the profitability of a company will have a negative impact on the stock price while that which improves profitability will have a positive impact on the price. An example of the latter is when the government decided to increase military spending, which had a positive impact on companies whose work involved the military.

The Business. Of course we don't want to forget that a great influence on share pricing is the performance of the company based on the decisions it makes, the products it develops and markets, and the way it handles its resources. Sometimes this is known as the business risk aspect of investing and is usually unique to each company. The caveat here is that quite often the bad misstep of a company in an industry can have an impact on others in the same industry. For instance the withdrawal of Vioxx by Merck has had a negative impact on the companies with similar products. Of course, sometimes a misstep by one in the industry can be a boon for another in the same industry. An example of this is when recently the company making the flu vaccine had difficulties in production that contaminated many doses of the vaccine. Its stock price went down but others that had similar products went up.

Perception. Sometimes this is known as market risk. That is, if the perception is that the market is a "bull market" and will continue to move up then most stock prices will be perceived as moving upward. If it is the reverse then it will be perceived as a "bear market" and prices will tend to go down. What happens is that whenever someone sees an event, trend, announcement, or the like, they formulate an opinion about it in relation to the stock price of a particular company or companies. For instance, a company only makes $4 million dollars in profit this year compared to $4.05 million last year. Should this be perceived as the company losing its profitability? Succumbing to competition? Having poor management? A one-time event? Great in relation to the rest of the competition? Depending on how the market perceives the profit announcement will influence which way the price goes on the stock. Be aware that this type of influence is extremely strong in today's market and does add a bit of volatility to stock prices.

In summary, there are many factors that influence the price of a stock and they really deal with the risk versus return of the investment that we have previously discussed in the text. The greater the risk related to these factors the lower the price. Keep these factors in mind as you consider which stocks to invest in. We will discuss this in more detail later in the chapter when we discuss how to choose stocks.

How Stocks are Sold

? **Exchange**

Once stocks have been through the IPO process (often referred to as the primary market) they then can be traded or exchanged on the secondary markets often through stock exchanges. These exchanges make it much easier for the stock to have liquidity allowing an investor to easily buy and sell stock by bringing many buyers and sellers together at the same time. Each exchange is independently run and companies must apply to be "listed" on the exchange. Each exchange has its own set of criteria that must be met to qualify for listing on a particular exchange as well as to remain listed. Members of the exchange have seats or membership at the exchange. Each exchange limits the number of members and in order to be a member you must buy one of the seats from another member. These seats give members direct access to trading and quite often are held by various brokerage houses. The two most well known exchanges are the New York Stock Exchange (NYSE) and the American Stock Exchange (AMEX). There are also regional and international exchanges that function in a similar way to these top well-known U.S exchanges.

? **Over-the-Counter**

Another type of secondary market that is well known is the over-the-Counter (OTC) market. Rather than being a physical place like exchanges they are virtual exchanges created by computer and phone hookups. This type of secondary market is highly automated by computers. An example of this is the NASDAQ (National Association of Securities Dealers Automated Quotations) which is really based on a system name that allows individuals to buy and sell stocks by posting bid prices to buy a stock and ask prices for selling a stock. As with exchanges NASDAQ has criteria for companies to be listed on its automated service. For companies that do not qualify to be listed on an exchange or the NASDAQ there are other over-the-counter secondary markets that are less liquid than the NASDAQ such as the OTC bulletin boards (OTC-BB). Companies listed on these systems do so because they are unable to qualify for one of the other avenues or decide not to. Usually these companies are known but have had financial troubles or are relatively unknown for a variety of reasons such as the inability to secure funding from standard sources. Stock in these companies is much more difficult to sell and much more volatile and should only be considered by the most seasoned investors.

So then, how does this secondary market really work? Well it is somewhat involved but let's take it a step at a time. Taking it from the request point every market request is precipitated by an "order." This order is either to buy or sell shares in a particular stock (or other instrument such as a bond which is discussed later). In order to get access to the market for your order you will need to use a broker who has access to the market or exchange where the stock is sold. Your broker will send your order request to the "floor" of the exchange electronically to an individual known as a "floor broker." The floor broker then directs your order to the exchange member who is the specialist for the stock your order deals with. The specialist then keeps track of your order until he can meet the requirements of the order. Once he can meet those requirements he will execute the order and your request will be satisfied. By the way, these specialists play an important role in keeping the market stable by buying and selling stock from their own inventories when supply and demand fluctuates at different times throughout the day. Thus the specialist can fulfill a buy order even if there is no seller and a sell order even if there is no buyer. Of course they can only hold this stability for so long as was clear from the crash of the market in 1987. Despite spending millions to stabilize the market by buying stock for which there were no buyers the market still lost a substantial amount. This whole process works similarly on the NASDAQ but the NASDAQ has market makers or dealers who act as the specialists for each stock and perform the same functions as the specialist. In this case there is no need for the "floor broker." The computer system itself in a sense becomes the floor broker. Exhibit 8-1 shows the basic sequence of events in a stock purchase from the exchange perspective.

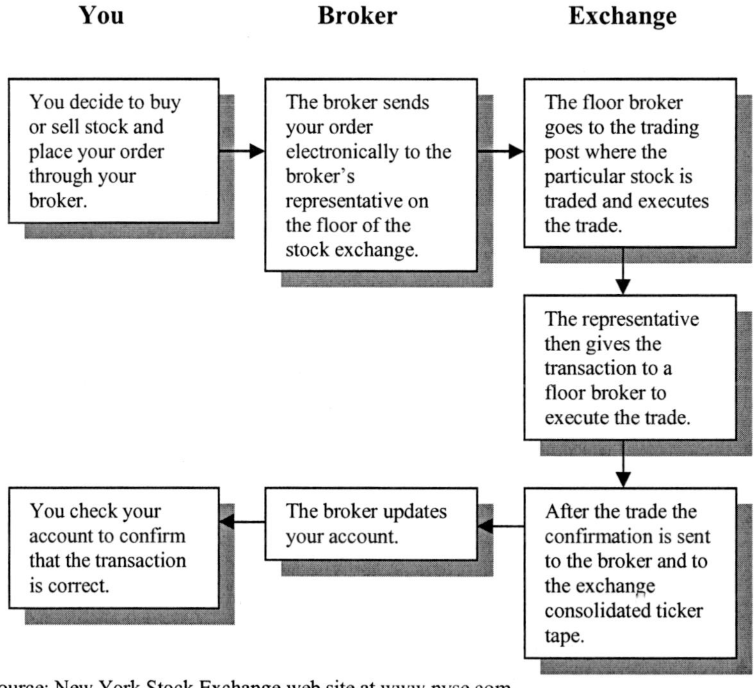

Source: New York Stock Exchange web site at www.nyse.com.

Exhibit 8-1. Stock Transaction Process.

Basics of Stock Orders

There are certain elements that you will include when making an order to send to one of the markets. First you will identify the stock you wish to place an order for. This is usually done using the ticker symbol. The ticker is the communications channel used for disseminating the current day's sales information about stock price, share volume, and the like. At one time this was done using a paper tape but is now done electronically. Each company is identified on the ticker using a one to four character code called the ticker symbol.

Your order will also provide a description of the number of shares involved in the order. This is sometimes called the lot. If your order is for an even number of 100 shares then it is considered a round lot. If it is less than 100 shares it is considered an odd lot.

? Good-till-Cancelled

You will also note how long the order is good for. That is, how long will the order be valid after which it will not be filled because the criteria for the order could not be met? The time given to fill an order is usually one of three possibilities: 1) a day order meaning that it is good for the trading day and if not filled will be cancelled when the market closes for the day; 2) open or good-till-canceled (GTC) order which means it will remain open until you cancel it; or 3) immediate or fill-or-kill orders that mean if it cannot be immediately filled to cancel it.

? Bid/Ask

? Limit

Of course you may also specify the price you are willing to buy (bid price) or sell (ask price) the stock for. If you do not specify a price you can put the order in as a "market" order that will be executed at the best available price. If you have specified a specific price for an order it is considered a "limit" order. With this your buy order will only be executed if the price is at your bid price or below and if it is a sell order the price will be at your ask price or above. Another type of order that deals with price is the stop or stop-loss order. This is an order to sell shares of a stock at the best available price when the price falls below a certain point. It can also be used to buy shares of a stock at the current price when the price of a share goes above a certain point.

Other Stock Instruments

There are other ways of "investing" in the stock market that are much riskier and from a steward's perspective would not be something to participate in. We do note them here just so that you will be aware that they are available and are best avoided.

Short selling. Short selling as its name implies, is selling that which you are short on. You sell stock you really do not own. To accomplish this feat you borrow stock from your broker with an obligation to replace it by a certain date. In addition, you would be responsible for any dividends missed by the broker. Of course the broker will want to protect himself by having you put up collateral in your account in addition to the funds you have received from selling the stock. Now, what is the purpose of doing this short selling? Well, it's basically the opposite of the way you normally consider stocks. Instead of looking for them to go up you are looking for them to go down. Thus, you are selling them now at a higher price and buying them back later at a lower price and giving the shares back to the broker. The key here is that the stock price must go down to make money and you must still cover any missed dividends.

This stock investment perspective should be avoided because of its extremely risky nature, as evidenced by the fact that the stock is borrowed, with no certain way to repay if the stock price goes higher rather than lower. In addition, the whole idea of desiring an organization's value to go down so you can make money seems to have an empty ring to it for the Christian. The other point is that the general tendency over time is for the market to go up. Short selling is more of a gamble rather than an investment and is usually spurred by the get rich quick mentality. It should be avoided.

Warrants. Offered by a company, warrants are instruments that allow the holder to purchase a stock at a predetermined price for a fee. These are quite risky since they have a time limit by which they can be used. The concept is similar to options discussed below. If the stock price never reaches a target that makes it worth exercising the warrant then you will have lost the fee for buying the warrant and the warrant will become worthless.

? **Warrant**

Options. An option as its name implies gives you an option of buying or selling stock at a predetermined price for a set period of time. The three most popular option time periods are three, six, and nine month agreements. A buy option is named a "call" option and a sell option is called a "put" option. The "call" option is similar to the warrant discussed above. Thus, if you believe the price of a stock will go up during a given period of time you could purchase a call option to buy shares of that stock later at an agreed on price that is lower than you expect the price to be at before the expiration of the option. If the price of the stock does go up before the expiration of the option period then you would exercise your option to buy the shares at the lower price. You could then immediately resell them at the higher price to lock in a profit. Of course, if you expected the price to go down over the short term you would purchase a put option that lets you sell a certain number of shares at a price that is higher than what you expect before the end of the option period. If the price does go down you can exercise your option to sell the shares by first buying them at the lower price in the market and then reselling them at the option's higher price and pocket the difference as profit.

? **Option**

? **Call/Put**

Several points should be made concerning options. First, options have a cost associated with them because of their high risk. That is, you must a pay the stockbroker who is willing to give you the option a fee for taking on some of the risk associated with option trading. If you do not exercise the option you lose the fee you paid. This is the only way the broker makes a profit on options. Otherwise, if options were free then the broker would be taking all the risk because if there is no profit in exercising the option for you, you can just let it expire. By paying the fee for the option you are risking losing that fee if you don't exercise the option. The fee is called the "option price" and is calculated using a computerized model that tries to adjust the price for risk. There are a number of different models for option pricing available for brokers. The second point is that it should be clear from this discussion that option trading, like short selling, can be extremely risky. Again, it is more akin to gambling than investing. Even if the price moves as you predicted you must hope it moves enough to cover your fee for the option.

What we have been discussing here is "buying" options for a set price. These prices may not be cheap and the risk is great. You could also sell a call option for shares you own and you would be the one receiving the option fee and the possible sale of your stock at a price you would like. Selling options is much less riskier because you are already the owner and can set the terms. Whether buying or selling options there will be brokerage fees involved as well.

Since buying options is highly volatile, and as Christians we are called to proper stewardship of our financial resources, this is another trading avenue that should be avoided. Many more lose than win with this strategy. Even selling call options has risk and we would recommend that you consider other avenues of investing. In any case, options and short selling are not for the inexperienced. Also, options and short selling generally fan the flames of the get rich quick mentality that Christians should avoid. There are better options available for the Christian.

Types of Stocks

Before leaving this section we should note that there are several types of stocks you may encounter as you do your research on a company. Each provides certain benefits to the holder of the stock.

? Common Stock

Common. The vast majority of stock is what is known as "common stock." This is usually the stock that has the voting privileges as owners of the company. Occasionally, the common stock is split into different classes such as class A, class B, and so on. In this case, usually one of the classes is designated as the voting stock class. If you are interested in having a vote in the company's affairs you will want to make sure the stock you purchase has voting rights.

? Preferred Stock

Preferred. Some companies issue what is called "preferred stock." The preference is related to the fact that these stockholders are paid dividends first and sometimes at a higher rate than the common stockholders. They may or may not have voting rights in the company.

? Cumulative Stock

Cumulative Preferred. Preferred stock can also have an additional designation as "cumulative." This means that any unpaid dividends accumulate until the company is able to pay them. This can happen when a company runs into difficulties and must conserve its funds. So if a dividend is supposed to be paid but is not instead of losing it the cumulative designation allows it to be noted as to be paid in the future. This also means that these stockholders will receive all of their accumulated dividends before the common stockholders get theirs.

Convertible Preferred. This type of preferred stock has the additional feature of being able to be converted to common stock at a predetermined conversion ratio.

? **Convertible Stock**

Evaluating Stocks & Finding Stock Information

Now that we have discussed what stocks are and the process by which they are purchased we are now ready to do some research and try to find companies that would be worth investing in. In this section we will explore the sources of information that can be useful in our decision making process and then follow that up with a discussion on what to look for in a company and what strategies are used to determine which stocks to select.

Using the Web

The quickest way of securing information about companies and stocks is through the resources on the web via the Internet. Before raving about all the great information available on the web we must first issue a warning that just because it is on the web does not mean it is true. There are many hoaxes and scams run off the web and via email that prey on the flesh's desires to get something for nothing or get rich quick. Investors have lost millions of dollars responding to "too good to be true" opportunities and found that they were. Anyone can setup web sites or post information on the Internet, so get your information from reputable sources and double-check information you find. Many of the stock tips you see are individuals trying to get you to buy shares of stock in a company that they already own stock in to try and get the price higher so they can sell. Again, keep in mind, that although the web has much good available there will always be those who will exploit it for their own vile desires. With this in mind let's look at some places to find information.

Company Web Sites. If you have an idea of what companies would interest you then each company's web site can be helpful in getting current investor information, securities filings, product information, and management team information. Keep in mind that most things provided on a company's web site are going to paint a rosy picture of the company but it can at least give you some basic information about the company.

Securities and Exchange Commission (SEC). The government organization that oversees the selling of stock and bonds (securities) by companies and stock exchanges is the Securities and Exchange Commission.

Their website is available at www.sec.gov. This site can provide a wealth of information about company related activities that might influence the price of a stock and will include all of the required governmental legal filings. Mutual funds, discussed later in the book, also must file appropriate documents through the SEC. The SEC uses something known as the Edgar project to make available all of the electronically filed reports, free of charge. You can access it from the SEC site address or directly from www.edgar-online.com.

Yahoo! Finance. For a great breadth of stock and financial news as well as historical market data and charts you might find Yahoo's Finance portal, Yahoo! Finance helpful. It can be accessed at finance.yahoo.com.

Bloomberg. Well known for its web site at www.bloomberg.com, it is a company that provides financial news, tools, analysis, and recommendations based on its other products and services including several magazines.

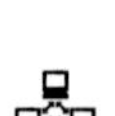

MarketWatch. This company provides real-time business and financial market news for free to investors via its two well-known web sites. These sites can be accessed at www.marketwatch.com and www.bigcharts.com. MarketWatch has recently agreed to be purchased by the Dow Jones Company.

Quicken. Quicken is best known as the software that manages your finances but it also manages a website for all aspects of personal finance including investments. Its investment section provides many helpful tools as well as a portfolio tracking service. It is a good reminder that we need to keep careful track of all our investing transactions, especially for tax purposes.

Using Newspapers and Magazines

Perhaps the best-known source of company and financial information is the Wall Street Journal. It is the most thorough newspaper in providing financial information and a complete look at stock information. The New York Times and other major city newspapers may also be good sources of information on companies. If you can not afford these you can read them at most major libraries.

There are also many financial and business magazines and newspapers that provide helpful insights, discussion, and recommendations related to purchasing stocks. Some of these include Barron's (www.barrons.com), Financial Times (www.financialtimes.com), Forbes (www.forbes.com), Fortune (www.fortune.com), Kiplinger's Personal Finance (www.kiplinger.com), Money (www.money.com), and Smart Money (www.smartmoney.com). Each of these company's web sites provide online access to articles and information. Some may require you to register or pay a fee to access the content. The magazines and websites can also be accessed at most major libraries.

One of the primary purposes of a paper is to look at the stock listings for the previous day to see how various stocks are doing. The fine print and numerous columns may seem hard to decipher so Exhibit 8-2 shows a sample portion with relevant items identified.

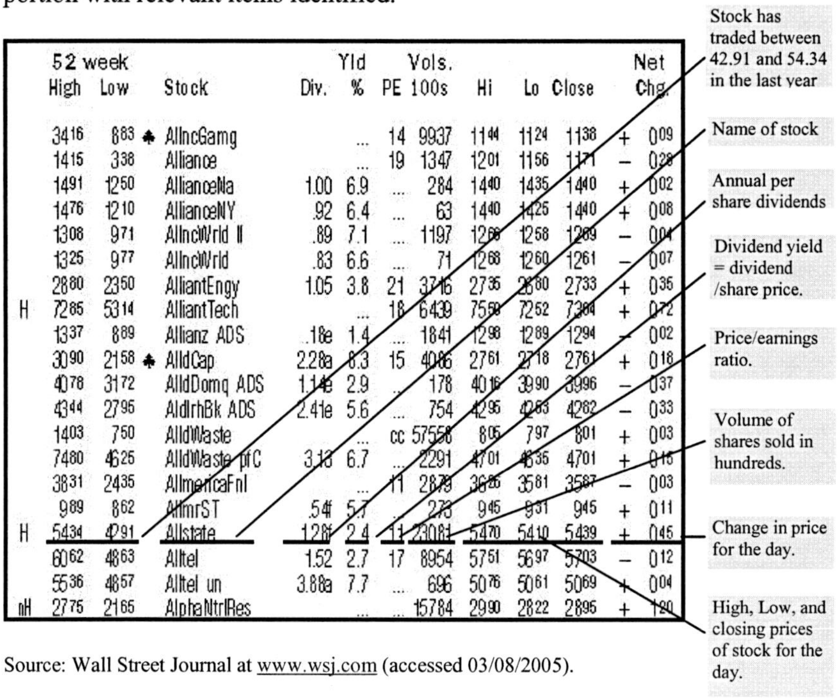

	52 week High	Low		Stock	Div.	Yld %	PE	Vols. 100s	Hi	Lo	Close	Net Chg.
	34^{16}	8^{83}	♣	AllncGamg		...	14	9937	11^{44}	11^{24}	11^{38}	+ 0^{09}
	14^{15}	3^{38}		Alliance		...	19	1347	12^{01}	11^{56}	11^{71}	– 0^{28}
	14^{91}	12^{50}		AllianceNa	1.00	6.9	...	284	14^{40}	14^{35}	14^{40}	+ 0^{02}
	14^{76}	12^{10}		AllianceNY	.92	6.4	...	63	14^{40}	14^{25}	14^{40}	+ 0^{08}
	13^{08}	9^{71}		AllncWrld II	.89	7.1	...	1197	12^{66}	12^{58}	12^{69}	– 0^{04}
	13^{25}	9^{77}		AllncWrld	.83	6.6	...	71	12^{68}	12^{60}	12^{61}	– 0^{07}
	28^{80}	23^{50}		AlliantEngy	1.05	3.8	21	3716	27^{35}	26^{80}	27^{33}	+ 0^{35}
H	72^{85}	53^{14}		AlliantTech		...	18	6439	75^{58}	72^{52}	73^{04}	+ 0^{72}
	13^{37}	8^{89}		Allianz ADS	.18e	1.4	...	1841	12^{98}	12^{89}	12^{94}	– 0^{02}
	30^{90}	21^{58}	♣	AlldCap	2.28a	8.3	15	4086	27^{61}	27^{18}	27^{61}	+ 0^{18}
	40^{78}	31^{72}		AlldDomq ADS	1.14e	2.9	...	178	40^{16}	39^{90}	39^{96}	– 0^{37}
	43^{44}	27^{95}		AldlrhBk ADS	2.41e	5.6	...	754	42^{95}	42^{63}	42^{62}	– 0^{33}
	14^{03}	7^{50}		AlldWaste		...	cc	57558	8^{05}	7^{97}	8^{01}	+ 0^{03}
	74^{80}	46^{25}		AlldWaste pfC	3.13	6.7	...	2291	47^{01}	46^{35}	47^{01}	+ 0^{15}
	38^{31}	24^{35}		AllmericaFnl		...	11	2879	36^{26}	35^{81}	35^{87}	– 0^{03}
	9^{89}	8^{62}		AllmrST	.54f	5.7	...	273	9^{45}	9^{31}	9^{45}	+ 0^{11}
H	54^{34}	42^{91}		Allstate	1.28f	2.4	11	23081	54^{70}	54^{10}	54^{39}	+ 0^{45}
	60^{62}	48^{63}		Alltel	1.52	2.7	17	8954	57^{51}	56^{97}	57^{03}	– 0^{12}
	55^{36}	48^{57}		Alltel un	3.88a	7.7	...	696	50^{76}	50^{61}	50^{69}	+ 0^{04}
nH	27^{75}	21^{65}		AlphaNtrlRes		...	...	15784	29^{90}	28^{22}	28^{95}	+ 1^{20}

Stock has traded between 42.91 and 54.34 in the last year

Name of stock

Annual per share dividends

Dividend yield = dividend /share price.

Price/earnings ratio.

Volume of shares sold in hundreds.

Change in price for the day.

High, Low, and closing prices of stock for the day.

Source: Wall Street Journal at www.wsj.com (accessed 03/08/2005).

Exhibit 8-2. Sample Stock Listing.

Using Specialized Services and Newsletters

Motley Fool. The Motley fool was created by the Gardner brothers as a tool to educate and amuse the individual investor rather than the institutional world that many target. As a result they have built a cadre of educational tools including online seminars, books, newspaper columns, and an online web site at www.fool.com. They also offer an investment newsletter Motley Fool Income Investor that is available by paid subscription. Overall, the site provides many solid perspectives on investment matters.

Moody's Investor Service. This is a well-known investor service that provides a variety of printed matter including the Moody Handbook of Common Stock and the Moody's Manuals that present information, backgrounds, and historical data on companies. They also host a website at www.moodys.com.

Standard & Poor's. This company is best-known for its market tracking index the S & P 500. They also provide a number of publications that provide company information and analysis including Standard & Poor's Corporate Records and Corporation Reports. They also host a website at www.standardandpoors.com.

Dow Jones. This company is best known for its market-tracking index, the Dow Jones Industrials Average (DJIA). But the company also plays a significant role in providing financial information and analysis to the world. Many do not realize that they also publish the Wall Street Journal and Barron's.  Their website can be reached at www.dowjones.com. They also recently agreed to purchase MarketWatch, which is well known for its two free websites MarketWatch.com and BigCharts.com

Value Line. The best-known and most useful service for investors is known as Value Line. The company publishes a quarterly Value Line Investment Survey that covers analysis, forecasts, and company ratings for some 1700 companies. In addition, Value Line also makes recommendations to investors and provides advice on where rates, industries, and markets are headed. It is quite expensive but can usually be viewed at major libraries.

Using Professional Advice

Brokerage Firms. Many brokerage firms will provide free information to their clients about companies they have researched and can provide professional advice on various investment options and strategies. Examples of firms in this category would be Merrill Lynch and Charles Schwab.

Online Brokerages. Some brokerages have been created as web-based only entities. Some of these also can provide professional analysis and recommendations to their clients based on their own research or that of others. Usually, those who provide more research also charge more in fees for trading. Examples of companies in this group include Ameritrade, and e-Trade.

Strategies for Buying and Selling Stocks

Now that we have an idea of where we can go to get company information, as well as analysis and recommendations, we are ready to build a stock portfolio. There are many ways of determining which and how many stocks and how often one should buy and sell. We will take a look at some of these strategies in this section.

Market Index Strategy. One possible strategy is to invest in stocks that mirror the indexes that track the market. Since the indexes over the years have tended higher over the long haul your stock portfolio should increase in value. By matching your portfolio to a market index its value will on average move up or down with the index. The key indexes include:

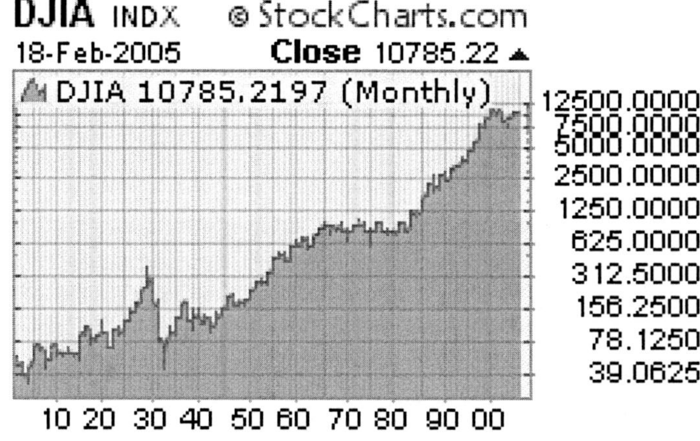

Source: Courtesy of StockCharts.com at www.stockcharts.com (accessed 03/08/2005).

Exhibit 8-3. Historical Picture of the Dow Jones Industrial Average.

Dow Jones Industrial Average (DJIA). This best-known index measures the performance of 30 large companies' (blue-chip) stock prices. The stocks change in the DJIA as companies and market segments change, but the average itself is adjusted based on a formula that takes into account these changes, rather than a sum of the stock prices. There are other Dow averages that some follow beside the DJIA. These include the transportation index, the utility index, and a composite of all three. Exhibit 8-3 gives a little history of the DJIA progress over time.

S & P 500. We have already noted that another common market tracking index is the Standard & Poor's 500 (S &P 500). Some investors like matching their portfolio stocks to this index because it has a wider variety of stocks and seems more representative of the overall market than the DJIA. Standard and Poor's also has a number of other indexes including an industrial index, a transportation index, a utility index, a financial index, a mid-cap index, a small-cap index, and another composite – the S & P 1500.

At this point we should note what the term "cap" means to the investor. "Cap" stands for "capitalization" or the market value of the company. The market value of a company is determined by multiplying the number of shares outstanding by the share price. The companies are then grouped into one of three groups based on their value. The market values assigned to each group may vary from one investment analyst to another but they usually fall into the following ranges: < $500 million – small-cap; between $500 million and $3 billion – mid-cap; and > $3 billion – large-cap. You may also hear of micro-cap companies. These are companies with a value less than $50 million. Generally, the less the value of the company the more risky owning the stock is.

NYSE Index. The New York Stock Exchange (NYSE) composite index is a measure of the performance of the market based on all the stocks listed on the exchange. The NYSE also has several other indexes including an industrial index, a utility index, a transportation index, and a finance index.

AMEX Index. The American Stock Exchange composite index is a measure of the market performance based on all the stocks listed on the exchange.

NASDAQ Index. The National Association of Securities Dealers composite index captures the market performance of the over-the-counter market of which the NASDAQ is a part. They also have a variety of other indexes to follow various segments of the market. Because of the concentration of technology stocks in the over-the-counter market the NASDAQ has been seen as a barometer of the technology stocks but it certainly is not composed of just that.

Other Indexes. Some investors use other indexes as guides to portfolio management. These include the Russell 1000, the Russell 2000, the Russell 3000, and the Wilshire 5000. Of these the Russell 2000 is more closely watched than the others.

Later we will discuss ways of actually incorporating in your portfolio all of the stocks noted in some of these larger indexes since to try and buy some shares of 500 or more stocks can be problematic, financially speaking. There are other strategies besides using a market index that we want to now look at as well.

? **Blue Chip**

The Blue-Chip Strategy. The blue-chip strategy means that as an investor you are going to stick with large well-known and profitable firms. Examples would include GE, IBM, GM, Johnson & Johnson, and the like. These companies have demonstrated consistent growth and profitability over a long period of time. The risk in such a portfolio is reduced because of the stability of the companies but the returns may also be lower because of mature product markets, larger cost structures, and bureaucracy that make them less nimble than smaller companies.

The Growth Strategy. The growth strategy involves creating a portfolio of stocks that involves companies that have excellent growth prospects. These may include companies, with new products or technologies, that are small but are quickly increasing in size and whose earnings outpace the market significantly. Recent examples of this type of company included Kohl's, Home Depot, and Starbucks.

The Income Strategy. Some investors desire plenty of income in their portfolio rather than appreciation so they look for stocks that provide great dividends that can either be taken out in cash or reinvested. The key here would be to find strong companies who have consistently declared dividends for many years and whose financial status supports continued dividend payouts. Examples of companies in this area include Pfizer, GE, and Washington Real Estate Trust. Bill Staton of Staton Institute champions this approach. He is known for his book *America's Finest Companies* that outlines the best companies to invest in. For more information visit his web site at www.statoninstitute.com.

Buy-and-Hold Strategy. With this strategy you decide to purchase stocks for your portfolio and keep them for a long period of time, usually many years. The rationale is that the market has a tendency to go up over time so it is highly likely that after many years your portfolio will have a greater value than when you first purchased it.

Dollar Cost Averaging. This technique involves investing the same amount of funds consistently for the same stocks over a period of time. This avoids the trap of buying high and selling low. If you buy $100 of Microsoft stock every month for 5 years you will have paid a variety of prices for the stock. In some months you will have paid more and in others less. The key is the average price paid for each share. Let's say the first time you bought the stock it was $50 a share, the most you paid was $53 a share, the least you paid was $35 a share and the current price is $48 a share. If after 5 years you had purchased 150 shares the average price would be $6,000 (5 years at $100 a month) / 150 = $40. That is, on average, you would have spent $40 for each share of Microsoft stock. Since it is currently selling for $48 a share you could still sell it all and make a profit. But what if you had bought it all up front and then sold it at its low of $35 a share? You would have sustained a significant loss. Dollar cost averaging helps you to avoid the effects of the market highs and lows to reduce the risk. The detractors of this strategy would suggest that you put the lump sum in all at once because the market's overall tendency is up. This is generally true but in recent years the volatility of the market has made this a better choice. So in a general bull market this approach is not as good as a lump sum investment but in a vacillating or down market this approach is better.

? **Dollar Cost-Averaging**

The buying on margin strategy. This strategy involves borrowing a portion of the funds needed to purchase the stock. Rather than get into the technical details we would recommend that you avoid the risk of using margin (borrowing based on the collateral in your investment account). If you don't have the funds to invest then you would certainly not have the funds to pay the loan back if the value of the stock went down quickly. We have also looked at short selling, which is another form of borrowing (the stock itself) that is to be avoided. As a Godly steward do not invest with borrowed funds or stock no matter how good the prospects look.

? **Margin**

The Hunch-and-Hot-Tip Strategy. This is synonymous with the "No one has a clue what the market will do" approach. More investors than you might realize do their investing based on hunches, what they overhear in the office, or based on some email or chat room conversation on the Internet. These rarely have any value and lead to constant buying and selling to hit that magic stock that takes off in price. Again, these strategies usually deal with either the get-rich-quick mentality or with "I don't have the time, knowledge, patience, etc." mentality. As Proverbs 4:26 notes "*ponder the path of thy feet, and let all thy ways be established*" (KJV).

? Fundamental Analysis Theory

The Market Theory Strategies. Basically these strategies involve various interpretations as to how the market actually works. The fundamental analysis theorists suggest that the value of a company's stock is determined by its future earnings. These folks carefully look at the financial statements, product developments, and anything that can be analyzed related to determining what the future earning of a company might be. We see much of this perspective in use today and the estimated future earnings are often noted when looking at future company growth and forecasts.

? Technical Analysis Theory

A second market theory strategy is the technical analysis theory. It suggests that future stock pricing can be determined by careful analysis of historical trends in the market. These folks are heavy users of charts and statistical tools to determine trends and correlations. They look at share volume, price, and number of orders trends to see what the future holds. We also see much of this technique used today by many investors especially as it relates to stock price. Most investment reports now at least include a chart showing the stock price over time.

? Efficient Market Theory

The last market theory is the efficient market theory, which suggests that the stock market is efficient as regards information about stocks so that it is impossible to beat the market average consistently. As a result they would advocate getting into the market in a broad way and you will likely match the market's growth over time. They would not advocate all the research the other two theories undertake to try to outperform the market.

Now that we have looked at various strategies for populating your stock portfolio you may wonder which way to go. Those who are consistently successful in the stock market are those who carefully consider the information available, consistently invest, and stay invested for a long period of time. Whatever strategy you decide on you should keep these things in mind. Certainly it is beyond the scope of this book to go into all the possible ramifications of choosing a particular approach. In fact, you may find, as some do, that a combination of approaches may help.

Stock Performance Indicators

In addition to the general approach or approaches you might decide on for your portfolio are indicators that help you identify which of the stocks to choose that may work with the approach you take. In this section we outline some of the indicators and factors that help determine whether a stock or company is worth considering for your portfolio.

? EPS

Earnings per Share (EPS). The earnings per share is determined by dividing the total earnings for a period by the total outstanding shares. Quite often this is given in investment information about the company. The EPS gives you an indication of the strength of the earnings. The earnings for the calculation is the net income minus the preferred stock dividends. So the calculation would look like the following:

EPS = (net income – preferred stock dividends) / number of outstanding common stock shares

The higher the EPS the better the company is in generating profits. You can compare the value to historical EPS values for the same company to see if earnings are growing. Keep in mind that "future" earnings per share are also considered based on expected earnings.

P/E Ratio

Price/Earnings Ratio (P/E). As its name implies, the price/earnings ratio is the result of dividing the price per share of the stock by the earnings per share of the company. The earnings per share is determined by dividing the total earnings for a period by the total outstanding shares as we calculated above. Quite often this is given in investment information about the company. This ratio is quite popular in determining the suitability of a stock especially when compared to the P/E ratio of the overall market. If the P/E ratio of the overall market is higher than the one for the stock you are looking at, there is a possibility the market undervalues it. Usually the lower the P/E ratio the better the investment may be.

Dividend Yield. The dividend yield is the percentage return on the investor's investment based on the dividends alone (no appreciation or depreciation in the price of the stock). If the stock cost $20 and the firm declares an annual $2.00 dividend then the investment earns a 10% return ($20/$2). This gives you a way of comparing the dividends of various stocks. The greater the yield you receive, the better the return on your investment.

Total Yield. The total yield is the total return on an investment including dividends and capital appreciation or depreciation. So, you could look at the previous year's number to calculate the total return for the pervious year or two to see what direction the total return is heading. As we noted before the formula is:

Total return = (annual dividend + annual capital gain (loss)) / share price.

Again, the greater the total return, the better the stock as an investment. It can also be a good tool for comparing with returns on other stocks.

Book Value. The book value of the firm is the booked or recorded assets minus its liabilities. We note this here because you may come across it in financial publications. It really is not all that helpful since the assets are based on when they were purchased and recorded by the firm and not their current value. Occasionally you will also see the "book value per share" where the book value is divided by the number of outstanding shares. Again this number may not be very useful since it deals with historical data on assets.

Net Profit Margin (NPM). This is another measure that is used to see how profitable a firm is. It is the net income or earnings divided by the sales. That is you are trying to see what portion of sales was attributable to profit. The higher the ratio is, the more profitability in the company. The formula is as follows:

Net Profit Margin = net income / total sales

Return on Equity (ROE). Another ratio that looks at profitability is the return on equity. It is a measure of how well an organization is managing and using its resources to produce profits. The formula for this ratio is:

Return on Equity = net income / total equity

Stock Purchase Vehicles

Most of you will be familiar with the fact that you can purchase individual stocks by using a full service broker or an online broker. In addition to these there are several other stock purchase instruments that you can use to try to reach the goals you have established for your portfolio whether they deal with the variety of stocks or the return. We cover some of these in this section.

Index and Mutual Funds

One way of setting up your portfolio to include many different stocks without purchasing each individually is to purchase shares in a mutual fund. We will cover these in detail in a later chapter but they are a way for small investors to pool their investment funds and purchase large numbers of many different stocks. These funds are managed by various brokers and they charge various fees for managing the fund. Of course those fees are shared as well. One type of mutual fund is an index fund. An index fund purchases stock to match the makeup of a particular market index. Thus if you wanted to have your portfolio track the S & P 500 you would locate an index fund whose holdings matched it. This is an easy way for an investor to broaden the base of stocks that are in the portfolio without having to purchase all of them (in this case 500). See the chapter on mutual funds to get a thorough understanding of how they work and the advantages and disadvantages of using them.

? Index Fund

Exchange Traded Funds (ETF)

? ETF

We want to note another type of mutual fund called the exchange-traded fund (ETF). This type of fund has been, up to this point, an index fund that has been created and then shares of the fund traded on an exchange just like stock. This gives the investor the advantages of an index fund that is professionally managed, has low costs, and low taxes as well as the flexibility of a stock where you can buy or sell from the fund at any point during the trading day. Of course, you will still need to pay commissions, as with a stock trade, to your broker. There are now over 100 of these funds available, like stock, that follow all types of different market indexes locally and internationally all of which trade on the AMEX. A few of the more popular ones include Spiders (SPD) that tracks the S & P 500, Diamonds (DIA) that tracks the Dow Jones Industrial Average, and Qubes (QQQ) that tracks the NASDAQ. Keep in mind when looking at the fund value of these shares that they are set as a fraction of the index value. So if the DJIA is at 7500 then the Diamonds might be at 750 or a tenth of the index it follows.

Dividend Reinvestment and Direct Plans

A great way of investing is through company sponsored direct stock purchase plans (DSPP). These plans allow you to establish an account with a plan administrator and then buy and sell shares of the company stock via the administrator. Another form of the direct purchase plan is the dividend reinvestment plan (DRIP). This is a direct purchase plan that will also automatically reinvest your dividends in additional company stock rather than receiving the dividends in cash. Some plans require you to already own shares to set up an account so you may need to create an initial investment outside of the plan to start one. There are many that do not have this requirement.

? DSPP

? DRIP

A good way of accomplishing your investment goals related to growth is to use dividend reinvestment plans. These plans allow you to take the company dividends that would normally come in the form of cash and buy additional stock for your portfolio of the same company from whom the dividend was issued. In reality you basically get your dividend in the form of more company stock. This is a great way of building your stock portfolio in an automatic fashion assuming you have stocks that pay dividends. For a comparison between automatic reinvesting of dividends and taking the dividends in cash, see Exhibit 8-4. As noted, these plans are developed by companies and usually managed by a third party plan administrator. Some popular administrators include EquiServe, Bank of New York, and Mellon. You can go to their websites to see what companies offer their plans from these administrators. You can also check the company website. Most have an investor's section that identifies whether they offer any stock plans and who administrates them.

Comparison of Cash and Reinvested Dividends				
Years	Shares	Stock Value	Cash Value	Total Value
Reinvested Dividends				
1	204.000	10710.00	0.00	10710.00
5	220.816	14091.18	0.00	14091.18
10	243.799	19856.13	0.00	19856.13
20	297.189	39426.61	0.00	39426.61
30	362.272	78286.00	0.00	78286.00
Cash Dividends				
1	200	10500.00	210.00	10710.00
5	200	12762.82	1210.07	13972.89
10	200	16288.95	2915.20	19204.15
20	200	26532.98	8703.65	35236.63
30	200	43219.42	20197.27	63416.69
Scenario: Jae has purchased 200 shares of stock at $50 each. The annual dividend is currently $1.50 per share annually and it increases at the rate of 5% each year. The value of the stock also increases at the rate of 5% each year.				

Exhibit 8-4. Reinvested Dividends versus Cash Dividends Comparison.

Another big benefit of these plans is that you can avoid having to pay brokers fees every time dividends are used to purchase stock for your account. Some brokers are beginning to offer dividend reinvestment as well but check to make sure there is no fee for doing so. Also there may also be a few companies that charge fees for reinvestment so again always check the fee structure. Some companies charge nothing at all for setting up an account, or buying or selling shares. Some also offer stock at a discount to these plans. Most plans do have fees related to selling. This is to encourage you to buy for the long term. The fees usually are not huge but enough to prevent constant selling of the stock. Be sure to look at all the costs related to a plan to make sure it will not cost you more than using your standard brokerage account. It shouldn't, but there are some that are more expensive and should be avoided.

Selecting a Broker

It is possible to avoid using a broker by using the direct purchase plans we noted above but your choices will be more limited and the benefits that come with using a broker may not be available for free. If you decide that you need a broker to provide greater access to the markets or need more research or advice then you will need to decide on what type of broker will meet your need. In this section we identify the types of brokers and what they have to offer and the tradeoffs of using the various types. Like with any purchase of a product or service check ahead on the company and comparison shop. Make sure you are receiving what you expected to get.

Types of Brokers

Brokers are basically intermediaries between you and the market, but because of their intimacy with and knowledge of the market they can provide more than just an avenue for you to place an order to the market.

? Broker

Full-Service Brokers. As the name implies the full-service broker provides a complete line of investment services to assist you in reaching your investment goals. Usually you will be assigned an individual from the firm who will work with you directly, give you advice, and oversee your account. The broker will also perform market trades for you.

Discount Service Brokers. A discount broker basically provides an avenue to send orders to the market. There is no advice or special help nor is there individualized service. There may be some service in the form of some research and a help line. Of course the big benefit is that the fees are 50-70% less than for full service brokers.

Deep Discount Brokers. Although the line may becoming more blurred with discount brokers, deep discount brokers really seek to minimize interaction and overhead and strictly perform trades. There is no research and usually the ways of making a trade are minimized to reduce overhead. Fees are up to 90% less than the full service brokerage.

Online Brokerage. These brokerage firms are usually discount type firms that reduce costs by making everything available via the web including automated trades. This again reduces the costs over a full service broker but relies more on you managing your own portfolio.

Influences on Broker Selection

So what should we look at when deciding which of the above brokers to select for our situation? There are several key factors that we should note that you will want to consider before deciding which way you will go.

Individualized Help and Advice. If you need individualized assistance and want someone to sit down with you and advise you on the best plan for your situation then you will need to select a broker that provides that service. That will usually be a full service broker. Another option is to hire a personal financial planner to help in the planning area and then a less expensive broker to create your portfolio. Keep in mind the personalized service will mean higher fees.

Research. Do you want a broker who provides plenty of research reports, news, and breaking events? If so, then using a deep discount broker is not likely going to work. If you would rather do your own research then the need for a full service broker is not necessary. Again, research takes time and as a result costs money. Usually the more research the broker provides the higher the fees.

Tools. Another area that increases the cost of a brokerage is the tools they provide. The more investment tools, calculators, and account management tools they provide the higher the fees for that broker.

Fees. For most a major concern are the fees paid for the brokerage service. As you can see there is no easy answer to that dilemma unless you go it on your own and use direct purchase plans that have no fees. The trade-off becomes between your time and that of the brokers. The more you do the less fees you will need to pay. Of course, you may not be an expert in investing either and so you may feel paying more is worth it.

Records. Some brokerages provide recordkeeping and safekeeping of your stock certificates. If you don't want to have to keep track of all the transactions and paperwork then paying a little more for record keeping might be a benefit for you. Keep in mind that record-keeping is very important especially for reporting taxes for dividends received and for capital gains purposes when selling stock.

As you can see there is no easy answer to the broker you should select. It is based on what you feel you are able to learn and do on your own versus seeking the help of professionals. If you are going to invest be sure to learn something of the area on your own so you can have some control of your portfolio. Too many are the stories where people have left their portfolio with a broker and not tracking it, only to find the broker getting rich off fees created by churning the portfolio; that is, buying and selling stocks from the portfolio for the sake of generating commissions. Whether you select a broker or not be sure you are watching your portfolio.

Outcomes and Chapter Summary

In this chapter we focused on what stock is as an investment how it is purchased, and how to invest in it. We also discovered where to locate information regarding companies that have stock and identified attributes that might be important in selecting a particular broker.

Learning Objective 1. Define company stock from an investment perspective and identify types of stock that a company can offer. Describe the elements that influence stock pricing and what the expected returns from a stock investment can be.

We explored the definition of what a stock is and discussed how it creates a return. We also reviewed the different types of stocks including common, preferred, cumulative preferred, and convertible preferred.

Learning Objective 2. Identify and locate organizational and stock information from a variety of sources. Identify and select a strategy for stock investing.

We explored the many avenues available for learning about stocks and the companies that they represent. These resources included the World Wide web, newspapers and magazines, newsletters and services, and professionals. We also reviewed the various strategies for investing in stock some of which included market index strategy, growth strategy, buy and hold strategy, dollar cost averaging, and income strategy.

Learning Objective 3. Identify and describe the vehicles available for purchasing and selling stocks as well as select a particular vehicle based on its particular benefits.

We explored the various vehicles by which stocks can be purchased. These included mutual funds, exchange traded funds, direct investment plans, and broker accounts.

Learning Objective 4. Be able to identify and select a stockbroker based on your investing needs and experience.

Our discussions on brokers looked at not only the types available but the characteristics that might be important for a particular investor. Some characteristics include individualized advice, research, tools, fees, and record-keeping.

Bible Texts Referenced

Proverbs 4:26 Matthew 25:14-30

Exercises and Research Activities

1. How do stocks create a return when they are invested in? Are the returns or your principal guaranteed?

2. Write a brief essay on the factors that influence stock price. Do you control any of the factors? How does your answer influence your thinking when investing in stocks?

3. You have been given $100,000 to invest in 8 to 10 stocks. Create a spreadsheet that lists the stock ticker symbol, the price per share, the number of shares you will purchase and the total cost of the purchase.

Include a rationale as to why you chose a particular stock. After several months go back and note the price per share and the current value of each stock. Did you gain or lose? How did you fair in comparison to the DJIA or S & P 500?

4. Perform some research and identify a stock that you believe, based on your research, has great potential for a significant return on investment. Explain why you chose the stock and what sources you used in your research.

5. Based on your current situation and your tolerance level, what type of strategy would you use for investing in stocks?

6. Do some research and find at least one stock that you can purchase direct from the company that has no fees to open an account or to purchase or reinvest stocks, and that offers automatic reinvestment of dividends.

7. Comparison shop for a broker using some of the criteria discussed in this chapter. Write a brief summary of your comparison and identify which broker you selected and why.

References and Resources

Web Sites:

Bank of New York. www.stockbny.com
Barron's. www.barrons.com
BigCharts.com. www.bigcharts.com
Bloomberg. www.bloomberg.com
Computershare. www.computershare.com
Dow Jones. www.dowjones.com
EquiServe. www.equiserve.com
Financial Times. www.financialtimes.com
Forbe's. www.forbes.com
Fortune. www.fortune.com
Kiplinger's. www.kiplinger.com
Market Watch. www.marketwatch.com
Mellon Investor Services. www.melloninvestor.com
Money. www.money.com
Moody's. www.moodys.com
Motley Fool. www.fool.com
Moody's. www.moodys.com
New York Stock Exchange. www.nyse.com
Security and Exchange Commission. www.sec.gov
SEC Edgar Reports. www.edgar-online.com

Smart Money. www.smartmoney.comwww.wsj.com
Staton Institute. www.statoninstitute.com
Wall Street Journal. www.wsj.com
Standard & Poor's. www.standardandpoors.com
StockCharts.com. www.stockcharts.com
Yahoo! Finance. finance.yahoo.com

CHAPTER 9

Investing in Bonds

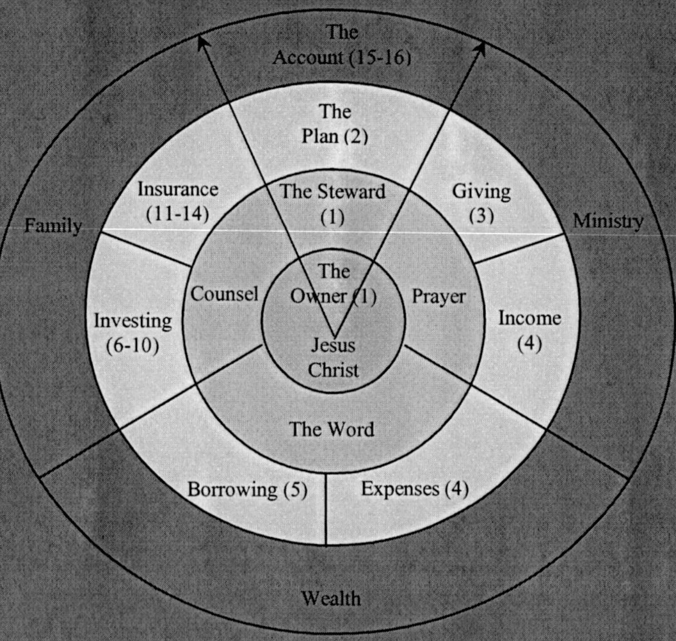

Learning Objectives

1. Define the term bonds and be able to differentiate bonds from company stock. Identify the types of bonds that a company can offer.

2. Describe the elements that influence bond pricing and what the expected returns from a bond investment can be.

3. Identify and locate organizational and bond information from a variety of sources. Identify and select a strategy for bond investing.

4. Identify and describe the vehicles available for purchasing and selling bonds as well as select a particular vehicle based on its particular benefits.

Lord, I commit to keep in view assets that will generate future income.

Lord, although I may be fairly young now there will be a time that I will need to make sure that my assets are generating income. I commit now to keep the income generation aspect of assets in view as I invest for the future. Thank you for the understanding you have given me thus far concerning all of the different investment vehicles. Help me by thy Spirit to be a wise master builder for the future.

Introduction to Bonds

We now embark on our third chapter dealing with investing. In this chapter we will seek to understand the function of bonds and how to identify offerings that can benefit our investment portfolio. Keep in mind much of what we discussed in stocks applies to bonds. When this is the case during the chapter we will for the most part refer you back to the previous discussion rather than repeat what has already been stated.

What is a Bond?

? Bond

? Coupon

? Maturity

We learned in our discussion concerning stocks that owning stock makes you an owner in the company. Bonds, on the other hand, make you a lender to the company. That is, a bond is an IOU for money you have given to the company. Bonds are the way various institutions fund major projects and other initiatives. They could, of course, borrow from a bank but sometimes they will borrow from investors. The investors are just another source of funding for the company when they have a need. Institutions that issue bonds include corporations, municipalities, and the federal government. Bonds have a variety of face values usually from $1,000 to $5,000. So when you buy a $1,000 bond from a company you give them $1,000 and in exchange they agree to pay you back by the date noted on the bond plus a certain amount of interest each year until it is paid. The interest rate noted on the bond is often called the coupon. The date noted by which the borrowed funds must be repaid is the maturity date. Maturity dates on a bond can run from 6 months to 30 years or more

? Bond Call

Bond interest is usually paid semi-annually or every six months. That continues until the bond matures, is sold, or is called by the company. The call is when a company decides to retire the debt early and pay you back what you lent to them. This can happen if the company wants to take advantage of lower rates by offering a new bond issue at those rates and save money. Basically the company may desire to either reduce its debt or refinance it just as people do.

In summary, then, a bond is a debt instrument and the lender or investor becomes a creditor of the organization. If the company falters the bondholders will have priority over the stockholders in any bankruptcy proceeding.

Understanding the Return on a Bond Investment

As with stocks there are two basic forms of return on a bond. First and foremost bonds return interest each year on the bond amount. For example if we have a $1,000 bond that pays interest at 8% APR we will receive $80 a year in interest income. Of course that income will usually be taxed unless the bond is tax-exempt as with some municipal bonds we discussed earlier in the book. Bonds held to maturity will be paid their full face value by the company to the holder of the bond. If held to maturity the bondholder does not sustain any loss in the principal. The risk of loss only occurs if the company is unable to meet its debt obligations or you sell the bond for less before maturity.

What if you needed your money back before the maturity date? Well, that is one of the things to be careful of when investing in bonds. Their liquidity is less than that of stock. This has been tempered by the development of the bond market which allows for the resale of bonds to others before their maturity. If you decide to sell a bond before maturity you could sell it to somebody else via a broker. Your expectation might be that you should sell it for $1,000 since the new bondholder will receive that amount back when it reaches maturity. Unfortunately it does not quite work that way. The value of the bond to another person will be different based on the interest rates available on other bonds being sold at the time you wish to sell yours. If your bond pays 8% and other bonds are paying 10% when you go to sell your bond then you will not be able to fetch $1,000 for it since your bond pays less interest. The value of your bond is less than the others currently selling for $1,000. So in this example the 10% bond will return $100 a year to the investor while your bond will only return $80 a year to the investor. Which bond would you buy for the $1,000? Of course the one that pays more interest. So, if that is the case how can you get your money back? Well, the answer is to sell your bond for less than $1,000 so it becomes more competitive with the other current bonds and more appealing to other investors. Of course this means you will not get your full principal back but that is the price you are going to pay for liquidity now. How much does the price have to be reduced to make it competitive? Enough so that a current bond earning 10% is the same as buying your bond that pays 8%. We will show you the formulas in the next section that will help you to determine the approximate value of a bond at any given time.

This leads us to the second way of gaining a return on a bond by selling it for more than what you bought it for. Let's take the example we have been using and assume the current rates for new bonds is 6% instead of 10%. So a $1,000 bond receives $60 annually in interest. If you wish to sell your bond that pays 8% you can actually make more than the face value since the buyer will receive more interest than with the new bonds currently being offered on the market. So, your bond will sell for more than $1,000 to make up for the better return the investor will receive. If you have been following our discussion closely you will realize that bond prices seem to behave strangely. That is, as interest rates go up bond values go down and as rates go down the values of bonds go up. This is because the bonds themselves are interest rate based instruments whose return will need to compete with the current market if they are to be sold. We again provide the formulas in the next section to show how to calculate the current value of a bond.

Determination of Bond Prices

What determines the interest rate that is placed on a bond or the value of a bond that has already been purchased? We must first note that many of the same factors that influence stock pricing also influence bond pricing. Certainly supply and demand can affect bond rates and pricing. If a company makes a bond offering that is desired by many investors the rate will be lower because it is already able to attract investors for other reasons such as stability, business model, and the like. If the company struggles to attract investors to a bond offering they may need to raise the interest rate in order to attract additional ones. Other risk factors including external events, inflation, business events, and perception can influence rates and pricing as well. Be sure to review these factors in our similar discussion under determining stock prices. Also, current interest rates most definitely have an effect on bond prices and new bond offering rates. As we have noted this is because the primary return on a bond is based on the interest rate it carries. As with stocks these influences comprise the risk of investing in a certain debt instrument or bond. The higher the rate paid, usually, the higher the risk associated with the bond.

Maturity. The bond maturity is the date at which the debt is due to be paid in full. Usually, the longer the maturity is, the greater the risk so a longer maturity requires a higher interest rate on debt issue.

Yield. You can determine the current yield on your bond by dividing the current annual interest income by the current market price of the bond. Basically it is the same formula for determining the dividend yield on stock. As with a stock you would have to look up the current price of your bond on the market. The formula then is:

Current yield = annual interest income / market price of bond.

Keep in mind that current yield is just a reflection of what your return is in relation to the value of the bond in the market. If you keep the bond until maturity then your annual yield or return will be the stated interest rate on the bond (sometimes called the coupon).

Yield to Maturity

Yield to Maturity. Sometimes it could be helpful to know what the approximate annual current yield of a bond investment is until its maturity. This would take into account not only the current interest rate, but the current value and number of years remaining on the bond. Although a little more involved, it is still basic math that allows us to calculate this value. Exhibit 9-1 shows an example of using this formula. The formula is:

Yield to maturity = (annual interest income + ((face value of the bond – current value of the bond) / the number of years to maturity)) / ((the current value of the bond + the face value of the bond) / 2).

Scenario: Barbara is considering purchasing a $5,000 bond that currently pays 11% annually and has 7 years left to maturity. The bond is currently valued at $4,300.

YTM = (550 + ((5000-4300) / 7)) / ((4300 + 5000)/2)

YTM = (550 + (700 / 7)) / (9300 / 2)

YTM = 650 / 4650

YTM = .1398 = 13.98%

Exhibit 9-1. Yield to Maturity

Without getting into any technical details the result of these calculations would allow the investor to determine if the rate of return until maturity meets or exceeds his desired return. The higher the yield to maturity the more attractive the bond is to the investor.

Current Value. Although you can look up the current market value of a bond in some newspapers or on the web you may want to calculate it just to see if the price is just reflecting a change in the interest rate or some other factor is influencing the price as well. The formula is:

Current price = current annual interest / current comparable market interest

For example, if the $1,000 bond currently pays a 5% annual rate (or $50) and the current market rates for comparable bonds is 7.5% then the value of the bond is reduced to $667. Here is the calculation: 50 / .075 = 666.67. So the bond on the market should be priced around $665. If it is not, then there may be other factors that are influencing the price to be higher or lower. Of course, if the rates have gone down it is possible to sell a bond at a profit.

Bond Ratings. Part of the risk of lending to a company is the possibility that you will not receive your money back. To help investors determine the level of risk associated with the debt instruments of a particular company there are financial strength ratings. These ratings are assigned by well known financial services firms who look at the company's business and finances and make a determination as to the default risk on the bond issue. Moody's and Standard & Poor's, companies we have previously identified in the stock arena, are the best known for giving ratings to company bond issues. The rating indicates the ability of the borrower to service the debt issue in a timely manner. The higher the rating the lower the interest rate on the debt because there is less risk.

Exhibit 9-2 provides a comparison of the three most popular rating scales used by investors including scales by Moody's, Standard and Poor's, and

A. M. Best Company. Most investors look for an investment grade rating which means having some type of "A" rating. Some will also include a high "B" rating in the investment grade category. Anything below a high "B" rating is considered a poor investment because of the danger of default of the issuer. The low "B" grades are known as the "junk bond" category which means they are speculative. Anything below a "B" is considered poor and means the company is likely to default or is already in default on debt. These sometimes have the "zombie bonds" label.

Financial Strength Ratings			
	Moody's	Standard & Poor's	A. M. Best
Strong	Aaa, Aa, A, Baa,	AAA, AA, A, BBB	A++, A+, A, A-, B++, B+
Weak	Ba, B	BB, B	B, B-, C++, C+
Poor	Caa, Ca, C	CCC, R	C, C-, D, E, F

Exhibit 9-2. Financial Strength Ratings.

Callability. The ability of the borrower to call back the bonds and pay them off is a feature that can also affect the value and rate of a bond. If the bond can be paid off at any time then the return is not guaranteed until maturity leaving a bit more risk as far as the expected return goes. The more flexible the call for the borrower the higher the rate will need to be to compensate the lender for the uncertainty of the future return.

Convertibility. Another influence on bond rates and prices is their convertibility to stock of the corporation. If the company allows the bond to be converted to stock then usually the interest rate on the debt will be lower. This is because the investor gains the option of converting the bond into stock and realizing gains in the company stock (assuming of course that the stock goes up in value). The terms of the conversion are set at the time the bond is issued so that for each bond either so many shares can be purchased or each share can be purchased at a particular price. There is also a time period specified in which the conversion must occur. So the investor can watch and see how the stock does and determine if the conversion would create a profit or not. If the stock has gone up markedly then the bond could be converted to stock and then the stock sold for a nice profit since the price of the stock is set at the time the bond is issued.

Although investors gain an advantage with convertible bonds, companies quite often like them for the advantages they gain. Important to the organization is the reduced interest rate they can sell the bond at because of the convertible option. This can be 1 to 2 percent below the usual rate. It also attracts more types of investors since the conversion aspect adds a different wrinkle to the investment. Also, if the conversion does occur then the company is no longer required to pay off the bond at maturity.

Bonds versus Stocks

Some may ask which investment vehicle is better. You, of course, expect us to say it depends. In reality the advantage of bonds is their safety compared to stocks. For creditors, companies will make every effort to pay their debts to avoid being forced into bankruptcy. Companies rarely will default on an interest payment to its bondholders but dividends for stockholders are not as safe. Also in bankruptcy bondholders are more likely to recover more of their investment than stockholders who are often wiped out after a bankruptcy and new stock is issued.

Stocks in general have beaten the bond market over time although the recent market troubles for stocks have brought the averages closer together. Usually the capital appreciation of stock is a benefit that is hard to beat but, of course, when the market is not doing well capital depreciation can occur very quickly as well. So, stocks have more risk and they usually pay higher returns than bonds. In summary, then, we buy bonds for our portfolio to reduce risk or to provide income.

How Bonds are Sold

Bonds are sold very much like stocks. There is the primary market, where the initial bond offerings are made by a company in conjunction with an investment bank. So in that market you would purchase the bonds from the investment bank or a similar representative of the corporation.

There is the secondary market where, like stocks, most of the business of trading occurs. Most major bond issues are listed on the New York Bond Exchange or the American Bond Exchange. You can purchase a bond using the same steps we discussed under stocks in the previous chapter. You use a broker to execute the buy or sell order on the exchange floor. Keep in mind that as with stocks there will be commissions that must be paid to the broker for handling the transaction for you.

The federal government and other political entities, such as cities and states, also offer their own bonds. As we have noted, many times the income on these is tax-exempt. As a result the rates are sometimes lower than for other bonds. Of course these are also adjusted for risk using the same factors as other bonds. Bonds issued by the government are seen as very safe and usually are sold at a rate lower than other bonds on the market.

Bonds issued by the government and other political entities can be purchased through an investment broker or many times through the entity itself. Buying directly from the entity may reduce or eliminate the brokerage fees that are normally assessed.

Basics of Bond Orders

We will be brief here and state that the bond order is achieved for the most part the same way a stock order is executed over the OTC. Most bond orders are executed through the OTC market. As with stocks you can make the various types of orders including market and limit orders. Of course, with bonds the parameters passed with the order are slightly different. They include the bond, face value of the bond you wish to purchase or sell, and either the total face value of the bond order or the number of bonds involved. Of course you will specify a price as well.

For a look at the basic process involved in bond order execution, review the process discussed in the previous chapter under stocks. Although there may be some slight differences depending on the broker or exchange used, it gives you an idea of the process involved.

The process may be different if you are investing directly with the bond issuing entity. In this case you will likely receive a prospectus first. A prospectus describes the bond (or stock) offering and the risks and rules related to its issue. It should be reviewed carefully to gain an understanding of the investment and the organization offering it. Look for company viability, ratings, maturity, call criteria, convertibility (if non-government), fees, and rate. After you have reviewed the prospectus you can then apply to purchase the number of bonds you desire at the face value of the bond. There may or may not be fees so be sure to check the prospectus.

Sources of Bonds

Corporate Bonds. Bonds issued by corporations account for about half of the bonds issued. These, unlike many other bonds, appeal to the smaller investor because their face value (sometimes called the par value) can be in increments of $1,000 and occasionally less.

If the bonds are for a mortgage type arrangement such as purchasing land or a building, then the bond issue is considered secured. This reduces the risk to the lender so it is more appealing than the other more common form of bond, which is unsecured (sometimes called a debenture). Of course, the rates payable on the bond usually reflect this risk. So, secured bonds might have a lower rate. Also, sometimes companies have several outstanding bond issues. As a result, they establish an order as to who will get paid first in case of financial difficulties. Any bond issue that falls under another in priority is considered a "subordinated debenture." This means that subordinated bond issues are riskier than unsubordinated issues and usually command a higher rate.

Government Bonds. It should be no surprise that the government is a big borrower of funds. You have likely heard about the annual budget deficits which mean we are spending more than we are taking in for income. As a result the balance must be financed. To do this the government, like the corporation, offers bonds which are, as we have noted, an IOU to repay us for the money we lend to the treasury. The plus with government bonds, at least so far, is that they are considered safe and virtually risk free since they are backed by the ability of the government to tax and print money.

With that in mind you might raise the question as to why the government doesn't just print some more money and pay off the debt. Well, we could get a little long winded but do you remember the issue of supply and demand and their effect on value? The more a supply of something there is the less valuable it is. That's why collectors collect items that are scarce. There will be more people who want the item than there are copies of the item available. If the government were to print enough money to pay off the debt the flood of additional currency would make the value of the currency worth substantially less.

The government issues treasury securities (another term for bonds or stocks) in many denominations and many time periods. The maturity period can run from 3 months to 30 years. Of course, generally, the longer the maturity period the higher the rate paid on the security. Now, you may have heard the term treasury bills, or treasury notes, or treasury bonds and you were probably confused as to what the difference was. They key is the maturity. Securities with one year or less are called Treasury Bills (or T-Bills for short). Bonds with a maturity of 1 to 10 years are called Treasury Notes. Bonds with a maturity of greater than 10 years are called Treasury Bonds.

? **T-Bills, T-Notes, T-Bonds**

Treasury Inflation Protected Securities (TIPS). The federal government also sells a special type of 10-year bond called TIPS which are like other government bonds but they are adjusted for inflation every six months. If you have purchased a $1,000 bond and inflation is 4.5% for the year then at the end of the first year your bond will be valued at $1,045. This type of investment can be quite good for the investor who is risk averse and would like to have protection against inflation. The one caveat is that the bonds often sell at a lower coupon or interest rate than standard government bond issues.

? **TIPS**

Agency Bonds. There are other entities in the government besides the Treasury that offer bonds. Others include the Federal Home Loan Bank and the Federal National Mortgage Association. These bonds usually have a slightly higher rate than the bonds issued by the Treasury despite being about as safe as those offered by the Treasury. Denominations can vary and the maturity dates can run from 1 to 40 years.

Types of Bonds

Savings Bonds. The federal government issues a form of bond called an E or EE savings bond. These have a variable interest rate and have many denominations running from $50.00 to $10,000. This flexibility in denominations makes it easy for small investors to participate. In addition, the bonds are tax-exempt at a state and local level. If used for educational purposes they may also be tax exempt at the federal level. What makes these bonds different from other bonds is that they are purchased at half their face value. A $50 bond is purchased for $25. The interest is then applied to the bond for a period of time until the bond is worth its face value at which time it can be redeemed. Since rates are variable this time frame will vary. The bonds are also very liquid and can be redeemed at any time but you will only receive what the bond is worth at redemption, which may be less than the face value.

The government also at one time offered H and HH bonds that were only issued in exchange for E and EE bonds. The difference between the two was that federal taxes on the interest on the E and EE bonds were deferred until it was cashed but interest on H and HH bonds was taxed annually.

The government now also offers an I bond. These bonds are purchased at face value and the interest is added to that value. The total including interest is returned when redeemed. The same tax advantages as the E and EE bonds apply. The denominations are from $50 to $30,000 and can be purchased for maturities as long as 30 years. As with the other bonds they can also be easily redeemed.

Treasury Bonds. We have already noted that the Treasury issues many types of bonds having different names based on their maturity. They are called T-bills, T-notes, and T-bonds. Other government agencies also issue bonds. There is a special type of bond called a pass-through certificate that is issued by what is called "Ginnie Mae." That is the Government National Mortgage Association (GNMA). Rather than pay the principal at maturity it pays the principal and interest monthly to the bondholder until the entire principal has been paid. It works like you were the lender for a mortgage (which in essence is what you are doing, that is, pooling your funds with others to purchase a pool of mortgages so you appear to be the lender). As they are paid the interest and principal are returned to you.

Treasury Inflation Protected Securities (TIPS). As we have already noted, the Treasury also provides special bonds that are indexed for inflation sometimes called Treasury Inflation Indexed Bonds. These not only have the tax advantages of other government bonds but also take into account the inflation rate. The inflation rate is used each year to increase the underlying value of the bond. If the bond were for $1,000 and the inflation rate was 5% then the bond's underlying value will be increased to $1,050 for the coming years. Future interest and inflation increases will be based on the new value. Taxes are paid annually on the interest and the inflation increase unless the bonds are part of a tax-deferred portfolio such as a 401K.

? Zeroes

Zero Coupon Bonds. Another type of bond issued by many organizations is a zero coupon bond (sometimes called zeroes). If you recall, the coupon is the interest rate of the bond. A zero-coupon bond pays an interest rate of 0%. The return on the bond is based on purchasing the bond at a discount (similar to E and EE bonds) and then at maturity the face value of the bond is paid. These can be sold in the market place as with other bonds if you do not wish to hold it to maturity. Two things to keep in mind: taxes are paid on the appreciated value of the bond unless it's in a tax-deferred portfolio and the value of these bonds has a tendency to fluctuate much more than other bonds. The federal government plays a big role in this market and sells many zero-coupon bonds called STRIPS which reflects the fact that they have been "stripped" of their coupon (interest rate). These are sometimes referred to as Certificates of Accrual on Treasury Securities (CATS) and Treasury Investment Growth Receipts (TIGRs).

Evaluating Bonds & Finding Bond Information

Bond Specific Information

As with stocks there are many available sources of information to help you identify and select bonds for investing purposes. These include the web, newspapers and magazines, services and newsletters, and professionals. You can use some of the same sources noted in the chapter on stocks for finding information on bonds. We will not cover those sources again in this section but many of them will include bond information so you may want to go back and review them.

There are several sources on the web that specifically deal with bonds and may be of help in your bond search. The first site that we should note is www.investinginbonds.com, which is specifically developed for the individual investor. This site provides information on how to invest in bonds as well as provides bond prices, market information, and investor guides. The site also provides links to many other sites that will likely be of help to you. Another related site is www.bondmarkets.com. These sites are both managed by the Bond Market Association (BMA). These sites will also provide you with a list of all the bond dealers that are members of the association.

Another great site, for learning about United States government securities, is www.ustreas.gov which is maintained by the Department of the Treasury. It also contains a link to Treasury Direct, which allows you to buy various government bonds directly from the government without having to pay a broker.

Other bond specific sites include www.bondknowledge.com, www.bondheads.com, www.bondpage.com, and www.bondtalk.com. Some sites such as www.bondpage.com also provide services for purchasing bonds. Many of the investing sites such as www.morningstar.com also provide bond information in addition to their stock offerings.

In addition to the newspapers such as the Wall Street Journal and magazines such as Financial Times mentioned in the stock chapter, there is a newspaper dedicated to bonds called BondWeek. It can be accessed at www.bondweek.com. There are other bond related magazines and journals that may be of interest that serve specific segments of the market. For instance, Institutional Investor Magazine is geared toward the institutional investor and can be reached at www.institutionalinvestor.com. For those more research oriented there are Journals such as The Journal of Fixed Income available at www.iijournals.com.

As we have noted, there are various investor newsletters published by investing organizations some of which deal with both stocks and bonds such as Morningstar FundInvestor (www.morningstar.com). As with stocks there are various professional newsletters published for bond investors such as Distressed Debt Securities published by Jack Colombo. In fact, there are literally hundreds of investment newsletters many covering both stocks and bonds. To get a feel for the breath and depth of these newsletters visit Select Information News at www.sienews.com. They offer trial subscriptions to many of the newsletters that are available for a much smaller price than would normally be available.

For more personal advice you can seek out a professional. Keep in mind, of course, investment professionals may charge a fee or expect you to buy products from them that generate fees that you must pay. You can seek out a standard investment firm such as Charles Schwab or seek a bond specific professional using one of the web sites or newsletters mentioned above.

Bond Strategies

As with stocks, you can choose a variety of strategies based on your investment goals. Many folks use bonds as part of their asset allocation for their entire investment portfolio in order to reduce the risk of an all stock portfolio. Others have a strategy to generate as much income as possible, perhaps because they are in retirement. The various strategies fall into at least several categories.

? **Bond Ladder**

Laddered Strategies. These strategies attempt to set up a stream of income over a period of years by buying bonds equally across a range of maturities so that each year some of the bonds mature and the funds are made available. This can be an effective strategy for those desiring steady income with a decreased exposure to interest rate risk (due to the range of maturities used). Thus, if rates go up those bonds on the short-term part of the ladder will mature soon and can be reinvested at higher rates mitigating the reduction in value of the long-term bonds at the other end of the ladder. If rates go down, the value of the bonds on the long-term part of the ladder go up mitigating the lower returns that would result from those bond funds that need to be reinvested if they mature soon.

Income Strategy. The goal of this strategy is to purchase bonds that generate the maximum amount of income. Of course risk must be considered in selecting the appropriate bond portfolio but the emphasis is on generating income rather than looking for capital appreciation in the bond so it can be resold.

Growth Strategy. Investors that use this strategy are looking for bonds that will likely have an increased value so they can be resold. This approach becomes more popular when investors believe that the interest rates will be going down forcing the value of the bonds up. This strategy is not a concern for those who plan on holding their bonds to maturity. At maturity the borrower pays the face value of the bond regardless of the current interest rates.

Tax Advantaged Strategies. As we have previously discussed under tax-advantaged investments, some investors develop their portfolios to minimize the taxes paid. Certain types of bonds can provide support for this type of strategy. Some municipal (sometimes called "munis") and government bonds provide tax advantages but many times carry lower rates so you will need to carefully look at the actual return. Some bonds are tax-exempt at the federal level (municipal bonds) while others are tax-exempt at the state and local level (savings bonds). Some types of savings bonds such as the I bond also provide inflation protection. A semi-annual inflation rate is added to the standard fixed rate for the bond. As we have noted, the federal government also has a treasury bond that is also indexed for inflation that has tax advantages at the state and local level. They are called Treasury Inflation-Protected Securities (TIPS).

Bond Performance Indicators

You can use the formulas covered earlier in this chapter to gain an indication as to the quality of a bond issue. The yield and the yield to maturity calculations would be quite helpful in this regard. You may also want to look at other issues that are important to your investment goals. These might include the liquidity of the bond investment – that is, how quickly can you cash it in. The safety and tax implications may be of interest as well.

In order to gain insight into the current values of bonds it will be important to consult a resource such as the Wall Street Journal to see what the current interest rates and bond values are. Exhibit 9-3 gives a sample bond listing as you might find in the Wall Street Journal and identifies the key elements for a bond listing.

There are no easy sure-fire ways of picking a bond. Just as with stocks, careful consideration of your investment goals as well as the bond offerings available will lead to a successful outcome. It will be important to contrast the yields, yields to maturity, and the other characteristics of the various bonds you are interested in before investing.

BONDS ❶	CUR YLD ❷	VOLUME ❸	CLOSE ❹	NET CHG ❺
AT&T 7 3/4s07	7.3	4	106.88	.25
AT&T 6s09	5.7	51	104.75	-.38
AT&T 6 1/2s13	6.0	50	107.63	-.25
AT&T 8.35s25	8.1	139	103.63	-.13
AT&T 6 1/2s29	6.3	88	103.75	.13
ATTBdb 9.45s22	6.8	52	139	-1.63
AForP 5s30	6.7	20	74.25	.25

❶ The bond name appears confusing but it is usually abbreviated and includes the annual interest rate, whether it is secured (s), and the year of maturity. The highlighted bond is from AT&T, has a 6% coupon or annual interest rate, is a secured bond, and matures in 2009. At 6% interest the bond pays $60 a year per thousand dollars of face value ($1000 x .06).

❷ The current yield is determined by taking the annual interest amount (60) and dividing it by today's price. For this bond the current yield is 60 / 1047.50 or 5.7%.

❸ Volume is the number of bonds that have sold for the day. For this bond 51 have sold.

❹ The close shows the percentage of the bond face value that the bond is worth today. For this bond it is 104.75% or $1000 x 1.0475 or $1047.50.

❺ The net change is the difference between the price of the last bond sold the previous trading day and the last one sold today. Here it is 38 cents less than the previous day.

Source: The Wall Street Journal web site at www.wsj.com (accessed (03/09/2005).

Exhibit 9-3. Sample Bond Listing.

Bond Purchase Vehicles

If you seek bonds in the secondary market (that is, you purchase them from the current owners) then will you will likely use an investment broker of some type. This can be a standard broker that you can walk in and meet with or through an online trading site. You can review the web sites noted earlier in this chapter to find sites that allow for trading of bonds. An example of one site is HarrisDirect, which gives investors a low cost way of buying bonds directly. It can be reached at www.harrisdirect.com. For municipal bonds you can check out FMSBonds.com at www.fmsbonds.com.

A real benefit of the government bond offerings (a primary issuer) is that you can purchase them directly from the treasury at www.ustreas.gov. This can save you substantial amounts related to fees for buying them through a broker. Of course the Treasury only sells its own bonds. If you desire to buy other bonds directly you will need to consult the issuing organization. Other government agencies and municipalities also use direct purchase programs but most corporations use a banker or investment firm to sell a primary bond issue, which usually requires a fee for purchase.

Outcomes and Chapter Summary

In this chapter we focused on what a bond is and how it creates a return for the investor. In addition we have discussed the various types of bonds that are available and identified ways of finding information on various bond issues.

Learning Objective 1. Define the term bonds and be able to differentiate bonds from company stock. Identify the types of bonds that a company can offer.

We explored the definition of a bond and how it differed from a stock. In addition we reviewed the various types of bonds such as savings bonds, treasury bonds, and zero-coupon bonds.

Learning Objective 2. Describe the elements that influence bond pricing and what the expected returns from a bond investment can be.

We explored the many characteristics that influence the price of a particular bond. These included bond ratings, callability, convertibility, interest rates, and the like.

Learning Objective 3. Identify and locate organizational and bond information from a variety of sources. Identify and select a strategy for bond investing.

We discussed the availability of various sources of bond information including general investment sources as well as those that cater specifically to the bond investor.

Learning Objective 4. Identify and describe the vehicles available for purchasing and selling bonds as well as select a particular vehicle based on its particular benefits.

We reviewed the sources of various bonds including those used for purchasing stock. We also discussed buying bonds direct.

Exercises and Research Activities

1. Based on your current situation and point in life how do you view bonds as an investment vehicle?

2. Your broker has notified you of a great deal on a $1,000 bond. which is currently paying 6% but is selling for only $700. Current bonds are paying around 8%. Is this a great deal for you?

3. How is the current yield of a bond figured?

4. Research the current bond market and find the best tax-exempt bond issue available. Write up a brief summary of how you went about finding the bond and why you believe it is the best.

5. Research the current government debt offerings that are available and provide a brief summary of the benefits/costs of purchasing them in relation to other current bond offerings on the market.

References and Resources

The Bond Market Association. www.investinginbonds.com
BondHeads.com. www.bondheads.com
BondKnwoledge.com. www.bondknowledge.com
BondMarkets.com. www.bondmarkets.com
BondPage.com. www.bondpage.com
BondTalk.com. www.bondtalk.com
BondWeek. www.bondweek.com
FMSbonds.com. www.fmsbonds.com
Harrisdirect. www.harrisdirect.com
Institutional Investor. www.institutionalinvestor.com
Institutional Investor Journals. www.iijournals.com
Morningstar. www.morningstar.com
Select Information Exchange Company. www.sienews.com
U. S. Treasury. www.ustreas.gov
Wall Street Journal. www.wsj.com

CHAPTER 10

Mutual Funds and Other Investment Vehicles

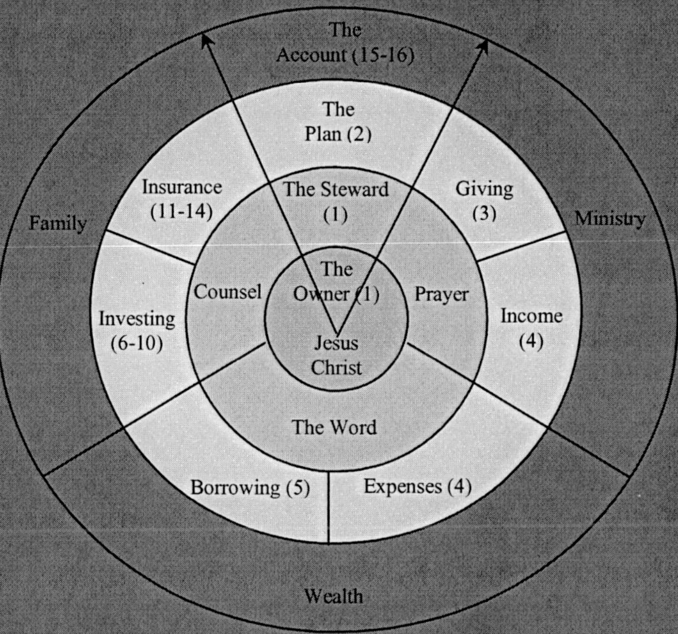

Learning Objectives

1. Describe what a mutual fund is and what the advantages and disadvantages are in using it as an investment vehicle.

2. Determine the return on a particular mutual fund and the components that are represented by it.

3. Evaluate and select appropriate mutual funds based on investment goals.

4. Identify other investment choices and describe the tradeoffs in considering them as part of an investment portfolio.

Lord, I commit to saving for the future.

Lord, I realize the future is in your hands and you know the end from the beginning so I trust you for it. I commit to save some of the resources you provide and invest them wisely and will trust you for the increase. I thank you for the reminder from the physical blessings that you provide, of the great spiritual blessings I have in Christ.

Introduction to Mutual Funds

The most common way for most individuals to invest in various securities is through mutual funds. In this chapter we explore the reasons for mutual fund popularity as well as discuss some of the disadvantages that are often overlooked when individuals look to invest in these funds. We will also review some characteristics of good mutual funds that you might wish to consider before investing in a fund.

What is a Mutual Fund?

? Mutual Fund

As the term "mutual" implies these types of funds involve sharing. That is, investors pool their funds together in order to purchase a portfolio of stocks that is professionally managed by another individual, usually from an investment company. As a result, investors can attain a more diverse and less expensive portfolio of stocks than if they tried to invest on their own. The key difference with mutual funds is that the investors own shares in the fund and not in each individual security owned by the fund. Thus the fund becomes the investing entity. Keep in mind that funds can invest in all types of vehicles including bonds, stocks, and real estate.

The number of mutual funds has mushroomed over the last 30 years from about 500 to over 8,000. You might wonder why there would be so many and the reasons are many. First, each fund has a particular strategy it focuses on. For instance, some might be growth oriented while others might be income oriented. Some only invest in certain industries while others are socially conscious and only invest in companies that benefit society. So there are thousands of funds to meet just about any kind of investment objective you could envision. In addition, there is competition and so it is possible that one fund could be similar to another but is just competing for the investor's funds perhaps by offering lower fees or better service.

We should note here that the objectives of a fund and information on how it is managed are contained in a document called the prospectus. These documents can be large and not worth the time to look at, but the investor should be warned that the prospectus is the legal documentation that guides the investment and its relationship to you. Be sure to seek out the sections that explain the objectives of the fund, who will manage it, and all of the fees involved. Too many assume all mutual funds must be good when in reality there is a difference among the funds and some can be quite a bit better than others.

The popularity in mutual funds is well-founded. In the harried pace of life most individuals just do not have the time to carefully plan and manage a portfolio of investments. Planning a portfolio, as we have seen in the previous chapters on investing, requires significant consideration of many factors and certainly should not be rushed into. Even if there is time available some find the task of selecting investments arduous. Unfortunately, few realize that the same careful process of selecting stocks and bonds is also true of mutual funds. Many individuals invest in mutual funds without having carefully considered which fund to use. In the following sections we will touch on the benefits and drawbacks of mutual funds as well as give you guidance in what to look for in selecting a fund.

Advantages of Mutual Funds

Asset Diversification. One of the biggest benefits of a mutual fund is that an investor can truly diversify his portfolio. As an individual it is usually difficult to select and track more than a dozen stocks or bonds. On the other hand, a mutual fund can select and manage hundreds of stocks and bonds thus making the investment portfolio much more diverse. If one stock in the mutual fund slumps badly it is usually offset by the stability of the others in the fund portfolio and the effect is minimized by the shear number of securities owned by the fund. In an individual's portfolio a slump in one stock can have a significant effect on the value of the entire portfolio since the stock is only one of a few in the portfolio. Concerning an investment portfolio, then, we can say that the larger the percentage of a particular security in the portfolio, the greater the risk. Mutual funds, by being able to be more diverse, reduce risk.

Lower Commissions. Another big advantage of mutual funds is that they can reduce the cost of investing for the individual. That is, since the fund is buying shares using funds pooled from many investors the cost of the transactions is shared by all the investors. An individual, regardless of how few shares he adds to his portfolio usually pays the same fee. In a mutual fund that same fee can purchase thousands of shares, usually for the same fee as the cost of ten shares. The difference is that rather than paying the full fee yourself the fund pays the fee which ends up reducing the fund's overall value but that decrease for the fee is shared by all in the fund. This makes investing much more affordable for the average person.

Time. As we have noted, we live in a busy world where there seems to be little time left to properly weigh investment scenarios and make decisions. Mutual funds offer the obvious advantage of time savings. Rather than select and track many stocks in your own portfolio, you select and track one or two mutual funds. Since the mutual fund is responsible for selecting and managing the portfolio there is much less for the individual investor to worry about. Of course, there is no free lunch and the caveat we will discuss later in this section is that the tradeoff for this benefit are the fees related to having another manage the portfolio.

Professional Management. Another major advantage of mutual funds is that they are professionally managed. The fund officer is usually well educated and trained in the evaluation and selection of securities for investment portfolios. In addition, they may become more quickly aware of changes in the market and make appropriate moves to benefit the portfolio that an individual might not be able to accomplish in a timely manner. The caveat besides the fees that are charged to the fund for the management services is that just because it is professionally managed does not mean it will beat the market. As we will see this is not always the case. Another benefit of professional management is that all of the record keeping is handled by the fund which makes it easier for the investors.

Improved Liquidity. Mutual funds also offer another benefit, especially if the fund invests in liquid assets, that is, the liquidity of mutual funds is usually quite good. If you needed your funds you could call the mutual fund service and ask for a check and they could easily get it for you. Keep in mind, though, that this may not always be true. For instance, some real estate funds may require a certain amount of time if your request for funds is large. Be sure to check the prospectus if liquidity is important to you.

Other Services. Mutual funds often provide other services as well. They provide account statements, reinvestment of dividends, plus some provide automatic deposits and withdrawals from the fund. They also provide easy access to buy or sell shares in the fund usually via a phone call or on the web.

Disadvantages of Mutual Funds

Market Performance. The biggest disadvantage of mutual funds is that they underperform the market on average. Unfortunately, many individuals do not realize this. Many funds tout their great returns over the past year or past 5 years and this has made it seem that mutual funds automatically do better than the market average. In reality about two-thirds of all funds underperform the market which is not a very exciting record. Of course, one of the key reasons that they underperform the market is that they must pay brokerage and management fees, whereas the market does not. The question becomes whether your return is greater with a mutual fund versus another investment methodology such as managing you own portfolio. As we have noted in previous chapters, it is possible to have low or no cost investing thus boosting your return but there will be the tradeoffs of portfolio diversification, time, and managing your own portfolio that the mutual fund would normally deal with. Alas, as we have previously noted nothing is truly free, there are only tradeoffs of things of value. You will need to decide which will give you the greatest overall return.

Fees. In return for its services the mutual fund company charges the fund various fees that reduce the fund's value and thus the return on the fund's assets. This can be a significant disadvantage to the average investor. Few individuals realize that fees can take a huge part of the fund's return. The prospectus will usually list fees as an annual percentage of the fund's value. Fees usually fall into three areas: sales fees, expense fees, and 12(b)-1fees. We cover these in more detail under evaluating mutual funds but keep in mind that you want to minimize the fees charged otherwise your return will be seriously impacted.

Taxes. Another disadvantage to keep in mind is that you do not control the sale of the securities in the fund. As a result, when there are any capital gains from the sale of securities in the fund you must pay taxes for the portion of capital gains that is yours. The fund will provide this information for you. Of course, if the fund is part of a tax-deferred instrument then taxes can be deferred. Since funds will likely trade more frequently than an individual investor would trade, the tax issues as well as the fees from more frequent trading can be significant disadvantages.

Types of Mutual Funds

Open-end. The term open-end means that the mutual fund does not have a limited number of shares as with most corporate stock today. As individuals request more shares of the fund new shares are created and sold. The reverse is also true; as investors sell shares in the fund the fund buys them back. The key here is that the investor deals with the fund rather than the underlying market for the stocks in the portfolio. Thus, investors are not selling shares in the fund to others or buying shares of the fund from other investors as in the market for stocks. Basically the fund is "the company." The number of shares does influence the value of the fund and the per-share price just as the number of shares of stock influences the value of a company and the per-share price of its stock. You might wonder how the price of the fund's shares is determined, which is an excellent question. The price is based on the value of the assets the fund currently owns, minus its liabilities. This is known as the Net Asset Value (NAV) and is usually calculated at the end of each day. By dividing the NAV by the number of outstanding shares we can get a per-share price for the fund. For example if a fund has $8,000,000 in assets, and $1,000,000 in liabilities, and 300,000 outstanding shares we could calculate the per-share price of the fund as follows:

$$NAV = (8{,}000{,}000 - 1{,}000{,}000) = 7{,}000{,}000$$

$$PPS = 7{,}000{,}000/300{,}000 = 23.33$$

Each share of the fund in this case would be worth $23.33. This, then, would be the price at which shares in the fund would be bought or sold. The NAV is also sometimes provided as the value per share which can lead to confusion. The true NAV is the total net worth of the fund but sometimes is communicated as the net worth of a share in the fund.

Closed-end. A vast majority of mutual funds are open-end but there are some that are closed-end. That is, they have a limited number of shares available. Basically a closed-end fund is like a corporation. It has a fixed number of shares and they are traded on the open market between investors. So, unlike open-end funds where you are dealing with the fund (company) directly, with closed-end funds you invest in shares of a fund by using the stock market with each fund having a ticker symbol on a particular exchange. Most of these types of funds trade on the NYSE. So, unlike an open-end fund, there is no need to worry about having too many shares to buy back or too much money coming into the fund. As a result, the fund manager can be more focused on a long-term portfolio that has a fixed amount of money and perhaps also reduce expenses since there are no new funds to invest. Keep in mind one key difference in closed-end funds is that the price is set by the market. Although the NAV is important, the other issues that influence the market, such as supply and demand, also influence the price of a share of the fund.

Exchange-Traded Funds (ETFs). These are mutual funds that are a cross between an open-end and a closed-end fund. These funds are closed-end in that they trade as a close-ended fund would on a stock exchange. These usually trade on the AMEX. These funds are open-end in that the number of shares is not limited, thus, they are not subject as much to the market forces and so they trade fairly close to a price based on the net asset value. These funds provide a nice combination of advantages of both types of funds. There is easy access for trading during the day (open-end mutual fund trades are all completed at the end of a day) while having the advantages of shared low fees and no taxes until you sell the shares. Many of these funds are based on a particular market index such as DJIA or the S & P 500 and so they are sometimes referred to as exchange traded index funds. Index funds were touched on in the chapter on investing in stocks.

? **Investment Trust**

Investment Trusts. These are sometimes called a Unit Investment Trust (UIT). A unit investment trust is a fixed investment portfolio controlled by a trust agreement that is created by a trust sponsor that in turn sells shares or ownership units in the trust to investors. Most trust sponsors are large investment firms. Of course, they do not do this for free and as a result there can be significant fees withdrawn from the assets of the funds for sales and maintenance fees (the funds really are not managed since the trust agreement established the assets up front). Again, check the prospectus before investing in these investment vehicles. These trusts are for the most part fixed and last for a certain number of years based on the trust agreement. For the most part the goal of UITs has been a high, steady stream of income using bonds as the security in the portfolio. Now there are also stock trusts that focus on growth, dividend yields, and market indexes.

There is another type of trust available for investing called the Real Estate Investment Trust (REIT). As with unit trusts the portfolio is more fixed and closed-end but in this case contains real-estate related investments such as mortgages and commercial real estate. If you were interested in income you would invest in the mortgage oriented REITs while if you are interested in growth you would invest in the ones that invest in properties in hopes of gaining capital appreciation. There are hybrid trusts that invest in both. Unfortunately, dividends distributed from a REIT are taxed as ordinary income rather than at special capital gains rates. REITs, though, on average have significantly higher yields than other investments such as stocks and bonds. Units or shares in the trust can be acquired through the open markets, on the exchanges, like closed-end mutual funds.

Money Market. There are some mutual funds that specialize in short term income instruments such as T-bills that have very short maturities. As a result these types of mutual funds are considered quite safe or pretty close to risk-free. They also have very low fees. The caveat is that the funds returns are quite small compared to other investment vehicles. You can gain slightly better returns with a tax-exempt money market mutual fund that invests in municipal bonds but even here the returns may not be great. The return generally follows the trend of short-term interest rates.

Stock and Bond. As we have noted under the open and closed-end funds, mutual funds can invest in stocks (equity funds), bonds, or a combination of the two (hybrid funds). The more growth oriented funds will emphasize their stock holdings while the income related funds will emphasize their bond holdings and dividend yielding stocks.

Balanced and Asset Allocation Funds. As the term implies, balanced funds try to balance capital appreciation with steady income by having a combination of stocks and bonds. These are sometimes called hybrid funds. The prospectus will detail what balance of the two the fund will have. These types of funds provide less risk than stock funds but their returns may also be lower as a result. Asset allocation funds are balanced funds where the manager tries to time the market so when stocks are on the rise the fund is more in stocks and when bonds are on the rise the fund is more in bonds. As we have noted, market timing is generally a losing proposition, so you might want to steer clear of asset allocation balanced funds.

Life Cycle Funds. These types of funds allocate their assets based on certain characteristics of investors. Younger investors generally have greater tolerance for risk and do not need income from their assets to live on, so a fund that catered to this group would be growth oriented and include substantially stocks, whereas a life-cycle fund that caters to senior citizens would focus on returning income and thus have a strategy of investing in bonds and short term financial instruments. These funds are often based on characteristics such as the investor's age and risk tolerance.

Social. Some mutual funds are created to invest based on certain social, ethical, or moral characteristics of the companies being invested in. Social funds invest in companies that create products that are for the public good or do not harm the public or the environment. Companies that are quite often excluded, depending on the funds, are those that are involved with tobacco, alcohol, polluting the environment, abortion, guns, and product testing on animals, among a host of others. Some people do not want to be part owners of companies that participate in things that are against their beliefs or are unethical in their business dealings. Social fund returns have generally lagged behind other stock fund returns.

Sector. Some mutual funds specialize in a particular industry or sector. For instance, there are many "technology" mutual funds which focus on investing in technology companies. Of course, because of the emphasis on the concentration in a single industry's stocks this type of fund is much riskier since a major downturn in the industry can devalue the whole portfolio. For instance, the recent difficulties by Merck with the Vioxx drug resulted in a substantial hit on the stocks in the pharmaceutical industry. Funds which emphasized the pharmaceuticals sector took major hits on their portfolios values.

Other Funds. Mutual funds come with a host of monikers and it is beyond the scope of this book to be able to identify them all. Some funds may be able to be called several different name types based on the characteristics of that fund. The prospectus should guide you in identifying into which fund categories or types the fund falls. Other names that are quite common that we have not discussed separately include growth (capital appreciation), value (selects stocks that are undervalued by the market), aggressive growth (speculative capital appreciation), and equity income (dividend income from stocks), among others. Whatever the type that is included in the name, confirm the fund has the characteristics you desire in a fund. One other type of fund to note is the international fund. International funds, as the name implies invest in foreign securities. These are often referred to as global funds. They attempt to take advantage of the economic growth in foreign countries and the possible exchange rate benefits related to the U. S. dollar. The risk of these funds is greater so caution is in order here.

Mutual Fund Information

Every mutual fund has a prospectus it has filed with the Securities and Exchange Commission, which governs the securities markets in the United States. Be sure to get a copy of the prospectus for any funds you are interested in and make sure you understand the goals of the fund, as well as any fees involved. The prospectus will provide a good starting point for any particular fund. If you need help in identifying funds first, then you can reference some of the links given below. Reading a prospectus can be a very daunting task the first time you look at one but it does contain the guidelines by which the fund will be administered.

As with stocks and bonds there is no shortage of information on mutual funds available to you to help in selecting the right investment fund. The Wall Street Journal does provide a Monthly Mutual Funds Review that lists mutual funds, their NAV (as a price per share), and their return over the last ten years. There are many web sites, magazines, and newspapers that assist you in evaluating the over 8,000 mutual funds. Many of the sources noted in the chapters on stocks and bonds, such as www.morningstar.com and www.thewallstreetjournal.com, should also be checked for information on mutual funds since many also provide that type of information. In this section we will examine some sources that have yet to be mentioned in the text.

Consumer Reports which is produced by Consumers Union each year has some research related to mutual funds to offer within its pages. Usually its March issue has an in depth look at some types of mutual funds. Its research, analysis, and ratings are quite good and they give some good guidelines for looking at mutual funds. It can also be reached at www.consumerreports.org. Standard & Poor's runs a web site that can be quite helpful in researching mutual funds and can be reached at www.funds-sp.com. Some sites offer mutual fund screening tools to help you sort through the thousands of funds. MSN Money (moneycentral.msn.com/investor/finder/mffinder.asp), Quicken (screen.yahoo.com/funds.html?quicken=2), and Zack's at www.zacks.com provide free screeners. Morningstar also provides a free basic screener and an advanced screener which is available only to members (requires a fee). You can also access a number of mutual fund related sites through www.mutualfunds.com.

There are several publications dedicated to mutual funds that may be of help in understanding and analyzing mutual funds. Tom Maddel puts out a free electronic mutual funds newsletter at funds-newsletter.com called the Mutual Fund Research Newsletter. Tom had a career in computing before going into the financial area and now spends a great deal of time in the mutual fund arena. The Mutual Fund Prospector is available at www.ericdany.com. Brill's Mutual Fund Interactive is available as a mutual fund resource at www.brill.com. The Investment Company Institute (www.ici.org) publishes the Mutual Fund Fact Book each year along with a number of newsletters. The Securities and Exchange Commission also provides some helpful publications for mutual fund investors (www.sec.gov).

Along with the sites noted in the earlier investment chapters there is plenty of free information available for both beginner and advanced investors. Keep in mind some sites and publications may have fees to access some portions of their materials. The screeners can be valuable in helping you whittle down the thousands of funds on your own or you can use one of the newsletters or Consumer Reports, who have done some of the work for you. In either case there is help in this area of investing.

Participating in a Mutual Fund

There are three basic ways to participate in mutual funds. You can directly participate in open-ended funds by contacting the fund directly which is usually accomplished via a toll-free telephone number, buy exchange traded funds on the market, or buy mutual funds through a mutual fund supermarket. Whatever approach you take, be sure to do your research first before investing. Although many companies have at one time or another offered top-rated funds in the past, this does not mean that it will happen in the future.

Direct. The largest purveyors of mutual funds are Fidelity (www.fidelity.com) and Vanguard (www.vanguard.com). As open-end funds they provide a direct way for investment either via the phone or online. These companies as well as others provide toll-free numbers to allow you to create and change your account settings. If you only want to invest in a few funds and don't need to be able to trade them during the day then this approach will work well.

ETFs. If you want the immediate liquidity of being able to sell your shares during the day then closed-end exchange-traded funds will likely be better. Keep in mind that the fees on closed-end funds may be higher. You can buy and sell shares of these mutual funds through your broker just like stocks and bonds.

Supermarkets. If you want to buy shares from many mutual funds then you might want to consider a mutual fund supermarket. Schwab pioneered this concept in 1992. Schwab developed a market for 600 mutual funds from which you could choose even though the funds belonged to many other investment firms. Schwab receives a small portion of the management fee in exchange for making an organization's mutual fund available in the supermarket that you can pick from. This way you can pick a variety of funds from a variety of sources without having to open and track separate accounts for each. There are other players in the supermarket arena now so look carefully to be sure you are getting what you expect and at the fees you expect. Some are now charging a transaction fee.

Evaluating Mutual Funds

In this section we will look at and briefly discuss how we evaluate mutual funds and what makes a good mutual fund for investing in. The key areas to be considered include fees, returns, and services. In addition, though, you will want to look at the fund's objectives to make sure they match your investment needs. You may also want to look at the fund manager's past performance and experience as well.

Mutual Fund Fees

As you embark on investing in mutual funds keep in mind that the companies are in the business to make a profit. As a result you must carefully evaluate all the costs related to investing in these funds. Many funds have poor returns because of the fees that eat away over time at the investment. Let's take a look at some of these fees.

Front-End Loads. Some mutual funds charge an up-front fee for the right to purchase the shares in the fund. This is usually identified as a percentage of the investment. If you invested $1,000 n a fund with a 3% load, $30 of your funds would be allocated to the fee and $970 to investment in the fund. There are many excellent no-load funds on the market so there should be no reason to pay load fees to participate in a fund. Keep in mind that load

? **Front-end Load**

charges are not considered a part of any expense ratio given by the fund since they are taken directly from you.

? Breakpoint

Breakpoints. Some companies will reduce the sales load charge if you purchase a large lot of shares in the fund. For instance, some funds might reduce their load by 1% if you purchase a thousand shares. They may reduce it in tiers as you purchase more shares. This reduction in sales load based on the number of shares purchased is called a breakpoint. If you avoid front loaded funds you will not need to worry about this. Also, you may qualify for a breakpoint based on your investments in the company's other funds but may not be told about it. This happens in about one-third of cases.

Management Fees. These are fees that may be charged for the management of the fund's assets. They are usually included in the expense ratio given in the prospectus.

? Back-end Load

Back-End Loads. Also known as Contingent Deferred Sales Charges (CDSC), these are charges based on the sale value of any shares you sell in the fund in the future. It is also expressed as a percentage of the amount withdrawn from the fund. These fees usually expire after you have held the shares for a predetermined length of time. Be aware that they are not included as part of the expense ratio.

Other Fees. There may be other fees such as 12(b)-1 fees (based on the rule that allows fees for the marketing and distribution of fund shares) that the fund charges that can reduce your return. Sometimes these fees are called asset-based sales charges. These are usually included in the expense ratio. Be careful. Some companies still charge these fees even though their funds are no longer marketed to the public – they are added on for pure profit but few investors realize it. No-load funds have their 12(b)-1 fees capped at 0.25 percent which is a plus as well.

? Expense Ratio

Expense Ratio. The expense ratio is usually given in the prospectus as an annual percentage of the fund's value that is deducted for expenses. This ratio does not include other investment expenses related to the mutual fund that are taken directly from your funds before and after investment such as front and back end loads. So it is important to take into account all costs of investing in a fund. When this is done you will find that there are many funds that are not worth investing in.

Mutual Fund Classes

For most people the key issue that arises when considering the purchase of an investment is "what will it cost me"? In the mutual fund arena this can sometimes be difficult to decipher. The mutual fund industry has made this more difficult and confusing by the introduction of mutual fund "classes." That is, the mutual fund can sell different classes of shares in the same fund even though all those in the fund basically get the same "share." The difference is in the expenses and fees that are charged for the different classes. Some funds can have 5 or more different classes so check the prospectus carefully. Usually the class is determined by the combination of the load, the deferred sales charges, breakpoint discounts, and asset-based sales charges. Some classes end up paying fewer fees and the fund may not give you the best deal or steer you toward a class that you might qualify for that would reduce your fees.

Don't be afraid to ask about the other classes or to ask to have your shares be a certain class even if you do not qualify. Someone at the fund may give you some leeway if they believe you might give them more business in the future. Also keep in mind that you might qualify for lower expenses by being a member of several funds owned by the same company. The SEC provides a mutual fund cost calculator to help compare various mutual fund scenarios. It can be reached at http://www.sec.gov/investor/tools/mfcc/mfcc-int.htm. This calculator will allow you to compare the costs of multiple funds or multiple classes in the same fund.

Mutual Fund Returns

Now that we have looked at how investment companies profit off investing by charging fees the question becomes: "what is left for your return on the investment?" If we assume reinvestment of dividends, which is usually a good idea unless you are living off the income, a normal total return formula might look like this:

Total return = ((end shares * end PPS) – (start shares * start PPS)) / (start shares * start PPS)

If we assume we started with 100 shares at $19 a share and ended with 120 shares at $21 a share the total return would be calculated as follows:

Total return = ((120 * 21) – (100 * 19)) / (100 * 19)
= (2520 – 1900) / 1900
= 32.6%

This total return would have to be divided by the number of years invested to get the annual return. If in this case the investment was over a 5 year period then the annual rate of return would be 32.6/5 which equals 6.5%. This may seem like a decent annual return but keep in mind that these calculations did not take into account the front and back-end loads or taxes. The expense ratio would be included here as well as any fees taken directly from the fund. If we take into account the other fees the return does not looks as good. If there were a 2 percent front end load in our example then there would have been an initial fee of $38 which, if you could have invested at the total return of 32.6% for five years, would have been worth $50.39. So the up front load fee would have cost $50.39, $12.39 of which we would say is foregone earnings. That is, the earnings we did not receive on our $38 because we had to use it to pay the load fee. The 1% load fee at the end of the five years would be 2520 * .01 or $25.20. Now our total return would be as follows (we won't deal with taxes since we have looked at those in a previous chapter):

Total return	= (2520 – 1900 – 50.39 – 25.20) / 1900
	= 544.41 / 1900
	= 28.7% (5.7% annual return)

As you can see the additional load fees had a significant impact on our rate of return for the investment. We lost nearly 8% on what may have seemed liked two small fees of 2% and 1%. As you can see from this example, you want to avoid as many fees as possible. We looked at a very small investment here over a short period of time. If this investment were much larger with a much longer period the lost return would be quite large. The lesson of this example is to avoid funds with loads and excessive fees. In reality fees are a good predictor of return. Research sows that the smaller the fees the greater the return. Said another way, paying larger fees does not guarantee a larger return and in fact will likely result in a smaller return. If you have the time and record keeping skills you can earn more by using DSPPs or DRIPs that charge no fees or by using a low fee online brokerage. Just be sure that you don't just buy one or two stocks or stocks in a single industry.

One final note here is that the rates of return published by mutual funds for 1, 5, and 10 year periods do not contain the load fees so be careful to calculate the return based on whatever loads and fees you must pay or would have paid had you invested during that period of the return. Generally, the returns are much lower than advertised on mutual fund investments.

Mutual Fund Services

Another area to look at when considering which mutual funds to invest in are the services they offer. You may find some services more important than others and will want to verify those that you desire are available.

Easy Access. Many funds offer easy access to switch investment money among the various funds available. This access can be in the form of a telephone call or via the web. These access mechanisms usually have no additional cost associated with them or at least they shouldn't.

Check Writing. Mutual funds of the money market variety usually include some minimum type of check writing privilege. Sometimes there are restrictions on how small the check can be written for or how many times a month you can write checks.

Reporting. All mutual funds provide some type of investment account tracking for you but some may go beyond the standard record keeping and give you tax related reports that can help you during the tax season.

Bank Account Access. If you are interested in being able to transfer funds to and from your investment funds via a bank account you will want to make sure that the fund supports that capability and be sure there are no additional charges for processing the bank transaction.

Automatic Investing and Reinvesting. You will want to make sure that, at a minimum, your fund has dividend reinvesting so that if you desire, your dividends can be used to purchase additional shares in the fund allowing your money to compound. The fund may also allow for an automatic investment of a certain amount of funds from a bank account each month or other period that you select. That can be handy for those who procrastinate about making deposits or need a "forced" way of investing.

Other Investments

Real Estate

Perhaps you have seen the ads or have read the books that scream "make a fortune in real state" or "become rich in real estate with nothing down." Well we don't have time in this text to go into much detail but we should at least discuss some of the issues related to real estate as an investment.

First as we have noted that although your home is accounted for as an asset, as a steward you do not use it as that. You treat it as a place to shelter your family and it requires a great deal of expense to support. Beyond your home there are several ways you can invest in real estate.

Vacation or Second Home. Sometimes families will invest in a second home perhaps to use as a vacation home occasionally and then to be rented the rest of the time. This is certainly one form of real estate investment that could generate income from an asset. If you decide to purchase a second home make sure that you could repay any loan on it by reselling it if you had to. The same rules apply with real estate investment and borrowing as they do with buying your home. Any funds borrowed should be able to be repaid by giving the bank the home with no further liability or by selling it and repaying the loan. If you do purchase a vacation home then you will want to make sure the asset is generating a return that is not negative. That is, does the income or appreciation in the value of the property outpace the cost of maintaining it? Include in your calculation any savings related to using the home instead of staying at a hotel, traveling, and eating out. Make sure that the home is truly worth having from a financial perspective. Also make sure that you have the time to maintain the property or can afford to have someone else manage the property, if it is not near you (which is likely). Be sure to count the cost to maintain the property or to have someone else do it when considering whether the return on the property makes it worth purchasing.

Rental Properties. The same points apply here that are noted under vacation homes. Do not let the world's fixation on zero percent down real estate deceive you into making wrong choices. There are many who can tell their horror stories of what they have been through. Just consider the story of brother, Dave Ramsey, who knew and used all the world's tricks in real estate to create a fortune only to lose it all. Thankfully he has found riches far greater in Christ and has been used of Him in a Christian financial ministry. To repeat then, if you invest in rental properties the questions are: Can you repay any loan if it were necessary to do so within a short period of time? Does the investment have a positive return after factoring in all the costs including maintenance, taxes, and insurance? Do you have the time to keep up with the investment as a good steward? Keep in mind that renting properties can also present many headaches especially in finding good tenants who will pay their rent. You may need to budget for a management company to handle the property but then make sure the asset is generating a positive cash flow.

Businesses. Should you invest in your own business such as a store? Well, consider the same questions as we have noted under the other real estate investment options. Also consider whether you will be an employee of the store or whether others will run the store or business while you work elsewhere. Before taking this avenue you should carefully review your financial goals and consult with other Christian brothers who have undertaken this type of venture. Every situation is unique and we cannot begin to touch on all of the issues in this text but as a steward such endeavors must be carefully considered and abundant prayer applied.

Collectibles

There is much interest today in collectibles especially when significant values are frequently placed on items. Millions see that items can be worth considerably more than they thought. In the past relatively few had access to this type of information, but today with eBay and the Antiques Road Show we have instant access to information on collectibles and many who perhaps just enjoyed collecting an item as a hobby now see an opportunity to cash in and reap financial rewards. The steward must be careful not to get caught up in the hype of finding treasures for a few dollars that might be worth much more. This mentality harks back to the idea of getting rich quick which as we have seen is not Biblical.

Collectibles by their very nature require time to appreciate in value and many items never do actually appreciate in value. The reason time is required in the areas of collectibles is because over time the supply of a particular item dwindles increasing the values of those that are left. But as we noted earlier, there are many factors that can affect value and events can sometimes occur that render some items that had great value less valuable. Take for instance the value of signed baseballs. When Mark McGwire hit 70 home runs in a season the ball for the 70th home run sold for $3 million. The home run ball for Barry

Bonds record 73rd sold for $500,000 only a few short years later. What happened? Why did one home run ball sell for so much more than another seemingly equally important collectible ball? Obviously the value was influenced by events surrounding the home run chase, the individuals involved, the demand for the ball, and the time that the current record had stood. None of these events can be controlled by the collector. As a result collecting is generally extremely risky and certainly much more risky than other investments such as stocks and bonds.

I would not recommend collecting as an investment unless you have become an expert in a particular collectible domain such as paintings. Even for the expert there is no guaranteed return in cash flows. That is there are no dividends, rent payments, or interest on a collectible. The entire return is bound up in hopes that the item will appreciate over time. The market for collectibles is also quite illiquid. For anyone other than an expert in an area collecting for investment is really speculation and you have no idea what your return might be. Borrowing for collectibles should be avoided.

Timeshares

Another item often hawked as an investment by the world is what is known as a timeshare. A timeshare represents your portion of ownership in a portion of real estate (usually a condominium). That is, you are sold a share of a single living unit for which you pay a price. In exchange you have so many weeks a year to use or in some cases rent this real estate. Usually these are sold at high-pressure sales events that you are drawn to by a promotion that allows you to have a free or reduced rate vacation in a resort area (where many of the timeshares are). In exchange you are required to attend the sales event.

Many unsuspecting couples have gone thinking that they will just go to the event and not buy anything. In reality many leave having bought a timeshare when they could not afford to pay for it and I know of couples who have had them foreclosed on. These events are carefully planned and staged to entice you to bite on the "great offer" or the "can't miss opportunity."

Never buy timeshares as an investment. They lose a substantial amount of their value immediately after being sold. The secondary market for timeshares is weak and, although you will be told of the great appreciation properties of resort real estate, you will not be told that timeshares have not shared in that appreciation. Generally timeshares at resale usually fetch 50 to 70 cents on the dollar and sometimes less. The motto then is to avoid timeshares as an investment. They are not an investment.

Some will buy timeshares off of the resale market or buy new ones for trading with others so they can visit other locations around the world. The timeshare market is changing and you will need to do a great deal of reading and researching in order to understand all of the timeshare sales permutations available today especially now that some resorts have introduced point systems that can be redeemed for other accommodations. For the Christian the question becomes one of whether the cost represents a good use of funds. Keep in mind that even if you buy the timeshare on the resale market, inexpensively, there are annual maintenance fees that must be paid. Unless you find a great deal on a timeshare that you plan on using or trading for an extended period of time, the cost is likely not worth it. Good stewardship stories related to timeshares are hard to find while the reverse are in abundance. Usually there are cheaper ways of providing a vacation for the family.

Others

In this section on other investments we discussed those areas that you will most likely encounter as investment vehicles. You may find others marketed to you that are surefire ways of increasing your wealth. These may include precious metals such as silver and gold, gems, coins, stamps, sports memorabilia, and the list can go on for pages. It isn't that some don't make a profit off of these it's that very few do. That is, they are more like speculation rather than investment and should be avoided by the steward. For instance we are often encouraged to invest in gold as a hedge against inflation and the great benefits of it as an investment are touted by some. But if you were to look at the price of gold over the last ten years you would see that gold was nothing to write home about as an investment. It did have some strength in the early eighties when inflation was very high but such gains were short lived. Unlike other investments, such as stocks that tend to appreciate over time because the underlying asset produces more or becomes more efficient, these do not and should be avoided.

Outcomes and Chapter Summary

In this chapter we focused on investing in mutual funds. We explored the many different types and goals of mutual funds. We also looked at the many advantages and disadvantages of mutual funds. We reviewed the other well known investment vehicles as well.

Learning Objective 1. Describe what a mutual fund is and what the advantages and disadvantages are in using it as an investment vehicle.

We started the chapter by discussing what a mutual fund is and discussed in detail the advantages and disadvantages if investing in mutual funds. We found that investing in mutual funds should not be undertaken lightly.

Learning Objective 2. Determine the return on a particular mutual fund and the components that are represented by it.

We explored how mutual funds are valued and looked at how the net asset value of a fund is calculated. We also reviewed the differences between open-end and closed-end funds.

Learning Objective 3. Evaluate and select appropriate mutual funds based on investment goals.

We explored resources that are available for determining what mutual funds are available and also reviewed some sources that will help us assess the suitability and return of a fund.

Learning Objective 4. Identify other investment choices and describe the tradeoffs in considering them as part of an investment portfolio.

We had an opportunity to discuss the other options for investing beyond stocks, bonds, and mutual funds. These included real estate, collectibles, and timeshares, along with a number of others.

Exercises and Research Activities

1. Now that you have had an opportunity to consider mutual funds what are the advantages and disadvantages of investing in them?

2. Do some research and find the top 10 mutual funds based on reported returns in the past year. What were the top funds when loads and all fees are taken into account?

3. Research the mutual fund market and find the fund that currently has the lowest total fees including loads? Is the fund worth investing in? Explain your answer.

4. What is the net asset value of a fund and how does it influence the price of a share in the mutual fund?

5. Do some research and find the mutual fund with the largest total fees. Would you invest in this fund? Explain your answer.

6. Explore what other avenues there are for investing in addition to bank instruments, stocks, bonds, and mutual funds. Are there any other options that would be worth considering? Write a brief summary supporting your decision.

References and Resources

Brill Mutual Funds Interactive. www.brill.com
Consumer Reports. www.consumerreports.org
Fidelity. www.fidelity.com
Investment Company Institute. www.ici.org
Morningstar. www.morningstar.com
Mutual Fund Prospector. www.ericdany.com
Mutual Fund Research Newsletter. funds-newsletter.com
Mutualfunds.com. www.mutualfunds.com
MSN Money Mutual Fund Screener.
moneycentral.msn.com/investor/finder/mffinder.asp
Quicken Mutual Fund Screener.
screen.yahoo.com/funds.html?quicken=2
Securities and Exchange Commission. www.sec.gov
Standards & Poor's. www.funds-sp.com
Vanguard. www.vanguard.com
The Wall Street Journal. www.thewallstreetjournal.com
Zack's. www.zacks.com

PART FOUR

Determining and Managing Insurance Needs

Chapter 11
Introduction to Insurance

Chapter 12
Personal Insurance

Chapter 13
Property and Liability Insurance

Chapter 14
Other Forms of Insurance

CHAPTER 11

Introduction to Insurance

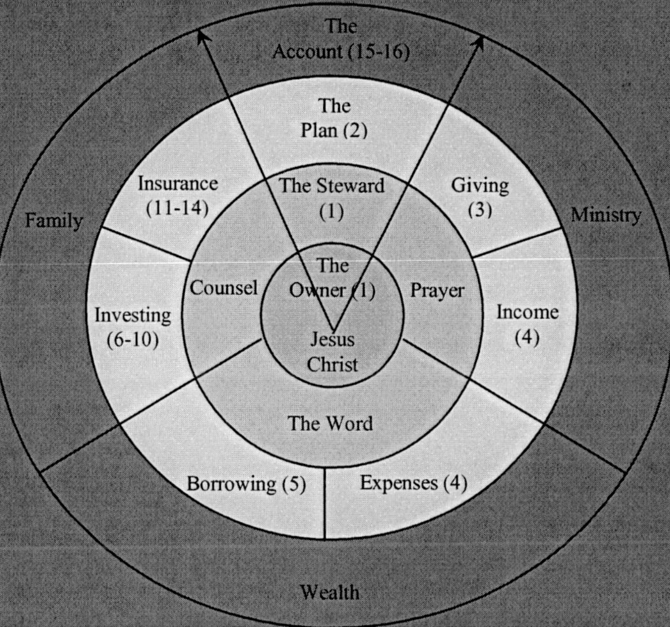

Learning Objectives

1. Be able to show the Biblical basis for the concept of insurance.
2. Describe the purpose and history of insurance and how it relates to the Biblical concept of making another whole.
3. Describe the important forms of insurance that Christians should consider.

Lord, I commit to trusting in you.

Lord, I realize that you are the source of life and you know what the future holds for me and my family. As I set aside funds and plan for the unexpected I commit to trusting you for my needs. Help me by thy Spirit to understand the role insurance plays in that plan and to wisely choose the avenues that would best protect the assets that you have and will provide to me. Help me not to rely on insurance as a means to take away my trust in you but recognize, as a good steward, that it is a financial tool to be carefully used.

Insurance – Making Things Whole

We now embark on a topic that can have a profound effect on your financial planning. That topic is insurance. There is much that is misunderstood about insurance and from the Christian's perspective the question of whether it is Biblical to rely on insurance rather than God is often raised. In this section we explore the history and purpose of insurance as well as look at the Christian's perspective on insurance.

The Biblical Perspective

We should first note that the word insurance does not occur in the Bible. The definition we would be most familiar with is a contract by which one party agrees to indemnify or reimburse for a loss of another. Insurance comes from the Latin word for "security." That is, there is an assurance that if there is a loss it will be reimbursed. The question that will be raised by many Christians is whether acquiring insurance shows a lack of faith. Unfortunately, this question causes unnecessary duress for the believer. To raise the question as one of faith would lead us to question whether we need to work or invest since they may show a lack of faith as well. The reason we do invest and work without casting doubt on our faith in God is because we see in the scriptures the importance of doing these things as part of our faith. As we shall see this is the same for insurance.

? **Insurance**

Did you ever notice that our English word invest is not mentioned in the Bible? Yet based on the Scriptures it is very clear that we should invest properly. The same is true of insurance. The word insurance is not mentioned but we do see the principle of insurance at work. The objective of insurance is to indemnify or reimburse for a loss; that is, to provide a substitute for something lost; whether you do it yourself (self-insured) by not buying insurance, or whether you purchase that protection from another. By not having insurance you have implicitly agreed to reimburse others for any losses they sustain as a result of any error on your part. This is quite Biblical. First take a look at Exodus 21:18-19. It states "*if men dispute, and one strike the other with a stone, or with his fist, and he die not, but take to his bed,-- if he rise, and walk abroad upon his staff, then shall he that struck him be guiltless; only he shall pay for the loss of his time, and shall cause him to be thoroughly healed*" (JND). Did you ever notice this verse? It basically says that if you were the cause for another to lose time that you must make it up – completely – by paying for the lost time. Let's take a look further down in the same chapter. In verses 33-35 it states "*if a man open a pit, or if a man dig a pit, and do not cover it, and an ox or an ass fall into it, the owner of the pit shall make it good, shall give money to the owner of them and the dead (ox or ass) shall be his*" (JND). Again we see the principle at work. If we cause the loss for another then we are required to make that individual whole by repaying for the loss. Exodus 22 also provides

many other examples including if you provide safe-keeping of something for a neighbor (7 ff.) or borrow something and it becomes hurt or broken (14-15).

God makes clear in His Word that making another whole by a fault of yours is Biblical. Our choices can lead to errors that hurt others and as a result we need to make them whole. Whether we do that implicitly (by being self-insured) or by the use of a financial instrument is also a choice we can make. The issue is not one of faith in God but recognizing that as humans we do err and we need to plan to reimburse those we cause to have losses. Acquiring insurance is just one way of providing for that situation. Others save some funds aside for that purpose. Others do not plan and as a result may go through grave difficulties and perhaps bankruptcy in order to make another whole they have wronged. Now, we should note here that insurance has gone beyond the initial goal of providing for the losses of others caused by you. We now have all types of insurance including life, long-term care, disability, natural disaster, and the like. These also reimburse for a loss but not for one necessarily caused by you. That is, many of these indemnify for actions of others or nature in its operations. These do not appear to cause any issue either as we must understand that events that have resulted in the creation of these forms of insurance do occur over time as part of the way the world operates. We can also see these same events in the Bible. The difference is in how the provision for the loss occurred in the past – usually through the support of the community. As we will discuss under the history of insurance, in the past insurance was acquired by becoming part of a community. In highly developed nations this in many ways has been at least partially replaced by insurance. We see, though, that areas where insurance is not prevalent the community still plays an important role as in the recovery from the recent tsunami that created a disaster in many nations in the Far East.

Based on our discussion here, then, Christians should at a minimum have no difficulty in acquiring insurance that provides for losses to others caused by their actions. This would include automobile insurance, home insurance (at least to some degree), liability insurance, and other insurances that cover actions of yours that may cause harm to others (such as boat insurance). Some of these policies, such as home insurance, also provide for you in case of the loss of the home. The only ones that Christians are usually required to purchase actually fall under the group we have mentioned – automobile and home (if you have a mortgage). If you live in a flood plain you may be required to purchase flood insurance if you have a mortgage. Of course the Christian is not required to live in a flood plain if they wish to avoid this type of insurance. Whether you wish to acquire other forms of insurance such as life, long-term care, and disability should be a decision between each family or individual, and the Lord. If your heart is right with the Lord and you carefully use these as a part of being a good steward and not for the wrong purpose then these other forms of insurance would be fine for the Christian to consider. As we will discuss in a later chapter not every form of insurance is necessary and the good steward needs to be aware of which ones a steward should use and those to avoid.

The History of Insurance

Although it may be impossible to trace the history of insurance back to its origins it has been around for a long time. Earliest recorded instances of the idea go back to Babylon and its merchants who would pay a premium to the one who provided capital for his goods in return for the cancellation of the loan if the merchant were robbed of his goods. Before this type of arrangement the merchant would lose all he owned and he and his family would become slaves. Basically the banker took on the risk of the loan for the payment of some additional amount from the merchant.

Over the years there have been various societies and clubs that have been formed for the purpose of sharing in any losses. Especially when we get to the times of the Romans, the idea of sharing losses became very pronounced in the form of guilds and burial societies where the cost of burial was shared by the members of the society. In these early efforts of insurance, profit was not the motive but the sharing of any risk related to an event. This idea of the community sharing in the losses was also evident in the early days of America.

Insurance as we know it was instituted after the Great London Fire of 1666. It burned over 400 acres of the city destroying thousands of buildings. Nicholas Barbon who had witnessed the tragedy of the London fire was moved to open an office to insure buildings. He established the first fire insurance company, the Fire Office in 1680. Soon after that was the establishment of the first "mutual" insurance company in 1696. Its title, although long, does convey the idea of sharing. Its name was "Contributorship for Insuring Houses, Chambers, or Rooms from Loss by Fire by Amicable Contributions."

The key difference we see today from what insurance used to be is that insurance companies now play the role of pooling together funds to be shared. Of course, they also take a portion for their work in making this a reality and taking on the risk associated with making members feel secure against a loss. As a result, we don't have near the level of community support and sharing we once had, although we do still see glimpses of it in major disasters or when a particular family has suffered a horrendous loss that moves people to action.

As this brief history then shows, insurance really is a shared way in dealing with reimbursement for loss. I would not be able to call this unbiblical since the idea of making one whole is Biblical. If the intent of insurance is other than this then we have a Biblical problem. Some have erred in trying to become rich off insurance by trying to find ways to collect on their policies even if no loss has actually occurred (feigning disability, staging accidents, etc.). When our heart seeks to go beyond the intention of the provision we have gone beyond where God would have us to go.

The Purpose of Insurance

Now that we have seen the Biblical perspective and the brief history of insurance we see that its purpose is to provide for a loss. We have seen that losses caused by us are certainly something we should seek to provide for, while providing for other types of losses should be carefully weighed, as a good steward, trying to keep his Lord's assets intact and earning a return.

Since the purpose of insurance is to provide in the event of a loss, it becomes clear that whatever insurance we do acquire we should hope that we never have to use it. That is, it is one expense that you pay into a pool that you hope you never get a return on. In order to get a return on insurance you must suffer a loss. So the lesson here is do not purchase insurance for any reason other than to plan for a possible loss. God can provide through the use of insurance when considered as an appropriate part of the financial planning portfolio and used in the proper way.

Although there is one purpose for insurance, the world has sought to abuse the opportunity provided by insurance by adding other features or using it as a replacement for careful stewardship. This is why many Christians have difficulty with insurance. They see the world's view of let's insure anything and everything so we can feel secure. The Christian recognizes that he is secure in Christ and that regardless of events or level of insurance that security in Christ remains. The problem is not insurance itself but when we remove our trust from Christ and put it in ourselves. By at least planning for losses or insurance we recognize that neither we nor the world is perfect. By not planning we make the assumption that nothing will go wrong (the world is perfect) or we think that God will fix whatever goes wrong. Some call this having faith in God but this thinking usually signifies a misunderstanding of how God operates in the world. The Bible and experience shows that although God can, and will at times intervene in the events of the world, He also allows men to make poor decisions and nature to run its course. The wise steward prepares for the events that emanate from these before they occur.

One example we can review is that of Joseph in Egypt. He learned from God that there would be a famine. God foreknew the event and just made Joseph aware of the fact that was what nature would bring to bear. Now keep in mind that God did not show Joseph anything about what to do about the famine in the dream (at least we are not told He did). Joseph could have told the Pharaoh about the dream and let it go at that and figure that God would take care of it from there. Rather, Joseph, likely after careful prayer, devised a plan to neutralize the natural event by storing up grain as security against the famine. Yet, certainly Joseph was trusting in God. Again, the issue is one of the heart. I want to encourage you to seek God's guidance on what insurance is appropriate as part of the larger plan of being a good steward of what God has provided. We do not want to lose all of what He has provided to an event that we could have planned for.

Insurance – Your Plan

Your Plan for Insurance

After reading the previous sections on insurance, you may be convinced of its appropriateness as a part of the personal financial planning process as a Christian. Your next question might be – what kinds are appropriate as part of the plan? In this section we will note the key insurance vehicles to consider and then go into more detail in the chapters that follow on how to determine how much coverage and the type of policy to acquire.

Automobile Insurance. It probably goes without saying that people make mistakes when driving and cause losses of their own as well as to others. Biblically as we have seen, we are enjoined to at least make the others that we affect whole. Also most states require some kind of automobile insurance to drive a vehicle. The recommendation then is to purchase appropriate automobile insurance for your vehicle or vehicles. We look at automobile insurance in detail in a coming chapter.

Home/renter's Insurance. Home insurance not only provides coverage for you if you should lose your home to a natural event but it also helps you make others whole who might suffer a loss on your property. If someone injures himself on your property then it is normally expected that you will pay the appropriate medical expenses and perhaps lost time out of work. Again, purchasing this type of policy is appropriate to cover others at a minimum. You may also be required to carry certain coverage for your home if there is a mortgage on the home. If you have no mortgage you will need to decide whether you can afford to pay any claims against you or rebuild your home if something does happen on your property. If you are a renter you will need to decide whether you can cover the loss of all your personal belongings or for another who is hurt through your fault in your apartment or home. Your personal property is not normally covered by the owner's policy if you are renting.

Health Insurance. This one is more difficult in several ways. First, the goal is not to make another whole but to provide for yourself or a family member. Second, no matter how you look at it healthcare is expensive. For a family with children today having healthcare coverage is worth pursuing in order to protect the family's other assets. We will discuss the many options in the next chapter but the goal should be to reduce the insurance costs as much as possible by keeping a savings for a large deductible. Premiums are much lower for health insurance if the company knows that it won't be paying for every visit to the doctor's office. Here your goal is to protect your assets against a major claim from a major health disease or accident. An operation today can cost many thousands of dollars and quickly wipe out an emergency fund or other assets.

Life Insurance. As with health insurance the goal of this form of insurance is to protect those in your family. Here, the protection is also in a sense related to assets since the goal of life insurance is to provide funds for those living if the one who earns money for the family dies. If there is no life insurance then the family must live off of the assets that are left. Whether to acquire life insurance should again be a personal decision based on your situation. If purchased, it should be for those who earn the income since the intent is to provide for a loss of income. Life insurance policies on children make no sense since they are not earning an income and their life expectancy is quite long. In addition, the policies are ridiculously expensive. Life insurance makes sense for a young family until they have built their assets enough where they could survive the loss of the income of the earning family member. As you get older your need for life insurance should wane as your assets grow and your expenses go down with children out of the home and on their own.

Disability Insurance. Research shows that many do become disabled at some point in their life, even if it is for a brief time. Again, this form of insurance is to protect the family's income when the wage earner cannot work. Since this is not to protect others outside the family the decision is up to the family or individual whether to pursue this form of insurance. It is best to try to get this kind of insurance through your employer. Otherwise, the policies are quite expensive. I would recommend having insurance in this area as a way of protecting assets if a disability were to occur.

Liability Insurance. Your home and automobile policies likely have some form of liability insurance that pays another when you are at fault. The goal of additional liability insurance is to protect assets that you would be required to use if you were served with a judgment where you were at fault. Those with significant assets should consider acquiring an "umbrella policy" that covers most types of liability especially since it helps to make another whole that you have harmed.

Long-Term Care Insurance. Over the last 20 years long-term care insurance has become very popular. This is because people are living longer and the cost of healthcare as people age is increasing. As people age they are also more likely to end up in an assisted living facility or nursing home. These are very expensive places to live. This, again, is something the individual or family must carefully consider. If it is possible for the loved one to remain at home and receive care from outside the home such as hospice care, then that could be an inexpensive option. There is no easy answer to this one since each family is different and has a different number of members to help support it.

There are many other forms of insurance, but these are the only ones a Christian needs to seriously consider. Many others are just money-making ventures for the companies who purvey them with little value to the policy holder.

Reducing Premiums. A key component of your plan, in addition to having adequate coverage in the area of insurance, is to keep the amount of premiums you pay to a minimum. The more you save on premiums the more that is available for investing and building your assets – which of course can lead to further reductions in premiums. We touch on what factors contribute to the premiums and how you might be able reduce them as we look at each type of insurance. You should also keep in mind, as a general point, that credit scores are now often used in determining premiums, especially in the areas of auto and home insurance. A correlation has been identified that those who are poor credit risks also file more claims for insurance. It's a good idea to check your credit report and make sure it is right. If you have had problems in the credit area start now to build good credit so your premiums can go down in the future.

Finding Insurance

There is an enormous amount of information about insurance available on the web, through libraries, and from various insurance companies around the country. You will need to weed through all of the material carefully to make sure the facts are correct. Several of the sites we have already noted in the text provide some good insurance information. Sites such as www.fool.com and many of the large financial sites such as www.quicken.com provide insurance related information in addition to their other financial offerings. CNN Money also has a good section for the essentials of insurance at money.cnn.com/pf/insurance/.

As you might expect there are many sites for insurance information and quotes. Some of these include www.netquote.com, www.insure.com, www.insweb.com and insurance.yahoo.com. You can get to many of the insurance company web sites directly by prefixing their name with "www." and suffixing it with ".com". Some of these sites include www.statefarm.com, www.progressive.com, www.allstate.com, and www.geico.com.

You may find it best to work with an independent agent who can shop for the best price for you and help you understand the contents of the policies. Keep in mind though, that they still sell based on commission. Also double check your policies occasionally since sometimes rates change for the better.

Don't forget to look at other independent sources as well. Consumer Reports regularly looks at various forms of insurance and usually has excellent points to consider when buying policies. They have covered almost all the major forms of insurance in the last five years. Visit a local library or order the articles from their site at www.consumerreports.org.

Christian Support

Before closing this chapter we need to note that some of the needs for insurance can be offset by Christians' willingness to support each other. Before the modern era families would care for one another in their homes or support the widows and infirmed. Today, as we have noted, the community aspect has been for the most part replaced by companies that provide the sharing of the funds through insurance. For the church, though, there are many examples especially in the New Testament that show how the saints cared for and supported one another. I would like to encourage those who have the means to be a support for those who are widows indeed, or for those who are infirmed or disabled. Some of the costs of insurance could be reduced by Christians working together to support one another.

Share Plans. Some Christians have made efforts to get back to the original community sharing aspect of Christians helping one another in the body of Christ. For instance, Medi-Share is one group where members support one another's healthcare costs. They can be reached at www.biblicalhealthcare.com. It is not considered insurance but considered medical cost sharing. Like insurance there is a monthly "share" that you pay based on the coverage you desire. There are also amounts you must pay first before being allowed to share in the pooled monthly shares. These are similar to the insurance "deductibles." The real plus of this type of approach is that members of the share group are expected to live according to Biblical principles, which encourage a healthy, less risky lifestyle. This type of plan may be worth investigating but be sure you understand all the requirements and rules before you sign up. The Medi-Share plan also has an application and annual renewal fee for some of its plans.

Outcomes and Chapter Summary

In this chapter we focused on the Biblical perspective of insurance and found that the Bible does support the idea of making others whole that we have wronged in some way. We also briefly looked at the history of insurance and the different types that are available.

Learning Objective 1. Be able to show the Biblical basis for the concept of insurance.

We explored the Biblical basis for insurance noting that the Bible emphasizes taking responsibility for our errors that cause others harm. The idea of making others whole as a result of our actions or inactions is important.

Learning Objective 2. Describe the purpose and history of insurance and how it relates to the Biblical concept of making another whole.

We reviewed the historical foundations of insurance as a joint effort to help one another in the community when there were needs. Insurance developed as communities became larger and the need for coordination of assistance became important.

Learning Objective 3. Describe the important forms of insurance that Christians should consider.

We discussed the key forms of insurance that might be appropriate for the Christian to consider. These included automobile, home, health, life, disability, liability, and long-term care.

Bible Texts Referenced

Genesis 41
Exodus 21:18-19
Exodus 21:33-35
Exodus 22:7
Exodus 22:14-15

Exercises and Research Activities

1. Research an example from the Bible that shows that we are responsible to right any wrong that we have committed. Write a brief summary and be prepared to share your thoughts.

2. By reading or interviewing others, find out why individuals buy insurance. Write up a report on your findings and be sure to include a comparison to the Biblical perspective.

3. Create an insurance plan for you, and if you have one, your family. Include the types of insurance and the amounts of coverage you believe you need. Identify why you chose the amount of coverage you did for each.

References and Resources

Web Sites.

Allstate Insurance. www.allstate.com
CNN Money Insurance. money.cnn.com/pf/insurance/
Geico Insurance. www.geico.com
Insure.com. www.insure.com
Insweb.com. www.insweb.com
Medi-Share. www.biblicalhealthcare.com
Motley Fool. www.fool.com
Progressive Insurance. www.progressive.com
Quicken Insurance. www.quickeninsurance.com
State Farm Insurance. www.statefarm.com
Yahoo! Insurance. insurance.yahoo.com

CHAPTER 12
Personal Insurance

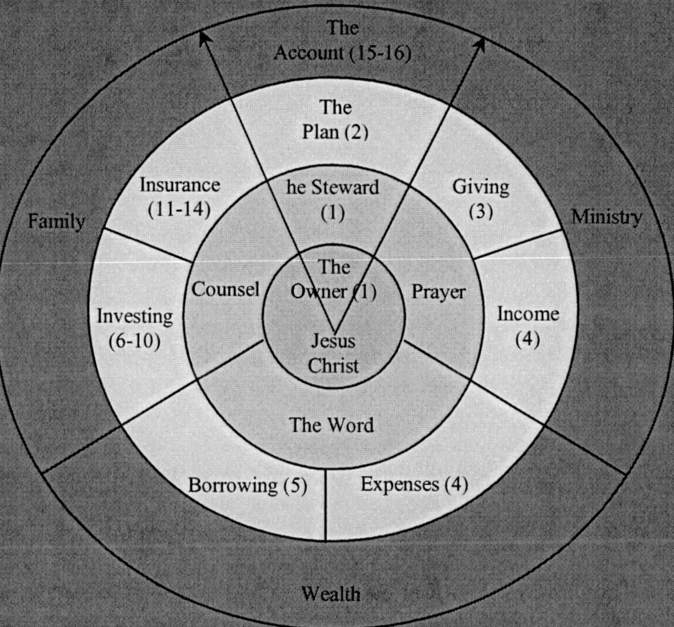

Learning Objectives

1. Describe and research various healthcare plans and explain their various characteristics.

2. Be able to determine the proper amount of life insurance coverage for an individual or family and identify the key components of a healthcare plan.

3. Describe the key components of disability insurance and the tradeoffs related to costing its components.

Lord, I commit my life to you.

Lord, you have shown me in thy Word that life is but a vapor that is here for a time. I thank you for that time you have given me and my family here. Help me to plan according to thy will so that whether I am here many years or few, those that rely on the income you have provided me will be taken care of if I should be unable to work or if you should call me home. Provide as you see fit for the health needs of my family. Help me once again to use insurance as an appropriate financial tool to help those you have given me the care over in this world. I commit my life and that of those I care for into your hands for safekeeping according to thy will.

Insurance - Healthcare

Most likely the highest cost insurance you will encounter is for health insurance. This makes sense since of all insurance types this would be the most likely used and just about everybody uses it at some point or another. In order to deal with this probability, insurance companies must make sure there are enough funds pooled together in order to provide for the various medical claims that arise. Sharing the costs helps since those who remain free of sickness have their portion of funds used to help those whose healthcare costs exceed what has been contributed. As we will discuss in our next section, healthcare insurance can play an important role in our financial planning when we view it from the right perspective.

Purpose

There is no question that the costs of healthcare are rising dramatically and this is the result of various market forces including the demand for healthcare services, improvements in healthcare technology, and the costs of supporting research and liability related to healthcare. Unfortunately, many individuals and families seek to have their healthcare costs completely covered. As we will see, though, healthcare is not free and the funds must come from somewhere. You might pay higher premiums for your healthcare insurance or your employer may pay higher premiums on your behalf among other options. So, for many, healthcare insurance is viewed as a way of avoiding expenses. In reality, we should take the view that the insurance is there to protect our assets. When this view is taken we are not seeking to eliminate all healthcare expenses by getting every healthcare item covered by insurance, but seeking to limit the effect of large healthcare expenses on our assets.

We are brought up, quite often, with the idea that healthcare is free or should be paid for by insurance and as a result, we really don't take the time to carefully consider the costs of it, its purpose, and how we live our lifestyles. More and more Americans today see healthcare as a right. Although this thinking is well-intentioned the Bible makes it clear that there will always be those who are poor and unable to have healthcare. Indeed, with good intentions the state of Tennessee implemented TennCare to help those who were unable to afford or secure healthcare. As should have been expected, the costs soared as more and more individuals tried to find a way to take advantage of the program. Many from other states moved to Tennessee to take advantage of the free program. Recently, the governor has had to make the arduous decision to cut the program significantly. This should be no surprise since human and market forces were bound to create the behemoth it had become. That is, the same forces that affect personal solvency affect organizations as well. Just as individual income is limited so is state income limited. No doubt one of the biggest difficulties in a program like TennCare is that the population it covers is likely to need more services thus driving up the costs. The advocates of such programs are well-intentioned but these market altering efforts are bound to fail because they attempt to do something and assume that no other changes will occur as a result of their implementation. The TennCare program is an example of where many other market aspects did change making it impossible for the program to continue as created.

With that review we should have a decent understanding of the purpose of insurance. Currently, rather than being a right for all, healthcare and healthcare insurance are services available for those who have the means to pay for them. As an individual or family your purpose in having health insurance should be to protect your assets in case of a major healthcare event such as a significant operation that requires hospitalization. If at all possible, budget some funds each month to take care of the smaller medical expenses such as doctor visits and medications. Of course, these can be expensive as well but they are generally smaller than hospital related costs.

As we noted in the Medi-Share plan in the previous chapter, as Christians we should tend to be healthier if we separate ourselves from the world's loose lifestyles. You can help reduce your health costs by refraining from smoking, drinking (not speaking about an occasional glass of wine), illicit drugs, and sexual promiscuity.

Components

When we purchase insurance we secure what is known as a policy. A policy is the document that describes the contract for insurance that you have agreed to. It notes all of the items covered as well as excluded by the insurance and any rules that must be followed by the parties to the agreement. Here we briefly discuss some of the key financial components related to a healthcare insurance policy. We will discuss coverage items in the next section.

? Premium

Premium. As with any insurance you pay some funds into a pool in exchange for the coverage you receive. Claims for services are then paid from this pool. In the past employers would bear the full cost of a plan but now that cost is quite often shared with the employee. As a result, most individuals and families pay some type of insurance premium for healthcare. These funds that you pay, usually on a monthly basis, are called the premiums. Usually the higher your premium the more coverage you have for healthcare expenses. Obviously one of the goals would be to keep your premiums to a minimum, keeping in mind the primary goal of protecting your assets from depletion by a major healthcare event.

? Deductible

Deductible. The deductible is the amount that you must pay first for a healthcare expense before the insurance will begin paying. Deductibles can vary widely. Generally, the lower your deductible, the higher your premiums. If you can afford to pay most of your own small healthcare expenses, a high deductible may be the way to go and avoid a large outlay in premiums. It is usually very expensive in premium payments to get a low deductible because the insurance company is more likely going to have to pay funds out of the shared pool for healthcare.

Co-Pay. Another feature of many healthcare insurance policies is the co-pay. This is usually a percentage of the amount that you agree to pay for a healthcare expense. Thus, if you had a $100 healthcare expense and had a 20% co-pay agreement then you would pay $20 of the expense and the insurance company would pay $80. The higher the co-pays the lower your premiums will be. Some policies also have a fixed per visit co-pay of $10-$25. So, every time you visit a doctor you pay the first $10-$25 and the insurance company will take care of the rest (subject to your deductible and co-pay rules).

? **Co-pay**

Limits. Look carefully at limits the policy places on how much you can use from the pool in a given year. Most policies limit their payouts for an individual or family. One million dollars is a fairly popular limit but they do vary. Also keep in mind that some policies have a lifetime limit. So if you have a chronic disease you may end up exhausting your insurance fairly quickly.

Determining Need and Coverage

Healthcare coverage is one of the most difficult to determine as far as the extent and need for coverage goes, since there are so many different healthcare related events and costs and few, if any, are known in advance. If you are able to build an emergency fund and you can budget for basic necessary healthcare needs then it might be best to secure a policy (on your own or through your employer that has higher deductibles but will protect your assets if something major occurs). Some of the high-deductible policies available today have deductibles as high as $5,000 annually but, as a result, the insurance company has low premiums and picks up all costs after $5,000. That may be worth looking at if you can afford such deductibles on an annual basis. Most employers don't currently offer those plans but they are becoming more popular and you may see more of them in the future.

If you have chronic healthcare conditions in the family it may become more difficult over time to find insurance unless you can get it through an employer. Even with insurance some of these conditions can exhaust lifetime limits on policies leaving you without any coverage. Saving while you are young can help develop assets that can then produce income to help in these situations. Since most chronic problems occur with age, planning ahead by building assets is key to having income in such situations.

If you have children, usually your premiums are not much more than they would be for a couple. The reason is that children usually have fewer medical expenses since while young they are fairly healthy and by the time they are done with college they are off the plan. It may seem strange that a family of 8 can have a premium that isn't much more than a family of 2 but that is how it works. Health insurance, again, can be helpful with children to protect assets, even if you can afford the smaller doctor visits.

Since there are many plans even from the same employer, you will need to choose from a combination of services, premiums, deductibles, and co-pays. The more healthcare services you use, the likely the lower the deductible you will want. The key will be to estimate what your usage of healthcare will be and then calculate your cost for the various policies available.

Keep in mind that employers and individuals may also have Health Savings Accounts (HSA) or Flexible Spending Accounts (FSA) available so that any funds you use for healthcare are not subject to tax, saving you some money. Be sure to check all the rules of the HSA as with many employer-based HSA accounts whatever funds remain at the end of the policy year are lost.

You should also consider dental and eye needs. These are usually excluded from healthcare policies except when surgery related or an accident is involved. You may be able to get these through your employer or some participating association more cheaply than privately. Some policies will also cover preventive care such as cleanings and exams (dental and eye) which can be helpful in avoiding large expenses later.

Exclusions. You will also need to look at you and your family's needs as well. Some policies have exclusions for pre-existing conditions. Others may exclude certain forms of medicine or care that you may need. Make sure you know what you are getting before signing up for a particular policy. For instance some policies exclude treatments related to fertility or cosmetic type surgery. Also experimental treatments are often excluded. All policies have some type of exclusions to reduce the risk of the fund pool being dried up by unnecessary, optional, or overly expensive healthcare options.

Tradeoffs

As you can see, the choice of a health insurance plan can be a daunting task. Be patient and consider carefully what would be best for you and your family. Invariably there are tradeoffs between cost (premiums), co-pays, deductibles, and limits when comparing policies. In addition, you will need to weigh the needs and funds you have available to contribute toward your healthcare. Keep in mind that your total monthly healthcare budget should contain the following:

> Healthcare budget = monthly premium + monthly deductible expenses + monthly co-pay expenses + non covered healthcare expenses

To arrive at a monthly figure be sure to divide your annual estimated expenses by twelve. Also do not forget to include dental and eye care as part of those totals. Although you may have insurance policies for those as well, they will similarly have deductibles and co-pays that must be met.

Is there a best tradeoff on adopting a healthcare plan? As you might expect there is no easy answer because every individual's and family's needs are different. This text can not begin to address all of the possible scenarios. I would suggest that you seek the counsel of a Godly Christian who is familiar with the tradeoffs and can look at your individual situation in more detail. As a general rule of thumb I would encourage the following if practical:

1. Live Biblically and you are likely to improve your health and reduce your healthcare expenses. In addition to the obvious things that we have mentioned previously, such as avoiding tobacco and drugs, we need to do other things in moderation such as eating. Overeating or eating improperly can cause health problems as well. This does not mean you have to be a vegetarian as some might claim. It's interesting to note that when I was a manager that my employees who were vegetarians also were sick more often. There may not be a correlation and this does not mean you can not be one but that it is important to get the proper nutrients in some way. Also appropriate exercise can help.

2. Estimate your healthcare expenses for the coming year based on previous experience. Again, be sure to include pharmacy, eye and dental costs.

3. Consider your plans for the next few years and identify any major healthcare costs you may have. Do you plan on having children in the coming few years? Surgery to repair something that you have been putting off? Looking at these costs can also help you in differentiating among policies.

4. Identify any current medical conditions so you can compare against the list of exclusions for any insurance policy that you consider.

5. If after your analysis you can handle your normal healthcare expenses via your normal monthly budget then consider a policy that has a higher deductible but covers you and your family in case of an unplanned healthcare event. This will reduce your premium significantly while giving you some protection. Just keep in mind that you will be responsible for all of the smaller expenses. Medi-Share works along these lines and expects the smaller expenses to be handled by you which keeps the share amount low. These options are good for the healthy individual or family.

6. If you find that you cannot afford many of the smaller expenses then you may need to try to find a plan that covers most of them. As a result, though, you will have increased premium costs. You will need to figure out if the increased premium costs you pay are less than the costs of paying the smaller healthcare expenses. This will depend on the nature of your healthcare expenses. If you find

it difficult for you or your family to stay healthy or have many smaller healthcare issues then this is more likely the way you would lean.

7. If possible use pre-tax dollars to pay for your healthcare by using a well-planned Health Savings Account (HSA) either through your employer or now on your own. For further information on using your own HSA see www.ustreas.gov/offices/public-affairs/hsa/.

8. These accounts allow you to set aside funds before taxes for qualified medical expenses including insurance premiums. As a result, you don't pay any taxes on the money that is used to pay your healthcare expenses which can save you hundreds of dollars a year.

Non-traditional Healthcare Insurance

Carefully consider alternate plans as well if they make financial planning sense for you and your family. Below we note a few of the possible alternatives to traditional healthcare insurance.

Christian Sharing Plans. Medi-Share, the Christian sharing network for healthcare expenses for Christians has over 50,000 members and seems to be working well for its members. This type of network might be especially helpful for those desiring to enter the ministry. We should note here that, officially, plans like Medi-share are not considered insurance plans, are not subject to insurance laws, and do not guarantee payment. So the motto here is be careful that you understand the plan before diving in.

High Deductible (HD) Plans. High deductible plans are usually coordinated with a healthcare savings account (HSA). These plans have deductibles of thousands of dollars which means they would only come into play if there were a major healthcare need such as hospitalization. As a result, their premiums are very small compared to standard insurance plans. If you are a healthy person or your family is generally healthy this might be an option.

The Bottom Line

The bottom line is to carefully weigh all of the factors and figure what perspective will cost you the least while protecting your assets and health. Building small healthcare expenses into your budget and relying on insurance for large healthcare issues is usually the best way to go for the average healthy individual or family.

Insurance - Disability

As we continue our look at personal insurance we come to an area of insurance often related to healthcare and that is the area of disability. It is possible that if a wage earner becomes disabled that loss of income can have a significant negative effect on the financial plan of the family. Disability insurance helps to protect your income in a similar way to life insurance.

Purpose

The only purpose of disability insurance is to protect the income of a wage earner in the event that he or she should become disabled and unable to work. This form of insurance is quite often abused by the world as a means of getting income without working. Many are those who have been caught doing activities outside of work that they were receiving benefits for not being able to do at work.

One who becomes disabled may also have healthcare or long-term care issues and expenses to deal with as well. The medical related expenses should be handled through your healthcare plan. The long-term care expenses may need to be dealt with through income on the disability insurance or other income, or perhaps a long-term care policy which we discuss later in this chapter.

Components

Qualification. Disability policies normally define very specifically what qualifies as a disability. Be sure to read a proposed policy carefully - the broader the definition, the better off you are.

Waiting Period. Most policies have a waiting period from when the disability starts to when you can begin collecting benefits. Be sure you can cover expenses during that period. The shorter the waiting period is the larger your premium will be since you will be more likely to collect for a short disability.

Non-Cancelable. Be sure any policy you purchase can not be terminated nor have its premiums changed by the insurance company.

Benefits. Check that you are covered for your occupation otherwise you may be required to work in any occupation and lose your benefits. Some policies provide funds for training or rehabilitation to prepare you for work even if it is in a new area but be sure you understand whether you have to work in that area. Some policies also provide a rider that pays residual benefits or loss of income so that if you must take a lower paying position they will pay the difference between your old salary and the new.

Waiver. Most policies offer a waiver of the policy premium if you do become disabled.

Length. Policies normally are in force as long as you pay the premium or until a certain age is reached. The premium usually remains static and is smaller the younger you are (because you will be paying longer and your chances of disability are less). Some policies have inflation clauses that allow you to increase the coverage because of inflation or increased salary. Taking advantage of such a clause also increases the premiums. Be sure your policy goes to age 65.

Benefit Period. The benefit period may vary depending on what age you became disabled. Usually policies will only pay benefits for a disability until your normal retirement age is reached at which time you will receive Social Security. As a result, disability policies are best for those who are younger (25-55) with significant incomes to protect and a significant period of benefits can be expected. For folks that are older the shorter benefit periods may not be enough to consider paying the higher premiums.

Determining Need and Coverage

Most disability policies provide for an income of up to two-thirds of what your salary was when you became disabled. So it may not fully meet your income needs if the wage-earner does become disabled. Social Security may provide some benefits to meet your living expenses, if you qualify, since that program also provides income for the disabled. Check any disability policy carefully as some will reduce what they provide by the amount you receive from Social Security making it a no-gain situation.

Since policies are written based on a percentage of your income there is not much planning needed other than planning with an emergency fund that can help you through any waiting period required before receiving benefits.

Most places you may work at provide for short-term illness or disability through sick-days or by self-insurance. Others also provide a short-term disability policy that is good for up to six months after which the long-term policy would start. These usually pay about two-thirds of your salary so you will need some emergency funds to see you through. Many also provide free long-term disability policies (40-50%). Some may provide a policy if you pay the premium. It may be worth looking into since the group premium is likely to be significantly less than doing it on your own.

Worker's compensation plans will pay for injury suffered on the job but not for illness, so a long-term policy could still be of help. Plans for worker's compensation vary widely by state so be sure to check the one for your state if you plan on relying on it.

As far as whether to purchase disability insurance, if it is not available at work, is a difficult question to answer. Factors such as the type of profession you are in and family history will likely play a role in your decision. The younger you are when you acquire the insurance the cheaper the premiums. The policy stays in force until you stop paying the premiums or until an age noted on the policy. Also keep in mind that benefits are usually only paid until a certain age – usually retirement age at which time Social Security retirement benefits start for many. Also, you may also qualify for Social security disability benefits if you become disabled. Your annual Social Security benefit analysis should identify how much you would receive both at retirement and if you were disabled. You can also go to the Social Security Administration web site and use a calculator to check benefits. If they are sufficient for your needs then you can avoid paying for your own policy.

The Bottom Line

Disability insurance can be expensive for an individual policy and needs to be carefully considered in light of possible need. High risk jobs will normally provide for a policy without the need to pay. If not, you may want to consider a policy anyway since research shows that 3 out of 10 individuals will become disabled before retirement. That is not meant to be a scare tactic although some use it as that. If you are single then disability insurance may still be necessary since it also covers you (unlike life insurance, you will still be living). The other forms of insurance such as health, auto, and home are more important so they should be considered first.

Also, consider whether you could save the premiums you would put into a disability policy and invest them as a fund to provide assistance to yourself if you have a disability, from the investment account. As we have noted before if you can build the income from your assets you can self-insure yourself in some ways and avoid enriching the insurance companies.

If you find that you need to purchase a policy, find some way of doing it through work or as a member of another organization. Group policies for disability insurance are significantly less than for private policies. It may be worth joining an organization to take advantage of a good group disability policy. If you decide to acquire a private policy you may want to have it reviewed by one who is familiar with the area and will look out for your best interest. The policies can be somewhat complex.

Insurance - Life

Another form of personal insurance that we hear a great deal about is life insurance. The marketing for these products is extensive and so in this section we discuss the purpose of this form of insurance and what we should look for in a policy.

Purpose

The only purpose of life insurance is to replace the income of one who leaves this world to go home to be with the Lord. That is, it is income protection for those who rely on the income of the insured individual. Some also consider insurance for burial expenses but this is not the primary purpose of life insurance and burial expenses do not need to be as large as many are today.

Components

Premium. As with other forms of insurance the purchaser of a life insurance policy must pay a premium into the pool which is shared and redistributed as individuals die. The premium can be based on your age, medical condition, length of policy, type of policy, and other factors. As you get older or the policy increases in length, then the premiums will likely be higher.

Face Value. A life insurance policy usually has a face value noted on its front declaration sheet. The face value is the amount that will be paid to the beneficiary after the death of the one being insured. The beneficiary is the one who has been identified to receive the proceeds of the policy. If the face value of the policy is $50,000 then the beneficiary would receive that sum after the death of the insured. The larger the face value on the policy the higher the premium.

Disability Waiver. Most life insurance policies come with what is known as a disability waiver. This means that if you should become disabled while the policy is in force then the insurance will waive the right to collect the premium but still keep the insurance in force. This can be helpful since many disabled folks are unable to work and likely would loose the life insurance benefits because they would be unable to pay the premium.

Exclusions. As with other forms of insurance there may be exclusions in the life insurance policy. For instance, most policies do not cover suicide of the insured in the first two years of coverage. Other policies may exclude death by highly risky endeavors such as sky diving. It's always good to read the details of the policy before securing it.

Determining Need and Coverage

Life insurance coverage is available to most assuming they are willing to pay the premium. If you have health conditions you may find it more difficult to secure life insurance or find it more expensive. The question might be raised, who should be insured? The answer is the one who provides the income for the family. Remember the purpose is to protect the income so that those who rely on it for sustenance will have something available if it is lost. Let's then look at possible individuals to cover:

Children. Covering children is not worth the cost. Especially if you purchase the small $1,000 to $10,000 policies that many companies try to sell to new parents. These are not only outrageously expensive for the amount of coverage, they serve little useful purpose. Even when the child is off on his own it is unlikely that such a small policy will be adequate to cover his needs. Most families would be able to find enough funds to bury a child if he should die so these policies just do not make sense. They are a great money making venture for the insurance companies but of little value to the steward. Since children do not normally provide the income for the family there is nothing to protect by insuring the life of a child. In addition, thankfully, a vast majority of children survive making the likelihood of the insurance company ever paying a claim miniscule.

Singles. Since most single individuals are only providing for themselves it is unnecessary to have life insurance. If they are providing for a child as a widow, widower, or for another who relies on their income it may make sense to purchase a policy. Policies are cheaper at a younger age, as well, so if you are single and your income provides for another then you may want to explore obtaining life insurance.

Married. For married couples life insurance is a good idea to cover the one or both that provide the income for the family. If there are no children then perhaps life insurance on one would be best. When you first get married and have children your life insurance needs will be much greater. The needs will slowly decrease as you pay off your home, children graduate from college, and you build your assets.

Seniors. I know the politically correct term might be "mature adults" but then that would seem to indicate that other adults are not so mature. So we will use the term seniors. Once the children have left the home and graduated college and your home is paid for your insurance needs are minimized. We should keep in mind, though, that if you have not built any assets to support you or your spouse then you may still need it. If a senior is alone then obviously there is little need for life insurance with one exception. Some seniors purchase an insurance policy as part of their inheritance planning to pay taxes and burial expenses after their death. This may be helpful although there are other ways for most. We touch on this in the chapters dealing with estate planning and inheritance.

There are various formulas and calculators available for calculating your insurance needs and Lead Fusion provides a good one at www.leadfusion.com. Fill in the values based on your best estimates. The result should give you an idea of how much you will need to cover for the loss of income if the earner in the family were called home to be with the Lord. Keep in mind that even if there are two wage earners you may need to figure the amount as if there were only one and the entire income is lost. For instance, if both husband and wife work and the husband dies, the wife may need to leave work as well to take care of the children or spend funds to have them taken care of (not as good an option) so losing the one income may be the equivalent of losing both. There are many factors, though, and you will need to look at you situation carefully. Use the following general guidelines when filling out the estimator:

1. Acquire life insurance only if necessary based on your income providing for others as noted above.

2. If there are no children and two wage earners then it may not be necessary to have insurance unless the income of one could not sustain a current or reduced expense layout.

3. If both husband and wife both work determine what one would do if the other were to die. When children are involved you will likely need to plan for the loss of some or all of the income of the second spouse as well, unless that spouse can work from home or has another arrangement that lets him or her continue to work.

You will need to revisit the estimation of life insurance as your situation changes. Your income may rise meaning more needs to be protected, you may have additional children, or you may take on the care of another. Of course, your needs could be reduced as a result of children leaving the home, income needs being reduced, or the availability of greater assets to support losses.

Types of Life Insurance

There are many forms of life insurance and it is important that you understand what it is that you are acquiring in a policy. Remember, for the most part insurance agents, no matter how well meaning they may be, seek to make a commission from selling a policy and there are certain types of policies where they will make more on than selling others. Remember that insurance is only good if it provides for your needs – protection of lost income. If you are being sold life insurance for any other reason, look elsewhere. Let's look at what influences the cost of a policy before looking at each type.

Time. If you buy insurance that has a specific length of time then it will likely be cheaper since once the term is up the insurance company's responsibility ends. The longer the period you desire the more expensive the premium for the policy. If you purchase an annual renewable term policy then you will continue to have coverage as long as you pay the premium for that year. This premium will rise over time (since you will be getting older and your risk of dying increases). You can also purchase guaranteed term which means you will pay the same premium each year for the length of the term; again, the longer the term the higher the premium.

Age. The younger you are the less life insurance will cost you. There is less risk that you will die while young and so the insurance company has time to collect your premiums while you are young to offset the future years when people normally age and die.

Health. The healthier you are the lower your premiums will be. As you age medical conditions may arise and it may become more difficult to acquire life insurance – at least at good rates or enough protection. Some policies will have reduced rates for those who pass medical exams that put them in the class of the healthiest (and thus the least likely to die). The lower the medical class as a result of the tests the higher your premiums. Usually the tests look at weight, blood pressure, cholesterol level, medical conditions, and medications among other items to determine what class you fall in. When young you might be able to secure some life insurance without a medical exam. But the size of the policy may not meet your needs. Your place of employment may provide free or low cost life insurance regardless of condition so you will want to consider that as part of your protection.

Size. The size or face-value of your policy will obviously affect how much you pay for premiums - the larger the amount, the greater your premium. It is usually cheaper to buy one large policy than many small ones but check carefully to see if two smaller policies from different companies might be cheaper. Also check at your place of employment where you might be able to get insurance at a reduced rate.

As you can see, there will be tradeoffs in making decisions about what policy to choose, especially since we do not know what the future holds regarding our earthly life. There are two basic types of insurance policies: "cash-value" types and "term" types. Despite all the sales tactics and reasons in the industry I can't find a really good reason to go with anything but a term insurance policy. Suffice to say, there are many forms of life insurance with many variations to choose from and you will need to evaluate the tradeoffs associated with selecting one over the other. We summarize these in the following paragraphs.

Term. As the word implies term insurance is in force for a specific period of time or term. Some call it renting life insurance seeming to think it is a bad thing. On the contrary, term insurance is fine if it meets your needs and for a vast majority (if not all) it is the best option. This is because it is less expensive and allows you to normally provide full coverage based on your estimated needs. Many buy other types of policies that cost more because they are "permanent" or have no ending date but usually are unable to afford the full protection necessary based on their estimates.

There are many types of term insurance for varying periods of time. Some have inflation riders that allow the face value to increase over time and others have a "decreasing" option that reduces the face-value as time goes by (the thinking being that your needs for insurance will decrease with age). Although guaranteed term is likely the best choice for most you will need to weigh your specific situation to see if that makes the most sense. If you stay healthy using a series of two, twenty or thirty year guaranteed term policies starting at age 25, that would cover you until you were between 65 and 85 depending on which term you chose. With proper planning that should be sufficient to cover your needs. Another option might be to acquire an annual renewable term policy first while the premiums are extremely low then change to a guaranteed policy around age 45. The premium being paid by that time on the annual policy will be about the same as the rate for the 30 year guaranteed policy. The difference being that the rate on the guaranteed policy will not change. Beyond age 50 the rates on annual policies get quite large.

Cash Value. This type of insurance policy provides both a death benefit as well as a cash value benefit. This is considered a "permanent" policy. That is, as long as you pay the premium the policy remains in force. The premium stays the same throughout the life of the policy. As a result, the premium will be more in the early years than with an annual term policy, but less in later years. The extra benefit of cash value means that a portion of your premium is returned to the policy so that its value builds over time. The face value remains the same but unlike term insurance you can get access to the "cash value" that builds up in the policy over time. Usually you can access this value either by taking a loan on the policy, or by returning the policy to the company for the value and ending the policy's death coverage. Some insurers try to sell these policies as "investments." These generally are very poor investments. By the way, once you die the cash value in the policy belongs to the insurance company not your beneficiaries - so much for being an investment. Acquire insurance for its intended purpose – to protect as much of your income as possible. For most young folks that can only be accomplished by term insurance because of the low rates available on those policies.

Term versus Cash Value. The question that invariably will be asked is which of the two types of policies should one consider? Invariably the answer is term insurance. In every case – at least from a cost perspective – term insurance wins. It is far better to purchase term insurance and invest the difference in the price between the term and cash value policies. Using insurance as a forced savings plan is a poor investment and you lose it all once you die.

Whole Life. Whole life insurance is a form of "cash value" policy. As the term implies the policy is in force for your entire life assuming you pay the premiums when due. It has the standard cash value features and the cash value earns income (interest rate that is usually not tied to competitive rates) while it remains with the policy. There are several forms of whole life such as limited payment life that allow you to choose a period of payments that pay the insurance off early but it stays in force. Of course these premiums will be higher since they are paid over a shorter period of time. Other policies reduce the premiums over time by using the cash value to pay the premiums. There is really nothing to recommend in these policies since you could buy term insurance at a much cheaper rate and invest the difference on your own.

Variable Life. This is a form of cash value where both the death benefit and cash account vary based on the underlying investment account. Usually, there is a minimum death benefit guaranteed regardless of the performance of the underlying investments. As with other cash value insurance instruments it tries to make an insurance policy into an investment vehicle, in this case with more risk. Term insurance is a better choice.

Universal Life. Another form of cash value (whole life) that pays competitive interest rates on the cash value rather than a standard policy crediting rate that is usually lower. Usually better than whole life but not worth pursuing in relation to term and your own investment.

Variable Universal Life. Another form of cash value that is sometimes called flexible life or Universal Life II. It combines the supposed benefits of both universal life (competitive interest rates) and variable life (premium payment flexibility). Usually better than other cash value policies but still not worth it.

Joint Whole Life. This is another form of cash value that provides coverage for two or more people and ends when the first of the group dies with the death benefit being paid to the survivors. Get term for the wage earner and save the difference.

The Bottom Line

Don't be fooled by the bells and whistles that agents will try to point out on a policy because usually they do not relate to the purpose of life insurance – which is to protect income. The vast majority of individuals should seek a term life insurance policy. Some exceptions might include:

1. Cases related to estate planning where permanent insurance is used as a tool to minimize taxes on a large estate. This applies to very few people since as of 2005 estates must be over a million dollars to be taxed.

2. Another case might be where you are older and your health is not too good. You might be able to convert your current term policy to a permanent one without evidence of insurability before the term of the current policy ends.

In summary, then, term insurance policies have several key features that make them attractive:

They are simple. You pay the premium and you have death benefit coverage. The only options worth looking at are a premium waiver for disability and an option for convertibility to another type of policy. There are no complex rules, loan options, and the like to make the product confusing.

Lower prices. Prices on average are lower than other types of insurance, especially for policies with level or guaranteed premiums (level term). You pay a lower rate over the whole term because the insurance company knows you are less likely to switch. Keep in mind, though, that if you purchase a guaranteed premium term policy, to get the price benefits you must hold it for the length of the term. Switching policies half way through in this case would be more expensive since you could have had a lower rate for the shorter term in the first place.

Flexibility. If you select a guaranteed level premium policy or a renewable term policy then as long as you pay the premiums and the term of the policy has not expired you can keep the policy regardless of your health condition. Some policies also offer a convertibility feature that allows you to convert from term to another type of policy without a medical exam. You may pay slightly more for this option but if your health deteriorates it may prove to be a big benefit to avoid having to perform a medical exam after the term of the current policy expires.

The goal of acquiring insurance must be kept in mind when evaluating policies; otherwise you will most likely purchase the wrong thing. Be sure to calculate carefully your needs as best you can and then find a policy that meets those needs at the lowest cost keeping in mind the discussions we have had in this section.

Insurance – Long Term Care

The last of the major forms of insurance that is worth considering for the Christian is long-term care insurance. This type of insurance usually provides some type of daily sum or income to be used for one who needs assistance with basic daily activities such as bathing or getting dressed. This can be quite a complex topic but we review the basics in this section and you are encouraged to explore it further using the references given at the end of the chapter and in the section on finding insurance in the introductory chapter to insurance.

Purpose

The purpose of this form of insurance is not to just provide "nursing home" care but rather to provide assistance or custodial care in the activities of daily life by providing regular income to make it possible. Many of these activities we take for granted such as bathing, dressing, and eating. The location of the custodial care may be in a nursing home, an assisted living facility, or in your home. An additional purpose is to protect assets that can be quickly depleted by this form of specialized care since it is quite expensive. This insurance is not required and must be considered in relation to the total financial plan of the individual or family. Some families decide to take care of loved ones themselves without getting this type of insurance and, of course, this was the predominant way it was done several hundred years ago. Others recognize that they are unable to provide the level of care they think is appropriate and decide to seek others to either help in the home or by using another facility.

Process

Perhaps it might be helpful here to note what normally happens without this type of insurance in place and consider several scenarios, keeping in mind that costs related to this type of care can be anywhere from $40,000 to over $100,000 annually. The optimum scenario is the one where the individual starts young to build assets so that if long-term care is necessary later in life there is enough income from the assets to pay for any care necessary. As a result, the only question would be where the best care would be for the individual. This is the scenario that we should work toward as good stewards.

The usual scenario occurs as follows whether you are still working and you become disabled, or you are retired. First, current income from various sources is used to try to cover the cost of the care which is the goal. Second, normally there is not enough income to cover the cost and so any assets or savings are used to supplement the income to pay the cost of the care. Third, once the savings or assets are gone then the individual is put on the program called Medicaid (not Medicare, although it can also help with professional medical care) which provides care for the needy. The Motley Fool provides a nice breakdown of the sequence based on age in their article *"Doesn't Medicare Pay for Long-Term Care?"* at www.fool.com.

The sequence of sources differs depending on the expense item and age. In any case Medicaid is always last because it assumes and has requirements that you are in a needy state. Medicare is designed for medical care and does not pay for custodial care unless it is part of the medical care in a nursing home. In every situation with the exception of medical expenses incurred after age 65 your savings are considered as part of the sequence of income sources. Protected savings are those you would like to save for your heirs so if you have enough long-term care insurance then it is not necessary to use your savings.

Components

Long-term care policies are very complex and require far more review than this text can touch on. Be sure to check out every aspect of the policy carefully and make sure it meets your needs if you decide to purchase one. Below we review some of the key components of the policies. For more information see the fine set of articles at http://www.fool.com/insurancecenter/longterm/longterm01.htm.

Activities of Daily Living (ADLs). Most policies define a list of activities that one should be able to perform without assistance. Usually policies require that an individual be unable to perform a number of these unassisted before qualifying for benefits, The more activities on the list and the fewer required for qualification, the better.

Duration. The longer the benefits period allowed by the policy, the better. Many last for four or six years but some are for life. Of course, additional length usually means more cost.

Location. Most policies limit where the care can be given. Be sure that home or assisted living facility care is provided for and that they are not limited in some way.

Inflation protection. As with disability insurance some policies provide for inflation protection which with the cost of healthcare rising might be a good idea.

Premiums. Keep in mind unlike life insurance policies where premiums can be guaranteed they are not for long-term care policies. They can and have risen significantly for a whole class of policies.

Determining Need

If you are in a situation where you can barely make ends meet then long-term care insurance is not going to be an option for you and since you likely have few assets Medicaid will provide the coverage you will need. The difficult situation is that if you can afford it, it can be fairly expensive and it takes away from your ability to save.

There is no easy answer here but if you are young try to save the amount you would have spent on long-term care insurance and invest it. You will likely have a much larger asset base to earn income off of later in life when you might need assistance. If you are older and have significant assets to protect for your spouse or heirs then long-term care insurance might be of some benefit but only if you would have dipped into the assets to pay for long-term care otherwise.

Keep in mind, as well, that long-term disability insurance will be of help, as we have discussed, and may reduce some of the need for long-term care insurance. Remember, as a steward you are trying to make the best use of resources and balancing the risk of various events happening. You can insure against just about every event and if you did you would soon be poor from paying all of the insurance premiums. Seek insurance for the most important areas of auto, home, health, disability, and life first and then consider whether long-term care insurance would be a wise choice in light of your circumstances.

The Bottom Line

For most people, long-term care insurance will not be worth the cost and limitations placed on the type of care that is provided for. Despite the scare tactics of those interested in the business side of long-term care insurance – about how many of us will end up needing long term care – a careful study will show that for most it is after age 75 and the individual is likely to be a widow. Not exactly the situation that calls for long-term care insurance. Of course, if the widow has assets the kids may lose some of the inheritance, but this is of small consequence in relation to paying long-term premiums for a lifetime for that "just in case it happens," situation.

The toughest decision will be for those who are in the middle between those who have little and have little to lose and those who are rich and will remain rich despite paying for services. Each will need to look at his own situation to determine what is best for him and his family. Although I would love to be able to provide an easy formula for you to determine if you should purchase long-term care insurance, it is not possible. You will need to take into account the things we have noted here and then carefully do some research. Several excellent references are provided at the end of the chapter to help you get a better understanding on long-term care insurance and the associated organizations involved in the long-term care insurance business.

Outcomes and Chapter Summary

In this chapter we focused on insurance plans that deal with the individual or family. We looked at the tradeoff and characteristics of purchasing healthcare plans, disability plans, life plans, and long-term care plans.

Learning Objective 1. Describe and research various healthcare plans and explain their various characteristics.

We explored the many components of healthcare plans and the key factors that influence the premiums that must be paid for coverage. We discussed the importance of evaluating your situation to determine the actual need. We noted that as Christians we should be living a healthier lifestyle than the world which should reduce our costs.

Learning Objective 2. Be able to determine the proper amount of life insurance coverage for an individual or family and identify the key components of a healthcare plan.

We discussed the components of a life insurance policy and reviewed the factors that are important in determining need and coverage. We also explored the wide variety of life insurance policies and came to the conclusion that life insurance should be bought for its intended purpose and not as an investment.

Learning Objective 3. Describe the key components of disability insurance and the tradeoffs related to costing its components.

We also reviewed the components of disability and long-term care policies. We also discussed how to determine the need and coverage related to them.

Exercises and Research Activities

1. Find several web sites that have life insurance calculators and compute your life insurance needs. Write a brief summary that compares the results and the perspectives each calculator took. Were the results different? Do you know why?

2. Assume you need to find health insurance for you and your spouse. You current healthcare bills run about $350 a month but you can only afford to spend $250. Find the best healthcare policy you can that comes closest to achieving your goal.

3. You need to get a $250,000 life insurance policy for you to provide for your family in case of your death. Locate the lowest cost policy you can for your situation. Write a brief summary that includes any factors that influenced the price of your policy.

4. Research a disability insurance policy and identify all of the key components and their purpose. Identify the ones that you feel are important and give your rationale for your thoughts.

5. You have been asked to perform a comparison of a $100,000 life insurance policy using term, whole life, and universal life. Use a

spreadsheet to perform the comparison and then write a brief summary about the one you would choose to go with.

6. Research an article about long-term care and long-term care insurance and present your findings to the class or group.

References and Resources

Web Sites:

Motley Fool. www.fool.com
LeadFusion. www.leadfusion.com
Medi-Share. www.biblicalhealthcare.com

Health Savings Accounts:

U. S. Treasury. www.ustreas.gov/offices/public-affairs/hsa/

Long Term Care Articles:

http://www.fool.com/insurancecenter/longterm/longterm01.htm

CHAPTER 13

Property and Liability Insurance

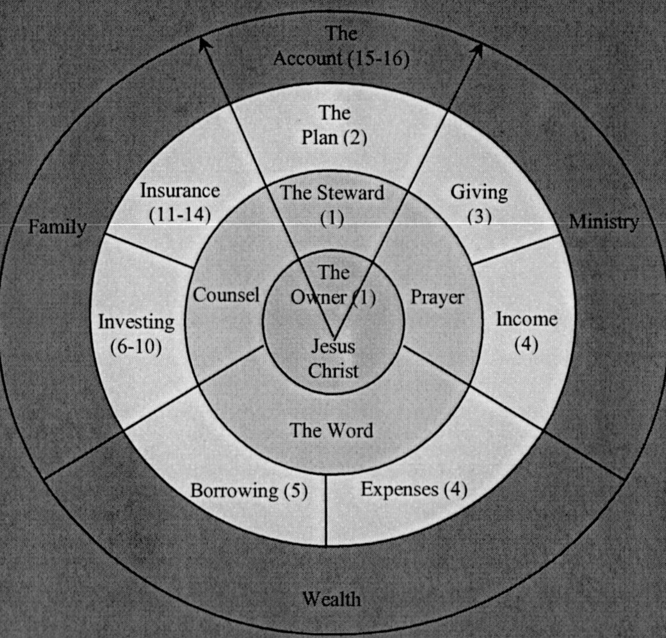

Learning Objectives

1. Describe and research the types of personal property and liability insurance products available.

2. Explore and research renter's insurance and what it covers.

3. Understand the rationale for "umbrella" liability and what it is used for.

Lord, I commit my resources to you.

Lord, you have so blessed me with all that I have. I appreciate all that you have given me in this world and recognize that I am not to become attached to these things. I also know that over time we are subject to the effects of nature and to the sin of this world which can cause loss of the assets you have provided. Help me, as a good steward, to provide appropriately for these assets that they might be available for my family and your work in the future. I commit these assets and resources you have given me, to you. Thank you, again, for them.

In the last chapter we took a fairly detailed look at insurance that protected you or your income for others. We looked at healthcare, disability, life, and long-term care insurance. In this chapter we explore insurance that relates to protecting your property and assets. Of course, the forms of insurance we discussed in the previous chapter also indirectly protect your assets from being used up but here we deal with insuring property and its use. We will look at automobile, home, renter's, and liability insurance in this chapter.

Insurance – Automobile

We have already looked at the Biblical concept of making another whole and realize that it is important to take on that responsibility if we have caused another a loss. Probably one of the most common ways individuals cause loss to another is through the use of an automobile (car) or vehicle of some type. In most, if not all, jurisdictions in the United States you are required by law to have some form of automobile insurance. As Christians we need to make sure we have at least the minimum coverage required by the law and perhaps more if we truly want to make another whole as a result of our use of a vehicle that causes loss.

Purpose

Automobile insurance, like other forms of insurance, gets down to the root of protecting your assets from being used up – in this case because of the requirement to make another whole. The key difference here is that even if you have the assets to protect yourself you may be required by law to have an insurance policy on your vehicles. If you use your car for work you may also be required to have certain levels of automobile insurance. Most automobile policies provide for restoration of any vehicles, other personal property, payment of medical expenses, and other services.

Components

There can be many components in an automobile policy and we can only cover the major ones in this text to give you an idea of the types and characteristics of the coverage available. You will need to perform some research and read actual policies before making a decision as to which insurance to purchase. Let's take a look at some of the key components related to an automobile insurance policy.

Premium. As with other forms of insurance, car insurance is not free. You pay a premium that goes into a shared pool from which claims for losses can be paid. Premiums can vary greatly and are influenced by many factors. Some of these factors include:

1. Age. If you are under 21 your premiums will be significantly higher. This is because experience shows that this group has a greater risk of being in an accident. This results from less experience driving as well as the tendency to take more chances in making maneuvers with the car. A student with a good grade point average (usually a B or better) can also get reduced premiums.

2. Gender. Although you may not want to hear it there are differences in men and women and this carries over into driving as well. Young men are more likely to get speeding tickets and to push the limits when driving and as a result are more likely to file claims from accidents. Unfortunately, this means that young male drivers will pay more in premiums for their policies. This difference eventually dissipates and the gender of mature adults has little influence on the premiums.

3. Car. The make and model of car can also have a significant effect on your premium. Unfortunately, many young drivers like vehicles (speedy and sporty) that are also the most likely to be involved in accidents or stolen which results in increased premiums. There are sites on the web that list the most stolen vehicles as well as let you know how your car or the one you want to purchase compares with others. See the section earlier in the text on purchasing an automobile for more information on this. Those on the lower end of the scale, spend less on insurance. Sporty vehicles and other cars valuable for their parts will have higher premiums. Check insurance information before purchasing a vehicle and consider autos that will keep your premiums low.

4. Location. Premiums are also influenced by where you live. If you live in an area where cars are stolen quite often then you will likely pay higher premiums for living in an area with that risk. If you live in an area of heavy traffic congestion then accidents will be more plentiful and your premiums will be higher. If you plan on moving considering the insurance rates in the area can be included as a factor in determining where you move. Generally, large cities have higher premiums as well as coastal areas where cars can be stolen, dismantled, and the parts shipped out of the country quickly. If you house your car in a garage rather than on a street then your premium may be reduced, as well, since it is less likely to be stolen.

5. Training. Drivers education and defensive education courses can also help reduce your premiums with some insurance companies. Be sure to compare and ask for any discounts related to driver's education.

6. Driving record. The more tickets and accidents you have the more likely you are to have others and this increases your premium. Getting caught speeding results not only in the financial pain of paying for the ticket (which can be substantial) but in higher premiums for many years to come. Let's say you get a $100 ticket for speeding. If your premiums only increase $50 a year as a result of the ticket then it will have cost you $350 to go a little over the speed limit before the premiums would no longer reflect the speeding ticket (3-5 years). Few folks take the time to think about the total cost of such an action.

7. Age and cost of car. The newer the car the more it will cost to insure it. This is because it costs more to replace the vehicle if it is in an accident. Consider buying a used vehicle to keep premiums lower. Related to this is, the more expensive the car is, the more it will cost to insure.

8. Usage. How the car is used and how many miles a year it is driven also influence the premium. The more you drive the more likely that you will be in an accident. If you drive to work then the chance of an accident increases because of all the other people on the road at the same time and the hectic pace of trying to get to and from work. The pressure is much less if you are driving a car for leisure purposes or to go to the local store (at least usually).

9. Safety and security features. Most insurance companies will give you discounts for having safety and security features. This is because the features will reduce the number of thefts and the severity of injuries in an accident which will reduce the costs related to claims. Keyless entry systems, alarms, airbags, and good crash protection will reduce the cost of insurance.

Taken together you can reduce your premiums significantly by carefully considering all aspects of the factors that influence the premium. With the exception of age you can control the factors noted.

Liability/Bodily Injury/Property Damage (L/BI/PD). Liability and bodily injury pay for medical expenses, pain and suffering, and lost wages for others. Property damage pays for others' property such as wrecked cars, fences, poles, and the like. Since the premium for these is usually together we note them together here. It is usually the most expensive part of your premium. On your declarations page (usually the front page of your policy that declares what coverage is in force) you will see an amount next to each of these areas that identifies how much coverage you have for either each individual and each accident, or just a total for each accident. It is quite common to see 100,000/300,000 for liability and bodily injury. This means that your policy will cover up to $100,000 of your liability for each person affected in an accident not to exceed a total of $300,000 for any one accident. Another common combination is $250,000/$500,000. The higher the liability coverage, the greater the protection and the premium. Property damage coverage will vary but will be $50,000-$100,000 on most policies. The property damage component will have just an amount covered for each accident. Your state law will likely require a minimum amount in these areas. To check your state requirements check insure.com/auto/minimum.html. Your state may have low amounts so you will want to consider increasing the minimums the state requires. Even in no-fault law states you will want to have coverage since the reason for no-fault laws is to expedite the cases rather than take away your liability.

Uninsured or Underinsured Motor Vehicle/Bodily Injury/Property Damage. Similar to the previous paragraph it provides the same coverage for yourself and your passengers in case an uninsured motorist causes the accident you are involved in or if you are involved in a hit and run accident (where the other guy runs). Since the uninsured motorist is driving without insurance (and likely does not have any assets to pay your claim) your insurance company will pay to make you whole. The property damage portion would only likely be used if an uninsured motorist damaged property other than your car (like your home) since collision and comprehensive coverage would take care of your vehicle. So you may feel comfortable dropping the property damage component of the uninsured motorist coverage to save on the premium. Otherwise, the other two components coverage overlaps some of the other coverages for you and your passengers noted below. It makes sense though, to take this coverage especially since it has a broader scope and is fairly inexpensive (about 10% of your premium). In some states you are required to have it.

Medical Payments. Your policy may allow for a maximum amount of medical payments per accident. $5,000 is a common amount that will be listed on the declarations page. Up to this amount can be claimed for medical or burial related charges incurred by you or your passengers in an accident.

Personal Injury Protection (PIP). This is common in no-fault states where your policy usually takes care of your own losses regardless of fault. This coverage goes beyond medical payments and includes lost wages. Your disability and health policies may provide some of this coverage so double check so you are not paying for the same thing twice.

Comprehensive Coverage. This portion of your policy provides coverage in case your car is stolen, damaged by storm, and other events not related to a collision. There is usually a small ($100) deductible for this type of coverage. That is, you pay the first $100 and the insurance company pays the rest. The glass on your car such as windshields and windows are usually protected under this part of the policy. If your windshield gets damaged by stones from the road and it can't be repaired, the insurance will pay for the repair of the windshield. Keep in mind the higher your deductible and the lower the market value of your vehicle the lower your premium.

Collision. This covers your vehicle if you are in an accident. The insurance company will pay up to the current market value of your vehicle as if it had not been in an accident. If the repair would cost more than the market value they would then consider the car "totaled." They would then pay you the market value and take the vehicle. The older your vehicle gets the lower the premium for collision. There is also a deductible for this portion of the insurance. The higher the deductible, the lower the premium. At some point, depending on the total depreciation on your vehicle, paying collision may not make any sense since any accident would either not reach the amount of the deductible or cause the insurance company to "total" the car as long as the repair bill were more than the market value of the car. The company could then resell the car for parts or have it fixed and resell it and recoup its funds paid to you or perhaps even make a profit.

Emergency Service. This is a small premium to provide you emergency road service and towing if you should become stranded. Most individuals already have this coverage through an automobile club such as the American Automobile Association (AAA). If you have AAA then this would be unnecessary. If not, then this is an inexpensive way of getting such coverage. Be sure to check what is covered in your policy and how much they will pay. Sometimes the coverage is not as good as the auto clubs.

Car Rental and Travel. Some policies allow you to include a line item for receiving help with rental car expenses or transportation after your vehicle has been in an accident. Look carefully; there are usually restrictions on when this feature can be used and there are daily and maximum limits on the amount paid out. If you have more than one car then this option may be unnecessary especially since the coverage usually is quite small for the amount you pay in premiums.

Using Another's Car

It's a good idea to consider your use of other vehicles in determining your automobile insurance coverage. If you use a friend's car then you will likely be covered first by the friend's policy and then by yours. You should verify this with the company or agent. The question of rental car insurance is bound to come up and we cover that in detail in the next chapter. Suffice to say here if you have appropriate vehicle coverage for your own car then the policy should also cover any rental car you use. Check with your company or agent to verify that you are covered for a rental car that you are going to drive. Most policies do cover it today.

Determining Need

Although car insurance policies can have various options, most do carry the basic ones noted above making it easier to comparison shop for the best deal. As far as determining need you will need to look at how much of your assets you would like to protect and make sure that you have at least the minimum required by your state law. If you have a loan on your vehicle then the bank may also have certain requirements such as carrying collision and comprehensive coverage. For most, a basic policy will have:

L/BI/PD – 100,000/300,000/100,000
Medical – 5,000
Comprehensive
Collision
UIM/BI/PD – 100,000/300,000/100,000

As we have already noted, you can control the type of car, the amount of the deductible for comprehensive and collision, the place you live, and the amount of coverage beyond what the law requires. If you also have a liability policy it may require higher limits on some of the items.

You will need to determine if you desire other options such as road service and rental car services. You may already have some of these features via an auto club or your auto dealership where you bought the car. Many people end up paying double by paying for the same feature in two places losing valuable funds that they could invest.

There are other ways of reducing premiums, such as having your auto and home insurance with the same company. Also adding safety features to a car or buying a car that has many safety features such as an alarm and air bags will usually provide discounts on your policy. If you have multiple cars and/or drivers then premiums can be reduced by combining them into a single policy. You may also get a discount for being a loyal customer after a number of years of purchasing insurance from the same company.

Also consider what other coverages you have for yourself and your family in other policies you own. Especially look at health and disability policies to see if there is any overlap. You might be able to reduce your coverage here if the items are covered elsewhere. Health and disability would only apply to you and your family, not others involved in a claim.

The Bottom Line

Research carefully the various policies that are available. Auto insurance is easier to compare since many of the components of a policy are standard. Keep in mind that just about all premium quotes are for six-month periods. Make sure you meet the needs of your state law as a minimum or your liability policy if that has greater limits (it usually does). Use the web sites listed in the first chapter on insurance to help in your research.

If you have other types of vehicles such as campers, motorcycles, boats, and trailers then you will need to make sure that you have appropriate insurance for them as well. Your state laws may also require minimum coverage on some of these vehicles as well.

Insurance – Home

Hopefully everyone that reads this book will have a place they call home. It may be a place that you have purchased or perhaps you rent it from another. In this section we will look at insuring a place that you own. We cover insurance for those who rent in the following section.

Purpose

The primary purpose of home insurance is to provide for the replacement of it and its contents if they should be lost. In addition, it covers you for accidents that occur on your property or in your home. As with other forms of insurance you are indirectly protecting your assets from being used up to either replace your home or to pay a claim to someone who was injured on your property.

Since this form of insurance provides the first avenue of payment for making another whole that has been injured on your property it is a good idea to have home insurance. If you have a mortgage you may be required to have insurance to protect the bank's interest in the home. If you live in a flood plain you will also need to have flood insurance to protect the bank's interest in the home.

Although just about all home insurance policies will cover for fire or hurricane damage some exclude natural disasters such as earthquakes and floods. Be sure you get what you need. Coverage is available for the other types of perils but they will need to be added as a rider (add on) to your policy or as a separate policy.

Components

There are many components that can be part of a home policy so you will need to review carefully those that you want to incorporate and be sure when comparing policies that you are comparing the same coverage. Some of the key components are noted below.

Premium. There are many factors that influence your premium. Obviously the extent of the coverage you need for your home and its contents will influence the cost. In addition, there are other factors such as how old the home is, the materials that were used to build it, how near to a hydrant and the firehouse it is, and its condition that will influence the premium. Your premium can be reduced if there are smoke and fire alarms, a security system, and deadlock bolts on the doors. Premiums will likely be higher if you rent part of the home, have a pool, have special recreation items such as trampolines, or use your home for business.

Dwelling. The most significant item on the declarations page of your policy will be the actual coverage for the replacement of your home if it is lost in a covered event. Be sure to check for exclusions as they can be many. You will want to make sure that you have current replacement cost coverage so that if you had to rebuild, you could, based on current costs. This will require that you have full coverage on the dwelling.

Contents. The premium for contents coverage is usually included with the amount related to replacing the dwelling. The amount of contents coverage can be adjusted based on what you would need replaced if you were to lose any or all of the contents of your home. Be sure you have replacement value on the contents otherwise you will receive only the market value which for many home related items is much less than what it will cost for you to replace the items. Much of our clothing, kitchenware, and furniture would fetch little at a sale so the insurance company would only give you a small amount (market value) for items that may cost you thousands to replace if you do not have replacement coverage.

Most policies will also include coverage for some jewelry and furs, a home computer, silverware, firearms, and a small amount of business property. The amounts for these are usually limited so check carefully if there is enough coverage. If not, you can request a rider to increase the coverage in a particular area.

Liability. Another major component is in the area of liability. This would pay for a claim against you related to lost time or other loss someone suffers on your property. The cost of this coverage is usually quite small because the risk of a claim is small.

Loss of use. Most policies will also provide a certain amount of coverage for expenses of living if you lose the use of your home. This will cover rental expenses related to having a place to live until you can replace your current dwelling.

Medical Payments. This feature provides for medical payments to individuals that are injured on your property. The coverage is usually small with a small premium.

Sewer/Drain Backup. If you are in an area that might be subject to a drain or sewer backup you might want to secure a rider to your policy to protect you for such a loss caused by one. It is not usually covered in a home policy. Coverage will likely run $10 a year.

Other Coverage. Most home policies include some coverage for credit card and bank card forgery, building ordinance problems, and damage to others' property. Check the level of coverage and make sure those things that you need coverage for are included or added as riders to the policy.

Determining Need

There is no magic formula for determining your home insurance needs because it will vary by family based on your own assets, location, and amount of goods owned. The following are the key recommendations related to considering your need:

1. If you have a mortgage or other home loan at least provide for the bank's requirements based on the loan papers you signed.

2. Be sure to have coverage for natural perils that occur in your area on a regular basis and be sure that you have replacement cost coverage for your dwelling.

3. Be sure that you have enough coverage for the contents of your home and that you also have replacement value coverage on it.

4. Provide liability coverage for you and your property. You may need to have a minimum amount if you also have a separate umbrella liability policy.

5. If you have any antiques or special collections or items not normally covered in a home policy be sure to secure appropriate policies or riders to provide for their replacement if lost or stolen.

6. If you have a home business you will likely need business insurance to cover professional liability and business equipment losses.

Condominium owners will need to check with their association to see what the association covers and what they must cover with their own insurance. At a minimum you will need to cover for personal liability and the contents of your condo. You may also need replacement insurance for the interior walls and mechanicals so check carefully.

Once you have identified the areas of coverage you need and how much coverage you need for each you can then have a basis for doing some comparison shopping. Be sure to use the numbers you develop for your needs when asking for quotes otherwise you will end up with different coverages that will be difficult, at best, to compare.

The Bottom Line

As you can see, there are many components that can influence the cost of a policy but the cost is most affected by the cost of replacing things and the risk of loss in the area you live. If you live in Florida, it is likely that your insurance rates will be higher since hurricanes reach shore on somewhat of a regular basis. So, just living in an area that is inexpensive and not prone to natural perils or theft will result in much lower premiums.

Be sure to look for replacement cost rather than cash value. You may have a nice $3,000 computer that still might cost $2700 to replace but the insurance company will only give the cash value of $500 for it unless you have replacement cost coverage which means you would have to provide the other $2200 to replace the computer from your own assets.

Consider taking an inventory of your home with pictures so you have proof that you owned the items. An insurance company may request proof that you owned an item before they will pay a claim for it. Be sure you store the inventory in a safe place that will not be destroyed if your home gets destroyed.

Insurance - Renter's

It is surprising how few people who rent have insurance to cover their assets against fire or from a judgment of liability. In this section we explore the importance and components of insurance for renters.

Purpose

Renters need the same basic type of coverage as home owners with the exception they have no building to cover. The building will be covered by the landlord's insurance which would also likely cover any rent he loses because of lost apartments, but his insurance does not cover your loss or the cost of finding a new apartment. The purpose of renter's insurance then is to cover the replacement of personal belongings and provide personal liability protection for your assets. As with other insurances, if you have enough of your own assets to self-insure yourself then the insurance would not be necessary or you could secure an umbrella liability policy with a high deductible in the case of some type of catastrophic liability.

Components

Renter's insurance, like home insurance can have a number of different components and riders depending on the need. Rather than repeat what we covered under the home insurance area you should review all of the areas in that section related to personal contents and liability. The only area you don't need to consider is the dwelling coverage. If you own a condo you may also want to cover any improvements you have made to the dwelling which would not be covered by the landlord's policy.

Determining Need

As with home insurance your needs will be based on the amount of personal goods you need covered and the risk in the area you live. The less expensive your living style and the less prone the area you live in to perils of any kind the less expensive the premiums for the policy.

The Bottom Line

If you rent be sure to consider renter's insurance at least for the liability aspect. Liability can be difficult to cover with your own assets. Unlike home insurance, insurance for renters can be relatively inexpensive and is worth having to protect assets and to make others whole that you wrong. Keep in mind you want to get replacement coverage on your personal belongings and not cash value so that you are able to replace anything that is lost or damaged.

Insurance - Liability

As we have noted previously we need to be able to make others whole as a result of mistakes we make. That is, we are liable or assume responsibility to make whole another because of an action (or non-action) on our part. Sometimes our mistakes can be quite significant resulting in great loss for others. To be able to handle these situations we need to have either adequate assets to cover that possibility or have a liability policy that protects what assets we have and provides for the loss. In this section we touch on issues related to liability insurance policies.

Purpose

Although your other forms of insurance such as automobile, renter's, and home, may cover some forms of liability sometimes the cost related to your liability is much greater than what is covered by those policies. In addition, you may wrong others in ways not covered by those policies. The purpose of liability insurance is to provide broader financial protection on a larger scale that protects your assets when you have acquired a responsibility to repay another for a loss that you had a hand in creating. Your part may have been as a result of inaction such as not properly storing tools that you left in the yard (and another tripped on them resulting in a major injury) or as a result of something you did such as injuring your neighbor as a result of a stone thrown from your lawn mower while you were mowing the yard.

No matter the event or the characteristics of the event you bear some responsibility to make the person whole when you have caused a loss to occur. In today's litigious age and with costs of reparations soaring it is a good idea to have a liability "umbrella" policy that covers for costs that go beyond what your other conventional insurance policies will cover. This is especially true if you could end up with a substantially reduced asset base after paying for a significant claim.

Determining Need

Liability insurance should be acquired to cover personal liability as well as other work or professional liability that you are not covered for by insurance provided by your employer or in your own business. As with other forms of insurance you will need to determine how much in assets you wish to protect as well as determine what types of liability must be covered for. Many policies have exclusions on certain types of liability or provide certain types of coverage with the payment of an additional premium.

There are no special formulas for determining the amount of umbrella liability coverage. On average it costs $250-$350 per $1 million of liability coverage beyond your basic insurance policies. The higher the coverage of your basic policies, the lower the cost of the umbrella policy. You will need to consider the extent of your assets and how much of them you would wish to keep if a large judgment were issued against you. For instance, assume you have $400,000 in assets, a basic liability coverage on your home or car of $200,000 and $500,000 of umbrella or extended liability coverage. What would happen if you were delivered with a $1 million judgment against you? Well, the first $200,000 would likely come from the base policy and the next $500,000 would come from the extended policy. The other $300,000 would have to come from your assets which would leave you with $100,000 when you were done paying the judgment.

It might be best to plan based on what you would be willing to give up from your assets if you were served with a minimum of a $1 million judgment keeping in mind what your basic liability coverage will cover. Also, the basic liability under your home and auto policies may be different. Some insurance companies will require that the basic limits on both policies be at a minimum level before issuing an umbrella policy. In simplistic terns, then, the formula would look like this:

Umbrella coverage = largest judgment covered – basic liability coverage – amount from own assets.

Using the example we used previously if it was our desire not to use any of our assets to cover a judgment of $1 million or less then the formula would be:

Umbrella coverage = 1,000,000 - $200,000 – 0 = $800,000

Based on this example you would need to have extended liability coverage of at least $800,000 to avoid using any of your own assets to pay a judgment of $1 million. Basically, the higher the judgment you want to plan for or the fewer the assets you want to contribute the higher the umbrella liability coverage must be.

The Bottom Line

Because liability insurance relates directly to the Biblical perspective of making another whole that you have caused a loss to, it makes sense to acquire the coverage if you can afford to. A minimum of $500,000-$1,000,000 of extended coverage seems appropriate to cover possible claims arising out of liability attributed to you. Consider if you have more assets you would like to protect. It is important that if you have limited income and assets to be sure to provide appropriately for your family by having home, auto, health, and life insurance first.

Outcomes and Chapter Summary

In this chapter we focused on insurance instruments that protect property or its use. We have reviewed several types of policies including automobile, home, renter's, and liability. We looked at the purpose and components of each and touched on determining the needs and type of coverage.

Learning Objective 1. Describe and research the types of personal property and liability insurance products available.

We took a significant look at the components of automobile and home insurance. In addition, we discussed the characteristics of renter's insurance and umbrella liability policies.

Learning Objective 2. Explore and research renter's insurance and what it covers.

We discussed the importance of renter's insurance, recognizing that it is often forgotten or overlooked by many. We explored how this form of insurance is different than home owner's insurance and what it actually covers.

Learning Objective 3. Understand the rationale for "umbrella" liability and what it is used for.

We explored the purpose of liability insurance and the rationale for an umbrella policy.

Exercises and Research Activities

1. You have decided to buy a new car. You have narrowed your choices to a 2002 Saturn LW 300 and a 2002 Cadillac Escalade EXT. Comparison shop using the same set of coverage factors and find the lowest insurance you can for the two vehicles. Write a summary report that includes the insurance components and their cost comparisons. Is there a difference? Explain your answer.

2. You and your spouse have decided that you would like to purchase a home. You have found this great home on the water in Tampa, FL. It's a great value at $160,000. You need to determine how much it will cost you in insurance because with the new mortgage payments things will be a bit tight. Your mortgage payment will be $710.00 a month before the insurance. You have also found that you are in a flood plain since you are on the water. Do some research and find out what it will cost to insure your property. Assume you have $30,000 in personal property to insure.

3. You have decided it might be best to secure a renter's insurance policy while you save to purchase a home. You have about $25,000 in personal belongings to insure. Locate the best policy for your needs. Assume you plan on living either in Chicago or Boston and compare prices for the two. Are there any differences? Why?

References and Resources

State Auto Insurance Requirements:

Insure.com. insure.com/auto/minimum.html.

CHAPTER 14

Other Forms of Insurance

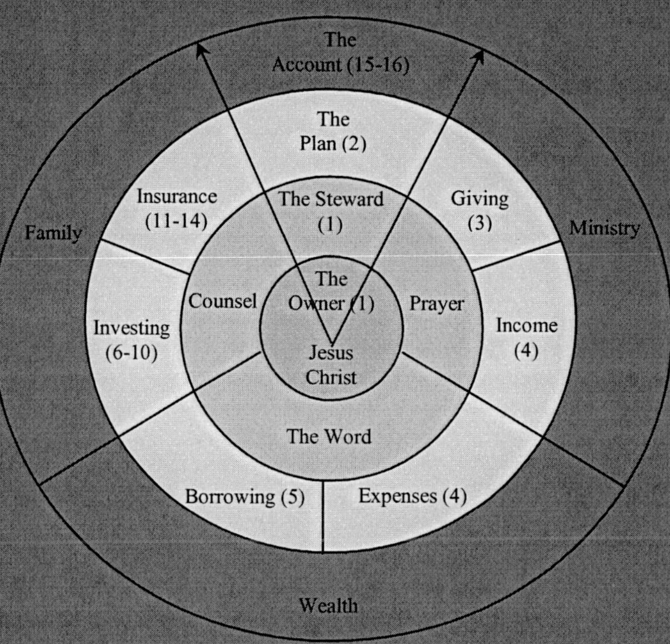

Learning Objectives

1. Understand the various forms of rental car insurance and what they are used for. Identify ways of avoiding this insurance.

2. Identify forms of insurance to avoid and the rationale for avoiding them.

3. Describe the trade-offs of securing travel insurance.

Lord, I commit to being watchful.

Lord, thank you for the insights you have given me on insurance. Help me to use insurance appropriately. I know there are many in this world that are seeking to insure everything or provide the ability to do so. I commit now to being watchful so that I am not carried away by these efforts. As many things in this world, insurance can be used for good, or abused. By your Spirit I will seek to use it for good and use it appropriately.

Insurance - Rental Cars

There will likely be some time in your life when you will need to rent a car whether because yours is in for repair or you are on vacation far away from home. When picking up the rental car you will be confronted with a host of insurance options that can prove confusing and stressful since you must make a decision on the spot as to whether you want the various forms of coverage. Prepare yourself now so you will know what to do when the time arrives. You will feel much better for having done so. Below we discuss the key forms of insurance that you should expect to be offered and what you should do.

Types of Coverage

Check your policy to be sure that it will cover you for driving a rental car. Most do today but you should know in advance. If not, it may be worth adding the coverage. Rental insurance rates, are to say the least, outrageous and if all the insurance options are taken they can cost more than the actual rental of the car itself. Here are the types of coverage offered and how they will be covered:

Loss or Collision Damage Waiver. The first rental car insurance type is known as the loss damage waiver or LDW or the Collision Damage Waiver (CDW). If you accept this insurance then it will cover the vehicle if you have an accident or it is lost to theft. This is basically the same as the collision and comprehensive coverage you have in your auto policy. If you have comprehensive and collision in your auto policy and your policy covers a rental car then there is no need to take this insurance. It can cost $10 a day or more for this type of coverage which you can save if your auto policy has the appropriate coverage. Your credit card company may also provide coverage if you use its card to pay for the rental. Check the fine print to make sure you will be covered as expected.

Liability. Another insurance coverage you will be offered is liability. This will pay on your behalf for any damages assessed to you by a loss you have caused to another party. Of course, since you have liability insurance included in your auto policy there would also be no need to accept this insurance. If for some reason you do not have auto insurance (you don't own a car) then it may be worth your while to accept the LDW and the liability coverage despite the expense.

Personal Accident Insurance. Also known as PAI this coverage is basically an accidental death policy which only applies if the vehicle you are driving is in an accident and you or your passengers need medical care or die as a result. This insurance is unnecessary since this is the same coverage that you would have under your auto, life, and/or disability insurance policies. Of course, check to make sure before hand.

Personal Effects Coverage (PEC). This insures against the theft or loss of your personal belongings from the rental car. This coverage is not necessary since your home and/or auto policy will cover such losses. Confirm that your policy covers the items. If it does not, it may be worth covering them yourself if the value of them is not that great and you have the assets available to cover the loss.

Additional Liability Insurance (ALI). This insurance provides coverage for liability and bodily injury beyond the limits offered in the CDW/LDW. If you have a good auto policy that covers rental cars and you have an additional liability policy that also covers driving a rental car you will already have sufficient coverage and can decline this coverage.

The Bottom Line

Rental car companies and insurance companies make a great deal of money off the various forms of rental car insurance. Some may even require that you purchase some of it. Find another company if that is the case. For the most part if you plan ahead you do not need to take any of these insurance options unless you have very specific circumstances such as not owning a car so you don't have an auto insurance policy, or you don't carry a credit card that provides for it. Even then, you might be able to find a cheaper rental car rate by shopping ahead of time on the web and securing the insurance before you get to the rental car counter.

The key is being ready and knowing what you will do when you get to the rental car counter. Much of this insurance is sold to individuals based on a lack of knowledge and a fear based on a sales pitch by a rental agent describing what can happen if you don't signup for the insurance options.

Insurance - Other Forms

We now come to our final section on insurance. Here we want to discuss all the other forms of insurance that you may see pass your way that for the most part are money making opportunities for the insurance companies and those who purvey the products. It does not mean that some do not collect on them but the number is so few and the risk so small that few if any need take advantage of them.

Types of Coverage

Travel Insurance. One of the more difficult decisions deals with travel insurance. This type of insurance usually covers trip cancellation and/or medical evacuation. The benefit of the insurance is that if for a "qualified reason" you must cancel your trip you can get your deposit or funds back. The medical option allows you to be covered for any transportation needs from where you are to a decent medical facility as well as some medical needs and a possible home if needed.

As far as the trip cancellation goes, you will need to be careful since there are many exclusions and very few reasons that qualify for the cancellation. So if work intervenes and you need to cancel your trip the trip cancellation insurance will not help you. For most people, trip insurance for this reason is usually not necessary unless the trip is extremely expensive and you still plan on taking it at some point and will need the funds that would have been lost with the cancellation. If it is just a small deposit then that may not be an issue. The cost of the insurance will be from 5 to 7 percent of the trip cost so it is not cheap insurance. As we have noted before, if you have built your assets then such insurance will likely not be necessary and you can absorb any loss using your own funds. If not, then you may want to consider it for expensive, once in a lifetime, types of trips. Just be certain that the reasons you might cancel are covered by the policy.

The medical evacuation aspect of the insurance, if it is offered, would likely only be of value if you are traveling internationally or on some high-risk adventure where the nearest medical facilities are far away and/or you are more likely to become injured. Hunting in the African Sahara might be a good example where such insurance might be handy. This will have to be determined based on individual trips and needs. Check to see if your medical plan will cover this as well.

In summary, travel insurance is an expensive form of insurance that should be carefully reviewed before being purchased to make sure that it will meet your unique needs. People often find out too late that what they thought they had for a claim turns out to be excluded.

Flight Insurance. This usually provides a sum to a beneficiary if you should die or perhaps become disabled as a result of a plane crash. This type of insurance is not worth the cost and you may get the same coverage through your credit card company if you use its card for booking the flight. Needless to say the collection rate on such policies is almost nil since there are so few plane crashes (thankfully). Also, invariably airlines are insured in the event of a crash so that they can help those affected by it. Pass on this form of insurance.

Mortgage Insurance. This type of insurance will pay off your mortgage if you die. This is a very expensive form of insurance that usually duplicates the insurance you have with your life insurance policy. Even if you do not currently have a life insurance policy, it would be cheaper to get one to cover the amount of the mortgage than to pay an insurance company for mortgage insurance for 30 years. Pass on this form of insurance as well.

Credit Life Insurance. Similar to the mortgage insurance it will pay off your credit cards if you should die. As we noted with the mortgage insurance it is very expensive and certainly not worth the cost for the small amount of coverage afforded. You are better off having a decent term life insurance policy that will cover your needs if you should die. Avoid this type of insurance.

Identity Theft Insurance. This form of insurance will allow a company to track your credit report and will notify you when there has been activity against it. What will they think of next? This of course you can do on your own for free (by the end of 2005 in all parts of the country) by ordering the reports on an annual basis from the credit bureaus. This type of insurance is not worth it.

The Bottom Line

These forms of insurance are sold using mostly "FUD.' That is, what we would call "Fear, Uncertainty, and Doubt." With the exception of travel insurance, which we elaborated on, these other forms of insurance are for the most part money making gambits for the companies involved. You have better things to do as a steward of the Lord's resources than spend on such solicitations.

Outcomes and Chapter Summary

In this chapter we focused on how the world has formulated a host of insurance products that will insure just about anything. We looked at some of those that you are likely to encounter sales pitches for and analyzed whether they make sense to use.

Learning Objective 1. Understand the various forms of rental car insurance and what they are used for. Identify ways of avoiding this insurance.

We explored the various types of insurance rental car companies offer at the time of rental and what their purpose is. We discussed several ways to avoid the significant charges imposed for these insurance instruments by preparing ahead of time.

Learning Objective 2. Identify forms of insurance to avoid and the rationale for avoiding them.

We looked at many forms of insurance that have little use except for those that sell them. These included flight insurance, mortgage insurance, credit insurance, and identity theft insurance.

Learning Objective 3. Describe the trade-offs of securing travel insurance.

We reviewed the issues and tradeoffs related to securing travel insurance for major trips.

Exercises and Research Activities

1. You are planning a $4,000 25th anniversary cruise. You are considering purchasing travel insurance. Do some research and locate the 3 best policies you can find and then contrast what they offer. Summarize your findings in a brief report. Also, note if you would purchase any of them and why.

2. Locate some offers for various forms of credit or identity theft insurance. How much per thousand dollars of coverage do these types of insurance cost?

3. You need insurance to cover your mortgage if you should die. Currently your mortgage is $85,000. Research mortgage insurance and find what appears to be a good deal. Calculate how much a year the insurance will cost and compare that to how much mortgage is being covered each year. Is this a good deal? Why?

PART FIVE

Giving an Account: Planning for Retirement and an Inheritance

Chapter 15
Life Planning

Chapter 16
Will We Have Been Found Faithful?

CHAPTER 15

Life Planning

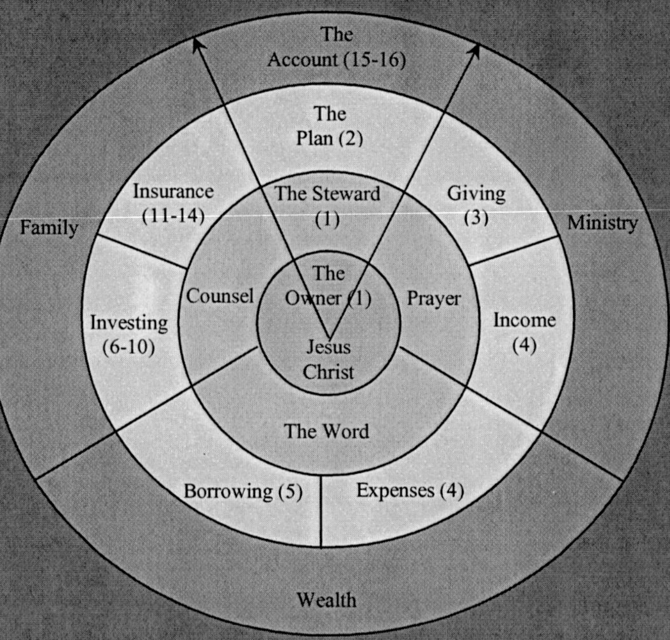

Learning Objectives

1. Be able to show the Biblical perspective on retirement.
2. Identify and describe the key retirement planning documents and tools.
3. Explain the role Social Security plays in the retirement years.
4. Discuss the options for retirement housing and identify the advantages and disadvantages of reverse mortgages.

Lord, I commit to being used of you in retirement.

Lord, I know I may be young now but at some point, if you so will, I will be older and my body will get to a point that it will be ready to retire from the physical labors it once could endure. I commit now, though, to not languish in retirement or just take my ease, but to be used of you as you would see fit. Help me to build assets so that I might be a help to my family and to your work when it becomes time to retire. Please let your Spirit guide me now and in the future as I seek to glorify you in this life whether young or old.

Life Planning – The Retirement Years

Many of you reading this book may be college age and thinking that retirement is so far away that it is something that can wait for a later time. As we noted earlier, the time value of money has a profound effect on your future assets and what you will have available to support you, your family, and the Lord's work. By ignoring the issue while young you will lose out on the opportunity to better provide in the future. These next two chapters, then, are included to encourage you to take a more significant look at this area while you are young so that you may be an instrument of the Lord when you are older. The fact that people are living longer should also give us pause to consider how we will support those extra years of retirement and yet still be of service to Him.

The Biblical Perspective on Age

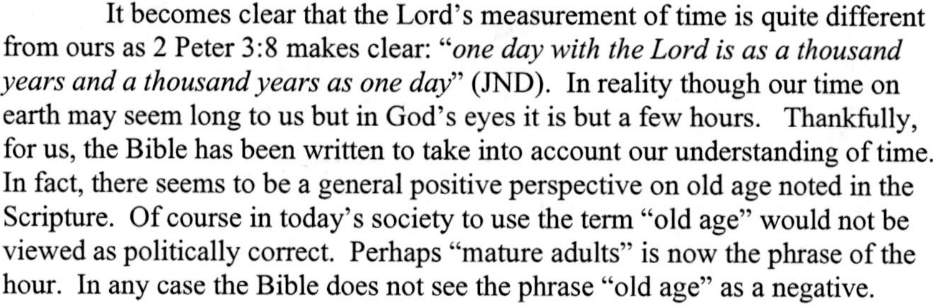

It becomes clear that the Lord's measurement of time is quite different from ours as 2 Peter 3:8 makes clear: "*one day with the Lord is as a thousand years and a thousand years as one day*" (JND). In reality though our time on earth may seem long to us but in God's eyes it is but a few hours. Thankfully, for us, the Bible has been written to take into account our understanding of time. In fact, there seems to be a general positive perspective on old age noted in the Scripture. Of course in today's society to use the term "old age" would not be viewed as politically correct. Perhaps "mature adults" is now the phrase of the hour. In any case the Bible does not see the phrase "old age" as a negative.

We would do well to understand that "old age" is seen as a positive in the Bible. Genesis 25:8 notes that Abraham lived 175 years and that he "*died in a good old age, old and full of days*" (JND). That God looks at old age as an honor is clear by the instructions He gave to Moses for Israel. In Leviticus 19:32 he notes that "*before the hoary head thou shalt rise up, and shalt honour the face of an old man and thou shalt fear thy God: I am Jehovah*" (JND). I wonder if this is how we view those who are older – one to whom honor is due for their maturity. Evidently, not to have an old man in the house was not seen as a good thing. 1 Samuel 2:31-32 records Eli being told that because of his sons' sin that "*there shall not be an old man in thy house…there shall not be an old man in thy house forever*" (JND).

There is no question of course that at times age also brings a reduction in the body's ability to maintain itself against disease. Eli, just as is common today as people advance in age, could not see as he was dim in the eyes (1 Samuel 3:2). That those who are older can be of help due to their experience and many years of walking with the Lord is clear. Rehoboam sought the counsel of the old men but forsook their counsel to his detriment (1 Kings 12:6-8). We don't have the space to go through the entire Bible and look at each verse related to those who are old but it becomes clear as you read that for the Israelites a long life was a blessing from God to those who followed Him. In the same vain Christians are blessed with a lasting Spiritual life if they continue to follow Christ. Our physical life may not be assured as being long but our spiritual life is if we follow Him for that life will continue into eternity.

In summary, then, old age is normally seen as a good thing and a time when one can still be used of God in helping others along the right path as counselors who have had many years of experience to draw on. Though the physical body may tire, the believer's spiritual life can continue to flourish and can still be used of God for His service.

The Biblical Perspective on Retirement

? Retirement

Seeing, then, that older age is a good thing, it is important to understand what God has to say about what we do during that time. In our society we call that time retirement. For many, this has the unfortunate connotation of taking our ease and traveling with little regard of being of service to God and others. The Biblical mandate is quite different. Although there is the indication that our physical labors to support us may be reduced or cease, our other labors of love in the Lord should not. The one time that retire comes out in the Bible as we know it seems to occur in Numbers 8:24-26. It is a great lesson for what retirement is about. It says "*Jehovah spoke to Moses, saying, This is that which concerneth the Levites: from twenty-five years old, and upward shall he come to labour in the work of the service of the tent of meeting. And from fifty years old he shall retire from the labour of the service, and shall serve no more; but he shall minister with his brethren in the tent of meeting, and keep the charge, but he shall not serve in the service*" (JND).

There does come a time when the "labor" ceases as we know it but the "ministering" continues. The Biblical perspective is never seen as one of taking your ease but rather reducing the labor that is difficult for the body and increasing the opportunity to minister in the things of the Lord. That we should bring forth fruit for the Lord during retirement permeates the Bible. Psalm 92:13-15 states "*those that are planted in the house of Jehovah shall flourish in the courts of our God. They are still vigorous in old age, they are full of sap and green; to shew that Jehovah is upright: he is my rock, and there is no unrighteousness in him*" (JND). Proverbs 20:29 notes that the beauty of old men is their grey head. That is, in symbol the grey hair identifies one who has a mature understanding from years of being in the presence of God.

The New Testament continues on the same theme concerning the aged. In fact, the church, as described in its functioning, is headed up by a plurality of "elders" rather than by a pastor as many know it today. That is, it was men who were mature in the Lord and had devoted themselves to the Word and demonstrated by their life and their handling of their family that they were capable as men over God's house. Paul in his letter to Titus also recognizes that the aged men and women play a continued role in God's work even if they may not work for their sustenance. He notes "*that the elder men be sober, grave discreet, sound in faith, in love, in patience; that the elder women in like manner*

be in deportment as becoming those who have the say to sacred things, not slanderers, not enslaved to much wine, teachers of what is right, that they may admonish the young women..." (Titus 2:2-4 JND).

It becomes clear that as we prepare for retirement that we must be prayerfully considering what that retirement will involve. The idea that retirement will just be a time to relax and watch television is foreign to Scripture. Scripture sees older men and women still as able ministers for the Lord. The beauty of retirement is that it allows you more time to help others in the Lord's name or to minister with your spiritual gifts more frequently than when you had to work full-time. So although retirement can provide some rest for the body as it ages, it does not preclude the steward from continuing to minister for the Lord. You can be used greatly of the Lord in your retirement if you plan ahead.

Living Beyond Our Ability to Earn

Retirement as we have noted usually involves a reduction or elimination of our employment for purposes of providing income for the family. This of course does not eliminate the need for funds to continue to live. These must be provided by the funds that the good steward has developed over time while able to work. The funds for living beyond your ability to earn will come from savings, income on assets, and Social Security. Although in this text it is impossible to provide details on every possible source of funds most recognize that these three will provide a majority of the funds. Sometimes, if there is a greater need than there are financial resources then other members of the family or the church may help support an individual. The church clearly plays a role in helping those who are in need, indeed (1 Timothy 5:16).

Social Security. The Social Security system was implemented in the 1930s to help provide for those who work during their life and then need income during their older years. It basically became a forced savings plan for workers so they would have something to rely on when they retired from work. Currently 6.2 percent of earned income (up to $87,900 for 2004) is deducted and saved in this government plan (there is also a 1.45 percent Medicare tax on all income that is often included as part of this Federal Insurance Contributions Act (FICA) tax). In addition, the place of employment also contributes an equal portion on behalf of the employee into the system (plus 1.45 percent for Medicare). So, a total of 15.3 percent of your income is saved in the Social Security and Medicare funds. You must have put funds into the system for a certain period of time before you can collect from it. This is based on a credit system for the amount of time worked. You can receive up to four credits a year and you need 40 in order to qualify for benefits. Once you qualify you can receive funds either when you become disabled or retire. The earliest you can collect is at age 62. The more you put into the system the greater your monthly income from the system when you start collecting. The longer you wait to collect the larger your monthly payment is when you start collecting. This is because you will not collect as long as you would if you started earlier. Of course, there is no guarantee that you will collect anything from the system if you wait because you do not know how long you will live. The issue all goes back to risk which we have already discussed in detail earlier in the book. You can collect full benefits starting sometime between the ages of 65 and 67 depending on your year of birth.

Although Social Security will provide some income for you when you retire it may not be enough to meet your needs. You need to carefully look at what your needs will be when you retire and plan accordingly. Usually Social Security will provide about 42 percent of your average annual income over your working career. Unlike other types of pension plans that take your last number of years or your few highest years of income this takes into account the highest 30 years of income. Also there are adjustments that do help lower wage earners and reduce what higher wage earners can collect. You can also work while collecting Social Security but some of your Social Security may be taxed depending on your income and age.

Pension Plans. A second source of income during retirement will be the pension plans that either you, your employer, or both funded while you were working. We have already discussed these in detail earlier under tax-advantaged instruments and include 401K, 403B, IRA, and retirement accounts. Most of these can be accessed at 59 and a half and many require distribution starting at 70. You will need to estimate how much will be in these accounts at the time of retirement and then figure your withdrawal rate based on the income earned by the accounts. You could use an amortization calculation if you have a specific number of years in mind that you would like each fund to last. That is, how much can you take out each month to exhaust the fund based on a certain number of years and at a particular rate? For example, if you had a fund with $140,000 and you want it to last 25 years at 7% interest and you wanted to know how much you will take out a month to meet these criteria you could perform the following calculation:

Withdrawal amount = interest rate per period / (1-(1 / (1 + interest rate per period)^{periods})) * 140000

WA = (.07/12) / (1-(1/(1+.07/12)$^{(25*12)}$)) * 140000

WA = .00583 / (1-(1/(1+.00583)^{300})) * 140000

WA = .00583 / (1-(1/5.7197) * 140000

WA = .00583 / (1-.1748) * 140000

WA = .00583/.8251 * 140000

WA = .007 * 140000

WA = 989.13

You would be able to withdraw almost $990 a month from your $140,000 fund for 25 years at 7% interest before it would be exhausted. Now the formula may appear complicated and if you do not want to use it you can consult an online calculator or use an amortization table like the one that is included in Appendix A.

Savings. A third source of income is your savings or other assets that can be sold to put into your savings. As with the retirement accounts noted above you can use the same calculation to determine how much you can withdraw based on the parameters you decide to use.

Earnings. As we have already noted you may decide to continue to work in some capacity usually part-time or doing a hobby that generates income. This income can also be used as part of your retirement planning. If you do not wish to rely on this income in retirement then you will need to plan carefully so that it will not be necessary.

These will likely be the key sources of income for your retirement plan. You may receive support from others which, if it is regular, you could include as possible income. Otherwise you want to plan based on known sources that are consistent. We discuss the retirement financial plan in the next section.

Retirement Planning Tools and Documents

In this next section we will look at how to bring the retirement income together into a financial plan while also exploring some other tools and documents that will be important for retirement planning.

The Financial Plan

As you would do as a steward before retirement you should also do as a steward after retirement. Just because you enter retirement does not mean you no longer have to be a good steward. At times people look at retirement as an opportunity to spend all that they have saved but this certainly does not follow the Biblical perspective of being a good steward and providing for His work.

If we are going to be good stewards in retirement then we must have a financial plan as we would if we were not retiring. Of key importance, for those retiring, is that their income may be more limited than before retirement. As a result, they will need to be sure that their expenses are budgeted so that they are in line with the income expected. Retirees should use the same methodology covered earlier in this text for developing a financial spending plan or budget. If you have been careful with your expenses as you have matured then it is likely that most if not all your costs related to children are past and you have hopefully paid off any debt related to your home and credit cards.

As you plan and budget keep in mind that there will likely be increases in spending for healthcare as you get older and your insurance premiums may rise for health and auto related insurance policies. If you own a home then you may be able to reduce your taxes as some communities have reductions for senior citizens.

Exhibit 15-1 provides a checklist of items to review in preparation for your retirement years. Be sure you have reviewed all of the appropriate documents and know how things will be covered and be taken care of if you should become unable to take care of your finances on your own. Good planning using this checklist can save your family from much consternation when having to deal with unexpected difficulties you might have. We cover most of these documents briefly either in this chapter or the next.

Retirement Documentation Checklist	
Retirement Spending Plan	☐
Estate and Inheritance Plan	☐
Medical Directives/Living Will	☐
Power of Attorney	☐
Trusts if Appropriate	☐
Last Will and Testament	☐
Funeral Instructions	☐

Exhibit 15-1. Retirement Documentation Checklist.

The Medical Directives

One of the documents that can play an important future role is that of the medical directives. This document declares who will be responsible for making medical decisions on your behalf if you are unable to make them. It also expresses your desires concerning the means that should be used to extend your life if you can not make such a decision at the time the decision is necessary. Having this type of document in place can save much heartache for your family if they are confronted with such decisions. Although it is noted here under retirement planning it is an excellent idea for all adults to have such documents in place.

The medical directives usually deal with the extent of life support systems that should be used, whether you should be resuscitated, and what types of extraordinary means should be used to save your life if necessary. Without these instructions healthcare providers must rely on the family or various state laws to determine their course of action. Such actions taken may not be what you would have wished if you have not given guidance ahead of time via medical directives.

Medical directives are usually accomplished via two documents. The first is known as the living will which, as we have noted describes the level of care you wish or do not wish to receive if you become terminally ill and unable to make known what you would like done medically. It also includes definitions for the term "terminally ill." The living will can be accomplished by filling out a form that is specific to each state.

The second document is the healthcare power of attorney or the durable power of attorney for healthcare. This document is important not only to reinforce your living will but identifies an individual who can make healthcare decisions on your behalf when you are unable to do so, even if it is temporarily. This means it applies whether you are terminally ill or not. Be sure to review your documents with the individual you have selected as well as other family members that should be aware of it.

The Power of Attorney

? Power of Attorney

Power of attorney means that you grant another the authority to make decisions on your behalf based on the scope of the authority you have granted. For instance, in the previous section we looked at a healthcare power of attorney which gives a selected individual the power to make decisions as if you were making them, when they relate to healthcare. That is, a power of attorney basically acts on your behalf or in your place as your representative. Beyond healthcare it is also wise to have a power of attorney for your financial matters. It can become messy and expensive for your loved ones to get access to accounts to pay bills or expenses on your behalf or provide for your needed medical care, when you are unable to perform these functions yourself, if appropriate planning has not occurred beforehand.

The power of attorney document can be either a standard legal form or one you have specifically created for you. If you do have one made, be sure you have an attorney review it. In the document you can describe the breadth of powers delegated to your power of attorney or limit the powers that are given to the individual or individuals you select. Keep in mind that healthcare and financial powers of attorneys are important to set up in advance regardless of age.

Annuities and Planned Giving

? Annuity

Part of your retirement planning may involve the selection of a payout plan for your employer's pension plan or investing some retirement funds in such a way that you receive a guaranteed annual payout. Company sponsored plans may give you the option of a one-time lump sum payment or the option of taking an annuity which means it will guarantee a periodic payout for a certain period usually until you die or you and your spouse both die. The decision of which to take is not easy since if you take the lump-sum payment your investment choices will need to outperform the annuity to get ahead. If you take the annuity there are several options available.

Single Life Annuity. This type of annuity provides you a monthly payout guaranteed for the rest of your life. This can be an excellent choice if you live to a very old age because this type of annuity keeps on paying regardless of how old you become. The tradeoff is that if you only live a year or two after it starts then it ends regardless of how much you would have received if you had lived longer.

Annuity for Life. This type of annuity performs like the single life annuity with the exception that there is a certain period of time over which the annuity must continue to payout regardless whether you are living. Sometimes referred to as "Certain Period Annuity," it pays for your entire life but, if you should die before the certain period is up, then the annuity will continue to pay your designated beneficiary. Usually these types of annuities are for a period of 10 or 20 years.

Joint and Survivor Annuity. With this type of annuity the period covered is for the life of both you and your spouse. Although there are variations, the most common are to have the annuity pay the same benefit to the surviving spouse as you had received or pay 50 percent to your spouse of the amount you had received. Your spouse then would continue to receive the benefit until he or she died at which point the annuity would end.

Purchased annuities and planned giving. You can also purchase an annuity from an insurance company or other organization that has the same characteristics of the one we noted above. Many Christian organizations today also offer these as a means to provide funds for the organization's use while providing a monthly income to you. This way the organization has use of your funds to develop ministry while providing monthly income for your financial needs. It also can serve as an avenue of planned giving to an organization once you go home to be with the Lord.

Be careful that you fully understand the terms of an annuity before purchasing it – even from Christian organizations. Unfortunately, many older people are taken advantage of by solicitors, insurance agents, and others, some Christian in name, with little regard for the person who is providing the funds. Their goal is to fill their own pockets or that of their organizations. This does not mean there are not good Christian organizations that you should not consider helping in this way, but you should look for them rather than they looking for you. That is, giving in this way should be initiated by you. An organization can certainly list their needs and the types of donations they accept but if the organization is continuous in its marketing and prospecting for funds then one must question whether it is the Lord's ministry.

Housing in Retirement

One of the most important aspects of retirement is planning for shelter. Issues of location, access, maintainability, and cost are important questions related to the selection of any home you might live in when you retire. We also need to keep these points in mind as we consider the fact that our bodies will age. Do we want a place that will be adaptable to our changing needs or will we want to move to another home when our physical needs change? It is better to think about these things as you plan rather than waiting for some event to occur that forces you to make rushed decisions.

Owning a Home

One option for retirement is to own your own home. This could be a house, co-op or condominium. If you own your home with no mortgage or other loans on it then you likely have something that will be cost effective unless you live in an area of high taxes. Owning a condo can minimize the need for maintenance of the yard and building that becomes more difficult with age with a normal single family house. Some homes are poor choices for wheelchair accessibility. Keep that in mind in case you at some point need to use one.

For many, it is best to own their own hone as long as they can. This provides independence and perhaps a psychological lift in being able to live in a place perhaps they have lived in many years. For some it may be best to own a home but in a different location to take advantage of the lower taxes, the better climate, or to be near family in the case of need. An owned home also provides an asset that may help in the future if financial need arises.

Senior Housing

Another housing possibility for senior citizens is what is often called senior housing or "mature communities." These developments or complexes have a breadth of living accommodations and have age related restrictions that keeps the residential community for the most part homogenous. Some complexes include single family homes, condos, assisted-living facilities and nursing care facilities or some combination thereof. If you purchase a home in a community that includes assisted living and nursing care facilities then you normally have the ability to move from one accommodation to another as your needs change. The arrangements for selling a home and moving into other parts of the community varies widely. In some communities you purchase a home for as long as you are able to stay in it. Once you move out of it whether to the assisted living facility or elsewhere the home reverts back to the community. Others will allow you to sell your home but then you must pay to enter the assisted living facility. The range of options is large so you will need to carefully look at the options and cost related to a particular community.

Skilled nursing care is quite expensive and unless you live in a community that allows you to move from one accommodation to the nursing facility, you may find it extremely expensive and perhaps too expensive to enter it. Medicaid does provide some support for nursing homes but it is limited and varies from state to state. It is only available, as we have noted previously under long-term care insurance, to those who have little in assets.

The key here is planning ahead based on the possible scenarios. It is always easier to plan in case of something occurring rather than trying to come up with a solution when something does occur. Proverbs 21:5 notes that "*the plans of the diligent lead surely to advantage*" (KJV).

Reverse Mortgages

It night be good to cover another topic that often comes up in relation to senior housing or providing income for seniors and that is the subject of reverse mortgages. Many of the aged own homes but financially can not take care of all their expenses. That is, much of the net worth is wrapped up in the illiquid form of the home. This has resulted in the creation of a mortgage product that lets those who have reached a certain age and own their home to tap into the equity it contains by receiving a monthly payment from the bank. This product is called a reverse mortgage.

? Reverse Mortgage

With a reverse mortgage the amount of the loan on a home increases each month as a payment is made by the bank to the owner of the home. Interest is charged on the amount of the loan currently outstanding which, of course, will also grow as the loan grows and the interest is compounded. The loan is paid off on the sale of the home with the remainder of the proceeds going to the owner or his beneficiaries.

The two key benefits for the aged are the increased income from tapping the equity in their home and the ability to continue to live in their home. The minus is, that depending on the type of reverse mortgage, they may need to sell it sooner than they wish to pay off the loan and they will have less of an inheritance to pass on, or a home that has been in the family for many years may have to be sold instead of remaining with the family. A reverse mortgage can be helpful but should only be considered as one of the final remedies to financial difficulties.

Outcomes and Chapter Summary

In this chapter we focused on what the Bible has to say about old age and retirement. We also discussed the various planning documents that should be created when considering the future beyond our earning years, especially those that deal with the end of our life on earth.

Learning Objective 1. Be able to show the Biblical perspective on retirement.

We discussed in detail what the Bible says about old age and retirement and looked at the important point that we can still be used of the Lord even if unable to perform the same labors we did in our youth.

Learning Objective 2. Identify and describe the key retirement planning documents and tools.

We looked at a number of planning documents that are important as we plan for the future. Some of these included medical directives, power of attorney, and the financial plan.

Learning Objective 3. Explain the role Social Security plays in the retirement years.

We explored the sources of income for when we retire which included a significant look at Social Security.

Learning Objective 4. Discuss the options for retirement housing and identify the advantages and disadvantages of reverse mortgages.

We discussed the various options that are available for housing during retirement. We looked at owning a home, securing senior housing, skilled and assisted living facilities, and the use of reverse mortgages to stay in your own home.

Bible Texts Referenced

Genesis 25:8	Leviticus 19:32	Numbers 8:24-26	1 Samuel 2:31-32
1 Samuel 3:2	1 Kings 12:6-8	Psalm 92:13-15	Proverbs 20:29
1 Timothy 5:16	Titus 2:2-4	2 Peter 3:8	

Exercises and Research Activities

1. Write a brief abstract on what your hopes for the future are and what you expect to do during retirement if the Lord tarries.

2. Think carefully about the future and try to come up with an idea of how much you will need to live on each year during retirement. Assume you live 25 years during retirement. How much would you need at the beginning of retirement to have enough to get you through it assuming a 7% return on your assets?

3. Research the various powers you can give via a power of attorney. Which ones do you feel are important and why?

4. Research medical directives and living wills for the state you live in. Create a medical directives document.

CHAPTER 16

Will We Have Been Found Faithful?

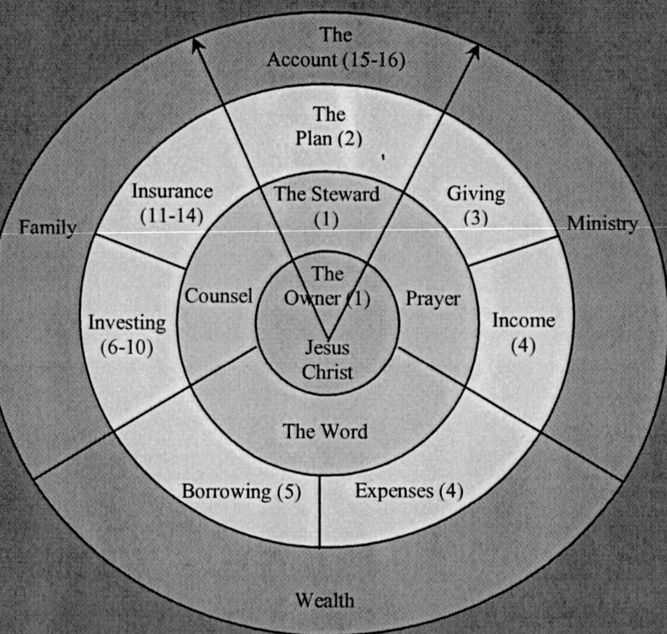

Learning Objectives

1. Describe the purpose of a will and identify the components commonly found in the document. Give the Biblical perspective on wills and inheritance.

2. Identify the issues related to estate planning including tax related concerns.

3. Understand the purpose and relationship between probate, trusts, and joint tenancy. Describe the major forms of ownership of property.

4. Discuss the components of funeral directives and the tradeoffs related to pre-paid funerals.

5. Create an estate plan.

Lord, I commit to being a faithful steward.

Lord, as I come to end of my life here on earth I hope that you will have found me faithful to you as a good steward of what you have provided. I hope that the legacy I leave to those in this world will be one that speaks loudly of your sustaining grace and provision in my life. I give you the honor and glory for all that you have done and intend to do in my life. I find it hard to express in words what you mean to me so I will simply say "thank you" for your love to me.

Estate Planning – Inheritance

We now come to our final chapter of study together and it is fitting that it deals with the final chapter in our earthly lives of dealing with the future of our estate that is left once the life in our physical bodies dies. Although at this point you may be quite young and feel that such things are a long way off, experience shows that no one knows ahead of time when the precise time will be that death occurs. So it is important as a good steward to prepare in advance for this certainty of life. This chapter will help you to prepare for that time.

The Biblical Perspective of Wills and Inheritance

As we have done throughout the text, as we have embarked on various personal financial planning topics, we have made an effort to study what the Word of God has to say about a particular matter first. As with most financially-related topics the Word is not silent concerning the issues of estates and inheritance.

We should first note that as Christians we have a spiritual inheritance that the world cannot know. Our hope is an inheritance in the heavenlies and not on the earth. The Jews, of course, looked for a physical inheritance such as the land in Canaan flowing with milk and honey and were to keep that inheritance in the family (Numbers 36:7-9). It is interesting to note, though, that the Levites received no inheritance in the land. They were priests to God and God was their inheritance. It says that "*to the tribe of Levi, Moses did not give an inheritance; the Lord, the God of Israel, is their inheritance, as He had promised them.* The Levites, of course, are symbolic of the Christians who are also priests as 1 Peter 2:5 makes clear: "*yourselves also, as living stones, are being built up a spiritual house, a holy priesthood, to offer spiritual sacrifices acceptable to God by Jesus Christ*" (JND). So today for Christians, we are more concerned with our spiritual inheritance, or at least we should be. Paul in Galatians notes "*but because ye are sons, God has sent out the Spirit of His Son into our hearts, crying Abba, Father. So thou art no longer bondman, but son; but if son; heir also through God* (4:6-7, JND).

Beyond the spiritual inheritance that we look forward to, we will leave earthly property or an estate when we die. If we look at the issue of estates, most recognize that once death occurs the future disposition of the estate is most likely controlled by a will or other similar document such as a trust. Some may be surprised to know that the importance of estates and wills is noted in the Bible. The parable of the prodigal son brings out how the estate is divided among the living heirs after the death of the father. In the culture of the prodigal son, a son evidently could request his inheritance in advance. Both sons in the parable received their inheritance early and one went as the parable states "and squandered his estate" or literally "dissipated his property" (Luke 15:13, JND) Now this parable has many lessons that we do not have the time to get into here, but it becomes clear that one's estate or property does have a future beyond your death. Do you know what it is?

In Hebrews 9:15-18 we see how the Greek word for "disposition" is either translated "covenant" or "testament." The context usually will provide the appropriate translation. In verses 16-17 it states "*for where there is a testament, the death of the testator must needs come in. For a testament is of force, when men are dead, since it is in no way of force while the testator is alive*" (JND). Rather than debate whether "covenant" is the better term here it becomes clear that the writer understood the concept of wills and that the provision for an estate after the death of the testator is important. Thus God, through His Son, has provided an inheritance to all those that are called sons. To make that inheritance available required the death of Christ. In addition, under this testament God has given time to allow others to become sons by accepting that the mediator's death was on their behalf. Once that time noted in the testament for becoming sons has ended, the inheritance is lost to those who have not become sons.

In this section on Hebrews we see a picture of how a will or testament works. The steward recognizes that the future of his estate must be provided for so that the inheritance goes to the appropriate place. For God, he has decided that it will only go to those who have become His children through Christ. What will it be for our estates? Will we be pleased to see how the remainder of our earthly estate is used? You can use it for His glory and the future support of your family if you plan ahead.

The Will

One of the most important documents related to the planning of your future estate is your will. Keep in mind, that no matter how little or how much you have for earthly possessions when you die it is still considered your "estate." We often think that "estate planning" is for those who have big homes with lots of land or have a great deal of earthly wealth. In reality whether you're rich or poor your possessions are considered your "estate." The "disposition" of your estate can be guided by you if you plan ahead by using a will. There are other ways of planning the future of your estate such as with the use of trusts. These are also legal documents that allow you as a grantor to grant your possessions to a trustee to manage for the benefit of your beneficiaries.

The will is a legal document prepared by you before your death that describes how your estate is to be distributed after your death. If you do not leave a will (sometimes called a last will and testament) then your estate will be considered intestate. That is, you have an estate for which you did not leave a testament for. Every state has laws on how an estate is to be distributed on the death of the estate owner. The difficulty is that the state's laws or court determinations on the distribution of your estate may not be as you would have planned. For instance, states care little about providing some of your estate for the benefit of the Lord's work even if that is what you would have desired. It is

? Will

better to plan ahead and draw up a will. This can initially be done using samples available online or through a software package such as Quicken WillMaker Plus, which is created in partnership with Nolo (www.nolo.com). Nolo provides legal support books and information on most legal topics so that individuals can understand what to do in various legal situations. Their site is quite good for legal information and their books are quite good as well. You should use the services of a professional (lawyer) to review your will or other legal documents to be sure that they are correct for the state you live in and that they are properly signed and witnessed. You could, of course, have the lawyer create the will based on your desires but the more you can do up front the less expensive it will be to use the lawyer.

Whatever you put in your last will and testament will be become available for public review as part of the probate court documents. Probate is the process that a will goes through in the court in order to distribute the estate according to your wishes. So be careful what you put into the document since you never know how what you say might be used at some point in the future. Wills in most states must be typed and the individual making the will must be of sound mind and not under undue influence of others in creating it. Wills must be signed and witnessed by others who are not beneficiaries of the will. Wills usually have several sections. We discuss these briefly in the following paragraphs.

Introduction. In the introduction the will describes the testator, declares the document as his last will and testament, and makes any personal remarks to the family and/or beneficiaries. Sometimes personal remarks are written separately and read as part of the reading of the will but not made part of it. Sometimes the names of the spouse and children are also listed in this section.

Payments. Just about all wills provide for the payment of any outstanding debts, medical bills, taxes, and the like. What remains after the payment of all outstanding claims is considered the "estate."

Distribution of the Estate. All wills contain a section that describes how the estate will be distributed. Be sure that you check your state laws since some may require a distribution to a spouse or children (they may not allow disinheritance). It is in this section that you will make bequests of special items of sentimental value, collectibles, or items that you want to go specifically to an individual. In addition, you will make general bequests concerning the remainder of your estate (sometimes called the residual – what is left after all specific bequests) usually in the form of a percentage of the remaining estate. This is where you would also include any bequest for the Lord's work, perhaps to your local church.

Some wills contain a provision for a trust, especially if there are children that need to be provided for by the estate. The section would also name the trustee and the portion of the estate to be included in the trust. In addition, this section would also include a note as to when the trust ends and what happens with the trust assets that remain. In some cases a trust is created ahead of time and the will references that trust document.

Executor. All wills name an executor. This is the individual who is responsible to make sure that the will is properly probated and becomes the administrator of the estate through the probate process. More generic terms are being used to today such as "personal representative" rather than executor but the role is the same. Basically he is representing the deceased. Quite often the executor is relieved of the need to post bond in this section if the court were to require it, and it details his powers as well. In addition, any compensation due the executor for administrating the estate is noted here.

? **Executor**

Guardians. If there are children it is imperative that your will provide for guardians for them. Even if you and your spouse are still both living there are many cases that both parents die at the same time leaving the state to determine who will bring the children up. Most Christians would want their children raised in the fear and admonition of the Lord but the state does not consider that when selecting guardians. Most likely it will be a family member even if you would not have approved of that family member becoming the guardian. In this section you identify who the guardians of your children will be especially if your spouse does not survive you.

Signature and Witnesses. There is always a section in the will at the end for the testator's signature as well as the signatures and addresses of the witnesses. Each state has different requirements in this area so be sure that it is properly signed, dated, and witnessed to alleviate any problems when it comes time to submit the will for probate.

In summary, then, the will is an important document in finalizing the stewardship of the earthly resources that God has entrusted to you when you die. Be sure you use it as an instrument to provide for your family and for the Lord's work when you die. There are many individuals and organizations that would want part of your estate but as a Christian be sure to provide in the way that best glorifies the Lord – that is usually by bequests to the Lord's workers or to the local church. Also, circumstances change as you age. Be sure to review your will periodically to make sure that it accomplishes your goals. If a simple change is needed you might be able to use a codicil (an addendum to your current will) otherwise if there have been major changes in your family or in your desires for the distribution of the estate then you will need to consider rewriting the will.

Ownership and Beneficiaries

In addition to your will and any trusts you might have, there are other ways that property is conveyed to another at your death. Most of these deal with ownership or pre-defined ownership as a beneficiary at your death. The following paragraphs note items that are influenced by ownership or a designation of beneficiary and are not covered by a will. As a result, there is no need for these to go through the probate process which can be somewhat time-consuming and expensive.

Insurance and Pensions. Most insurance policies, pensions, annuities, and the like have someone identified as the beneficiary of the account when the owner dies. For any such instruments that you have be sure you have identified a beneficiary to receive the benefits related to the account when you die. In fact, you usually can identify a second or third beneficiary in case the first does not survive you. By having beneficiaries identified the account or policy benefits go directly to the beneficiary rather than through your estate which is usually subject to some form of probate. If no beneficiary is noted or the noted beneficiary does not survive you then the benefits accrue to your estate and will be distributed according to your will. Using direct beneficiaries is better since it is faster and less expensive for your beneficiaries when you die.

Bank Accounts. More states are now providing a similar mechanism for bank accounts as with insurance and annuities. That is, you can identify a beneficiary of the account when you die. The person's name is associated with the account but they do not have access to the funds in the account until the account owner dies. These are often called "payable on death" or POD accounts. Of course the more traditional approach is to become a joint account holder with the beneficiary so that when you die the individual already has access to the funds. The key here is that once the accounts are jointly held then you cannot stop the joint holder from using the funds before you die. Obviously such an arrangement requires a certain level of trust that the joint holder will not use the funds while you are living.

Joint Tenancy with Rights of Survivorship (JTWROS). As we noted accounts can be held jointly and in actuality just about anything can be held jointly. There are several ways of holding property jointly. In some states there is a provision for automatic joint ownership for married couples. That is, if a spouse dies it is assumed, unless noted differently, that the other spouse automatically receives full ownership of the property. If you want to hold property jointly with someone so that they have full ownership of the property when you die then you want to be sure that it is Joint Tenancy with Rights to Survivorship. This setup will also avoid any probate proceedings related to the property. Keep in mind, though, that property held jointly can be sold or used by either owner even if it is a detriment to the other. Also keep in mind that a court could force one owner to liquidate the property to pay a debt even if the other owner does not want the property liquidated. Although it may not happen often it can so just be aware of that fact when you decide to use this approach to estate planning. There will be many factors that may influence your decision on whether to use this but married couples should use it unless there are complications arising from previous marriages or other family related issues.

Joint Tenancy in Common. This form of property ownership recognizes that each owner owns a portion of the property and when they die they can distribute their portion as they see fit. Since there are no rights to survivorship each owner determines what will happen with his portion through his will. Be careful with this form of ownership unless you are using it for a specific purpose such as keeping a portion of the property in a particular family (sometimes this happens when a widow or widower remarries).

Any property for which an owner has not been legally determined before death using one of the above mechanisms or through a trust will need to be distributed according to your will. Anything distributed through your will must be approved by a court of probate. Depending on the size of your estate in probate this can take a significant amount of time and expense. The larger your probated estate the longer it takes and the more expensive it is to probate.

The Inheritance

In this section we want to briefly review the purpose of an inheritance and what it is composed of. Proverbs 13:22 notes that "*a good man leaves an inheritance to his children's children*" (KJV). We often think of an inheritance as money and certainly that is part of it but we should also recognize that we leave an inheritance by the life we live as well. Children pick up on the legacy that you live. If you have a life honoring to Christ then it is likely that will be modeled by your children and then by your children's children.

You want to be seen as a faithful steward of all that God has given to you including the distribution of your earthly goods that remain after you die. A good inheritance (not necessarily a large one) demonstrates your faithfulness as a steward. The purpose of the inheritance is to provide for the future of your family as can be seen by the Proverbs 13:22 verse as well as provide for the future of the Lord's work. Ecclesiastes 2:21 states that "*there is a man whose labor is in wisdom and in knowledge, and in equity; yet to a man that hath not labored therein shall he leave it for his portion. This also is vanity and a great evil*" (KJV). Solomon's concern was that whatever he left after he died would go to one who did not labor the same way he did in wisdom and knowledge. Thankfully we, through the mechanisms we have briefly noted, can be sure that our estate is left to those who are of the same mind as we in the labor that glorifies the Lord.

The Bible has much to say about inheritance both physically and spiritually but in both cases the object is to provide for those we love in our physical family as well as those in our spiritual family. Plan now that the inheritance that you leave will produce fruit for the Lord for many years to come.

Estate Planning - The Plan

Up to this point we have been looking at what constitutes our estate and the mechanisms for transferring its ownership once we leave this earth. Now we need to discuss the steps involved in an estate plan and some related issues that can play a role in how much of your estate is left to be distributed after all your debts and expenses have been paid.

The Components of an Estate Plan

ⓘ The purpose of estate planning is to make sure that after your death your estate is distributed according to your desires at the lowest cost possible. This includes making certain that the estate goes to the appropriate beneficiaries. There are several components of an estate plan that can help to accomplish this. We have already noted that a will and/or trust can be instrumental in making your estate desires a reality. Be sure that you have an appropriate and valid will to start with. Other components might include tax planning instruments (such as trusts), funeral arrangements, gifts, living will, and power of attorney. Since we have looked at wills, healthcare directives (living will) and power of attorney previously we will only note here that it is important to create these documents. The others we touch on in more detail below.

The Funeral

During estate planning many forget to consider the plans and costs of the disposition of their physical body after death. It is a good idea to create a document that outlines your wishes regarding your body after death. If you consider this now it can save your family a great deal of anxiety when they must deal with it after you die. In addition to mourning the loss of a loved one, they are often presented with a myriad of questions and options in relation to funeral arrangements. As a result, hurried decisions are made that cost much more than necessary for the family or the estate.

Instructions. At a minimum it is important to have a set of instructions that describe the arrangements you would like to have relating to funeral options. Do you want burial or cremation? Where will your remains be located? What kind of service, if any, would you want to occur? Will there be calling hours? Remember whatever you decide on it should be a time of rejoicing if you know Christ as your savior because you are in a far better place. Though there may be some sadness because they will miss you, there is far more joy for those who know you are going to be with the Lord. This does not need to be a legal document but just a carefully considered set of instructions for your loved ones so they can know what decision to make as they move forward.

Final Place. You should try to plan ahead as to where your physical remains will be located after you die. Even with cremation there is still the need to determine where the ashes will go. If you will be using burial consider purchasing a plot (grave) or niche (place for an urn of ashes in a building). Some cemeteries can arrange for exchanges of plots if you have since moved to a new location. If the ashes are to be scattered then the location and method will also need to be determined. I am asked at times what is best for the Christian as far as choosing between cremation and burial. This is a choice best left to the individual since cremation is not really discussed in the Bible. I recommend burial since that is what was used throughout the Bible and those that were burned by fire were usually the wicked. That being said there is nothing saying that cremation is wrong and often it can be done at a reduced cost compared to burial (assuming the ashes will not be buried in a cemetery). The individual should choose based on what he feels God would have him to do.

Pre-Paid Funerals. Most funeral homes now offer pre-paid funeral services. The benefit of these is that you can lock in the current prices of a funeral and have most of the decisions about the arrangements made to save the family from having to make them in a hurried manner later. There are minuses as well. Obviously you lose the use of the funds that you pay to the funeral home. As a result, it is possible that you could have earned more on the funds than the cost increase of the funeral services. Also, there is not always a guarantee that the funeral services will be there. That is, companies can go out of business and you could lose your funds as well. Some companies have set up accounts at banks to deal with this issue so that if they were to go bankrupt your funds are still be available to you. Be sure to check the terms carefully. Also, if you move you may have to plan on transportation of your body. You may be able to find a funeral home chain that has services in multiple states which can take care of this issue. Be sure you understand all the terms of the pre-paid funeral and exactly what it covers and what happens to your funds. Some have lost their funds or have been overcharged for prepaid funerals.

The Taxes

Although you may be used to paying income and sales taxes most people are not familiar with estate taxes. Recently the laws regarding estate taxes have changed so you will want to check them carefully as you plan. Estate taxes are taxes on the value of your estate that exceeds a certain amount. The estate being defined as the value of the "probate estate" or the value of the property that goes through the probate process after payment of other expenses. Currently taxes on an estate do not occur until the value of it exceeds $1.5 million (2004-2005). This limit is scheduled to increase several more times over the next 5 years. In 2010 the tax is eliminated altogether but that can change in 2011 depending on what congress decides to do. When the tax does apply it can be significant – up to 50% of the portion over the limit. So it should not be taken lightly if there is a possibility it will affect you.

As you can see, then, for most people the tax issue is a non-issue. Few Americans have estates of that size when they die. We should realize, though, that it is easier than many realize to have such a significant estate. When the values of homes, automobiles, and other assets that are not jointly owned are combined the total can become large quite quickly. As a result estate planning is not just a one-time event but one that requires periodic review to make sure that your intentions of the plan will still be accomplished.

If you do expect to have a significant estate then there are ways to plan ahead that will reduce the amount of the estate that is subject to taxes. Remember anything over the limit will be subject to a significant tax which starts out at 37%. Also consider whether your state imposes inheritance taxes. If so, there may be ways of reducing these or you could retire to a state that does not have them. Usually there are four ways employed to reduce the tax burden on the estate that is passed on to your beneficiaries and we discuss these below.

Trusts. We have mentioned this several times and now we discuss them in a bit more detail. There can be many reasons for using a trust, such as providing for minor children in the event of the death of the parents, but they are also often used for tax purposes. As we have noted trusts are basically a legal document that outlines how the transfer of assets from one individual or entity to another will be administered. So creating a trust involves identifying assets that you (the grantor) wish to give to another entity (trustee) for safe keeping and administration on behalf of its beneficiaries which you identify. Basically the trustee is a steward of your assets for some particular purpose and aims to fulfill your wishes for the trust. Usually the trustee is a bank or investment company with experienced personnel in administering assets. Of course, administering the trust is not without costs and so there are fees paid to the trustee from the trust as payment for its administration of the assets.

There are a variety of trusts available and one of the most common is the living trust or revocable living trust. This trust is set up to manage your assets while you are living for the benefit of you and your family. It being revocable allows you, as still the legal owner of the assets, to take them back, and revoke or cancel the trust and resume management of the assets. The big benefit of living trusts is that they usually do not have to go through the probate process. The living trust is still subject to estate taxes since you are still considered the legal owner of the assets.

The type of trust that can avoid probate and save on estate taxes is the irrevocable living trust. The living trust by being irrevocable becomes the owner of your assets and it cannot be changed. You can benefit from the income of the trust while you are living but you have no legal control over the assets in the trust. Since the assets are no longer considered yours they are not subject to probate or to estate taxes when you die.

We have already noted that a trust can be created via a will for children or other purposes such as charity. These are known as testamentary trusts because they are created as part of your last will and testament. These trusts carry different names such as family trusts or charitable trusts. The benefits include reducing the estate that is taxed and controlling how assets are used after your death.

Trusts can be an excellent instrument for estate planning when carefully conceived and used appropriately. Created trusts should at a minimum be reviewed by a lawyer to make sure that all legal issues are dealt with properly before being signed. Also keep in mind that fees are higher to have a professional create a trust than with a will so budget accordingly. Be careful of companies which market their trust instruments. Seek appropriate professional Christian counsel when considering legal instruments such as this so that as a good steward the expected return will be realized.

Joint Ownership. A second way that can be used to reduce taxes is by owing assets jointly with right to survivorship. We have already discussed this in the previous section. It allows the other joint owner or owners to receive the property directly after your death. This will avoid probate but will not help you avoid the estate taxes unless you contributed toward the purchase of the joint property or the joint part is a gift that does not exceed the limit for which a gift tax is imposed (currently $11,000 for an individual and $22,000 for a couple).

Gifts. If you are getting older and will have a taxable estate you can reduce estate taxes by gifting assets to others. As of 2005 you can give up to $11,000 as an individual or $22,000 as a couple to as many people as you would like. So, if you have five children, as a couple you could reduce your estate by $110,000 a year by giving the maximum amount without incurring a gift tax.

Insurance. Another tactic for dealing with estate taxes is to prepare ahead of time to pay for them so that the family is not stuck trying to figure out how to pay them. Some folks purchase a permanent insurance policy for the amount they expect to owe on the taxes so that on their death the insurance proceeds will pay the estate taxes. Of course, you would need to weigh the overall cost of such a policy with the other methodologies for reducing the actual taxes. That is, it's better to find legal ways of not paying the taxes rather than finding more money to pay them.

In this section then, we have looked at the tax issues associated with estate planning and the effect of trusts, gifts, ownership, and insurance have on the estate value and the benefits and drawbacks of each. It is best to consult a Christian professional who can give you guidance in this area.

Does What is Left Point to Faithfulness?

In this final subsection we briefly note a question to ask yourself, does what you will have left behind point to faithfulness? That is, when you die and those you leave on this earth start to go through all that you were steward of will they see through it all one who was the faithful steward? Consider the foolish man who rather than planning for his future estate thought he would take his ease. Luke 12 gives the parable and part of it says "*I will lay up all my produce and my good things; and I will say to my soul, Soul; thou hast much good things laid by for many years; repose thyself, eat, drink, and be merry. But God said to him, Fool, this night thy soul shall be required of thee and whose shall be what thou hast prepared*" (18-20, JND). Clearly the fool was not being faithful. Yes, he had stored up much, but his heart was not right and his plan for its use was not as God would have. Developing a plan to use it for God's glory rather than

frittering it away would have demonstrated a heart right with God and a faithful one at that.

Perhaps you have heard the song sung so well by Steve Green that is entitled "Find Us Faithful." The words and music are by John Mohr and speaks of the faithfulness in the race of life as described in 2 Timothy 4:7-9. Within that song we really get the message loud and clear that others can see our faithfulness in how we live our lives and in what we leave behind. It conveys that we are pilgrims on the narrow road in this world. Many others have gone before us with lives that are a testimony to God and examples to us. As a result, we run the race before us with a desire to leave evidence of God's faithfulness in our lives that others may be able to follow in our footsteps. When we part this earth it is hoped that what we leave behind is a testimony to God's sustaining grace and faithfulness that will lead many to seek Him. May, as the song notes, all that come behind us truly find us faithful.

Remember 1 Corinthians 4:2 – "*it is sought in stewards that a man be found faithful*" (JND). My hope is that whether by death or by His coming for you in the air, that you can stand before Him as one who has been faithful. It is my hope that in some small measure this book has been used of the Lord in your life to help you to become a more faithful person to Him. May He receive the glory for any benefit that you derive from these pages "*for of Him and through Him and for Him are all things: to Him be glory forever, Amen*" (Romans 11:36, JND).

Outcomes and Chapter Summary

In this chapter we focused on the importance of the will and inheritance as a testament to God's faithfulness and your faithfulness to Him. We discussed the key issues related to your estate that is left once the Lord calls you home from the earth.

Learning Objective 1. Describe the purpose of a will and identify the components commonly found in the document. Give the Biblical perspective on wills and inheritance.

We took a detailed look at wills and what is included in them. We noted that wills and inheritances are both Biblical concepts and are to be considered carefully as part of financial planning.

Learning Objective 2. Identify the issues related to estate planning including tax related concerns.

We explored the point that we must prepare now for the future of our estate after our death. If you do not prepare for this then your estate may end up being distributed in a way that would not be pleasing to the Lord nor would it be a testament to your faithfulness to Him.

Learning Objective 3. Understand the purpose and relationship between probate, trusts, and joint tenancy. Describe the major forms of ownership of property.

We explored the various ways property can be conveyed to others at your death and the tradeoffs of each. Probate was discussed along with ways to avoid the process and fees associated with it.

Learning Objective 4. Discuss the components of funeral directives and the tradeoffs related to pre-paid funerals.

We also reviewed funeral directives which are not legal documents, but basically a note to those you leave behind concerning what should be done as regards any funeral for you. We also discussed the tradeoffs of pre-paid funerals.

Learning Objective 4. Create an estate plan.

Having explored the key components of an estate plan over these two chapters the reader should be ready to undertake an estate plan.

Bible Texts Referenced

Numbers 36:7-9	Proverbs 13:22	Ecclesiastes 2:21	Luke 12:18-20
Luke 15:13	Romans 11:36	1 Corinthians 4:2	Galatians 4:6-7
2 Timothy 4:7-9	Hebrews 9:15-18	1 Peter 2:5	

Exercises and Research Activities

1. Research wills and try to write up a sample one. If you have access to will making software try using that. What things do you think are important for your will?

2. Create a portfolio that contains all of the estate planning documents that are on your estate checklist. Be sure to include funeral instructions and any other personal instructions that are important to you.

3. Consider how you would want the remainder of your estate distributed when you die. Would your ideas change based on your age? If, so how?

4. Write a brief report on what you believe it means to be a faithful steward and identify ways you believe that you can be more like the model you should give.

References and Resources

Nolo. www.nolo.com

APPENDICIES

Appendix A
Compound Interest Tables

Appendix B
Financial Worksheets

Appendix C
Bible References

Appendix D
Debt Payoff Analysis

APPENDIX A

Compound Interest Tables

Table A-1 – Future Value of $1

Formula: Future Account Balance = the base amount * $((1+i)^n)$

Using the table: Future account balance = base amount * table entry

Example: The future value of $3,000 invested now at 5% for 10 years.

Value = 3000 * **1.647009** = $4941.03

	Annual Interest Rate						
	5%	6%	7%	8%	9%	10%	10.5%
Months							
1	1.004167	1.005000	1.005833	1.006667	1.007500	1.008333	1.008750
2	1.008351	1.010025	1.011701	1.013378	1.015056	1.016736	1.017577
3	1.012552	1.015075	1.017602	1.020134	1.022669	1.025209	1.026480
4	1.016771	1.020151	1.023538	1.026935	1.030339	1.033752	1.035462
5	1.021008	1.025251	1.029509	1.033781	1.038067	1.042367	1.044522
6	1.025262	1.030378	1.035514	1.040673	1.045852	1.051053	1.053662
7	1.029534	1.035529	1.041555	1.047610	1.053696	1.059812	1.062881
8	1.033824	1.040707	1.047631	1.054595	1.061599	1.068644	1.072182
9	1.038131	1.045911	1.053742	1.061625	1.069561	1.077549	1.081563
10	1.042457	1.051140	1.059889	1.068703	1.077583	1.086529	1.091027
11	1.046800	1.056396	1.066071	1.075827	1.085664	1.095583	1.100573
12	1.051162	1.061678	1.072290	1.083000	1.093807	1.104713	1.110203
24	1.104941	1.127160	1.149806	1.172888	1.196414	1.220391	1.232552
36	1.161472	1.196681	1.232926	1.270237	1.308645	1.348182	1.368383
48	1.220895	1.270489	1.322054	1.375666	1.431405	1.489354	1.519184
60	1.283359	1.348850	1.417625	1.489846	1.565681	1.645309	1.686603
72	1.349018	1.432044	1.520106	1.613502	1.712553	1.817594	1.872472
84	1.418036	1.520370	1.629994	1.747422	1.873202	2.007920	2.078825
96	1.490585	1.614143	1.747826	1.892457	2.048921	2.218176	2.307919
108	1.566847	1.713699	1.874177	2.049530	2.241124	2.450448	2.562260
120	**1.647009**	1.819397	2.009661	2.219640	2.451357	2.707041	2.844630
180	2.113704	2.454094	2.848947	3.306921	3.838043	4.453920	4.797761
240	2.712640	3.310204	4.038739	4.926803	6.009152	7.328074	8.091918
300	3.481290	4.464970	5.725418	7.340176	9.408415	12.056945	13.647852
360	4.467744	6.022575	8.116497	10.935730	14.730576	19.837399	23.018509
480	7.358417	10.957454	16.311411	24.273386	36.109902	53.700663	65.479132
600	12.119383	19.935955	32.780414	53.878183	88.518264	145.369923	186.263877
720	19.960739	36.271412	65.877531	119.590183	216.989873	393.522414	529.851741

Table A-2 – Future Value of $1 Per Period

Formula: Future Account Balance = the base amount * $(((1+i)^n - 1)/i)$

Using the table: Future account balance = base amount * table entry

Example: The future value of $200 per month invested now at 5% for 10 years.

Value = 200 * **155.282279** = 31,056.46

	Annual Interest Rate						
	5%	6%	7%	8%	9%	10%	10.5%
Months							
1	1.000000	1.000000	1.000000	1.000000	1.000000	1.000000	1.000000
2	2.004167	2.005000	2.005833	2.006667	2.007500	2.008333	2.008750
3	3.012517	3.015025	3.017534	3.020044	3.022556	3.025069	3.026327
4	4.025070	4.030100	4.035136	4.040178	4.045225	4.050278	4.052807
5	5.041841	5.050251	5.058675	5.067113	5.075565	5.084031	5.088269
6	6.062848	6.075502	6.088184	6.100893	6.113631	6.126398	6.132791
7	7.088110	7.105879	7.123698	7.141566	7.159484	7.177451	7.186453
8	8.117644	8.141409	8.165253	8.189176	8.213180	8.237263	8.249335
9	9.151467	9.182116	9.212883	9.243771	9.274779	9.305907	9.321516
10	10.189599	10.228026	10.266625	10.305396	10.344339	10.383456	10.403080
11	11.232055	11.279167	11.326514	11.374099	11.421922	11.469985	11.494107
12	12.278855	12.335562	12.392585	12.449926	12.507586	12.565568	12.594680
24	25.185921	25.431955	25.681032	25.933190	26.188471	26.446915	26.577337
36	38.753336	39.336105	39.930101	40.535558	41.152716	41.781821	42.100932
48	53.014885	54.097832	55.209236	56.349915	57.520711	58.722492	59.335280
60	68.006083	69.770031	71.592902	73.476856	75.424137	77.437072	78.468912
72	83.764259	86.408856	89.160944	92.025325	95.007028	98.111314	99.711137
84	100.328653	104.073927	107.998981	112.113308	116.426928	120.950418	123.294329
96	117.740512	122.828542	128.198821	133.868583	139.856164	146.181076	149.476469
108	136.043196	142.739900	149.858909	157.429535	165.483223	174.053713	178.543972
120	**155.282279**	163.879347	173.084807	182.946035	193.514277	204.844979	210.814814
180	267.288944	290.818712	316.962297	346.038222	378.405769	414.470346	434.029805
240	411.033669	462.040895	520.926660	589.020416	667.886870	759.368836	810.504870
300	595.509708	692.993962	810.071693	951.026395	1121.121937	1326.833403	1445.468853
360	832.258635	1004.515042	1219.970996	1490.359449	1830.743483	2260.487925	2516.400990
480	1526.020156	1991.490734	2624.813398	3491.007831	4681.320273	6324.079581	7369.043601
600	2668.651971	3787.191085	5448.070915	7931.727477	11669.101862	17324.390796	21173.014500
720	4550.577421	7054.282437	11121.862503	17788.527472	28798.649722	47102.689667	60440.198972

Table A-3 – Present Value of $1

Formula: Amount needed = base amount $*(1/((1+i)^n))$

Using the table: Amount needed = base amount * table entry

Example: The present value of $6,000 needed in the future invested now at 7% for 6 years.

Investment = 6000 * **.657849** = $3947.09

	Annual Interest Rate						
	5%	6%	7%	8%	9%	10%	10.5%
Months							
1	0.995851	0.995025	0.994200	0.993377	0.992556	0.991736	0.991326
2	0.991718	0.990075	0.988435	0.986799	0.985167	0.983539	0.982727
3	0.987603	0.985149	0.982702	0.980264	0.977833	0.975411	0.974203
4	0.983506	0.980248	0.977003	0.973772	0.970554	0.967350	0.965752
5	0.979425	0.975371	0.971337	0.967323	0.963329	0.959355	0.957375
6	0.975361	0.970518	0.965704	0.960917	0.956158	0.951427	0.949071
7	0.971313	0.965690	0.960103	0.954553	0.949040	0.943563	0.940839
8	0.967283	0.960885	0.954535	0.948232	0.941975	0.935765	0.932678
9	0.963269	0.956105	0.948999	0.941952	0.934963	0.928032	0.924588
10	0.959272	0.951348	0.943495	0.935714	0.928003	0.920362	0.916568
11	0.955292	0.946615	0.938024	0.929517	0.921095	0.912756	0.908617
12	0.951328	0.941905	0.932583	0.923361	0.914238	0.905212	0.900736
24	0.905025	0.887186	0.869712	0.852596	0.835831	0.819410	0.811325
36	0.860976	0.835645	0.811079	0.787255	0.764149	0.741740	0.730789
48	0.819071	0.787098	0.756399	0.726921	0.698614	0.671432	0.658248
60	0.779205	0.741372	0.705405	0.671210	0.638700	0.607789	0.592908
72	0.741280	0.698302	**0.657849**	0.619770	0.583924	0.550178	0.534053
84	0.705201	0.657735	0.613499	0.572272	0.533845	0.498028	0.481041
96	0.670877	0.619524	0.572139	0.528414	0.488062	0.450821	0.433291
108	0.638225	0.583533	0.533568	0.487917	0.446205	0.408089	0.390280
120	0.607161	0.549633	0.497596	0.450523	0.407937	0.369407	0.351540
180	0.473103	0.407482	0.351007	0.302396	0.260549	0.224521	0.208431
240	0.368645	0.302096	0.247602	0.202971	0.166413	0.136462	0.123580
300	0.287250	0.223966	0.174660	0.136237	0.106288	0.082940	0.073272
360	0.223827	0.166042	0.123206	0.091443	0.067886	0.050410	0.043443
480	0.135899	0.091262	0.061307	0.041197	0.027693	0.018622	0.015272
600	0.082512	0.050161	0.030506	0.018560	0.011297	0.006879	0.005369
720	0.050098	0.027570	0.015180	0.008362	0.004609	0.002541	0.001887

Table A-4 – Sinking Fund – $1 Per Period for a Future Sum

Formula: Amount needed = base amount * $(i/((1+i)^n - 1))$

Using the table: Amount needed = base amount * table entry

Example: You need $8,000 at the end of 5 years. With a 6% rate of interest how much per month must be set aside?

Monthly Investment = 8000 * **.014333** = $114.66

	Annual Interest Rate						
	5%	6%	7%	8%	9%	10%	10.5%
Months							
1	1.000000	1.000000	1.000000	1.000000	1.000000	1.000000	1.000000
2	0.498960	0.498753	0.498546	0.498339	0.498132	0.497925	0.497822
3	0.331948	0.331672	0.331396	0.331121	0.330846	0.330571	0.330434
4	0.248443	0.248133	0.247823	0.247514	0.247205	0.246897	0.246743
5	0.198340	0.198010	0.197680	0.197351	0.197022	0.196694	0.196530
6	0.164939	0.164595	0.164253	0.163910	0.163569	0.163228	0.163058
7	0.141081	0.140729	0.140377	0.140025	0.139675	0.139325	0.139151
8	0.123188	0.122829	0.122470	0.122112	0.121756	0.121400	0.121222
9	0.109272	0.108907	0.108544	0.108181	0.107819	0.107459	0.107279
10	0.098139	0.097771	0.097403	0.097037	0.096671	0.096307	0.096125
11	0.089031	0.088659	0.088288	0.087919	0.087551	0.087184	0.087001
12	0.081441	0.081066	0.080693	0.080322	0.079951	0.079583	0.079399
24	0.039705	0.039321	0.038939	0.038561	0.038185	0.037812	0.037626
36	0.025804	0.025422	0.025044	0.024670	0.024300	0.023934	0.023752
48	0.018863	0.018485	0.018113	0.017746	0.017385	0.017029	0.016853
60	0.014705	**0.014333**	0.013968	0.013610	0.013258	0.012914	0.012744
72	0.011938	0.011573	0.011216	0.010867	0.010526	0.010193	0.010029
84	0.009967	0.009609	0.009259	0.008920	0.008589	0.008268	0.008111
96	0.008493	0.008141	0.007800	0.007470	0.007150	0.006841	0.006690
108	0.007351	0.007006	0.006673	0.006352	0.006043	0.005745	0.005601
120	0.006440	0.006102	0.005778	0.005466	0.005168	0.004882	0.004743
180	0.003741	0.003439	0.003155	0.002890	0.002643	0.002413	0.002304
240	0.002433	0.002164	0.001920	0.001698	0.001497	0.001317	0.001234
300	0.001679	0.001443	0.001234	0.001051	0.000892	0.000754	0.000692
360	0.001202	0.000996	0.000820	0.000671	0.000546	0.000442	0.000397
480	0.000655	0.000502	0.000381	0.000286	0.000214	0.000158	0.000136
600	0.000375	0.000264	0.000184	0.000126	0.000086	0.000058	0.000047
720	0.000220	0.000142	0.000090	0.000056	0.000035	0.000021	0.000017

Table A-5 – Present Value of $1 Per Period – Annuity

Formula: Amount needed = base amount * $(1-(1/((1+i)^n)))/i$

Using the table: Amount needed = base amount * table entry

Example: You need $100 a month for the next 20 years. With an 8% rate of interest how much must be set aside now to have enough for the 20 years?

Investment = 100 * **119.554292** = 11,955.43

	Annual Interest Rate						
Months	5%	6%	7%	8%	9%	10%	10.5%
1	0.995851	0.995025	0.994200	0.993377	0.992556	0.991736	0.991326
2	1.987569	1.985099	1.982635	1.980176	1.977723	1.975275	1.974053
3	2.975173	2.970248	2.965337	2.960440	2.955556	2.950686	2.948256
4	3.958678	3.950496	3.942340	3.934212	3.926110	3.918036	3.914008
5	4.938103	4.925866	4.913677	4.901535	4.889440	4.877391	4.871384
6	5.913463	5.896384	5.879381	5.862452	5.845598	5.828817	5.820455
7	6.884777	6.862074	6.839484	6.817005	6.794638	6.772381	6.761293
8	7.852060	7.822959	7.794019	7.765237	7.736613	7.708146	7.693971
9	8.815329	8.779064	8.743018	8.707189	8.671576	8.636178	8.618559
10	9.774602	9.730412	9.686513	9.642903	9.599580	9.556540	9.535126
11	10.729894	10.677027	10.624537	10.572420	10.520675	10.469296	10.443743
12	11.681222	11.618932	11.557120	11.495782	11.434913	11.374508	11.344479
24	22.793898	22.562866	22.335099	22.110544	21.889146	21.670855	21.562858
36	33.365701	32.871016	32.386464	31.911806	31.446805	30.991236	30.766918
48	43.422956	42.580318	41.760201	40.961913	40.184782	39.428160	39.057344
60	52.990706	51.725561	50.501994	49.318433	48.173374	47.065369	46.524827
72	62.092777	60.339514	58.654444	57.034522	55.476849	53.978665	53.251057
84	70.751835	68.453042	66.257285	64.159261	62.153965	60.236667	59.309613
96	78.989441	76.095218	73.347569	70.737970	68.258439	65.901488	64.766771
108	86.826108	83.293424	79.959850	76.812497	73.839382	71.029355	69.682229
120	94.281350	90.073453	86.126354	82.421481	78.941693	75.671163	74.109758
180	126.455243	118.503515	111.255958	104.640592	98.593409	93.057439	90.465078
240	151.525313	139.580772	128.982506	**119.554292**	111.144954	103.624619	100.162274
300	171.060047	155.206864	141.486903	129.564523	119.161622	110.047230	105.911817
360	186.281617	166.791614	150.307568	136.283494	124.281866	113.950820	109.320766
480	207.384291	181.747584	160.918839	143.820392	129.640902	117.765391	112.540338
600	220.197012	189.967875	166.198968	147.215942	131.827053	119.174520	113.672145
720	227.976397	194.486016	168.826340	148.745716	132.718865	119.695062	114.070021

Table A-6 – Payment to Amortize $1 – Loan Payment

Formula: Payment = base amount * $i/(1-(1/((1+i)^n)))$

Using the table: Amount needed = base amount * table entry

Example: How much per month do you need to pay in order to repay $3000 borrowed at 5% over a 9 year period?

Payment = 3000 * **.011517** = 34.55

	Annual Interest Rate						
	5%	6%	7%	8%	9%	10%	10.5%
Months							
1	1.004167	1.005000	1.005833	1.006667	1.007500	1.008333	1.008750
2	0.503127	0.503753	0.504379	0.505006	0.505632	0.506259	0.506572
3	0.336115	0.336672	0.337230	0.337788	0.338346	0.338904	0.339184
4	0.252610	0.253133	0.253656	0.254181	0.254705	0.255230	0.255493
5	0.202507	0.203010	0.203514	0.204018	0.204522	0.205028	0.205280
6	0.169106	0.169595	0.170086	0.170577	0.171069	0.171561	0.171808
7	0.145248	0.145729	0.146210	0.146692	0.147175	0.147659	0.147901
8	0.127355	0.127829	0.128304	0.128779	0.129256	0.129733	0.129972
9	0.113439	0.113907	0.114377	0.114848	0.115319	0.115792	0.116029
10	0.102306	0.102771	0.103236	0.103703	0.104171	0.104640	0.104875
11	0.093198	0.093659	0.094122	0.094586	0.095051	0.095517	0.095751
12	0.085607	0.086066	0.086527	0.086988	0.087451	0.087916	0.088149
24	0.043871	0.044321	0.044773	0.045227	0.045685	0.046145	0.046376
36	0.029971	0.030422	0.030877	0.031336	0.031800	0.032267	0.032502
48	0.023029	0.023485	0.023946	0.024413	0.024885	0.025363	0.025603
60	0.018871	0.019333	0.019801	0.020276	0.020758	0.021247	0.021494
72	0.016105	0.016573	0.017049	0.017533	0.018026	0.018526	0.018779
84	0.014134	0.014609	0.015093	0.015586	0.016089	0.016601	0.016861
96	0.012660	0.013141	0.013634	0.014137	0.014650	0.015174	0.015440
108	**0.011517**	0.012006	0.012506	0.013019	0.013543	0.014079	0.014351
120	0.010607	0.011102	0.011611	0.012133	0.012668	0.013215	0.013493
180	0.007908	0.008439	0.008988	0.009557	0.010143	0.010746	0.011054
240	0.006600	0.007164	0.007753	0.008364	0.008997	0.009650	0.009984
300	0.005846	0.006443	0.007068	0.007718	0.008392	0.009087	0.009442
360	0.005368	0.005996	0.006653	0.007338	0.008046	0.008776	0.009147
480	0.004822	0.005502	0.006214	0.006953	0.007714	0.008491	0.008886
600	0.004541	0.005264	0.006017	0.006793	0.007586	0.008391	0.008797
720	0.004386	0.005142	0.005923	0.006723	0.007535	0.008355	0.008767

APPENDIX B

Financial Worksheets

Worksheet B-1 – Personal Spending Plan

Personal Spending Plan

Income	Projected Income	Actual Income	Difference
ncome 1			
ncome 2			
nterest Income			
nvestment Income			
)ther Income			
Total monthly income			
Housing	**Projected Expense**	**Actual Expense**	**Difference**
lortgage/Rent			
teal Estate Taxes			
elephone/Cell			
lectricity			
as			
Vater			
ewer			
able			
tubbish Removal			
tepairs			
upplies			
)ther			
Total Housing Expenses			
Transportation			
ehicle Payment			
ublic Transportation			
arking/Tolls			
icense/Registration			
uel			
laintenance			
)ther			
Total Transportation Expenses			
Insurance			
lome/Renter's			
utomobile			
ealth/Dental/Vision			
ife			
isability			
ong-Term Care			
iability			
)ther			
Total Insurance Expenses			
Food			
roceries			
ating Out			
ending			
)ther			
Total Food Expenses			
Education			
uition			
ooks			
oom & Board			
ubscriptions			
rganization Dues			
)ther			
Total Education Expenses			
Personal Care			
ledical/Dental/Vision			
lair Care			
lothing			
ry Cleaning/Laundry			
ealth Club			
ther			
Total Personal Expenses			
Entertainment			
lovies			
VD/CD/Videos			
oncerts			
ports			
Veb Subscriptions			
)ther			
Total Entertainment Expenses			
Column 1 Totals			

Giving	Projected Expense	Actual Expense	Difference
The Lord's Work			
Charities			
Other			
Total Giving			

Gifts	Projected Expense	Actual Expense	Difference
Christmas Gifts			
Cards			
Other Gifts			
Total Gift Expenses			

Investing	Projected Expense	Actual Expense	Difference
Retirement Account			
Emergency Fund			
Investment Account			
Total Investment			

Miscellaneous	Projected Expense	Actual Expense	Difference
Bank Fees			
Professional Fees			
Other			
Total Miscellaneous Expneses			

Taxes	Projected Expense	Actual Expense	Difference
Federal Income Rax			
State Income Tax			
Local Income Tax			
FICA			
Medicare			
Personal Property Taxes			
Other			
Total Tax Payments			

Loans	Projected Expense	Actual Expense	Difference
Personal Loans			
Student Loans			
Credit Card 1			
Credit Card 2			
Credit Card 3			
Credit Card 4			
Credit Card 5			
Credit Card 6			
Credit Card 7			
Other			
Total Debt Payments			

	Total Projected Expense	Total Actual Expense	Total Difference
Column 2 Totals			
Column 1 Totals			
Spending Plan Totals			

Cash Flow Total	

Note: Adapted from the Monthly Family Budget Microsoft Excel template available on the Microsoft web site at http://www.microsoft.com.

Worksheet B-2 – Debt Analysis Worksheet

Debt Analysis

Extra Amount: 0.00 [Date]

Type of Consumer Debt	Balance	Minimum Payment	Payoff Months	Priority	Interest Rate	Monthly Payment	Months to Payoff
Auto Loans							
Education Loans							
Personal Installment Loans							
Home Improvement Loans							
Other Installment Loans							
Credit Cards							
Home Loans/Credit Lines							
Loans on Life Insurance							
Margin Loans from Broker							
Other Loans							
Totals							

Note: Adapted from the Consumer Debt Payoff Microsoft Excel template available on the Microsoft web site at http://www.microsoft.com.

Worksheet B-3 – Net Worth Worksheet

Net Worth

Assets	Estimated Value	Liabilities	Estimated Value
Personal Property Assets		**Loan Balances**	
Home		Mortgage loan	
Vehicles		Home equity loan	
Jewelry		Car loan 1	
Artwork		Car loan 2	
Furniture		Student loans	
Electronics		Real estate loan	
Antiques		Other loan 1 - ( )	
Other		Other loan 2 - ( )	
Liquid Assets		Other loan 3 - ( )	
Cash		Other loan 4 - ( )	
Checking account		Other loan 5 - ( )	
Savings account		**Other Outstanding Debt**	
Certificates of deposit		Credit card 1 - ( )	
Money market account		Credit card 2 - ( )	
Life insurance (cash value)		Credit card 3 - ( )	
Other		Credit card 4 - ( )	
Investment Assets		Credit card 5 - ( )	
Retirement account		Credit card 6 - ( )	
Bonds		Credit card 7 - ( )	
Mutual funds		Other debt 1 - ( )	
Individual stock shares		Other debt 2 - ( )	
Real estate other than home		Other debt 3 - ( )	
Other		Other debt 4 - ( )	
Assets Total		**Liabilities Total**	

Net Worth	

Note: Adapted from the Net Worth Calculator Microsoft Excel template available on the Microsoft web site at http://www.microsoft.com.

Worksheet B-4 – Financial Goals Worksheet

Financial Goals Worksheet

Date Set		Goal	Priority	Target Date	Cost	Biblical	Specific	Realistic	Measure
Near-Term Goals									
Mid-Term Goals									
Long-Term Goals									

Worksheet B-5 – Financial Goal Analysis Worksheet

Financial Goal Analysis

Date Set	Goal		
Scenario 1			
Cost	Benefits	Disadvantages	Risk Level
Scenario 2			
Cost	Benefits	Disadvantages	Risk Level
Scenario 3			
Cost	Benefits	Disadvantages	Risk Level

Worksheet B-6 – Account Reconciliation Worksheet

Account Reconciliation

Date: ____________________ Bank Statement Date: ____________________

Line 1	**Ending Balance from Bank Statement:**	
	Subtract Outstanding Checks and Other Payments:	

Check Number	Amount	Check Number	Amount

Line 2	**Total Outstanding Checks and Other Payments:**	
Line 3	**Subtotal (subtract Line 2 from Line 1)**	
	Add Outstanding Deposits and Other Credits:	

Deposit Date	Amount	Deposit Date	Amount

Line 4	**Total Outstanding Deposits and Other Credits:**	
Line 5	**Reconciled Balance (add Line 4 to Line 3)**	
Line 6	**Balance from Your Account Reguster:**	
Line 7	**Difference (should be zero)**	

APPENDIX C

Bible References

Bible Verses Referenced in the Text

Chapter 1

Genesis 2:10
Genesis 3:19
Genesis 39:1-4
Genesis 41:39-44
Genesis 45:4-8
Genesis 50:19-21
Deuteronomy 10:14
Job 1:21
1 Samuel 16:7
1 Kings 17:4-6
1 Chronicles 29:11-12
Psalm 24:1
Psalm 50:10-12
Psalm 135:6
Proverbs 11:14
Proverbs 16:9
Proverbs 21:1
Haggai 2:8

Matthew 6:24
Matthew 6:31-33
Matthew 25:14-29
Luke 12:31-34
Luke 12:42-44
Luke 14:26-27
Luke 14:28-32
Luke 16:1-13
Luke 16:13
John 3:16-18
John 8:36
John 14:14
Acts 17:26
Acts 18:3
Romans 8:9-16
Romans 8:28
Romans 14:12
1 Corinthians 1:25
1 Corinthians 1:26
1 Corinthians 2:11-14
1 Corinthians 3:11-15
1 Corinthians 3:19
1 Corinthians 3:16
1 Corinthians 4:2
2 Corinthians 5:10
2 Corinthians 8:1-2
Ephesians 1:3
Ephesians 4:17-24
Ephesians 4:30
Colossians 1:15-18
Colossians 3:1-4
Philippians 2:5-7
Philippians 2:21
Philippians 4:17
Philippians 4:19
2 Thessalonians 3:10
1 Thessalonians 5:19
1 Timothy 5:10
1 Timothy 5:18
1Timothy 6:8
1 Timothy 6:9
1 Timothy 6:10-11
2 Timothy 3:16-17
Titus 1:7
Hebrews 11:6
James 4:3
James 5:16
1 Peter 4:10

Chapter 2

Proverbs 19:2
Proverbs 22:7

Luke 12:16-21
Luke 16:1-8
Philippians 2:9
Colossians 1:7-8

Chapter 3

Genesis 4:3-5
Genesis 8:20-21
Genesis 12:1-8
Genesis 14:20
Genesis 22:1-14
Genesis 28:20-22
Exodus 23:10-11
Exodus 35:4-10
Leviticus 19:9
Leviticus 22:18-23
Leviticus 27:30
Numbers 18:10-11
Numbers 18:12
Numbers 18:17-18
Deuteronomy 12:10-18
Deuteronomy 14:28
Deuteronomy 16:10
Deuteronomy 25:14
Nehemiah 10:32-33
Psalm 127:3
Psalms 127:8

Matthew 23:23
Mark 12:41-44
Luke 6:38
Luke 7:37-38
Luke 11:42
Luke 18:12
Luke 19:1-10
Acts 4:32-35
1 Corinthians 9:9-11
1 Corinthians 9:14
1 Corinthians 13:3
1 Corinthians 16:2
2 Corinthians 8:2
2 Corinthians 8:4
2 Corinthians 8:8-15
2 Corinthians 9:6
2 Corinthians 9:7
2 Corinthians 9:12-13
Galatians 6:6
Galatians 6:10
Ephesians 6:4
Philippians 4:17-19
Philippians 4:18
1 Timothy 5:16-17
1 Timothy 5:18
Hebrews 7:1-9
Hebrews 7:4
Hebrews 13:15
1 John 3:17

Chapter 4

Genesis 2:18
Genesis 41
1 Samuel 8
2 Kings 23:35
Proverbs 31:10-31
Proverbs 31:24
Daniel 11:20

Matthew 6:19-21
Matthew 17:24-27
Matthew 22:15-22
Matthew 25:14-30
Luke 15: 11-24
Luke 16:1-8
Luke 22:15
Romans 13:3-4
Romans 13:6-7
1 Corinthians 11:2
Ephesians 5:21-24
Colossians 3:23
1 Timothy 3:4-5
2 Timothy 2:15

Chapter 5

Exodus 22:14
Deuteronomy 15:6
Psalm 37:21
Proverbs 6:1-2
Proverbs 11:15
Proverbs 17:18
Proverbs 22:7
Proverbs 22:26-27

Matthew 25:27
Luke 12:58-59
Romans 13:8

Chapter 6

Genesis 41
Proverbs 21:5
Proverbs 23:4-5
Proverbs 24:3-4,
Proverbs 27:1
Proverbs 28:20
Proverbs 28:22
Proverbs 31:16

Matthew 6:19-21
Matthew 7:22
Matthew 25:14-30
Ephesians 2:19
Philippians 3:20
1 Timothy 6:9-10
James 4:13-15

Chapter 8

Proverbs 4:26
Matthew 25:14-30

Chapter 11

Genesis 41
Exodus 21:18-19
Exodus 21:33-35
Exodus 22:7
Exodus 22:14-15

Chapter 15

Genesis 25:8
Leviticus 19:32
Numbers 8:24-26
1 Samuel 2:31-32
1 Samuel 3:2
1 Kings 12:6-8
Psalm 92:13-15
Proverbs 20:29

1 Timothy 5:16
Titus 2:2-4
2 Peter 3:8

Chapter 16

Numbers 36:7-9
Proverbs 13:22
Ecclesiastes 2:21

Luke 12:18-20
Luke 15:13
Romans 11:36
1 Corinthians 4:2
Galatians 4:6-7
2 Timothy 4:7-9
Hebrews 9:15-18
1 Peter 2:5

APPENDIX D

Debt Payoff Analysis

This appendix will help you to complete the debt analysis report discussed earlier in the text. It covers the calculations for determining the payoff of debt as well as discusses the various finance charge calculations that companies use. The following formula will calculate the debt balance after each payment. You will need to calculate it for each month until the debt is zero. The number of monthly payments will vary and will be the number of calculations you make to bring the debt to zero.

New balance = old balance + (old balance * monthly rate) – (old balance * percent payment)

Example: Assume a $1000 balance, an annual rate of 18%, and a minimum 3% payment on the balance.

Balance after first payment assuming no new charges =

$$1000 + (1000*(.18/12)) - (1000*.03)$$

$$1000 + (1000*.015) - 30$$

$$1000 + 15 - 30 = 985$$

So after one payment the balance will be $985. The $30 payment was evenly split between interest and the principal in this case. If we went through the calculation again using the new balance of $985 and a minimum 3% payment then after two payments we would have a balance of $970.22 If you want to know what the minimum percentage is for your case take the minimum monthly payment and divide it by the outstanding balance.

You can easily calculate the balance after a certain number of payments by using the formula:

$$\text{Remaining balance} = \text{Original balance} * (1 + \text{rate} - \text{minimum payment percent})^{\text{time}}$$

Example: What will the balance be above after 60 monthly payments?

$$\text{Balance} = \$1000*((1+.18/12)-.03)^{60}$$

$$\text{Balance} = \$1000*(1+.015-.03)^{60}$$

$$\text{Balance} = 1000 * .98560$$

$$\text{Balance} = 1000 * .40381$$

$$\text{Balance} = 403.81$$

The balance on this account after paying it for five years (60 monthly payments) will be $403.81. You increase the number of payments in the formula to see how long it would take to finally pay it off or just use a calculator available on a number of web sites. One that is quite good is at www.financecenter.com/products/calculators. For the payoff months just enter one and the result will display how many months it will take based on the minimum payment you entered. The difference with most of these is that they use a fixed payment rather than the minimum payment or percentage to calculate the length. So you would enter $30 a month whereas above we used the credit card company approach of a percentage of the balance. Cardweb.com provides a calculator that takes both a percentage and a fixed amount but as of this writing the percentage calculation seemed to produce an incorrect result for the number of months required to pay off the card. This may be because they stop after the remaining balance falls below a few percent of the original. Still, it is a useful tool.

In the credit card company case you might estimate, based on what we have seen, that it would take another three or four years to pay off this credit card. But you would be surprised at the result. If we try 120 for the number of payments (which is ten years) the balance is still $163.06. This is where credit card payments are different than most other loan payments that you will calculate. There is no difference if you use fixed payments to pay all credit cards and loans, but if you go by the minimum payment from a credit card company the payment amount becomes smaller because they are based on a percentage of the balance. But this does not help you, it helps the credit card company; by extending the length of time you pay interest on the balance. In fact by just putting various time frames in months into the formula you would find that it would take you 25 years to get the balance down to $10 using the card company's minimum payment amount. To make life easy, Exhibit D-1 is provided to quickly determine the payoff period for various interest rates using a fixed percent of the original balance which will help you to pay the balance off sooner. Avoid using the card company's minimum balance. In our example above, if you spent the 25 years paying the minimum balance you would

Percentage of Initial Balance Paid Each Month	Annual Interest Rate							
	9%	10%	12%	15%	18%	21%	24%	28%
2%	63	65	70	79	94	120	*	*
3%	39	40	41	44	47	51	56	66
4%	28	29	29	31	32	34	36	38
5%	22	22	23	24	24	25	26	28
7%	16	16	16	16	17	17	17	18
10%	11	11	11	11	11	12	12	12
12%	9	9	9	9	9	10	10	10
15%	7	7	7	8	8	8	8	8
20%	6	6	6	6	6	6	6	6

*Interest is more than the payment.

Exhibit D-1. Credit Card Payoff Chart (in months) Using Fixed Payment.

Minimum Payment Due Paid Each Month	Annual Interest Rate							
	9%	10%	12%	15%	18%	21%	24%	28%
2%	422	452	*	*	*	*	*	*
3%	233	243	263	301	351	422	*	*
4%	161	165	175	191	210	234	263	316
5%	123	125	131	139	149	161	175	197
7%	83	84	87	90	95	99	104	112
10%	56	56	57	59	61	63	65	67

*Interest is more than the payment. Or repayment period is greater than 40 years.

Exhibit D-2. Credit Card Payoff Chart (in months) Using Minimum Balance Due to Reduce Balance from $5,000 to $25.

have spent $1989.23. That amount is almost double what you had borrowed and it assumes that you don't use the credit card for 25 years.

Exhibit D-2 provides a sample chart showing the number of months it would take to pay off a $5000 balance if you paid the minimum balance due on the credit card. It is usually a percentage of the current balance so that is what is used in the table. As you can see the number of months is quite a bit larger than if you made a fixed payment based on the initial balance. Both tables assume you do not make any additional charges on the credit card. If you do, the credit card company computes your interest in one of a variety of ways usually for its benefit. Exhibit D-3 shows a comparison of the various interest charge calculations. The key methods include:

Average daily balance excluding new purchases. This approach is best for you. It basically takes the remaining balance from the previous month to determine the interest charge as in the tables above. It also includes any payments you have made. It is sometimes known as the adjusted balance method. If the payments are not allowed in the calculation then the interest is based on the previous balance and will result in higher finance charges. This variation is known as the previous balance method.

Average daily balance including new purchases with a grace period. This approach is the most popular for credit card companies. It takes the balance from the previous month and any new charges for the billing period and determines the average balance. This approach generates more interest since new charges make the average balance higher. The grace period option allows those who pay off their balance completely within the grace period to avoid any finance charges on new purchases. Another variation on this is to not have the grace period option and then regardless of whether it is paid in full you will be charged interest on new purchases. This variation is also known as the daily balance method.

Two-cycle average daily balance including new purchases. More credit card companies are starting to take this approach and it is the worst option for the consumer since it generates more finance charges (sometimes double) than the other methods. This method takes the average balance over two billing cycles which means that you must completely pay the bill for two months in a row to avoid the finance charges. Even if you pay off the bill the first month you will be charged interest on the amount paid off that month using this method. It is basically a way of raising the interest rate without having to advertise it. There is also a variation of this method that excludes new purchases.

Exhibit D-3, even with the small amount and the few months being used, shows a 45% difference in the finance charges assessed between the lowest and highest calculations from the various methods. These dollar differences can be extremely large when using larger balances and longer time periods. Also, when payments are received and when charges are made can influence these average balance figures greatly. You are better off not carrying a balance.

To see how the different finance charge methods can affect the finance charge you pay let's use an example where in the first month there is a $1000 balance, a $100 payment on the 15th of the month, and additional charges of $60 on the 10th of the month. In the second month you pay another $100 and have $40 in new charges on the same days as the previous month. In the third month you pay off the balance and have no new charges. The table provides the finance charges you would pay assuming an 18% rate so there will be a $15 interest charge due in the first month.

Method	Daily Balance 1	Daily Balance 2	Daily Balance 3	Finance Charges
Average daily balance including purchases with grace period	$997.50 ($1000 for 10 days, $1060 for 5 days, 975 for 15 days)	$981.65 ($997.50 for 10 days, $1037.50 for 5 days, $952.46 for 15 days)	Paid in Full by end of grace period	1- $14.96 2- $14.72 3- $0.00 T- 29.68
Average daily balance excluding new purchases with grace period	$957.50 ($1000 for 15 days, $915 for 15 days)	$925 ($975 for 15 days, $875 for 15 days)	Paid in Full by end of grace period	1- $14.36 2- $13.88 3- $0.00 T- 28.24
Average daily balance including purchases with no grace period	$997.50 ($1000 for 10 days, $1060 for 5 days, 975 for 15 days)	$981.65 ($997.50 for 10 days, $1037.50 for 5 days, $952.46 for 15 days)	490.83 ($981.65 for 15 days, $0.00 for 15 days)	1- $14.96 2- $14.72 3- $7.36 T- 37.04
Two-cycle average daily balance	$998.75 ($1000 for 40 days, $1060 for 5 days, 975 for 15 days)	$990.83 ($998.75 for 40 days, $1038.75 for 5 days, $953.73 for 15 days)	743.12 ($990.83 for 45 days, $0.00 for 15 days)	1- $14.98 2- $14.86 3- $11.15 T- 40.99

Exhibit D-3. Credit Card Finance Charge Calculation Comparison

Most other loans have a fixed payment period or identify when the loan must be paid by. If you want to calculate the payoff for a fixed payment instrument that does not have a fixed end date, such as a credit card or personal loan, then you can use loan calculators available for free on various web sites. Otherwise, you can also calculate an amortization schedule for them using a calculator.

This formula will calculate the debt balance after each payment. You will need to calculate it for each month until the debt is zero. The number of monthly payments will vary and will be the number of calculations you make to bring the debt to zero.

> New balance = old balance + (old balance * monthly rate) - payment

Example: Assume $1000 balance, an annual rate of 18% and a fixed monthly payment of $30 on the balance.

Balance after first payment assuming no new charges =

> 1000 + (1000*(18/12)) -30
>
> 1000 + (1000*.015) - 30
>
> 1000 + 15 - 30 = 985

So after one payment the balance will be $985 just like we did the first time. The $30 payment was evenly split between interest and the principal again. If we went through the calculation again using the new balance of $985 and a $30 payment, then after two payments we would have a balance of $969.76. Now you see the difference. Using a fixed payment will make the balance go down faster on these types of debt.

You can easily calculate the balance after a certain number of payments by using the formula:

> Balance remaining = Payment * $((1-(1+i)^{-n})/i)$

i = interest rate per period and n = number of payments left

For example, assume we were paying off a credit card balance of $4,000 over 3 years at 12% interest with a $132.90 a month payment and had 2 years remaining.

> Balance remaining = 132.90 * $((1-(1+.12/12)^{-24})/(.12/12))$
>
> Balance remaining = 132.90 * $((1-(1+.01)^{-24})/.01)$
>
> Balance remaining = 132.90 * (1-..787567)/.01
>
> Balance remaining = 132.90 * 21.2434
>
> Balance remaining = 2823.25

After completing the debt analysis you should have a complete picture of where you are concerning your liabilities. You also should be able to easily use an online calculator to help determine various scenarios later after you have set your financial goals.

GLOSSARY

401K. A pension plan that is based on Section 401(k) of the tax code and is used by for-profit employers.

403B. A pension plan that is based on Section 403(b) of the tax code. These are plans that are offered by non-profit institutions such as hospitals and universities.

457. A pension plan that is based on Section 457 of the tax code and is used by governments.

529 Plan. A higher-education savings plan that allows savings or pre-payment of tuition tax-free.

Accountable. Responsible to give a report of one's work.

Affinity Card. A credit card that is associated with a specific organization that usually receives a small percentage of the amount charged on the cards.

Annuity. An investment instrument that will guarantee a periodic payout for a certain period usually until you die, or you and your spouse both die.

Asset. Something of ownership having exchange value.

Bankruptcy. An individual in a state where he is unable to meet his financial obligations or the legitimate claims against him.

Blue-Chip. Large, well known, profitable firms.

Bond. A bond is an IOU for money you have given to the company.

Bond Ladder. A strategy to set up a stream of income over a period of years by buying bonds equally across a range of maturities so that each year some of the bonds mature and the funds are made available.

Broker. Brokers are basically intermediaries between you and the market.

Buyback. When a company purchases its own stock to take it off the market.

Call. When a company decides to retire debt early and pay you back what you lent to them.

Cashier's Check. A guaranteed check the bank makes out to a particular payee, and is signed by an officer of the bank.

Certified Check. A personally written check that the bank has certified as having the funds available to cover it and has indicated this by marking the check as "certified."

CD. Certificate of Deposit. An insured, timed bank deposit requiring the money to held for a specific period in order to receive the full return on the investment.

Collateral. The item that is given in pledge that you will repay a debt.

Common Stock. The stock that has the voting privileges of the company and is the primary ownership of the company.

Compounding. The act of combining, and from a financial perspective is the act of earning interest on the combined principal and interest thus far received. Also known as earning interest on interest.

Consumer. One who destroys or expends by use; uses up; eats or drinks up; devours, spends (money, time, etc.) wastefully.

Consumer Price Index. A measure of the cost of living for the average "consumer."

Coupon. The interest rate noted on the bond.

Closing. The event at which a home is paid for and legally transferred.

Conventional Loan. A fixed rate loan.

Credit. Credit comes from the Latin "credere" meaning to trust, loan, believe. The idea being that one could be trusted to return or repay that which they have borrowed. Today we see it as the ability to borrow based on the ability to repay.

Credit Card. A card instrument that allows the borrowing of funds quickly for a consumer transaction, based on a pre-approved limit of funds that are available.

Credit Line. A form of borrowing where the loan is taken from a predefined fund over a period of time after which it must be repaid according to a predetermined schedule.

Credit Report. A historical document that shows an individual's credit history.

Credit Union. Non-profit organization that is owned by, and formed for the benefit of its members.

Day Trading. An investing strategy that involves quickly buying and selling stocks during a given day in order to gain small profits on the small changes in the stock price during the day.

Debit Card. A card whose use creates a debit or subtracts the transaction amount from your account that is connected to the card.

Debt Consolidation. To combine various debt payments that usually involve several sources into a single monthly loan payment that is paid to a single source. As a result the monthly payment is reduced.

Deductible. The amount that you must pay first toward an insurance claim expense before the insurance will begin paying.

Defined Benefit Plan. A plan that specifies the benefits that the employee will receive based on their age at retirement.

Defined Contribution Plan. A plan that specifies the source of contributions for the plan. The benefit is whatever is in the account at retirement.

Deflation. A decline in the general level of prices.

Dividends. That portion of the profits that is given back to the owners of the organization.

Dollar Cost Averaging. This technique involves investing the same amount of funds consistently for the same stocks over a period of time.

Down Payment. The amount the buyer provides in cash toward the purchase of a home, car, or other major purchase.

DRIP. Dividend Reinvestment Plan. This is a direct purchase plan that will also automatically reinvest your dividends in additional company stock rather than distributing the dividends in cash.

DSPP. Direct Stock Purchase Plan. These plans allow you to establish an account with a plan administrator and then buy and sell shares of the company stock via the administrator.

Education IRA. Actually an education trust for saving for educational expenses tax-free.

Efficient Market Theory. This theory suggests that the stock market is efficient as regards information about stocks so that it is impossible to beat the market average consistently.

EPS. The earnings per share is determined by dividing the total earnings for a period by the total outstanding shares.

ESA. Education Savings Account. Also known as the Coverdell Education Savings Account. The same as the education IRA.

Escrow. An account where money is held for the payment of costs, usually related to a home.

ETF. Exchange traded fund. This type of fund is an index fund that has been created and then shares of the fund traded on an exchange just like stock.

Exchange. A secondary market where securities can be traded or exchanged.

Executor. The individual who is responsible to make sure that the will is properly probated and becomes the administrator of the estate through the probate process.

Expense. A cost or charge.

FAFSA. The Free Application for Federal Student Aid. It is a form that is filed with the federal government to determine if one qualifies for federal aid for college.

FDIC. Federal Deposit Insurance Corporation. Federally insures bank accounts including certificates of deposit.

FICO. Known best as an individual's credit score. It named after the Fair Isaac Corporation.

Fixed Rate. The interest rate on a loan that does not change and the payment schedule is fixed and known in advance.

Flexible Spending Accounts. Flexible Spending Accounts (FSA) allow you to set aside funds before taxes through payroll deduction for qualified expenses such as childcare, medical expenses, and other insurance premiums.

Fundamental Analysis Theory. The fundamental analysis theorists suggest that the value of a company's stock is determined by its future earnings

Grace Period. The number of days you have to make a payment before your payment is considered late

Grant. Financial award that does not need to be repaid.

Income. Returns as a result of labor, business, investment.

Index Fund. An index fund purchases stock to match the makeup of a particular market index.

Inflation. A rise in the general level of prices.

Insurance. A contract by which one party agrees to indemnify or reimburse for a loss of another.

Interest. Payment for the use of funds.

Investing. Investing deals with putting assets to use for a return in the future.

Investment Trust. A unit investment trust is a fixed investment portfolio controlled by a trust agreement that is created by a trust sponsor that in turn sells shares or ownership units in the trust to investors.

IPO. Firms will often make a first "public" stock offering called an IPO or Initial Public Offering to attract investors to invest in and become part owners of the corporation.

IRA. Individual Retirement Account. A tax-advantaged retirement account for an individual.

Keogh Plan. A pension plan designed for the self-employed based on the Keogh Act of 1962.

Lease. To rent. Also refers to the rental contract.

Liability. Something owed, debts, or obligations.

Liquid Asset. An asset that can be turned into cash at a reasonable price, quickly.

Living Will. A legal document that describes the level of care you wish or do not wish to receive if you become terminally ill and unable to make known what you would like done medically. It also includes definitions for the term "terminally ill."

Margin. Borrowing to invest based on the collateral in your investment account.

Market Timing. Timing an investment to occur just before the price of an investment goes up and timing the sale for just before the price goes down from its peak.

Maturity. The date noted by which the borrowed funds must be repaid.

Medicare. Funds the government healthcare program for retirees.

Money Order. A check that is purchased with cash funds.

Mutual Fund. A fund where investors pool their funds together in order to purchase a portfolio of stocks that is professionally managed by another individual, usually from an investment company.

Net Worth. What has been accumulated as wealth. Determined by subtracting total liabilities from total assets.

N.O.W. Account. These accounts are basically checking accounts that earn interest. NOW means Negotiable Order of Withdrawal which references the fact that a check can be written against the account.

Option. Gives the holder an option of buying or selling stock at a predetermined price for a set period of time.

Opportunity Cost. What is given up as a result of a financial decision. Sometimes called the time value of money.

Over-the-Counter. A virtual exchange that does not require an exchange floor to operate.

P/E Ratio. The price/earnings ratio is the result of dividing the price per share of the stock by the earnings per share of the company.

Perception. Decisions based on intuition.

PMI. Private mortgage insurance. It is usually required if the amount borrowed is more than 80% of the value of the home. This protects the bank in case the borrower is unable to repay the mortgage and they cannot get their money back on reselling the home.

Power of Attorney. A legal document that lets you grant another the authority to make decisions on your behalf based on the scope of the authority you have granted.

Preferred Stock. Stock holders are entitled to payment of dividends first if there is insufficient funds to pay all shareholders.

Principal. An amount paid each month that reduces the amount owed to the bank. Also sometimes considered the amount still owed to the bank as well.

Probate. The legal court process for validating a will and distributing the estate according to its plan, or by the law if there were no will.

Purchasing Power. A measure of the goods and services we can buy with whatever income we have.

Reconcile. To balance your accounts, so that the transactions and balance in your ledger match the transactions and balance on the financial institution's statement.

Retained Earnings. That portion of the profits that is retained by the organization to grow the business and develop new products and services.

Return. What the investor expects to get in return for the use of the investor's money.

Reverse Mortgage. A mortgage where the amount of the loan on a home increases each month as a payment is made by the bank to the owner of the home. Interest continues to accrue on the amount borrowed until paid, usually when the home is sold.

Reverse Stock Split. When 2 or more equal shares are united into one share reducing the number of shares available.

Risk. A measure of the degree of uncertainty.

Roth IRA. An individual retirement account that is funded by after-tax dollars but whose earnings are tax-exempt.

Scarcity. The inability to satisfy all needs and wants at the same time.

Secured Loan. A loan that has something that is pledged against it.

SEPP. An easy to administer pension plan option for small businesses, with no employees, which is called a Simplified Employee Pension Plan.

Share. That portion which represents part ownership in a company.

Smart Card. A card instrument where the funds available are stored on the card and deducted directly when used in a consumer transaction.

Social Security. Social Security is the government's funding vehicle for your retirement or for you and/or your family if you should become disabled or die. The system is funded by contributions by both you and your employer.

Spending Plan. A statement of cash flows. Also sometimes called a budget.

Steward. One who manages or administers the property or financial affairs of another.

Stock. Part ownership in a company.

Stock Split. When a share of stock is divided into 2 or more equal shares.

Tax Bracket. A division of income that is taxed at a predetermined rate.

Tax Deferred. Taxable income that is taxed at a later date than when it was first received.

Tax Exempt. Same as tax free.

Tax Free. A form of income that is not taxed.

Taxable. A form of income that is subject to tax.

Technical Analysis Theory. This theory suggests that future stock pricing can be determined by careful analysis of historical trends in the market.

Time Value of Money. Sometimes known as opportunity cost, it describes what has been given up in the future to have something else today.

TIPS. Treasury Inflation Protected Securities. The federal government sells this special type of 10-year bond which is like other government bonds but they are adjusted for inflation every six months.

Traveler's Check. A prepaid check that can be used as cash at most business establishments and must be signed when you purchase it and then signed again when you cash it.

TSA. Tax-sheltered annuities. Often given as a general name to a variety of pension plans and retirement accounts that defer or eliminate taxes.

Unsecured Loan. Borrowing based on your promise to repay without any collateral other then the promise itself.

Variable Rate. The interest rate on a loan that varies based on some financial index that is published in a national newspaper.

Warrant. A document that specifies that the holder can purchase stock at a predetermined price.

Will. The will is a legal document prepared by you before your death that describes how your estate is to be distributed after your death.

Zeroes. A zero-coupon bond. It pays an interest rate of 0%. The return on the bond is based on purchasing the bond at a discount and then at maturity receiving the face value of the bond.

INDEX

4

5

A

B

E

F

G

H

I

J

K

L

M

N

O

P

Q

R

S

T

U

V

W

Y

Z